TOEFL核心词汇

21天突破

Build Your TOEFL Vocabulary in 21 Days

李笑来　著

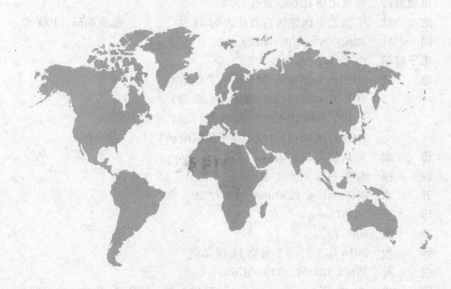

外文出版社

FOREIGN LANGUAGES PRESS

图书在版编目（CIP）数据

TOEFL 核心词汇 21 天突破／李笑来著. — 北京：
外文出版社，2012（2016 年重印）
ISBN 978 - 7 - 119 - 07646 - 1

Ⅰ.①T… Ⅱ.①李… Ⅲ.①TOEFL –词汇–自学参考资料
Ⅳ.①H313

中国版本图书馆 CIP 数据核字（2012）第 070194 号

责任编辑　李春英
印刷监制　冯　浩

TOEFL 核心词汇21 天突破

作　者	李笑来 著
出版发行	外文出版社有限责任公司
地　址	中国北京西城区百万庄大街 24 号　　邮政编码　100037
网　址	http://www.flp.com.cn
电子邮箱	flp@cipg.org.cn
电　话	（010）008610-68320579（总编室）
	（010）008610-68995883（编辑部）
	（010）008610-68995852（发行部）
	（010）008610-68996183（投稿电话）
印　制	北京信彩瑞禾印刷厂
经　销	新华书店／外文书店
开　本	880 mm × 1230 mm　　1/32
印　张	16.875
字　数	620 千字
版　次	2016 年 7 月第 1 版第 11 次印刷
书　号	ISBN 978 - 7 - 119 - 07646 - 1
定　价	39.00 元

建议上架　TOEFL 考试、出国留学

总　目

前　言

　　提起留学，没有人不想拿奖学金出国。要拿奖学金，就只好参加 TOEFL 考试。如果开始准备 TOEFL 考试，考生做的第一件事情就是去买一本 TOEFL 词汇书，因为"江湖"上传闻，想拿 TOEFL 高分，词汇量至少要 12000。

　　传闻通常只不过是传闻而已。传闻往往还有另外一个说法——"谣言"，因为传闻一般并不可靠。然而，谣言总是有蛊惑力的——不然怎么会有那么多人相信？这世界上确实了解真相的人并不多，真正多的是相信传闻并散布传闻的人。

　　然而矢志成功的人需要的是真相，永远只需要真相。还好，这世上有一样东西通常不会撒谎——数字。需要真相的人只相信可靠的数字。在可收集的数据范围之内（过去二十多年近 130 次考试中），总计出现过的词（Token）的数量为：13621。如果去除词汇的变形（例如：refuses；refused；refusing；应该算作一个词），余下的词汇数量为 9952。这其中有相当数量的词汇仅出现过一次，这些词汇的数量为 4152，这些仅出现过一次的词大多数是考生一辈子再也碰不到、在考场上不认识也根本无所谓的词汇，比如，Cajun："移居美国路易安纳州的法国的后裔"；或者 Callisto："【天文】木卫四（即，木星的第四颗卫星）"。余下的词汇量为：5800。出现过 17 次以上的词汇数量为 1004，这些词大多数都是常见词汇，比如：the、of、mean、paper、soft 等等。而出现次数在 2-17 次之内的词汇，就应该被我们认为是必须掌握的核心词汇。

　　在整理词汇的过程中，还需要考虑以下几点：

❶　有些词汇尽管出现次数很多，但是只出现在一篇文章中，即，这些

词汇不应被收录到核心词汇之中。例如以下词汇均出现过多次，却只是在一篇文章中出现：phlogiston（*n*. 燃素，热素）出现过 14 次；igneous（*adj*.【地】火成的）出现过 9 次；warbler（*n*. 刺嘴莺）出现过 6 次。这其中还包括：

* 人名，例如：Warren［13 次］；Charleston［5 次］
* 地名，例如：California［24 次］；Washington［17 次］；Whitney［11 次］；Calabria［2 次］卡拉布里亚区（意大利行政区名）
* 古怪的动物名，例如：wrasse［4 次］隆头鱼；gibbon［6 次］长臂猿
* 古怪的植物名，例如：cactus（*pl*. cacti）［4 次］仙人掌科植物

❷ 有一些词出现 17 次以上，却不是常见词汇，而是因 TOEFL 考试所使用的特殊题材而频繁出现：artisan、cotton、sediment、tropical、vessel 等等。这些词汇应当收录在核心词汇之中。

❸ 有一些词只出现过 1 次，然而其衍生词汇却出现过很多次，比如，anthropology 只出现过 1 次，可是 anthropologist 却出现过 6 次，anthropological 也出现过 1 次。这些词汇应当收录在核心词汇之中。

❹ 由常用的词缀构成的衍生词汇（往往只涉及词性的变化）应收录于同一条目之下，例如 abhor：abhorrence；abhorrent；abhorrently。常用词缀包括：-able, -al, -an, -ance, -ar, -ate, -ation, -ed, -en, -ence, -er, -ery, -ess, -ful, -ible, -ic, -ical, -ing, -ion, -ish, -ist, -ity, -ive, -ization, -ize, -less, -like, -ly, -ment, -ness, -or, -ous, -ry, -ship, -th, -ward, -wards, -work, -y 等等。

经过以上处理之后，核心词汇条目总计为 2140 个。所以，短期内迅速提高 TOEFL 成绩根本就不是什么不可能的事情——关键在于，不要做"无用功"。单词一定要背，不过要"精"、要"准"。传闻是 12000，而真相是 2140。最终这个数字的差异再次证明一个简单的事实：为了寻求真相，无论付出怎样的努力都是值得的。

从 2006 年 9 月开始，ETS 已在中国大陆地区推广 IBT（Internet Based Test）形式的 TOEFL 考试。尽管考试形式变了，考试的本质没有变——它依然是 Test of English as a Foreign Language。英语本身不会因

为 TOEFL 考试的形式发生变化而产生任何转变。针对 ETS 发布的考试样题的统计表明，这 2140 个核心词汇依然占考试中所出现词汇的 95.5%，即，**这个比例没有发生任何变化。**因此，对考生来讲，**词汇量越大越好，然而核心词汇最重要！**

编 者

www.xiaolai.net/blog

再 版 前 言

　　2003年11月本书第一版交付印刷至今，一晃已经10年了。其间又教了不计其数的托福班，学生数万人。常常慨叹时间过得太快，真是恨不得想个办法让所有的计时工具全部失灵。这几年总觉得学生年龄越来越小。后来突然想明白，其实不是学生越来越小，而是自己越来越老。这样看来，即便计时工具全部失灵，也不能消灭所有自己越来越老的证据，越是在乎，就越是束手无策。

　　最要命的还不是这个。当初把这本书稿交出去之后学校就组织体检，结果医生说我患有"中等程度脂肪肝"。我问医生"中等程度"意味着什么？医生问我喝不喝酒，我说从来不喝。医生又问了我的年龄，之后就说"你这个年纪就已经是中度，有点可惜了。"——我觉得我有点被吓着了。第二天早上就接到某医院的电话，推销他们的中医疗法，说是很轻松并很有效的。

　　不知怎么总是觉得轻松的办法很难有效。于是想了想，就找了一个健身俱乐部缴纳了年费，估计着锻炼不是轻松的事儿所以应该更有效。第一天是要做体能测试的，要很长时间。一做吓了一跳。原来还一直以为自己身体不错呢——还以为自己比大学刚毕业那会儿可以连续一个月每天只睡四个小时的状态差不了多少呢。结果可好，跑步机上刚跑5分钟就跑不动了；就算靠着墙，蹲马步也蹲不到半分钟！正在上气不接下气呢，教练突然问道：你能坚持下来吗？

　　我想，不就是每天来跑跑步、游游泳吗？推杠铃一组要推12个，一共6组，就算8组也超不过100下。一天最少200个单词都背过，这有什么不行？我就很自然地点了点头。教练笑了一下。不过我却觉得他笑得有点怪。后来我知道为什么我会觉得教练的笑容有点古怪了。我在健身俱乐部报名之后，大概有十几个朋友、同事都报了名，缴了年费。可是如今，只有我还在每星期去四次，每次两个小时以上。少数几个还偶尔去的，也不过大抵上一两个月只去一次。

最初的时候，我1.72米的身高，有75公斤。两个月减到65公斤，腰围从二尺八减到二尺四。到现在我已经长到85公斤——不过，脂肪换成了肌肉。去了健身房之后才知道原来男人也很在意自己的胸围。忽然开始有人夸我有毅力了。我知道不是那么回事儿。因为只有自己才知道：经常都是挣扎着从家里走出来去健身房的。但是，被别人夸有毅力，总是一件很能满足虚荣心的事情。于是也就不做解释。

后来读了 Nature 上的一篇文章才真正想清楚。原来，大多数人在经过一段时间的连续运动之后，大脑会开始分泌一种叫做"胺多芬素"（endorhine）的东西，而这种物质会使人产生快乐的感觉——简称"快感"。可问题是，每个人的情况不同。少数人只要连续一个星期的运动之后大脑就开始正常、稳定地分泌胺多芬素；而有些人（像我这种）却可能要连续运动半年以上才可能体会大脑分泌胺多芬素带来的快感。这样看来，说那些只要一个星期的坚持就可以享受快感的人"有毅力"或者说那些连续运动半年甚至一年大脑却从来没有分泌过胺多芬素的人"没有毅力"都是没什么道理的。

这样看来"毅力"这个东西甚至可能根本不存在。有些人到了清晨4点之后就再也睡不着了；而另外一些人只有午夜的时候才文思泉涌，因而根本没办法10点之前起床。没什么理由只因为后者不能早起就说他没有毅力吗？我想我应该老实一点。之所以我这种半年之后大脑才开始在运动之后稳定分泌胺多芬素的人可以坚持半年，而后开始享受运动，好像不是因为"有毅力"而更可能是因为当初我被医生对"中等程度脂肪肝"的解释吓着了——总是记得他说"你这个年纪就已经是中度，有点可惜了"。恐惧才是真正的动力。后来跟朋友谈起这件事儿，朋友说，估计这就是所谓的"因祸得福"吧。

突然想到当初玩命背单词的时候，其实也是恐惧充当了动力。并不是因为"有毅力"而是因为害怕失败而拼命努力。有的时候想想，中国学生很可怜：从中学甚至小学就开始学英语，直到大学毕业，近10年过去，竟然有越学越差的趋势。花费了10年却不成功，是件很可怕的事情。也许因为如此，才有一个韩国人写了一本书竟然很畅销，书名叫《千万别学英语》——估计大意是，学不好就不要学了，要学就一定要成功。也许正因为失败太可怕，我们才如此向往成功。

同样的道理，对时间流逝的恐慌迫使我让自己忙起来。每天都把时间表填得满满的，然后将每个任务逐一完成并逐一打勾：备课、讲课、读书、写书、查资料、写文章、跑步、游泳、推杠铃……到了晚上睡觉前看看画满了对勾的时间表就觉得"还好，没有让时间白白漂走"。一天一天过去，到了年底，竟发现自己做了很多事情就觉得很开心。正如正视自己的无知可以使我们如此渴求，直面恐惧竟然最终使我们体会更多的快乐。

背单词是很枯燥的事情。很多人都背过词汇书，却没有坚持到底。佐证就是中国学生都认识一个他们几乎从来不用的单词 abandon——这是几乎市面上所有词汇书中的第一个单词。然而用"没有毅力"去评价那些最终没能坚持下来的人真的公平吗？是不是有点把问题过分简单化了呢？不过，我的经历好像提供了一个解决方案，那就是在没有体会到学习乐趣之前，先用恐惧作为动力。找一张纸，尽量罗列如果不搞定这本词汇书可能导致的恶劣结果。比如：托福成绩很低，没办法申请到奖学金，只好在国内考研或找工作，低薪水，没前途……写得越吓人越好。一定要随身携带，如果觉得实在背不下去了，就拿出这张纸来看看。

李笑来

本书特色及其使用方法

（一）

准备 TOEFL 考试并不要求读者有"大学英语四级基础"。这是因为，TOEFL 考试中所出现的词汇与"大学英语四级词汇大纲"几乎是完全不同的词汇集合。由于 TOEFL 考试的特殊题材，很多所谓的常见词汇实际上很少出现，比如：beer、husband、loud、upset、yes 只出现过一次；同时也有很多词的使用方法很古怪，比如：兰花的"花"不用 bloom 而用 blossom，火山往外喷岩浆不用 erupt（出现过一次）而用 emit、issue、well……

本书"附录 1"包括一个"朗文定义词汇"（The Longman Defining Vocabulary）。朗文词典使用这 2300 个左右的词汇定义解释了朗文词典中的 70000 多个词条。这是朗文的研究机构根据其专门的语料库筛选出来的一个相对完整的基础词汇集合。换言之，一方面，这些词汇是认知的基础，另一方面，考生在 TWE 考试中，使用这个词汇集合就可以精确表达所有思想。建议读者在阅读核心词汇共 21 个单元之前，先用几天时间消灭附录 1 中的所有生词（注意，只需要了解这些词的最常用含义——多义词都标出了常用词性）。另外，有耐心的读者不妨抄写 2-3 遍，顺带练练英文书法，因为这是 TWE 考试之必需准备的项目。

（二）

本书核心词汇部分的词条分别由音标、释义、例句、衍生词、近义词五个基本单位构成。

* 本词之后加注国际音标。

* 词条释义的中文全部来自于《美国传统辞典》（American Heritage

Dictionary），词义过多的单词或一些过于常见的单词只收录了TOEFL 考试中常见的特殊含义，比如 succeed 只收录了"v. 接连，继承，继续，接着…发生"的含义。"精"、"准"是本书最重要的特色。

* 例句全部来自真实文章，保持原有考试的原汁原味。但是，也由于例句全部来自真实的托福文章，所以，很多例句整体偏难。不过，读者大可不必一定要看懂整个例句，只须关注单词本身的用法即可。

* 衍生词一般只涉及词性的变化，是指通过英语本族构词法衍生出的词汇。这些词放在一起记忆可以节省大量宝贵时间。

* 近义词的收录有时包括一些生僻词汇（包括 TOEFL 考试中只出现过一次的词汇）。

其中需要格外注意的是"近义词"条目。考生要了解的是，在准备TOEFL 考试的过程中，暂时没必要对近义词有辨析能力。例如：important、essential、critical、vital、indispensable 等等，只需要知道这些词全都是"重要"就可以了；ape、monkey、chimp、chimpanzee、primate 等等，只需要知道这些词全都是"猿、猴"就可以了；cave、cavity、chamber、pit、hole、crater 等等，只需要知道这些词全都是"坑、洞"就可以了。至于这几组词中的各个单词之间的具体差别，是无关紧要的——至少在 TOEFL 考试中。其次，通过单词书去背单词，实际上也是迫不得已的事情。使用单词书的过程中，最头痛的就是突然发现："哎呀，这个单词的意思我曾经背过，可是想不起来是什么了?!"近义词条的重要功用之一就是避免出现这种尴尬。读者可以使用近义词条确定并温习那些已经背过的"相近词义"的词汇。

(三)

背单词是一件很苦的事情，但却是绝对值得去做的事情。据说背单词有很多方法，谁也说不清楚哪个方法更好一些。"21 *Secrets of Self-made Millionaires*" 中有这样一段话：

The difference between successful people and failures is that successful people make a habit of doing the things that failures do not like to do. And what are those things? Well, the things that failures don't like to do are the same things that successful people don't like to do either.

But successful people do them anyway because they realize that these are prices that they must pay for the success that they desire.

Successful people are more concerned with pleasing results. Failures are more concerned with pleasing methods. Successful people do things that are goal achieving. Unsuccessful people do things that are tension relieving. Successful people do the things that are hard and necessary and important. Unsuccessful people, on the other hand, prefer to do the things that are fun and easy and which give immediate enjoyment.

Remember, everything in life is a test. Every day, every hour and sometimes every minute, you are taking a test of self-mastery, self-control and self-discipline. The test is to see whether you can make yourself do the things that are most important and stay with them until they are complete. The test is whether or not you can keep your mind on what you want and where you are going rather than thinking about things you don't want or problems that you have had in the past.

所以，实际上"方法"这个东西没那么重要——至少没有很多人想象的那么重要。事实上，很多人用很笨的方法同样成功了。因此，成功往往不是靠"方法、技巧"而是靠"勤奋、努力"。

不要认为一天背 100 个单词不可能。这本书中每个单元有 101 或 102 个词汇——有些词汇还包括若干个词义。乍看起来"每天一个单元"似乎有些过量，但并没有那么可怕——本书在编写过程中已经有很多学生使用本书的测试版在 21 天之内消灭这本书中的所有词汇，最终体会那种在考场上不再有大量生词的快感。过去有一位老师经常这样鼓励我："书怎么会看不完呢？你想啊，有人能写出书来，可你看书都看不完是不是太笨了呢？"

诀窍在于：尽快完成第一遍，然后重复很多遍。因为并没有人要求我们"第一遍就全部记住"——实际上也没有人能做到"第一遍就全部记住"。早上起来花一个小时重复一遍昨天的内容；上午用两个小时浏览新的单元，并把已经认识并且正确掌握的词汇划掉；下午用两个小时把剩下的部分反复过滤很多遍；晚上用一个小时复习一下白天的内容。——就是这么简单！

不要觉得一天背 100 个太累。一天 100 个，21 天结束。一天 10 个

210 天才能结束——更累!!! 事实上从来就没有人背单词可以坚持 210 天。钟道隆先生①以他 50 多岁的高龄，在 1 年内用 3000 个小时就从零做起攻克了英语难关，成为"首席翻译"。如果每天只学 1 个小时，大约要 8 年的时间；高手们都比较"凶悍"，每天狂练 8 个小时，甚至 10 个小时——钟道隆先生每天 15 个小时! 所以，他们只需要一年——这大概就是所谓的速成吧。

也别怕别人说你是疯了。背单词的人都是疯子。心理学家拉里·奎尔早就做出这样的总结："精神病患者的典型症状之一就是——他会不停地重复做一件事情，期望得到不同的结果……"

把自己当作一台机器吧——暂时别把自己当人看。因为人是有各种各样的感觉的——其实各种各样的感觉都是浪费时间的："沮丧"、"焦虑"除了浪费时间之外没有任何用处；即便是"开心"、"幸福"不也同样是 time-consuming 的嘛! 机器的好处是永远可以定时定量完成指定任务。"该干嘛就干嘛"是成功者朴素的信条。坚持到底，终将有所收获，成功之后，没有人说你是"机器"、"呆子"或者"疯子"，所有人对你只是"羡慕"。不要半途而废。这样"变态"的事情，我们这辈子只需要做这么一次——做就要做到最好，做就一定要坚持到底。坚持不下去的时候想想那个永不失败的 Bryan 曾经说过的话吧："失败只有一种，就是半途而废。"

---

① 钟道隆，《逆向英语学习法》的作者。

TOEFL 常见词汇障碍
设置方法及其应对策略

　　在语言水平测试中，出题者设置障碍的最直接手段就是在词汇上做文章。TOEFL 考试中，出题者最常使用的词汇障碍设置手段有三种：(1) 词性活用；(2) 熟词僻义；(3) 高难词汇。以下将分别举例说明这三种手段。

1. 词性活用

　　英文中的名词和动词都有复数形式，所以，这种障碍设置手段中，名词、动词的活用情况是最多的。不过，这种障碍设置方式很容易应付，无非就是注意"名词的复数"和动词的"一般现在时"。例如：

(1) The weight of a gibbon (a small ape) hanging below a branch arches the terminal leaves down so that fruit-bearing foliage drops toward the gibbon's face.

　　初读这个句子的考生往往一头雾水。因为 arch 这个词，绝大多数人是把它当作名词"拱门"记忆的。可是在这个句子里，出题者把 arch 当作动词使用了，相当于 bend。

(2) Near the end of this era, research studies demonstrated that rapid weight loss was associated with nitrogen imbalance and could only be rectified by providing adequate dietary protein associated with certain foods.

　　这个例子中，出题者完全可以写"..., research demonstrated ..."或者"..., studies demonstrated ..."，却偏偏要写成"..., research studies demonstrated ..."就是为了让考生读到 studies 的时候把这个词误解成谓

语动词，而后才发现说不通。

（3） The spectacular auroral light displays that appear in Earth's atmosphere around the north and south magnetic poles were once mysterious phenomena.

这句话，如果把 displays 当作是动词的话，就完全看不懂了。实际上，这句话的谓语动词是 were。"The spectacular auroral light displays"（啰嗦得很："辉煌的极光的光的演示"）是一长长的名词性词组，后接一个定语从句，做句子的主语。

2. 熟词僻义

背单词最苦的就是到达 3000 词汇量之前的那个阶段。因为，常用词的特征是一个单词有很多个意思。不经过专门的准备，谁会知道 condition 有 "*n*. 病痛" 的含义，exponent 是 "*n*. 典型"，fashion 是 "*v*. 制造"，issue 是 "*v*. 喷出"，season 是 "*v*. 风干" 呢？值得庆幸的是这类词汇数量并不是很多：总计 130 个左右——只要一个下午就可以完全搞定（参见附录 2）。

3. 高难词汇

无论考生背过多少单词，总会在考试中遇到不认识的单词。在可收集的数据范围之内（过去二十多年近 130 次考试中），共计有 4152 个单词只出现过一次。这些词中的绝大多数，都是出题者明知道应试者必然不认识的单词。

关于这一点，可以参照 BNC① （British National Corpus，大不列颠国家语料库）的词频表——尽管 ETS 使用自己的语料库（T2K-SWAL Corpus），但在本质上是相同的。目前我们可以得到的几种国际上权威的语料库包括 Collins、Cambridge 等等的词频表都与 BNC 词频表相似。这些词频表中排在前几位的单词分别是：the、of、and、a、in、to、is……而 TOEFL 文章中经常出现在 BNC 的词频表中排位在 30000 以外的词汇，比如：exorbitant（39336）、lethargic（36774）、rupture（33232）、chico（50566）、purveyor（52510）、quasar（56673）等等。

---

① BNC 官方网站地址：http://www.natcorp.ox.ac.uk/

这些词汇就算认识也没有什么用处，因为下次考试中仍然会出现新的陌生词汇。这些词大多与题目根本就没有关系。换言之，在考场上可以干脆跳过。如果词汇题中出现了高难度词汇，那么文章中一定会提供相应、确切的线索。处理这类词汇的对策总结有三：跳、换、猜。

(1) 跳

请仔细对照以下一段文字的两个版本：

a) Evaporated from the oceans; water vapor forms clouds, some of which are transported by wind over the continents. Condensation from the clouds provides the essential agent of continental erosion: rain. Precipitated onto the ground, the water trickles down to form brooks, streams, and rivers, constituting what is called the hydrographic network. This immense polarized network channels the water toward a single receptacle: an ocean. Gravity dominates this entire step in the cycle because water tends to minimize its potential energy by running from high altitudes toward the reference point, that is, sea level.

b) ~~Evaporated~~ from the oceans; water ~~vapor~~ forms clouds, some of which are transported by wind over the continents. ~~Condensation~~ from the clouds provides ~~the essential agent of continental~~: rain. ~~Precipitated~~ onto the ground, the water ~~trickles down to~~ form ~~brook~~, ~~streams~~, and rivers, constituting ~~what is called the hydrographic~~ network. This immense polarized network channels the water toward ~~a single~~ ~~receptacle: an~~ ocean. Gravity dominates this entire step in the cycle because water tends to minimize its potential energy by running from high altitudes toward ~~the reference point, that is,~~ sea level.

在 b) 版本中，尽管大量的单词被跳过了——以至于剩下的篇幅几乎都是由高中词汇所构成，然而我们仍然没有错过任何重要信息。

在考场上，应用这种跳跃需要信心。信心来自于何处呢？如果读者把这本词汇书中的 2100 多个词汇全部掌握了，就应该有十足的信心了。因为，在考场上如果出现了一个单词，连精心准备过的你都不认识，那么，几乎可以肯定，其他人估计也不认识这个词！

(2) 换

首先，考生要了解 TOEFL 考试中的一个特殊概念——"等价结构"。这是 TOEFL 考试的一个特色。在 TOEFL 中，我们经常会遇到上下文互相解释的现象，而这种上下文互相解释的结构，被我们称为"等价结构"。先让我们熟悉一些 TOEFL 中常见的"等价结构"：

* 同位语；that is；冒号"："；破折号"——"；括号"（）"
* and①；or
* includes/including；for example；such as；as
* called；named；known as

这些"等价结构"前后的词汇所表达的意思往往是近义，至少是同一范畴。比如，上下文曾经出现"twigs and branches"，那么我们应该知道 twigs 实际上至少应该与 branches 是同一范畴的东西（事实上 twig 就是"小树枝"）。而下一次再看到 twig 这个词的时候，就可以把它换成 branches。再比如，文章中说"Small animals, such rodent as mice and squirrel,..."那么，在这篇文章中，small animals = rodent = mice = squirrel——反正都是"小动物"。文章中说"... mammals of moderately large size, which may include monkeys, cats, civets, and porcupine."那么，mammals of large size = monkeys = cats = civets = porcupine 反正都是"大动物"。

大量地阅读 TOEFL 文章，读者就可以体会：除了在 TOEFL 文章中，一般不可能在其他类型的文章中遇到这样广泛存在的"等价结构"。在 TOEFL 文章中，"等价结构"前后往往连接着一个我们认识的以及一个我们不认识的词汇。"等价结构"前后哪一个更重要呢？答案是：我们看得懂的那个就是重要的。

另外，需要了解这样一个简单的道理，"有限的篇幅中将只能讨论有限的概念"。请仔细阅读以下的文章：

---

① 注意：大量的 and 并列时，除最后一个之外，其他的 and 将省略，而是用逗号"，"替代之。如：... which may include monkeys, cats, civets and porcupine.

— 15 —

Plants are subject to attack and infection by a remarkable variety of symbiotic species and have evolved a diverse array of mechanisms designed to frustrate the potential colonists. These can be divided into preformed or passive defense mechanisms and inducible or active systems. Passive plant defense comprises physical and chemical barriers that prevent entry of pathogens, such as bacteria, or render tissues unpalatable or toxic to the invader. The external surfaces of plants, in addition to being covered by an epidermis and a waxy cuticle, often carry spiky hairs known as trichomes, which either prevent feeding by insects or may even puncture and kill insect larvae. Other trichomes are sticky and glandular and effectively trap and immobilize insects.

If the physical barriers of the plant are breached, then preformed chemicals may inhibit or kill the intruder, and plant tissues contain a diverse array of toxic or potentially toxic substances, such as resins, tannins, glycosides, and alkaloids, many of which are highly effective deterrents to insects that feed on plants. The success of the Colorado beetle in infesting potatoes, for example, seems to be correlated with its high tolerance to alkaloids that normally repel potential pests. Other possible chemical defenses, while not directly toxic to the parasite, may inhibit some essential step in the establishment of a parasitic relationship. For example, glycoproteins in plant cell walls may inactivate enzymes that degrade cell walls. These enzymes are often produced by bacteria and fungi.

Active plant defense mechanisms are comparable to the immune system of vertebrate animals, although the cellular and molecular bases are fundamentally different. Both, however, are triggered in reaction to intrusion, implying that the host has some means of recognizing the presence of a foreign organism. The most dramatic example of an inducible plant defense reaction is the hypersensitive response. In the hypersensitive response, cells undergo rapid necrosis—that is, they become diseased and die—after being penetrated by a parasite; the parasite itself subsequently ceases to grow and is therefore restricted to one or a few cells around the entry site. Several theories have been put forward to explain the basis of hypersensitive resistance.

不要被这篇文章中的大量生词所吓倒。文章的第一句话告诉我们，"植物容易受到攻击，所以演化出了一系列的防御机制"。于是，这篇文章将只涉及两种事物："植物"和"攻击者"。

* 以下所有的概念本质上相对于"植物"来讲都属于"攻击者"的范畴：*symbiotic species*；*potential colonists*；*pathogens*；*bacteria*；*invader*；*insects*；*insect larvae*；*intruder*；*insects that feed on plants*；*Colorado beetle*；*potential pests*；*fungi* …
* "植物"发出的动作都是"防御"：*defense*；*prevent*；*render tissue toxic*；*puncture*；*kill*；*trap*；*immobilize*；*repel*；*inhibit*；*inactivate* …
* "攻击者"发出的动作都是"攻击"：*attack*；*infest*；*entry*；*breach*；*degrade* …

另外，在这篇文章中，preformed ＝ passive；inducible ＝ active；mechanism ＝ system。有了这样的了解，这篇看起来难之又难的文章实际上就变得非常简单了。

(3) 猜

猜测词义通常并不是一件容易的事情。然而，因为在 TOEFL 这种设计严谨的考试中，出题者一方面要中规中矩地设置障碍；而另一方面，出题者还要小心翼翼地提供逻辑清晰却又尽可能隐蔽的提示。于是，在 TOEFL 文章中猜测一个词汇的含义就变得相对简单一些。

需要我们猜测的词汇通常都是：名词、动词、形容词、副词。它们之间的相互关系如下：

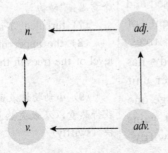

（1）特定的形容词将只能修饰一些特定的名词；反之，特定的名词将只能被一些特定的形容词所修饰；

（2）特定的名词将只能发出一些特定的动作；反之，特定的动词将只能接一些特定的名词作宾语；

（3）副词能够修饰的很多，包括 a) 形容词 b) 副词 c) 动词 d) 句子，然而，副词的特征是：通常情况下，如果删掉一个句子中的副词，句子的大意通常没有很大的变化。

以下通过一篇文章，具体说明"跳"、"换"、"猜"三个词汇策略的应用：

The canopy, the upper level of the trees in the rain forest, holds a plethora of climbing mammals of moderately large size, which may include monkeys, cats, civets, and porcupines. Smaller species, including such rodents as mice and small squirrels, are not as prevalent overall in high tropical canopies as they are in most habitats globally.

Small mammals, being warm blooded, suffer hardship in the exposed and turbulent environment of the upper most trees. Because a small body has more surface area per unit of weight than a large one of similar shape, it gains or loses heat more swiftly.

（1）canopy = the upper level of the trees in the rain forest。

（2）plethora、moderately 不认识可以跳过。

（3）civets、porcupines 都不认识，反正都是 mammals of large size。

（4）rodent = mice = squirrel，都是 smaller species。

（5）第二次出现 canopy 可以换成"the upper level of the trees in the rain forest"。

（6）这一段中的 mammals，上段的 species，以及后面段落中的 animals 都是同一个意思："动物"。

（7）turbulent 不认识可以暂时跳过。

（8）the upper most tress = the upper level of the trees in the rain forest = canopy

（9）小动物体表面积相对大一些，那么获得热量以及散失热量更怎么样呢？——更快（swiftly）。

Thus, in the trees, where shelter from heat and cold may be scarce and conditions may fluctuate, a small mammal may have trouble maintaining its body temperature.

Small size makes it easy to scramble among twigs and branches in the canopy for insects, flowers, or fruit, but small mammals are surpassed, in the competition for food, by large ones that have their own tactics for browsing among food-rich twigs. The weight of a gibbon (a small ape) hanging below a branch arches the terminal leaves down so that fruit-bearing foliage drops toward the gibbon's face. Walking or leaping species of a similar or even larger size access the outer twigs either by snapping off and retrieving the whole branch or by clutching stiff branches with the feet or tail and plucking food with their hands.

Small climbing animals may reach twigs readily, but it is harder for them than for large climbing animals

（10）这里说的 "shelter from heat and cold may be scarce" 实际上就是上文 "exposed environment" 的具体解释。

那么，conditions may fluctuate 就应该对应上文中的 "turbulent environment"。其实，turbulent = fluctuate（不要在意词性的不同）；environment = conditions。

（11）twigs 和 branches 应该是属于同一范畴的。以后看到 twigs 都可以被替换为 branches。

（12）小的动物在 branches 上可以发出的动作其实没有几个，并且还是为了获取食物，那这个动作可能是什么呢？——爬。

（13）gibbon = ape

（14）arches 不认识无所谓，因为 arches sth. down 的意思是说，把什么东西弄下来了（down 没有人不认识）。

（15）foliage = leaves。leaves 被 ... down 了，那么 掉下来的是什么呢？就是 leaves 嘛！

（16）别管是 "walking"，还是 "leaping"，都是 "larger size" 的。

（17）snapping off、retrieving、clutching、plucking 都是 access the outer branch（twigs）的手段而已。其中，clutching 是 feet or tail 发出的动作；plucking 是 hands 发出的动作。

to cross the wide gaps from one tree crown to the next that typify the high canopy. A macaque or gibbon can hurl itself farther than a mouse can: it can achieve a running start, and it can more effectively use a branch as a springboard, even bouncing on a limb several times before jumping. The forward movement of a small animal is seriously reduced by the air friction against the relatively large surface area of its body.

Finally, for the many small mammals that supplement their insect diet with fruits or seeds, an inability to span open gaps between tree crowns may be problematic, since trees that yield these foods can be sparse.

（18）终于出现了"tree crown"，实际上 canopy = tree crown。

（19） macaque = gibbon = ape = mammals of large size

（20） macaque 或者 gibbon 可以发出 hurl 的动作，而后面说，在 jumping 之前，它们还可以 bouncing。那么 hurl 是什么呢？其实 "hurl itself"（把自己猛投出去）就相当于 "jump"。

（21）是什么意思呢？上一次出现 gap 的时候，前面的形容词是 "wide"，等同于现在这个 "open"；而 "span" 就应该等同于上一次出现的 gap 前面的那个动词 "cross"。

（22）sparse 是 "稀疏的"，是个很难的词汇。然而，不认识这个词也没有关系，因为题目中没有涉及到文章最后一句话。

总之，考生在 TOEFL 考试中所面临的问题表面上看来是 "词汇问题"，实际上非完全如此。如果策略得当，正如上面分析的那篇文章一样，每一篇 TOEFL 文章都可以被简化成 "完全由高中词汇构成的文章"。只背诵单词书是不够的，背单词最好的方法就是根据上下文。很多人都背过 "turbulent—湍流的、激流的" 但是在文章中却根本看不懂；可是注意到上下文的联系，"turbulent environment = where ... conditions may fluctuate"，"turbulent" 这个词没有背过又怎么样呢？把 canopy 背成 "天篷、华盖"（其实应该是 "tree crown—树冠"）还不如不背呢！

所以，建议考生考前至少精读 25 篇 TOEFL 阅读文章，（1）寻找并分析第一个"等价结构";（2）认真琢磨上下文之间的联系，看看不认识的单词在上下文中有没有提供相应的线索；（3）分类整理出现过的名词概念，看看他们是不是只属于某一两个范畴；动词、形容词、副词也同样可能属于同一范畴。

注意，所谓的精读，最重要的是要把已经读过的文章反复阅读很多遍。很多人是没有耐心去读已经读过的文章的，可恰恰是因为如此，能力总是没有提高。其实，"反复阅读已经读过的文章"，才是提高阅读速度以及理解能力的不二法门，重复次数越多，才越可能看到更多上下文之间的联系，而这种对上下文联系的理解能力，才是最重要的。

Unit 1

abandon	entail	nebula	shrink
accumulate	etch	nostalgia	slide
adverse	exploit	occupy	solve
amazing	fantasy	orchid	spiky
approve	flap	overturn	squeeze
assemble	forage	passage	steep
avid	fuel	per capita	strain
barter	genre	photosynthesis	submerge
biography	gradient	plateau	summit
boulder	hang	portable	sustain
bulb	herb	precipitate	tail
can	household	primary	telescope
casualty	imagine	promise	theme
chance	incentive	provoke	tight
civilian	initial	quartz	tough
conceive	insult	ration	transparent
consecutive	invade	recognition	trouble
convention	journal	regenerate	undergo
crab	lathe	remnant	utility
curriculum	librarian	request	venture
defend	log	retire	visual
detect	magnify	risk	way
discipline	match	runoff	withdraw
divert	meteorite	scavenger	
dynamic	mission	secrete	
emanate	mosaic	sew	

abandon [əˈbændən]

【释】 *v.* 扔弃(地位等)，离弃(家园)

【例】 Haskin eventually *abandoned* the risky project.

【衍】 abandoned (*adj.*); abandonment (*n.*)

【近】 discard，forsake，cast off

accumulate [əˈkjuːmjuleit]

【释】 *v.* 积累，存储

【例】 Formation of a glacier is complete when ice has *accumulated* to a thickness (and thus weight) sufficient to make it move slowly under pressure.

【衍】 accumulating (*adj.*); accumulation (*n.*)

【近】 accrue，amass

adverse [ædˈvəːs]

【释】 *adj.* 逆的，相反的，不利的，有害的

【例】 This sharing enables lichens to resist the most *adverse* environmental conditions found on earth.

【衍】 adversely (*adv.*); adversity (*n.*) 逆境，苦难，不幸；adversary (*n.*) 敌手，对手，反对者；adversarial (*adj.*) 敌手的，对手的；adversative (*adj.*) (词等)意义相反的

【近】 detrimental，harmful，undesirable

amazing [əˈmeiziŋ]

【释】 *adj.* 令人惊异的

【例】 The electric eel is an *amazing* storage battery.

【衍】 amaze (*v.*); amazingly (*adv.*); amazement (*n.*)

【近】 astonishing，astounding，startling，marvelous，miraculous

approve [əˈpruːv]

【释】 *v.* 批准，认可；赞成，满意

【例】 Though some doctors *approved* of the women's desire to establish a nurses' training school，other medical men were opposed.

【衍】 approval (*n.*) 赞成，同意；disapprove (*v.*); disapproval (*n.*)

【近】 agree，grant，consent

assemble [əˈsembl]

【释】 ① *v.* 集合；聚集

【例】 When a food object or nest intruder is too large for one individual to handle，nestmates can be quickly *assembled* by alarm or recruitment signals.

【衍】 assemblage（*n.*）与会者；assembly（*n.*）集会

【近】 accumulate，amass，congregate，marshal

【释】 ② *v.* 装配

【例】 The modern factory used power-driven machines and *assembly*-line techniques to turn out large quantities of well-made goods.

【衍】 assemblage（*n.*）装配；assembly（*n.*）装配

【近】 compile，construct

avid ['ævid]

【释】 *adj.* 渴望的；贪婪的

【例】 A child is normally nature's *avid* student.

【衍】 avidly（*adv.*）；avidity（*n.*）；avidness（*n.*）

【近】 ardent，eager，enthusiastic，keen，passionate

barter ['bɑːtə]

【释】 *n.* 物物交换，换货，实物交易

【例】 Then the *barter* system was replaced by coins.

【衍】 barterer（*n.*）交易商

【近】 bargain

biography [bai'ɔgrəfi]

【释】 *n.* 传，传记

【例】 He wrote an auto *biography* in 1956，and also published several collections of poetry.

【衍】 biographer（*n.*）传记作者；biographical（*adj.*）

【近】 memoir

boulder ['bəuldə]

【释】 *n.* 圆石，卵石；冰砾

【例】 The spot continues to move across the shelter floor and down the butte，or hill，toward a group of small *boulders*.

【近】 pebble，rubble，rock，stone

bulb [bʌlb]

【释】 ① *n.* 球根；鳞茎，球状物

【例】 Thomas Hancock，an English settler，wrote thanking his plant supplier for a gift of some tulip *bulbs* from England， but his letter the following year grumbled that they were all dead.

【衍】 bulbed（*adj.*）

【近】 tuber，corm

【释】 ② *n.* 灯泡

【例】 Ordinary light，from the Sun or a light *bulb*，is emitted spontaneously，when atoms or molecules get rid of excess energy by themselves，without any outside intervention.

can ［kæn］

【释】 *n.* 罐头 *v.* 制罐头

【例】 In 1810 a French inventor named Nicolas Appert developed the cooking-and-sealing process of *canning*.

【衍】 canned（*adj.*）

【近】 container，canister，tin can

casualty ［'kæʒjuəlti］

【释】 *n.* 伤亡(人数)；事故，横祸

【例】 Troops fired on demonstrators near the Royal Palace causing many *casualties*.

【近】 wounded，victim

chance ［tʃɑːns］

【释】 *n.* 偶然；运气，命运

【例】 Only 0.1 percent of the species that have lived on Earth have survived to the present，and it was largely *chance* that determined which species survived and which died out.

【近】 possibility，fate，destiny

civilian ［si'viljən］

【释】 *n.* 市民，平民

【例】 Both governments made tremendous demands upon *civilians* and，in general，received willing cooperation.

【衍】 civil（*adj.*）市民的，公民的

【近】 inhabitant，resident

conceive ［kən'siːv］

【释】 *v.* 怀(胎)；想到，构想(计划等)

【例】 Under Macaulay's influence Mercy Warren *conceived* her plan to write a history of the American Revolution，living to complete it in 1805.

【近】 perceive，imagine，picture

consecutive ［kən'sekjutiv］

【释】 *adj*. 连续的

【例】 Durang continued his remarkable career for the next 20 years，performing in theaters and circuses and even managing his own dramatic touring troupe for nine *consecutive* summers.

【衍】 inconsecutive（*adj.*）；consecutively（*adv.*）；consecutiveness（*n.*）

【近】 successive

convention ［kən'venʃən］

【释】 ① *n*. 习俗，惯例

【例】 This new design concept, coupled with the sharp postwar reactions to the style and *conventions* of the preceding decades, created an entirely new public taste which caused Art Nouveau types of glass to fall out of favor.

【衍】 conventional（*adj.*）；conventionally（*adv.*）；unconventional（*adj.*）

【近】 tradition，custom

【释】 ② *n*. 会议

【例】 Many other early national political *conventions* were held there.

【近】 meeting，conference

crab ［kræb］

【释】 *n*. 蟹

【例】 They collected oysters，*crabs*，sea urchins，mussels，abalone，and clams，which they could gather while remaining close to their children.

curriculum ［kə'rikjuləm］

【释】 *n*. (［*pl.*］curriculums, curricula) 课程

【例】 As the student body changed，so did the *curriculum*.

【衍】 curricular（*adj.*）

【近】 course

defend ［di'fend］

【释】 *v*. 保卫(国家等)；防御,防守，保护…使免于(from, against)

【例】 Instead，they *defend* themselves from the consequences of

— 5 —

injury and infection by walling off the damage.

【衍】 defendable（adj.）；defendant（n.）【法】被告（人）（的）；defense（n.）；defenseless（adj.）；defensive（adj.）防卫的，防御的

【近】 protect，guard，secure，shield

detect ［di'tekt］

【释】 **v. 发觉，发现；检定**

【例】 These experiments were designed to **detect** consciousness.

【衍】 detectable（adj.）能发觉的；能检查出来的；detection（n.）

【近】 discover，reveal，ascertain

discipline ［'disiplin］

【释】 **n. 学科**

【例】 Archaeology is a source of history, not just a humble auxiliary **discipline**.

【近】 subject，field

divert ［di'vəːt，dai'vəːt］

【释】 **v. 使转向，使转移(from; to)；使消遣，使解闷，使娱乐**

【例】 Too often，the interest of children in the natural world is **diverted** by the example of their elders.

【衍】 diversion（n.）消遣，娱乐

【近】 avert，redirect，distract

dynamic ［dai'næmik］

【释】 **adj. 动(态)的；有生气的**

【例】 South Asia continues to be the most **dynamic** economic region in the world.

【衍】 dynamically（adv.）

【近】 active，energetic，lively

emanate ［'eməneit］

【释】 **v. (光、气体等)发出，发散，放射(from)**

【例】 a series of radiating diamonds of different colors **emanating** from the large central star

【衍】 emanative（adj.）；emanation（n.）

【近】 emit，radiate，issue

entail ［in'teil］

【释】 **v. & n. 使蒙受，使产生，带来**

【例】 All of this **entailed** tremendous risk, because France did not

— 6 —

have the military resources to control this much territory and
still protect itself and maintain order at home.

【衍】 entailment（*n.*）

【近】 cause，lead to

etch ［etʃ］

【释】 *v. & n.* 蚀刻，浸蚀

【例】 The pressure can be applied in various ways，such as
running the surface and the paper through an *etching*
press（etching press：铜版印刷机）.

【近】 engrave，scratch，carve，incise

exploit ［ik'sploit］

【释】 *v.* 利用，开发

【例】 With this invention Woods organized his own company，
the Woods Electric Company，to take over and *exploit*
his patents.

【衍】 exploitable（*adj.*）；exploitation（*n.*）

【近】 use，utilize，manipulate

fantasy ［'fæntəsi］

【释】 *n. & v.* 空想，幻想

【例】 In their generous conceptions，play harmlessly and
experimentally permits us to put our creative forces，
fantasy，and imagination into action.

【衍】 fantastic（*adj.*）；fantastically（*adv.*）；fanaticism（*n.*）
狂信，狂热

【近】 fancy，vision

flap ［flæp］

【释】 ① *n.* （鸟、昆虫）翼；（鱼）鳃盖；（狗等）下垂的长耳；
（菌类）张开的伞

【例】 ... providing support for a *flap* of stretched skin that
served as a wing.

【释】 ② *v.* 拍动

【例】 The bird *flaps* one wing in an apparent attempt to take
to the air...

forage ［'foridʒ］

【释】 ① *n.* 草料；饲料

【例】 In the eastern parts of the United States, the preferred grass for *forage* was a cultivated plant.

【近】 hay, straw, fodder

【释】 ② *v.* 觅食

【例】 During the day, parties of birds will have spread out to *forage* over a very large area.

【近】 feed, hunt

fuel [fjuəl]

【释】 *n.* 燃料,柴炭　*v.* (给…)加油

【例】 Sunlight is the only *fuel* solar cells need.

【近】 oil, gas, energy, petroleum

genre ['ʒɔŋrə]

【释】 *n.* (文艺作品的)类型,(诗、剧、小说、散文的)体裁

【例】 What type of subject matter does this art *genre* include?

【近】 type, sort, kind, genus

gradient ['greidiənt]

【释】 *n.* 倾斜度,坡度,梯度,陡度

【例】 This temperature *gradient* may be vital to successful hatching.

【近】 ascent, slope, incline, ramp

hang [hæŋ]

【释】 *v.* (hung, hanged)悬挂,垂吊(to; on; from)

【例】 A painter *hangs* his finished picture on the wall so that everyone can see it.

【近】 suspend

herb [həːb]

【释】 *n.* 草,草本植物

【例】 In addition to a few varieties of trees and tough shrubs, most deserts have grasses, *herbs*, and other annual plants.

【衍】 herbage(*n.*)[集合名词] 草本植物(尤指牧草);herbal (*adj.*) 草本植物的;草本植物制的;herbivore(*n.*)食草动物

household ['haushəuld]

【释】 *n. & adj.* 家庭(的),一家(的)

【例】 Articles for nearly every *household* activity and ornament could be bought in Rockinghigh.

【近】 family, house, home

imagine [i'mædʒin]

【释】 *v.* 想象，猜想，推测

【例】 Who could *imagine* a fairy-tale grass that required no rain and somehow made it possible for cattle to feed themselves all winter?

【衍】 imaginary（*adj.*）; imaginative（*adj.*）; imagination（*n.*）; imagist（*n.*）意象主义者；意象派

【近】 picture, envision, suppose

incentive [in'sentiv]

【释】 *n.* 刺激；鼓励；动机 *adj.* 刺激性的，鼓励性质的

【例】 There is little or no *incentive* to adopt such measures.

【近】 inducement, motivation, spur

initial [i'niʃəl]

【释】 ① *adj.* 最初的，开始的

【例】 His *initial* expedition, which sailed in 1578 with a patent granted by Queen Elizabeth, was defeated by the Spanish.

【衍】 initially（*adv.*）; initialize（*v.*）

【近】 first, original, primary

【释】 ② *n.* 词首字母，词首大写字母

【例】 She persisted in using her *initials* for the remainder of her career.

【近】 acronym

insult ['insʌlt]

【释】 *v. & n.* 侮辱，凌辱

【例】 Their behavior was an *insult* to the people they represent.

【衍】 insulting（*adj.*）; insultingly（*adv.*）

【近】 abuse, offend

invade [in'veid]

【释】 *v.* 侵入，侵略

【例】 Periodically, molten material wells out of the Earth's interior to *invade* the surface layers or to flow onto the surface itself.

【衍】 invader（*n.*）; invasion（*n.*）

【近】 intrude, assault

journal ['dʒəːnəl]

【释】 *n.* 日记，日志，航海日记

【例】 Townes and Schawlow published their ideas in a scientific *journal*.

【衍】 journalism（*n.*）新闻业；journalist 新闻记者；journey 旅行

【近】 diary, paper, magazine

lathe [leið]

【释】 *n.* 车床，镟床

【例】 In the late sixteenth century the glass *lathe* was introduced, making it possible to ground several lenses at once and also to produce—as objects of curiosity—powerful, thick concave lenses.

librarian [lai'brɛəriən]

【释】 *n.* 图书馆长，图书管理员

【例】 The most honored citizens are bankers, Carol, who has been to college and held a position as a *librarian*, comes to Gopher Prairie to live with her doctor husband.

【衍】 library（*n.*）图书馆；书库；藏书楼；藏书

log [lɔg]

【释】 ① *n.* 原木，圆木，干材   *v.* (把树)砍倒，锯成圆材；拖(木头)

【例】 *Logs* were piled up and burned in the open, and the ashes collected.

【衍】 logger（*n.*）伐木工，锯木工；logged（*adj.*）在水中泡重了的(圆木)

【释】 ② *v.* 航行；飞行；以…的时速飞行(航行)

【例】 During this time, the vessel *logged* 600,000 kilometers and took almost 20,000 core samples of seabed sediments and rock at 624 drilling sites around the world.

【衍】 logbook（*n.*）航海日志，飞行日志

magnify ['mægnifai]

【释】 *v.* 扩大，放大；夸张，夸大

【例】 Rapid industrialization and increased geographic mobility in the nineteenth century had special implications for women because these changes tended to *magnify* social distinctions.

【衍】 magnification（*n.*）扩大；放大率(倍数)；magnitude（*n.*）大小；数量；广大，巨大；量值

【近】 enlarge，expand，amplify

match ［mætʃ］

【释】 *v.* 相称，相适合，相配；结合

【例】 These two antagonists were poorly *matched*，in so far as they had very unequal strengths.

【衍】 matchable（*adj.*）能匹敌的，对等的；matchless（*adj.*）无敌的

【近】 correspond，equal，go with

meteorite ［ˈmiːtjərait］

【释】 *n.* 陨星，陨石

【例】 The most easily recognizable *meteorites* are the iron variety，although they only represent about 5 percent of all *meteorite* falls.

【衍】 meteoritic（*adj.*）陨石的；meteoric（*adj.*）流星似的；迅速的

mission ［ˈmiʃən］

【释】 *n.* 使命，任务，天职　*v.* 给…交代任务；派遣

【例】 But in the animal world，the homing pigeon alone can be trusted with its freedom and trained to carry out the *missions* that people demand.

【衍】 missionary（*n. & adj.*）传教士，传教（士）的

【近】 assignment，task，work

mosaic ［mɔˈzeiik］

【释】 *n. & adj.* 马赛克（的），镶嵌细工（的），拼花工艺（的），拼花图样（的），拼制物（的）

【例】 Each fall，billions of green leaves explode into a *mosaic* of reds，yellows and browns.

【衍】 mosaicism（*n.*）镶嵌性

【近】 mixture，variety，montage

nebula ［ˈnebjulə］

【释】 *n.* 星云；云状，雾影

【例】 Jupiter is the best-preserved sample of the early solar *nebula*，and with its satellites，might contain the most important clues about the origin of the Solar System.

【衍】 nebulae（*n.*）星云；nebular（*adj.*）星云的；nebulize（*v.*）使成水花，使成喷雾状

nostalgia [nɔ'stældʒiə]

【释】 *n.* 怀乡病，乡愁，怀旧，留恋过去

【例】 Her subjects are based on the New England countryside and evoke a strong mood of *nostalgia*.

【衍】 nostalgic（*adj.*）；nostalgist（*n.*）怀乡者，怀旧者

【近】 homesickness, reminiscence, melancholy

occupy ['ɔkjupai]

【释】 *v.* 占领，占据；侵占；占用；占有；占（时间、空间等）

【例】 Botany, the study of plants, *occupies* a peculiar position in the history of human knowledge.

【衍】 occupation（*n.*）占有，居住；职业；occupant（*n.*）占有人，居住者；occupancy（*n.*）占领，占用，居住

【近】 inhabit, engage, take up

orchid ['ɔːkid]

【释】 *n.*【植】兰科；兰花

【例】 Certain species of *orchids*, for instance, imitate female bees: other plants look and smell like dead animals, and still others have the appearance of stones.

【衍】 orchidaceous（*adj.*）兰（科）的；兰花般的

overturn ['əuvətəːn]

【释】 *v.* & *n.* 颠覆；推翻；打倒，（使）倒

【例】 Yet even the political *overturn* was not so revolutionary as one might suppose.

【近】 upset, abolish, reverse

passage ['pæsidʒ]

【释】 *n.* 通行，通过；经过；转变，演变

【例】 The *passage* of the Bill of Rights marked the end of their long period of political agitation.

【衍】 passageway（*n.*）过道，出入口

【近】 way, route, road

per capita [pəː'kæpitə]

【释】 人均；按人均分的

【例】 The average *per capita* wealth increased by nearly 1 percent per year—30 percent over the course of a generation.

photosyn-thesis [ˌfəutəu'sinθisaiz]

【释】 **n.** 光合作用；光能合成

【例】 The autotrophic green algae produce all their own food through a process called ***photosynthesis***.

【衍】 photosynthetic（*adj.*）

plateau [plæ'təu]

【释】 **n.** 高原，台地，高地

【例】 Pushing slowly backward into the ***plateau***, the side canyons expose new rocks, and the pattern of erosion continues.

【近】 upland, highland

portable ['pɔ:təbl]

【释】 ***adj.*** 可搬运的；便于携带的；手提式的，轻便的

【例】 They are durable, ***portable***, available in infinite variety.

【衍】 portability（*n.*）

【近】 moveable, handy, convenient

precipitate [pri'sipiteit]

【释】 ***v.*** 促成，促使，使沉淀；使（水蒸气）凝结

【例】 It dissolves, transports, and ***precipitates*** many chemical compounds and is constantly modifying the face of the Earth.

【衍】 precipitation（*n.*）降水，降水量

primary ['praiməri]

【释】 ① ***adj.*** 第一的，最初的

【例】 Thus they developed the ***primary*** economic activity of the entire ancient world and the basis of all modern life.

【近】 primitive, primal

【释】 ② ***adj.*** 主要的，第一位的

【例】 The ***primary*** reason was skepticism that a railroad built through so challenging and thinly settled a stretch of desert, mountain, and semiarid plain could pay a profit.

【衍】 primarity（*adv.*）

【近】 crucial, major, principle, prime

promise ['prɔmis]

【释】 **n.** 允许；诺言；约束；（前途有）希望；（有）指望

【例】This newer emphasis on archaeology as social history has shown great *promise*.

【衍】promising（*adj.*）有出息的；有前途的；有希望的

【近】assurance，warranty

provoke [prə'vəuk]

【释】*v.* 触怒，使愤怒；成为…的原因，引起

【例】This is a grand conception that excites and *provokes*.

【衍】provoking（*adj.*）

【近】antagonize，irritate，incite

quartz [kwɔ:ts]

【释】*n.* 石英，水晶

【例】The *quartz* is much less brilliant and more plentiful than true topaz. Most of it is a variety of amethyst that heat has turned brown.

ration ['ræʃən]

【释】*v.* （按额定分量）配给

【例】Prices are the means by which products and services that are in limited supply are *rationed* among buyers.

【衍】rationing（*n.*）食物的配给；rationed（*adj.*）

【近】distribute，dispense，apportion，assign

recognition [ˌrekəg'niʃən]

【释】① *n.* 认识；识别

【例】Much of the focus of this education was on the *recognition* of vitamin deficiency symptoms.

【衍】recognizable（*adj.*）；recognize（*v.*）

【近】identification

【释】② *n.* 承认，认可

【例】In *recognition* of his work for peaceful change，Dr. King received the 1964 Nobel Peace Prize.

【衍】recognizance（*n.*）保证书，保证金；recognized（*adj.*）

【近】acknowledgment

【释】③ *n.* 褒奖，赞誉

【例】In 1955 Martin Luther King, Jr. gained national *recognition* for his nonviolent methods used in a bus boycott in Montgomery.

— 14 —

Unit 1

【衍】	recognize（*v.*）
【近】	appreciation

regenerate [riˈdʒenərit]

【释】 *v.* 使再生，使复生，使新生

【例】 Sleep is essential because it *regenerates* the brain and the nervous system.

【衍】 regeneracy （*n.*）; regeneration （*n.*）; regenerative (*adj.*); regenerator (*n.*)

【近】 renew, revive, rejuvenate

remnant [ˈremnənt]

【释】 *n.* 剩余，残屑

【例】 Most astronomers agree that comets are primordial *remnants* from the formation of the solar system.

【近】 remainder, remains, leftovers, residue

request [riˈkwest]

【释】 *n.* & *v.* 请求，恳求

【例】 An interviewer can obtain a high response rate because people find it more difficult to turn down a personal *request* for an interview than to throw away a written questionnaire.

【衍】 requested (*adj.*)

【近】 demand, ask for, application

retire [riˈtaiə]

【释】 ① *v.* 退休，退职

【例】 When she *retired*, she ordered all of her papers burned.

【衍】 retirement （*n.*）; retiree (*n.*) 退休者，退职者; retired (*adj.*)

【近】 stop working, give up work

【释】 ② *v.* 就寝，睡觉

【例】 Birds that feed in blocks commonly *retire* together into roosts.

【释】 ③ *v.* 收回(纸币等)

【例】 While they levied heavy taxes to repay state war debts, their larger neighbors might *retire* debts out of land-sale proceeds.

risk [risk]

【释】 *n.* 风险，危险 *v.* 冒险

【例】	The birds on the edge are at greatest *risk* since predators find it easier to catch small birds perching at the margins of the roost.
【衍】	risky (*adj.*); riskless (*adj.*)
【近】	danger, venture, hazard

runoff [ˈrʌnɔf]

【释】	*n.* (被雨水)冲走的东西，流走之物
【例】	Water has trouble entering this impervious soil and *runoff* is very common during rainfalls.
【近】	overflow, surplus, excess

scavenger [ˈskævindʒə]

【释】	*n.* 食腐动物(指食腐物腐尸)
【例】	The tiny, delicate skeletons are usually scattered by *scavengers* or destroyed by weathering before they can be fossilized.
【衍】	scavenge (*v.*); scavenging (*n.*)

secrete [siˈkriːt]

【释】	*v.* 分泌
【例】	These glands *secrete* hormones, which are chemicals that control numerous body functions.
【近】	exude, emit, produce

sew [səu]

【释】	*v.* 缝；缝合；缝补
【例】	Electric power was available for lamps, *sewing* machines, irons, and even vacuum cleaners.
【衍】	sewer (*n.*) 缝纫者；sewing (*n.*); sewage (*n.*) 阴沟污物，污水，下水道
【近】	stitch, seam, embroider

shrink [ʃriŋk]

【释】	*v. & n.* 收缩，缩水；退缩
【例】	*Shrinking* oil and mineral reserves contract supply, and prices move up.
【衍】	shrinkage (*n.*); shrinkable (*adj.*); shrunken (*adj.*)
【近】	contract, minimize, reduce in size

slide [slaid]

【释】	*v.* 滑，滑动

【例】 As the plates diverge from a mid-ocean ridge they *slide* on a more yielding layer at the base of the lithosphere.

【衍】 slider（*n.*）滑雪（冰）者，滑翔者

【近】 glide，slither，slip

solve ［sɔlv］

【释】 *v.* 解释，解答，解决

【例】 In 1943 the federal government imposed rent controls to help *solve* the problem of housing shortages during wartime.

【衍】 solvency（*n.*）溶解力；偿付能力；solvent（*adj.* & *n.*）溶解的；溶剂

【近】 resolve，explain，work out

spiky ［'spaiki］

【释】 *adj.* 尖而长的，锐利的

【例】 The external surfaces of plants often carry *spiky* hairs known as trichomes，which either prevent feeding by insects or may even puncture and kill insect larvae.

【衍】 spike（*n.*）长钉；尖铁

【近】 thorny，sharp，spiny

squeeze ［skwiːz］

【释】 *v.* 挤，压，塞

【例】 This is because，generally speaking，the educational system of the United States is *squeezed* indoors to a degree that stifles young minds.

【近】 press，compress，constrict

steep ［stiːp］

【释】 ① *adj.* 陡急的，峻峭的，险峻的

【例】 In Japan and elsewhere，the trees are planted to stabilize soil on *steep* mountain slopes.

【衍】 steeply（*adv.*）；steepness（*n.*）；steepen（*v.*）

【近】 sheer，vertical，precipitous

【释】 ② *adj.* 急剧升降的，急转直下的

【例】 Whatever their merits of demerits，the traditional organizations went into *steep* decline during the 1950's and 1960's. The old organizations lost the ability to maintain internal discipline.

【衍】	steeply（*adv.*）；steepness（*n.*）
【近】	sharp
strain	［strein］
【释】	① *n.* 拉紧；紧张；使用过度
【例】	Skyscrapers put a severe *strain* on a city's sanitation facilities.
【衍】	strained（*adj.*）紧张的，不自然的；strainer（*n.*）粗滤器，滤网
【近】	tension，stress，pressure
【释】	② *n.* 品系，系；菌株；变种
【例】	Going still further，they succeeded in breeding new *strains* that were resistant to diseases，grew faster and larger，and flourished in water of different salinities and temperatures.
【近】	species，breed，sort
submerge	［səb'məːdʒ］
【释】	*v.* 使浸在水中，潜水；沉没，淹没；消失
【例】	There is no much of it that if all the mountains of the world were leveled，the surface of the globe would be entirely *submerged* beneath water to a depth several thousand meters.
【衍】	submergence（*n.*）；submergible（*adj.*）；submerse（*v.*）
【近】	sink，immerse，overwhelm，submerse
summit	［'sʌmit］
【释】	*n.* 顶，绝顶；顶点
【例】	Many of these buildings were shaped in the ziggurat form，a design that recedes in progressively smaller stages to the *summit*，creating a staircase-like effect.
【衍】	summitry（*n.*）最高级会议；summiteer（*n.*）最高级会议参加者
【近】	peak，pinnacle，apex，acme
sustain	［sə'stein］
【释】	*v.* 支撑，支持；补养；维持；使…持续
【例】	Population growth in turn created an even greater reliance on settled farming，as only systematic agriculture could *sustain* the increased numbers of people.

【衍】 sustainable（*adj.*）；sustained（*adj.*）持续的

【近】 maintain，keep up，carry on

tail [teil]

【释】 *n.* 尾巴，尾状物　　*v.* 装上尾巴

【例】 Comets grow *tails* only when they get warm enough for ice and dust to boil off.

【衍】 tailed（*adj.*）有尾的；tailcoat（*n.*）燕尾服

【近】 end，extremity，back

telescope ['teliskəup]

【释】 *n.* 望远镜

【例】 The most distant luminous objects seen by *telescopes* are probably ten thousand million light years away.

theme [θi:m]

【释】 *n.* （文章、讨论的）主题；论题；话题

【例】 In whatever literary form Warren wrote, she had but one *theme*—liberty.

【衍】 thematic（*adj.*）；thematically（*adv.*）

【近】 subject，topic，matter

tight [tait]

【释】 ① *adj.* 紧密的，正合身的

【例】 Actresses used to be very reluctant to wear *tight* corsets.

【衍】 tightly（*adv.*）；tighten（*v.*）

【近】 compact，close-fitting

【释】 ② *adj.* 严格的，严厉的

【例】 Mrs. McCullers, understandably, had not yet learned the *tight* control of her art that was to make her next book so memorable.

【衍】 tightly（*adv.*）

【近】 strict, stringent, harsh

tough [tʌf]

【释】 ① *adj.* 强韧的，弯折不断的（[*opp.*] weak）

【例】 Sometimes the muscle is not attached directly to the bone but to a *tough*, nonstretchable cord, or tendon, that is attached to the bone.

【衍】 toughen（*v.*）；toughly（*adv.*）

【近】 sturdy, durable, leathery

【释】 ② *adj.* 不屈不挠的，坚强的；顽固的，固执的

【例】 Often called "the wanderer," it is *tough* and powerful as butterflies go, and is capable of long flights at speeds of 20 miles per hour or more.

【衍】 toughen (*v.*)；toughly (*adv.*)

【近】 robust, strong, hard

transparent [træns'peərənt]

【释】 *adj.* 透明的，明了的，坦率的，显而易见的

【例】 It can be colored or colorless, monochrome or polychrome, *transparent*, translucent, or opaque.

【衍】 transparently (*adv.*)；transparence (*n.*)；transparentize (*v.*)

【近】 see-through, translucent, visible

trouble ['trʌbl]

【释】 *n.* 麻烦；困难，艰难

【例】 Water has *trouble* entering this impervious soil and runoff is very common during rainfalls.

【衍】 troubled (*adj.*)；troublemaker (*n.*)

【近】 difficulty, dilemma, nuisance

undergo [ˌʌndə'gəu]

【释】 *v.* (-went; -gone) 经受(考验等)；经验，经历(变迁等)

【例】 This was in 1925, all forms of art were *undergoing* a revolution.

【近】 endure, experiences, suffer

utility [juː'tiləti]

【释】 *n.* 公用事业；公共设施

【例】 The price system of the United States is a very complex network composed of the prices of all the products bought and sold in the economy as well as those of a myriad of services, including labor, professional, transportation, and public *utility* services.

venture ['ventʃə]

【释】 *n.* 冒险(行动)

【例】 Indeed, in all *ventures* Napoleon tried to take the offensive on all fronts, and at all costs.

【衍】 venturous (*adj.*)；venturesome (*adj.*)

【近】 risk, adventure, chance

visual [ˈviʒuəl]

【释】 *adj*. 视觉的，视力的

【例】 Localization of the signal is generally poorer than localization of a sound or *visual* stimulus and is usually effected by the animal's moving upwind in response to the stimulus.

【衍】 visualize（*v*.）；visualization（*n*.）

way [wei]

【释】 *adv*. …得多，远

【例】 *Way* down in the valley to the west is the town of Freiburg.

withdraw [wiðˈdrɔː]

【释】 ① *v*. (withdrew; withdrawn)撤消；取消

【例】 He stated that all foreign forces would *withdraw* as soon as the crisis ended.

【衍】 withdrawal（*n*.）

【近】 retreat，abandon

【释】 ② *v*. 回收(通货等)；提取(存款)

【例】 They *withdrew* 100 dollars from a bank account after checking out of their hotel.

【衍】 withdrawal（*n*.）

【近】 draw

Exercise of Unit 1

左列单词在右列中有一个同义词，请找出并在相应的位置写上正确答案。

Exercise 1：

(A) abandon _____ danger
(B) tough _____ sturdy
(C) adverse _____ detrimental
(D) spiky _____ thorny
(E) risk _____ perceive
(F) conceive _____ discard

Exercise 2：

(A) assemble _____ contract
(B) shrink _____ resolve
(C) journal _____ diary
(D) barter _____ compile
(E) genre _____ bargain
(F) solve _____ type

Exercise 3：

(A) boulder _____ press
(B) tough _____ feed
(C) forage _____ sink
(D) squeeze _____ pebble
(E) primary _____ robust
(F) submerge _____ primitive

Exercise 4：

(A) amazing _____ hay
(B) sustain _____ accrue
(C) accumulate _____ maintain
(D) forage _____ fancy
(E) emanate _____ astonishing
(F) fantasy _____ emit

Exercise 5：

(A) theme _____ inducement
(B) incentive _____ subject
(C) fuel _____ acronym
(D) magnify _____ oil
(E) initial _____ enlarge
(F) avid _____ ardent

Exercise 6：

(A) precipitate _____ use
(B) exploit _____ subject
(C) discipline _____ discover
(D) initial _____ first
(E) detect _____ abuse
(F) insult _____ hasty

Exercise 7:

(A) provoke _____ way

(B) mission _____ antagonize

(C) defend _____ assignment

(D) convention __ avert

(E) divert _____ protect

(F) passage _____ meeting

Exercise 8:

(A) nostalgia _____ crucial

(B) recognition __ homesickness

(C) slide _____ acknowledgment

(D) primary _____ assure

(E) promise _____ agree

(F) approve _____ glide

Exercise 9:

(A) invade _____ successive

(B) withdraw __ retreat

(C) recognition __ identification

(D) consecutive __ intrude

(E) dynamic _____ picture

(F) imagine _____ active

Exercise 10:

(A) convention __ engrave

(B) etch _____ sheer

(C) curriculum __ possibility

(D) plateau _____ tradition

(E) chance _____ course

(F) steep _____ upland

ANSWERS:

1	E B C D F A
2	B F C A D E
3	D C F A B E
4	D C B F A E
5	B A E C D F
6	B C E D F A
7	F A B E C D
8	D A B E F C
9	D B C A F E
10	B F E A C D

Unit 2

abhor	embellish	moss	sewerage
accuse	enterprise	necessity	shrub
advocate	ethic	nostril	slightly
ambition	exponent	occurrence	sophisticated
approximately	fascinate	orderly	spin
assert	flash	overwhelm	squirrel
aware	foremost	passion	steer
basement	functional	perceive	strand
biologist	gentle	phrase	submit
bounce	grain	plaza	sunlit
bulk	harbor	portion	sustenance
canal	herd	precise	tailor
category	hover	primate	televise
channel	imitate	promote	therapy
classify	incessant	pry	tile
comedy	initiate	quilt	travel
concerning	intact	rational	transplant
consequence	invariable	recommendation	trough
converge	juice	regime	undergraduate
craft	latitude	remote	utilize
curtain	lichen	requirement	versatile
deficient	logical	retract	vital
deter	maintenance	ritual	wear
discriminate	maternal	rural	withstand
doctrine	meteorologist	scene	
eager	mobility	sector	

abhor [əbˈhɔː]

【释】 *v.* (**-horred**；**-horring**)憎恶，厌恶，嫌弃

【例】 He was a man who *abhorred* violence.

【衍】 abhorrence（*n.*）；abhorrent（*adj.*）；abhorrently（*adv.*）

【近】 hate

accuse [əˈkjuːz]

【释】 *v.* 控告(告发)某人犯某罪(**of**)；把某事归罪于某人(**for**)

【例】 At the time when Main Street was published Lewis was *accused* of hating dull people.

【衍】 accusation（*n.*）罪名

【近】 blame，charge，indict

advocate [ˈædvəkeit]

【释】 *n.* 拥护者，鼓吹者，提倡者　　*v.* 拥护；鼓吹；提倡；主张；辩护

【例】 *Advocates* of organic foods frequently proclaim that such products are safer and more nutritious than others.

【衍】 advocacy（*n.*）拥护；鼓吹；主张；辩护

【近】 supporter，proponent

ambition [æmˈbiʃən]

【释】 *n.* 抱负，志气，雄心

【例】 People continue to build skyscrapers for all the reasons that they have always built them—personal *ambition*, civic pride，and the desire of owners to have the largest possible amount of rentable space.

【衍】 ambitionless（*adj.*）；ambitious（*adj.*）；ambitiously（*adv.*）；ambitiousness（*n.*）

【近】 determination，motivation，drive

approximately [əˈprɔksimətli]

【释】 *adv.* 近似，约计

【例】 In 1860 there were *approximately* 80,000 reapers in the country.

【衍】 approximate（*adj.*）

【近】 about，roughly

assert [əˈsəːt]

【释】 *v.* 主张，硬说；断言，声明

【例】 In snippets，politicians *assert* but do not argue.

【衍】	assertion（*n.*）；asserted（*adj.*）据称的，尚待证实的；assertedly（*adv.*）据说
【近】	allege，affirm

aware [ə'wɛə]

【释】	*adj.*［用作表语］知道的，意识到的
【例】	Neither the French nor the Americans were *aware* of the vast amount of land the sale involved.
【衍】	awareness（*n.*）
【近】	conscious，cognizant

basement ['beismənt]

【释】	*n.* 建筑物的底部，【建筑】底层；地下室
【例】	The lower concourse and *basement* level were set aside for shops.
【近】	cellar，crypt

biologist [bai'ɔlədʒist]

【释】	*n.* 生物学者
【例】	A molecular *biologist* would "explain" these events in terms of forces that bind various molecules together.
【衍】	biology（*n.*）生物学；biological（*adj.*）；biologically（*adv.*）

bounce [bauns]

【释】	*v.* 弹起，反弹，弹回
【例】	Then it receives the echoes produced when the waves *bounce* off objects.
【衍】	bouncing（*adj.*）
【近】	spring，leap，jump，rebound

bulk [bʌlk]

【释】	*n.* 体积，容积，大小
【例】	Most of their *bulk* is hidden below the water, so their underwater parts may extend far beyond the visible top.
【近】	volume，size，mass

canal [kə'næl]

【释】	*n.* 运河；沟渠
【例】	They also helped build the vast network of *canals* and railroads that crisscrossed the continent and linked important

Unit 2

trade centers essential to industrial growth.

【近】 channel，passage

category [ˈkætigəri]

【释】 *n.* 类型，种类

【例】 Moreover，ants specializing in particular labor *categories* typically constitute a caste specialized by age or body form or both.

【衍】 categorize（*v.*）；categorization（*n.*）

【近】 group，type，kind，sort

channel [ˈtʃænəl]

【释】 ① *n.* 水道，渠，沟

【例】 In sum，the science-technology-industry relationship may flow in several different ways，and the particular *channel* it will follow depends on the individual situation.

【近】 duct，ditch

【释】 ② *v.* 为…开辟途径，引导

【例】 Procedures and traditions can contain conflict and *channel* the political energies that converge upon the lawmaking process.

【近】 direct，guide

classify [ˈklæsifai]

【释】 *v.* 把…分类

【例】 Indeed，had it not been for the superb preservation of these fossils，they might well have been *classified* as dinosaurs.

【衍】 classification（*n.*）

【近】 sort，categorize

comedy [ˈkɔmidi]

【释】 *n.* 喜剧

【例】 Its emotional implications had to be danced out at great length in what remains the most exhilarating dancing... ever devised for the United States musical *comedy* stage.

【衍】 comedic（*adj.*）；comic（*n.*）连环漫画

【近】 farce

concerning [kənˈsəːniŋ]

【释】 *prep.* 关于，论及

【例】 A survey is a study，generally in the form of an interview or

— 27 —

a questionnaire, that provides information *concerning* how people think and act.

【近】 about, as to

consequence [ˈkɔnsikwəns]

【释】 *n.* 结果；重要(性)；重大意义

【例】 The ability of agriculture to smooth out the seasonal scarcities of wild foodstuffs had major *consequences* for the sizes of Native American populations in New England.

【衍】 consequent（*adj.*）; consequently（*adv.*）; consequential（*adj.*）重要的；因…而引起的

【近】 importance, significance, import

converge [kənˈvɜːdʒ]

【释】 *v.* 会聚，集中

【例】 Competitors from more than a hundred countries have *converged* on Sheffield for the Games.

【衍】 convergence（*n.*）

【近】 congregate, assemble

craft [krɑːft]

【释】 ① *n.* 技能，手艺；手工业

【例】 Although they often achieved expression and formal excellence in their generally primitive style, they remained artisans skilled in the *craft* of carving and constituted a group distinct from what we normally think of as "sculptors" in today's use of the word.

【衍】 craftspeople（*n.*）; craftsman（*n.*）工匠；craftsmanship（*n.*）技能

【近】 skill, expertise, dexterity

【释】 ② *v.* 熟练制作

【例】 Much of the political activity we see on television news has been *crafted* by politicians, their speechwriters, and their public relations advisers for televised consumption.

【近】 fashion, manipulate

【释】 ③ *n.* 船舶；飞机，飞船

【例】 These canals can carry 1,350-to-2,000-ton *crafts*.

【衍】 spacecraft（*n.*）; aircraft（*n.*）

【近】 boat, vessel

curtain ['kə:tən]
【释】 *n.* 帘幕；窗帘，帘子
【例】 Each aurora hangs like a *curtain* of light stretching over the Polar Regions and into the higher latitudes.
【近】 drape，shutter

deficient [di'fiʃənt]
【释】 *adj.* 不足的，缺乏的 *n.* 有缺陷的人(东西)
【例】 Among the alder's valuable ecological contributions is its capacity to fix nitrogen in nitrogen-*deficient* soils.
【衍】 deficiently（*adv.*）；deficiency（*n.*）；deficit（*n.*）亏空(额)，赤字
【近】 lacking，scarce，scant，sparse

deter [di'tə:]
【释】 *v.* (-rred)防止，阻止
【例】 In the words of an economist，this was a case of "premature enterprise," where not only the cost of construction but also the very high risk *deterred* private investment.
【衍】 deterrent（*n.* & *adj.*）阻碍物(的)，制止物(的)；威慑物(的)
【近】 prevent

discriminate [dis'krimineit]
【释】 *v.* 区别，识别；分别对待，歧视，排斥
【例】 The device can *discriminate* between the cancerous and the normal cells.
【衍】 discriminating（*adj.*）有辨别力的；区别对待的；discrimination（*n.*）鉴赏力，眼力；不公平的待遇，歧视；discriminatory/discriminative（*adj.*）
【近】 distinguish，differentiate

doctrine ['dɔktrin]
【释】 *n.* (宗教、政治方面的)教旨，教条，教义
【例】 According to Cherokee *doctrine*，east was associated with the color red because it was the direction of the Sun，the greatest deity of all.
【近】 canon，dogma，belief

eager ['i:gə]
【释】 *adj.* 渴望的，极想的，热衷的(after；about；for)
【例】 The low prices still pull in crowds of *eager* buyers.

【衍】	eagerly（*adv.*）
【近】	keen，enthusiastic
embellish	［im'beliʃ］
【释】	*v.* 装饰，修饰，美化
【例】	The weaving design was then *embellished* with a series of small chained diamonds or vertical and zigzag lines.
【衍】	embellishment（*n.*）
【近】	adorn，decorate，ornament
enterprise	['entəpraiz]
【释】	*n.* 努力，进取
【例】	All such work was done by collective *enterprise* in the workshops.
【衍】	enterprising（*adj.*）有事业心的，有创业精神的，大胆的
【近】	endeavor，venture
ethic	['eθik]
【释】	*n.* 伦理观，道德标准
【例】	People tend to credit Thoreau，an American，with the idea because civil disobedience is a hallmark of American *ethics* and politics.
【衍】	ethical（*adj.*）；ethically（*adv.*）
exponent	[ik'spəunənt]
【释】	① *n.* 典型
【例】	France produced a number of outstanding *exponents* of the Art Nouveau style.
【近】	model，exemplar
【释】	② *n.* 【数】指数；幂
【衍】	exponential（*adj.*）
fascinate	['fæsineit]
【释】	*v.* 迷住，使神魂颠倒
【例】	She spent a lot of time at the Bronx zoo，*fascinated* by animals.
【衍】	fascination（*n.*）迷惑力，魅力
【近】	captivate
flash	[flæʃ]
【释】	*n. & v.* （使）闪光，（使）闪烁

【例】 Crystal-clear icicles draping from the ceiling *flash* blue-green, as though they were carved from precious jewels instead of ice.

【衍】 flashback（*n.*）（电影的）闪回；（小说等的）倒叙

【近】 spark, flare, sparkle, twinkle

foremost [ˈfɔːməust]

【释】 *adj.* 最初的，最前的；第一流的；主要的

【例】 From the earliest colonial times throughout the nineteenth century, disease ranked as the *foremost* problem in defense.

【近】 primary, chief, principle

functional [ˈfʌŋkʃənəl]

【释】 *adj.* 从使用的观点设计（构成）的

【例】 Seventeenth-century houses in colonial North America were simple structures that were primarily *functional*, carrying over traditional designs that went back to the Middle Ages.

【衍】 functionalism（*n.*）机能主义：讲求实用，而不注重外观。

【近】 useful, practical

gentle [ˈdʒentl]

【释】 *adj.* 文雅的，有礼貌的，柔和的，轻柔的

【例】 A person conveys thoughts and ideas through choice of words, by a tone of voice that is pleasant or unpleasant, *gentle* or harsh.

【衍】 gently（*adv.*）轻轻地，逐渐地

【近】 kind, tender

grain [grein]

【释】 ① *n.* 谷物，粮食

【例】 By 1880 a self-binding reaper had been perfected that not only cut the *grain*, but also gathered the stalks.

【衍】 grainy（*adj.*）; grained（*adj.*）有木纹的; grainer（*n.*）画木纹者

【释】 ② *n.*（木材、大理石等的）纹理

【例】 Granite, for instance, is a coarse-*grained* igneous rock whose individual mineral crystals have formed to a size easily seen by the naked eye.

harbor ['hɑːbə]

【释】 *n.* 海港，港口，避难所，藏身处

【例】 Digging began on a *harbor* that would make Los Angeles not only an ocean port but also a fishing center.

【衍】 harborage（*n.*）避难所；harborless（*adj.*）无港的，无避难所的

【近】 haven，port

herd [həːd]

【释】 *n.* 兽群，(牛)群，(猪)群

【例】 Among mammals, allelomimetic behavior is very rare in rodents, which almost never move in flocks or *herds*.

【衍】 herder（*n.*）牧主，牧人

【近】 group，flock

hover ['hɔvə]

【释】 *v.* 翱翔，盘旋

【例】 Jupiter's puzzling Great Red Spot changes size as it *hovers* in the Southern Hemisphere.

【近】 float，drift，fly，linger

imitate ['imiteit]

【释】 *v.* 仿效，模仿

【例】 More likely, numerous assistants, who had been trained to *imitate* the artist's style, applied the paint.

【衍】 imitative（*adj.*）；imitation（*n.*）

【近】 copy，emulate，replicate，duplicate，mimic

incessant [in'sesənt]

【释】 *adj.* 不停的，不断的

【例】 *Incessant* rain made conditions almost intolerable.

【近】 continual，constant

initiate [i'niʃieit]

【释】 *v.* 开始

【例】 The second era was *initiated* in the early decades of the twentieth century and might be called "the vitamin period".

【衍】 initiative（*adj.*）起始的，初步的

【近】 begin，start

intact [in'tækt]

【释】 *adj.* 未经触动的，未受损的，原封不动的

【例】 This is not to imply that sunken ships are always found *intact*.

【衍】 intactness（*n.*）

【近】 whole，unbroken，untouched

invariable [in'vɛəriəbl]

【释】 *adj.* 不变的；守恒的　　*n.*【数】不变量；常数

【例】 This is probably the most common pattern，but it is not *invariable*.

【衍】 invariably（*adv.*）

【近】 constant，consistent

juice [dʒuːs]

【释】 *n.* (菜蔬、果实、植物等的)汁，液，浆

【例】 The worker bees go from flower to flower collecting nectar，or *juice*.

【衍】 juicy（*adj.*）；juicer（*n.*）榨汁器

latitude ['lætitjuːd]

【释】 *n.* 纬度；(以纬度而论的)地区，地方，地域

【例】 Each aurora hangs like a curtain of light stretching over the polar regions and into the higher *latitudes*.

【衍】 latitudinal（*adj.*）

【近】 coordinate，location，position

lichen ['laikən]

【释】 *n.* 地衣；苔藓

【例】 The *lichen*'s strong resistance to its hostile environment and its ability to live in harmony with such environments is one example that humanity should consider in trying to solve its own problems.

【衍】 lichened（*adj.*）生着地衣的；lichenous（*adj.*）苔藓的，生满地衣的；lichenology（*n.*）地衣学

【近】 moss

logical ['lɔdʒikəl]

【释】 *adj.* 逻辑的，逻辑上的；合乎逻辑的

【例】 As colleges ceased to cater more narrowly to candidates for the religious ministry and came to be seen as a *logical* continuation of secondary school, younger students began to predominate.

【衍】 logically (*adv.*); logicalness (*n.*)
【近】 rational, reasonable, sound

maintenance [ˈmeintinəns]
【释】 *n.* 保持，维持，保养；支持的手段
【例】 The same forces that create surface tension in any sample of water are responsible for the *maintenance* of these unbroken columns of water.
【衍】 maintain (*v.*)
【近】 preservation, protection, safeguarding

maternal [məˈtəːnəl]
【释】 *adj.* 母系的；母亲的；像母亲的([*opp.*] paternal)
【例】 M. L. , as he was called, was born in 1929 in Atlanta, Georgia, at the home of his *maternal* grandfather.
【衍】 maternity (*n.* & *adj.*) 怀孕；产科医院；产妇用的；maternally (*adv.*); maternalism (*n.*) 纵容，溺爱；matrilineal (*adj.*) 母系的
【近】 motherly

meteorologist [ˌmiːtiəˈrɔlədʒist]
【释】 *n.* 气象学家
【例】 As *meteorologists* have begun using these new technologies in weather forecasting offices, Now-casting is becoming a reality.
【衍】 meteorologic (*adj.*) 气象的，气象学(上)的；meteorologically (*adv.*)

mobility [məuˈbiliti]
【释】 *n.* 可动性，活动性，能动性；灵活性，可变动性
【例】 Rapid industrialization and increased geographic *mobility* in the nineteenth century had special implications for women because these changes tended to magnify social distinctions.
【衍】 mobile (*adj.* & *n.*) 可动的，可动物，汽车；mobilize (*v.*) 发动，调动；immobilize (*v.*) 使不动，使固定；demobilize (*v.*) 复员，遣散

moss [mɔs]
【释】 *n.* 苔藓；地衣

Unit 2

【例】 In the harsh conditions of the tundra, for example, low growing *mosses*, lichens, and a few flowering plants all hug the ground for shelter from icy winds.

【衍】 mossy（*adj.*）生了苔的；多苔的；苔状的

【近】 lichen

necessity ［ni'sesəti］

【释】 ***n.* 需要，必要性；必需品；必然(性)**

【例】 Wood carving began as a *necessity* in America and developed into an art.

【衍】 necessitate（*v.*）使成为必需；necessary（*adj.*）；necessarily（*adv.*）

【近】 requirement, inevitability, requisite

nostril ［'nɔstril］

【释】 ***n.* 鼻孔；鼻孔内壁**

【例】 Kiwis smell out earthworms thanks to *nostrils* located at the tip of their beaks.

【衍】 nose（*n.*）鼻

occurrence ［ə'kʌrəns］

【释】 ***n.* (事件的)发生，出现**

【例】 An environment favorable to the growth and later preservation of organisms is required for the *occurrence* of fossils.

【衍】 occur（*v.*）；occurring（*n.*）事变，事件，事故

【近】 incidence, rate, occasion

orderly ［'ɔːdəli］

【释】 ***adj.* 有秩序的，有规则的**

【例】 Statistics had a mother who was dedicated to keeping *orderly* records of governmental units and a father who relied on mathematics to increase his skill at playing the odds in games of chance.

【衍】 order（*n.*）

【近】 arranged, tidy, methodical

overwhelm ［ˌəuvə'welm］

【释】 ***v.* 压倒；压服；推翻**

【例】 Extensive falls of volcanic ash and coarser particles *overwhelm* and bury all forms of life, from flying insects to great trees.

【衍】 overwhelmingly（*adv.*）压倒性地，不可抵抗地
【近】 overpower, overcome, beat

passion [ˈpæʃən]
【释】 *n.* 激情，热情，感情
【例】 Naturalists brought to their writing a *passion* for direct and honest experience.
【衍】 passional（*adj.*）
【近】 excitement, enthusiasm

perceive [pəˈsiːv]
【释】 *v.* 察觉，发觉；看见，听见；领会，领悟
【例】 How a speaker *perceives* the listener's interest, or sympathy in any given conversation can drastically alter the tone of presentation.
【衍】 perception（*n.*）
【近】 distinguish, recognize, see, identify

phrase [freiz]
【释】 *n.* 短语；格言，箴言
【例】 The *phrase* "civil disobedience" is usually attributed to the nineteenth-century American philosopher Henry David Thoreau.
【衍】 phrasal（*adj.*）
【近】 expression, idiom, slogan, saying

plaza [ˈplɑːzə]
【释】 *n.* 广场；集市场所；购物中心
【例】 A sunken *plaza*, complete with gardens and fountains, was designed to provide access to these shops.
【近】 square, piazza, mall

portion [ˈpɔːʃən]
【释】 *n.* 一部分，一份
【例】 Heat is transferred from the bird's skin to the top *portion* of the eggshell.
【近】 piece, part, section

precise [priˈsais]
【释】 *adj.* 准确的，精确的
【例】 This information helps to identify the *precise* location of a hearing problem.

【衍】	precisely（*adv.*）正好
【近】	exact，accurate，specific，defined
primate	['praimit]
【释】	*n.* 灵长目动物
【例】	The basis of all *primate* social groups is the bond between mother and infant.
【衍】	primates（*n.*）灵长类
【近】	ape，chimp，chimpanzee，monkey，gorilla，orangutan
promote	[prə'məut]
【释】	*v.* 增进；提倡，发扬，促进
【例】	The leaf litter often *promotes* successful germination of acorns.
【衍】	promotion（*n.*）；promoter（*n.*）促进者，助长者
【近】	help，support，uphold
pry	[prai]
【释】	*v.*（用杠杆等）撬，撬起，撬动；（用尽方法）使脱离
【例】	Shorebirds such as oystercatchers use their bills to *pry* open the tightly sealed shells of their prey.
【衍】	pryer（*n.*）窥探者；prying（*adj.*）爱打听的
quilt	[kwilt]
【释】	*n.* 被子，棉被，鸭绒被
【例】	Among the whole-cloth *quilts* made by these wealthy settlers during the early period are those now called linsey-woolseys.
【衍】	quilted（*adj.*）；quilter（*n.*）
rational	['ræʃənəl]
【释】	*adj.* 理性的，推理的，合理的
【例】	Cubism，which brought about a major revolution in Western painting，overturned the *rational* tradition that had been built upon since the Renaissance.
【衍】	irrational（*adj.*）；rationalism（*n.*）；rationalist（*n.*）；rationality（*n.*）；rationalize（*v.*）
【近】	reasonable，logical，sensible
recommend-ation	[ˌrekəmen'deiʃən]
【释】	*n.* 推荐，介绍；介绍信

【例】 The plan impressed university officials, and in time many of its *recommendations* were implemented.

【衍】 recommend（v.）; recommendable（adj.）值得推荐的，可取的; recommendatory（adj.）推荐的，劝告的; recommended（adj.）被推荐的

【近】 proposal, reference, suggestion

regime ［rei'ʒi:m］

【释】 *n.* 制度，社会组织; 政权，政体

【例】 Paying close heed to the practical needs of society, the new universities trained men and women to work at its tasks, with engineering students being the most characteristic of the new *regime*.

【衍】 regimentation（n.）编制，类别; 组织化，规格化

【近】 government, rule, organization

remote ［ri'məut］

【释】 *adj.* 遥远的，偏僻的; 很久以前(以后)的

【例】 The study of fossil footprints is not restricted to examples from such *remote* periods.

【衍】 remotely（adv.）; remoteness（n.）; remotion（n.）移动，移居

【近】 distant, isolated, inaccessible

requirement ［ri'kwaiəmənt］

【释】 *n.* 要求，需要，必要条件，资格(for)

【例】 Even these minimal *requirements*, however, sometimes arouse controversy.

【衍】 require（v.）; required（adj.）; requisite（adj. & n.）; requisition（n.）

【近】 requisite, prerequisite, necessity

retract ［ri'trækt］

【释】 *v.* 缩进，收回

【例】 When disturbed, a sea anemone *retracts* its tentacles and shortens its body so that it resembles a lump on a rock.

【衍】 retractable（adj.）伸缩自如的; retractile（adj.）; retractility（n.）

【近】 draw back, withdraw, pull back

ritual	[ˈritjuəl]
【释】	*adj.* & *n.* 仪式(的)，礼仪(的)；典礼(的)；宗教仪式(的)
【例】	There are many theories about the beginning of drama in ancient Greece，the one most widely accepted today is based on the assumption that drama evolved from *ritual*.
【近】	rite（*n.*），ceremony，sacrament
rural	[ˈruərəl]
【释】	*adj.* 乡下的，农村(风味)的([*opp.*] urban)；地方的；农业的
【例】	In both urban and *rural* communities，a rich and varied repertoire of ballads，tales，and poetic forms is preserved in memory and passed from generation to generation.
【近】	country
scene	[siːn]
【释】	① *n.* 事件，史实
【例】	She transposes images and *scenes* from her past，combining cultural documentation with invention in an interplay of fact and fiction.
【近】	incident，event，occurrence
【释】	② *n.* 景色，景致，风景
【例】	It was the result of intense study，and it grew out of two earlier studies of the *scene*，a water color and a small oil painting.
【衍】	scenery（*n.*）全景；scenic（*adj.*）景色优美的
【近】	panorama，view，landscape
【释】	③ *n.* 场，(舞台的)布景，(戏剧中的)一场
【例】	His lack of formal training did not stop him from becoming an accomplished puppeteer，clown，Harlequin，dancer，ropewalker，equestrian，Shakespearean actor，*scene* designer，and pyrotechnist.
【衍】	scenery（*n.*）舞台面；(舞台)布景
【近】	background，arena
sector	[ˈsektə]
【释】	*n.* 部分；地区，分区
【例】	Agriculture must，therefore，industrialize urbanized *sectors* if a modern economy is to be achieved.

【衍】	section（n.）部分，部件；sectional（adj.）部分的，地方性(强)的
【近】	division，segment，part

sewerage ['sjuəridʒ]

【释】	**n.** 下水道(系统)，排水(系统)
【例】	Water and **sewerage** systems were usually operated by municipal governments，but the gas and electric networks were privately owned.
【衍】	sewer（n.）阴沟，污水管道；sewage（n.）

shrub [ʃrʌb]

【释】	**n.** 灌木，灌木丛
【例】	He and his brothers believed that parks should be adapted to the local topography，utilize the area's trees and **shrubs**，and be available to the entire community.
【衍】	shrubby（adj.）灌木状的，多灌木的；shrubbery（n.）灌木丛，灌木丛生的地方
【近】	bush，hedge plant

slightly ['slaitli]

【释】	**adv.** 有一点，略；轻微地，轻轻地([opp.] **considerably**)
【例】	Nevertheless，the ability of children to conform to grammatical rules is only **slightly** more wonderful than their ability to learn words.
【衍】	slight（adj.）；slighting（adj.）轻蔑的，无礼的；slightness（n.）
【近】	somewhat，faintly，to some extent

sophisticated [sə'fistikeitid]

【释】	**adj.** (技术、产品等)复杂的，尖端的，高级的；微妙的([opp.] **primitive**)
【例】	These strange adaptations to life represent just a few of the **sophisticated** means by which plants enhance their chances of survival.
【衍】	sophisticatedly（adv.）；sophistication（n.）混合；复杂
【近】	complicated，advanced，subtle

spin [spin]

【释】	**v. & n.** (使)旋转；自旋，自转

【例】 Newton's laws of motion assume that the total amount of *spin* of a body cannot change unless an external torque speeds it up or slows it down.

【衍】 spun（*adj.*）纺成的，拉成丝状的；spinning（*n.*）纺纱

【近】 roll，rotate，twirl

squirrel ['skwirəl]

【释】 *n.* 松鼠

【例】 Smaller species，including such rodents as mice and small *squirrels*，are not as prevalent overall in high tropical canopies as they are in most habitats globally.

steer [stiə]

【释】 *v.* 掌(舵)；驾驶(船、车)；操纵，控制

【例】 Even with the Sun or stars to *steer* by，the problems of navigation are more complicated than they might seem at first.

【衍】 steerable（*adj.*）可驾驶的，易操纵的；steerage（*n.*）(客船的)统舱；操纵；steerageway（*n.*）【海】舵效航速

【近】 maneuver，manipulate，control

strand [strænd]

【释】 *n.* (绳子的)股；一股绳子；纤维，绳，线；串

【例】 Mild steel and aluminum barbed wire have two *strands* twisted together to form a cable which is stronger than single-strand wire and less affected by temperature changes.

【衍】 strander（*n.*）绳缆搓绞机

【近】 thread，fiber，string

submit [səb'mit]

【释】 *v.* 提交；委托，提出，提供；请求判断

【例】 In 1918 she established the Whitney Studio Club where annual exhibitions gave members a rare opportunity to present their work to the public without first *submitting* it to a jury.

【衍】 submissiveness（*n.*）柔顺，服从

【近】 present，propose，put forward

sunlit ['sʌnlit]

【释】 *adj.* 太阳照着的，太阳晒着的

【例】 Perhaps one of the most dramatic and important changes

— 41 —

occurred late in that era，among the small organisms that populate the uppermost，*sunlit* portion of the oceans—the plankton.

【近】sunny，bathed in light，bright

sustenance ［'sʌstinəns］

【释】*n.* 食物；营养；生计；支持(物)

【例】But few birds are more intimately tied to their source of *sustenance* than are crossbills.

【近】nourishment，food，provisions

tailor ［'teilə］

【释】*n.* 裁缝　*v.* 缝制(衣服)

【例】It was an area of banks，insurance companies，builders，jewelers，*tailors*，doctors，lawyers，and other black-owned or black-operated businesses and services.

televise ［'telivaiz］

【释】*v.* 电视播送，实况播送

【例】Much of the political activity we see on television news has been crafted by politicians，their speechwriters，and their public relations advisers for *televised* consumption.

【衍】television（*n.*）；televisual（*adj.*）适于上电视镜头的

【近】broadcast，telecast，show

therapy ［'θerəpi］

【释】*n.* 疗法；疗效

【例】In the third era of nutritional history in the early 1950's to mid 1960's，vitamin *therapy* began to fall into disrepute.

【衍】therapeutic（*adj.*）治疗(学)的，疗法(上)的；therapeutically（*adv.*）

【近】treatment，healing，remedy

tile ［tail］

【释】*n.* 瓷砖，砖瓦　*v.* 铺瓦，砌瓷砖

【例】Obviously，any square can *tile* the plane，as many kitchen floors have demonstrated.

【衍】tiler（*n.*）制瓦工人；瓦匠；tiled（*adj.*）平铺的

【近】cover，overlay

travel ［'trævəl］

【释】*v.* 漫游，游览，周游　*n.* 旅行

【例】He left home at the age of 15 to tour as a dancer with a *traveling* performer.

【衍】tourism（*n.*）游览，旅行；旅游业；tourist（*n.*）旅游者

【近】trip，sightsee，excursion，journey，expedition

transplant ［træns'plɑːnt］

【释】*v. & n.* 移植（皮肤等）

【例】In the past oysters were raised in much the same way as dirt farmers raised tomatoes—by *transplanting* them.

【衍】transplantable（*adj.*）；transplanter（*n.*）；transplantation（*n.*）

【近】remove，resettle，transfer

trough ［trɔːf］

【释】*n.* 波谷；【数】凹点（［*opp.*］ridge）

【例】Sound moves from its source to the ear by wavelike fluctuations in air pressure，something like the crests and *troughs* of ocean waves.

【近】trench，depression，low

undergraduate ［ˌʌndə'grædjuit］

【释】*n. & adj.* 大学生（的）

【例】He returned to the United States and attended Lincoln University，where he won the Witter Bynner Prize for *undergraduate* poetry.

【近】apprentice，student

utilize ［'juːtilaiz］

【释】*v.* 利用

【例】He and his brothers believed that parks should be adapted to the local topography，*utilize* the area's trees and shrubs，and be available to the entire community.

【衍】utilization（*n.*）

【近】exploit，employ

versatile ［'vəːsətail］

【释】*adj.* 多面手的，多才多艺的

【例】Her unique background made her into an unusually interesting and *versatile* human being.

【衍】versatility（*n.*）

【近】	flexible，resourceful
vital	[ˈvaitəl]
【释】	*adj*. 重大的，紧要的
【例】	This temperature gradient may be *vital* to successful hatching.
【衍】	vitally（*adv*.）；vitality（*n*.）活力，生命力
【近】	essential，critical，indispensable
wear	[wiə]
【释】	*v*. 损耗，磨破(away；out；off)
【例】	Notwithstanding preening and constant care, the marvelously intricate structure of a bird's feather inevitably *wears* out.
withstand	[wiðˈstænd]
【释】	*v*. (withstood)抵挡；挡住
【例】	According to some scientists migratory birds should be able to *withstand* the winter.
【近】	endure，survive，resist

Exercise of Unit 2

左列单词在右列中有一个同义词，请找出并在相应的位置写上正确答案。

Exercise 1:

(A) herd	_____	group
(B) consequence	____	congregate
(C) discriminate	____	importance
(D) converge	_____	allege
(E) assert	_____	distinguish
(F) imitate	_____	copy

Exercise 2:

(A) latitude	_____	coordinate
(B) channel	_____	drape
(C) scene	_____	background
(D) perceive	_____	thread
(E) curtain	_____	distinguish
(F) strand	_____	duct

Exercise 3:

(A) embellish	_____	conscious
(B) undergraduate	___	adorn
(C) craft	_____	panorama
(D) harbor	_____	boat
(E) scene	_____	apprentice
(F) aware	_____	haven

Exercise 4:

(A) shrub	_____	about
(B) approximately	___	continual
(C) requirement	___	farce
(D) comedy	_____	bush
(E) incessant	_____	treatment
(F) therapy	_____	requisite

Exercise 5:

(A) occurrence	_____	keen
(B) craft	_____	skill
(C) eager	_____	incidence
(D) enterprise	_____	model
(E) exponent	_____	endeavor
(F) category	_____	group

Exercise 6:

(A) rural	_____	reasonable
(B) sustenance	_____	country
(C) maintenance	_____	preservation
(D) doctrine	_____	canon
(E) bulk	_____	volume
(F) rational	_____	nourishment

Exercise 7:
(A) deter _____ spring
(B) advocate _____ about
(C) bounce _____ supporter
(D) overwhelm ____ kind
(E) concerning _____ prevent
(F) gentle _____ overpower

Exercise 8:
(A) abhor _____ channel
(B) transplant _____ hate
(C) flash _____ spark
(D) hover _____ remove
(E) canal _____ square
(F) plaza _____ float

Exercise 9:
(A) foremost _____ cellar
(B) basement _____ distant
(C) remote _____ primary
(D) precise _____ exact
(E) intact _____ rite
(F) ritual _____ whole

Exercise 10:
(A) deficient _____ requirement
(B) necessity _____ flexible
(C) versatile _____ lacking
(D) sector _____ constant
(E) accuse _____ division
(F) invariable _____ blame

ANSWERS:

1	A D B E C F
2	A E C F D B
3	F A E C B D
4	B E D A F C
5	C B A E D F
6	F A C D E B
7	C E B F A D
8	E A C B F D
9	B C A D F E
10	B C A F D E

Unit 3

abnormal	embody	moth	shade
acid	enthusiasm	neck	shut
aesthetic(al)	evaporate	notable	slip
amendment	expose	odd	sort
aquatic	fashion	ore	spine
assess	flat	oxygen	stabilize
awkward	forge	pasture	stem
basic	fundamental	percentage	strategy
bipedal	genuine	physician	subsequent
boundary	grand	plentiful	superb
bumblebee	harden	portrait	swallow
candidate	heritage	precursor	tale
cater	humanity	primitive	temperate
chaos	immediate	prompt	thereafter
claw	inclination	psychologist	till
comet	inject	quotation	tow
conclusive	integral	rattle	trap
conservation	invertebrate	recording	troupe
converse	jumble	regional	underlie
cranial	latter	renaissance	utter
curve	lighthouse	resemble	verse
definite	lone	retreat	vivid
deteriorate	maize	rival	weary
dismay	mature	rush	witness
dogged	methane	scent	
earnest	mock	secure	

abnormal [æbˈnɔːməl]
【释】*adj.* 反常的，变态的，不规则的
【例】One or both wings are held in an *abnormal* position.
【衍】abnormally (*adv.*)
【近】atypical, anomalous, odd

acid [ˈæsid]
【释】*n.* 酸 *adj.* 酸性的；尖酸刻薄的
【例】It is speculated that the food might interfere with the *acid* that decays teeth or with bacteria that produce the acid.
【衍】acidic (*adj.*) 酸性的；acidity (*n.*) 酸性；acidly (*adv.*) 刻薄地

aesthetic(al) [iːsˈθetik(əl)]
【释】*adj.* 审美的；美的，艺术的
【例】Soon a distinct *aesthetic* code evolved: form should be simple, surfaces plain, and any ornament should be based on geometric relationships.
【衍】aesthetically (*adv.*)；aesthete (*n.*) 唯美主义者；aesthetics (*n.*) [动词用单数] 美学；审美学；美的哲学；aestheticism (*n.*) 唯美主义；艺术感，美感

amendment [əˈmendmənt]
【释】*n.* 改正，修正；修正草案
【例】An early *amendment* to the act even prevented husbands and wives from filing separate claims.
【衍】amend (*v.*)；amendable (*adj.*) 能改正的；amendatory (*adj.*) 改正的；修正的
【近】revision, adjustment, modification

aquatic [əˈkwætik]
【释】*adj.* 水生的，水栖的
【例】They feed on fish, frogs, crayfish, and other *aquatic* animals.
【衍】aquatics (*n.*) 水上运动；aquatically (*adv.*)
【近】water, marine

assess [əˈses]
【释】*v.* 评定，估定
【例】His annual income was *assessed* at ten thousand dollars.
【衍】assessment (*n.*)

【近】	evaluate, measure
awkward	[ˈɔːkwəd]
【释】	*adj*. 有毛病的，难使用的；笨拙的，粗劣的
【例】	But even with the *awkward* interior configurations of the early apartment buildings, the idea caught on.
【衍】	awkwardly (*adv*.); awkwardness (*n*.)
【近】	clumsy, gauche
basic	[ˈbeisik]
【释】	*adj*. 基础的，基本的，根本的
【例】	No two comets ever look identical, but they have *basic* features in common.
【衍】	basically (*adv*.)
【近】	essential, fundamental, necessary, vital
bipedal	[baiˈpedəl]
【释】	*adj*. 两足动物的；两足的
【例】	The result emphasized that there were at least seven points of similarity with modern *bipedal* prints.
boundary	[ˈbaundəri]
【释】	*n*. 边界，疆界，限界
【例】	The site of this destruction is another kind of plate *boundary* into the mantle.
【衍】	bound (*n*.); bounded (*adj*.)
【近】	border, frontier, edge, margin
bumblebee	[ˈbʌmblˌbiː]
【释】	*n*. 大黄蜂，土蜂，野蜂
【例】	At a more advanced stage of sociality are the *bumblebees*.
【近】	wasps, hornet
candidate	[ˈkændidət, ˈkændideit]
【释】	*n*. 候选人；候补人
【例】	Initially, 70 sites were proposed as *candidates* for sanctuary status.
【衍】	candidature (*n*.) 候选(人)资格(身份)
【近】	nominee
cater	[ˈkeitə]
【释】	*v*. 迎合，投合(**to**)

【例】 Not only did they *cater* to the governor and his circle, but citizens from all over the colony came to the capital for legislative sessions of the assembly and council and the meetings of the courts of justice.

【近】 pander（to）

chaos [ˈkeiɔs]

【释】 *n.* 混乱

【例】 These new urbanites, already convinced that cities were overwhelmed with great problems, eagerly embraced the progressive reforms that promised to bring order out of the *chaos* of the city.

【衍】 chaotic（*adj.*）; chaotically（*adv.*）

【近】 disorder, disarray

claw [klɔː]

【释】 *n.*（动物的）爪;（蟹等的）钳

【例】 Countless animals, including us, bear external structures without blood supply or nerves—for example, our hair and fingernails, or the scales, *claws* and horns of other animals.

comet [ˈkɔmit]

【释】 *n.* 彗星

【例】 It was not the *comet* of the century experts predicted it might be.

【衍】 cometic = cometary（*adj.*）

conclusive [kənˈkluːsiv]

【释】 *adj.* 结论性的，确定性的；无争论余地的

【例】 Although there are no *conclusive* answers yet, the way in which a society views its environment is sometimes apparent in its choice and use of artistic materials.

【衍】 conclusively（*adv.*）; conclude（*v.*）; conclusion（*n.*）

【近】 decisive, final

conservation [ˌkɔnsəˈveiʃən]

【释】 *n.* 保存，维持（健康），保护（森林、河道、动物等）

【例】 Biological diversity has become widely recognized as a critical *conservation* issue only in the past two decades.

【衍】 conserve（*v.*）

【近】 protection, preservation

converse	[kən'vəːs, 'kɔnvəːs]
【释】	① *v.* 谈话
【例】	After a few minutes of familiarization, pairs of deaf people are able to *converse* freely over television.
【衍】	conversation (*n.*); conversant (*n.*); conversational (*adj.*)
【近】	talk, communicate
【释】	② *adj.* 倒转的，逆(转)的 *n.* 逆转
【例】	What you do for a living is critical to where you settle and how you live—and the *converse* is also true.
【衍】	conversely (*adv.*)
【近】	opposite, contrary, reverse, opposing
cranial	['kreinjəl]
【释】	*adj.* 颅的
【例】	It is the peripheral nervous system, consisting of the *cranial*, spinal, and peripheral nerves, together with their motor and sensory endings.
【衍】	cranium (*n.*) 颅；头颅
curve	[kəːv]
【释】	*n.* 曲线 *v.* 使弯曲，成曲线
【例】	Market prices may move up or down (or remain the same) in response to a host of factors causing shifts in supply (the whole supply *curve*) or demand (the whole demand *curve*) or both together.
definite	['definit]
【释】	*adj.* 明确的；确定的
【例】	It began to run more swiftly and cut more *definite* courses.
【衍】	definition (*n.*) 定义；definitive (*adj.*) 决定(性)的；definitively (*adv.*)
【近】	specific, explicit, unambiguous, distinct
deteriorate	[di'tiəriəreit]
【释】	*v.* 弄坏，使恶化；堕落
【例】	But no matter what its condition on the way down, a ship *deteriorates* much more slowly as it sinks deeper into protective layers of sand and mud.
【衍】	deteriorative (*adj.*); deterioration (*n.*)

【近】	worsen，decline
dismay	[dis'mei]
【释】	*n. & v.* (使)灰心；(使)沮丧
【例】	The enemy retreated in perfect *dismay*.
【衍】	disappointment，sadness
dogged	['dɔgid]
【释】	*adj.* 顽固的，固执的
【例】	They were regarded as *dogged* in their insistence on their own way of life.
【衍】	doggedly (*adv.*)
【近】	determined，persistent，resolute
earnest	['ə:nist]
【释】	*n. & adj.* 热心(的)；诚挚(的)，真挚(的)，认真(的)
【例】	Despite their *earnest* efforts，they still struggle to win support.
【衍】	earnestness (*n.*)
【近】	serious，sincere
embody	[im'bɔdi]
【释】【例】	*v.* 包含，收录
	They *embody* snows that drifted down hundreds，or many thousands，or in some cases maybe a million years ago.
【衍】	embodiment (*n.*)
【近】	include，contain
enthusiasm	[in'θju:ziæzəm]
【释】	*n.* 热心，热情；热烈
【例】	In England，the *enthusiasm* for American plants was on reason why tulips dropped out of fashion in the gardens of the rich and famous.
【衍】	enthusiastic(al) (*adj.*)；enthusiastically (*adv.*)；enthusiast (*n.*)
【近】	eagerness，keenness，fervor，passion，zeal，zest
evaporate	[i'væpəreit]
【释】	*v.* 蒸发，挥发
【例】	Ices have *evaporated* from its outer layers to leave a crust of nearly black dust all over the surface.

【衍】	evaporation（n.）
【近】	volatilize
expose	[ik'spəuz]
【释】	*v.* 使暴露；使曝光
【例】	Small mammals，being warm blooded，suffer hardship in the *exposed* and turbulent environment of the uppermost trees.
【衍】	exposed（*adj.*）；exposure（*n.*）
【近】	bare，uncover
fashion	['fæʃən]
【释】	① *v.* 制造
【例】	Coppersmiths employed it to *fashion* pots and kettles for the home.
【近】	make，create，form
【释】	② *n.* 风气，潮流；时新式样
【例】	This attitude is now passing out of *fashion*.
【衍】	old-fashioned（*adj.*）过时的；守旧的；fashionable（*adj.*）（价格昂贵）高级的
flat	[flæt]
【释】	*adj.* 平的，平坦的，扁平的
【例】	Although its nesting habits are similar to those of gulls that nest on *flat* ground，there are a number of important differences related to the cliff-nesting habit.
【衍】	flattish（*adj.*）有点单调（呆板）的；flathead（*n.*）傻子，无知识的人
forge	[fɔːdʒ]
【释】	*v.* 打(铁)，锻制
【例】	Pennsylvania's colonial ironmasters *forged* iron and a revolution that had both industrial and political implications.
【近】	build，create，fashion
fundamental	[ˌfʌndə'mentəl]
【释】	*adj.* 基础的，基本的；根本的
【例】	Mass transportation revised the social and economic fabric of the American city in three *fundamental* ways.
【衍】	fundamentally（*adv.*）
【近】	basic，elementary

genuine [ˈdʒenjuin]

【释】 *adj.* 真正的，坦率的，真诚的，真心诚意的

【例】 The phrase, "the real McCoy", has become a common term for "*genuine*" or "authentic".

【衍】 genuinely（*adv.*）

【近】 real, authentic, true

grand [ɡrænd]

【释】 *adj.* 盛大的，宏大的；堂皇的，雄伟的

【例】 This is a *grand* conception that excites and provokes.

【衍】 grandeur（*n.*）

【近】 splendid, magnificent, imposing

harden [ˈhɑːdən]

【释】 *v.* 使坚固，使变硬

【例】 For the first time in the Earth's long history, very large quantities of silica skeletons, which would eventually *harden* into rock, began to pile up in parts of the deep sea.

【衍】 hard（*adj.*）；hardened（*adj.*）

【近】 solidify, consolidate, coagulate, congeal

heritage [ˈheritidʒ]

【释】 *n.* 世袭财产；(长子)继承权

【例】 One-room schools are part of the *heritage* of the United States.

【近】 inheritance, legacy

humanity [hjuːˈmænəti]

【释】 *n.* 人类，人性，人情，人道

【例】 Scientists are discovering that the living world hold many interesting secrets of electricity that could benefit *humanity*.

【衍】 humanist（*n.*）人道主义者；humanitarian（*n.*）人道主义

【近】 civilization, humankind, people

immediate [iˈmiːdiət]

【释】 *adj.* 即时的，立即的

【例】 It is important to be clear about the distinction between long-range and *immediate* goals because long-range goals often involve a different decision than short-range ones.

【衍】 immediately（*adv.*）

— 54 —

【近】	instant，instantaneous
inclination	[ˌinkli'neiʃən]
【释】	*n.* 倾向，爱好
【例】	Being so educable，individual birds have markedly different interests and *inclinations*，strategies and scams.
【衍】	incline（*v.*）使(某人)倾向于
【近】	tendency，penchant，peculiarity
inject	[in'dʒekt]
【释】	*v.* 注入，注射
【例】	A mid-ocean ridge is a boundary between plates where new lithospheric material is *injected* from below.
【衍】	injection（*n.*）
【近】	infuse
integral	['intigrəl]
【释】	*adj.* 完全的；缺一不可的，主要的
【例】	It is a lifelong process，a process that starts long before the start of school，and one that should be an *integral* part of one's entire life.
【衍】	integrality（*n.*）完整性
【近】	essential，primary
invertebrate	[in'vəːtibrit]
【释】	*n. & adj.* 无脊椎动物(的)
【例】	Furthermore，many *invertebrates* that live in the depths of the ocean never experience a change in the chill of the deep water，and their body temperatures remain constant.
jumble	['dʒʌmbl]
【释】	*v. & n.* 搞乱，(使)混杂
【例】	Most ships break up on the way down，hit the bottom at about 100 miles per hour，and become a chaotic，confusing *jumble*.
【衍】	jumbled（*adj.*）
【近】	mess，clutter，muddle
latter	['lætə]
【释】	*adj.* 后面的，末了的([*opp.*] first)；(二者中)后者的([*opp.*] former)

【例】 The principle difference between urban growth in Europe and in the North American colonies was the slow evolution of cities in the former and then rapid growth to the *latter*.

【衍】 latterly (*adv.*)

【近】 last, later, second

lighthouse [ˈlaithaus]

【释】 *n.* 灯塔

【例】 Not withstanding differences in appearance and construction, most American *lighthouses* shared several features: a light, living quarters, and sometimes a bell (or, later, a foghorn).

【衍】 light (*adj.* & *v.*); lightness (*n.*) 明亮，光亮度

【近】 beacon

lone [ləun]

【释】 *adj.* 孤独的；无人烟的，人迹稀少的

【例】 With the opposition of only one other person there was very little yielding and majority of three was nearly as effective as larger majorities against the *lone* dissenter.

【衍】 lonely (*adj.*) 孤独的，孤单的；loneliness (*n.*) 寂寞，荒凉

【近】 single, solitary, isolated

maize [meiz]

【释】 *n.* 玉蜀黍，玉米(美国、加拿大叫 corn)

【例】 Under such conditions. Mandan women had to grow *maize* capable of weathering adversity.

mature [məˈtjuə]

【释】 *adj.* 成熟的；仔细考虑过的　　*v.* 成熟；使成熟

【例】 Universities had to adjust to the needs of students who were less *mature* and less settled in their interests.

【衍】 maturely (*adv.*); maturation (*n.*) 成熟；maturity (*n.*) 成熟；完备

【近】 grow up, develop, become adult

methane [ˈmeθein]

【释】 *n.* 甲烷，沼气

【例】 They are composed predominantly of such substances as hydrogen, helium, ammonia, and *methane*, unlike terrestrial planets.

Unit 3

mock [mɔk]
【释】 *v.* 嘲弄，愚弄；嘲笑，挖苦
【例】 However, these achievements were *mocked* by the artistic elite of Paris as expensive and ugly follies.
【衍】 mocking (*adj.*); mockingly (*adv.*); mockery (*n.*)
【近】 ridicule, tease, scorn

moth [mɔθ]
【释】 *n.* 蛀虫；蛾
【例】 It pays such little attention to its personal hygiene that green algae grow on its coarse hair and communities of a parasitic *moth* live in the depths of its coat producing caterpillars which graze on its mouldy hair.
【衍】 mothball (*n.*) 卫生球，樟脑球

neck [nek]
【释】 *n.* 颈，脖子；(器物的)颈状部
【例】 The violin consists in essence of a hollow, varnished wooden sound box, or resonator, and a long *neck*, covered with a fingerboard, along which four strings are stretched at high tension.

notable ['nəutəbl]
【释】 *adj.* 值得注意的，显著的；著名的，显要的
【例】 Most *notable* of these is the Alaska Peninsula.
【衍】 notably (*adv.*); notableness (*n.*); notation (*n.*) 符号，标志(法)，表示法
【近】 distinguished, prominent, famous

odd [ɔd]
【释】 *adj.* 奇妙的，奇特的，古怪的
【例】 Certainly no creature in the sea is *odder* than the common sea cucumber.
【衍】 oddly (*adv.*); odds (*n.*) 胜算，差异；差距，优劣之差
【近】 strange, abnormal, peculiar

ore [ɔ:]
【释】 *n.* 矿石，含有金属的矿石
【例】 Iron production was revolutionized in the early eighteenth century when coke was first used instead of charcoal for refining iron *ore*.

oxygen [ˈɔksidʒən]

【释】 *n.* 氧，氧气

【例】 The particles in a clay soil are so fine that it tends to be compact and interferes with the *oxygen* supply for plant roots.

【衍】 oxide（*n.*）氧化物

pasture [ˈpɑːstʃə]

【释】 *n.* 牧场；草地

【例】 The tolerance of water loss is of obvious advantage in the desert，as animals do not have to remain near a water hole but can obtain food from grazing sparse and far-flung *pastures.*

【近】 meadow，grazing land，fodder，ranch，prairie

percentage [pəˈsentidʒ]

【释】 *n.*【数】百分法；百分数；百分比；【商】手续费，佣金

【例】 The weights of each size are then expressed as a *percentage* of the sample weight.

【衍】 percent（*n.*）

【近】 proportion

physician [fiˈziʃən]

【释】 *n.* 医生，内科医生

【例】 A *physician* was not supposed to attempt to repair the damage directly，but Dr. Williams dared to do so.

【近】 doctor，surgeon，practitioner

plentiful [ˈplentiful]

【释】 *adj.* 丰富的

【例】 For example，many northern species leave their summer homes while the weather is still warm and the food supply *plentiful*.

【衍】 plentifully（*adv.*）

【近】 abundant，plenteous，copious

portrait [ˈpɔːtrit]

【释】 *n.* 肖像，肖像画；相片

【例】 Although the colonists tended to favor *portraits*，they also accepted landscapes.

【衍】 portraiture 肖像画法；portraitist 肖像画家，人像摄影家

precursor [priːˈkəːsə]
【释】 *n.* 前辈，前驱；预兆，先兆
【例】 Carbon compounds might have been the *precursors* of life on Earth.
【衍】 precursory（*adj.*）
【近】 forerunner，ancestor，predecessor

primitive [ˈprimitiv]
【释】 *adj.* 原始的，上古的；早期的
【例】 They are an ancient and *primitive* group of mammals that probably originated in North America and migrated to South America before about sixty-five million years ago.
【近】 prehistoric，ancient，primordial，primal，primeval

prompt [prɔmpt]
【释】 *v.* 刺激，鼓励，怂恿
【例】 In time the increasing complexity of Neolithic societies led to the development of writing, *prompted* by the need to keep records.
【衍】 promptly（*adv.*）敏捷地，迅速地

psychologist [saiˈkɔlədʒist]
【释】 *n.* 心理学者；心理学家
【例】 Most *psychologists* deal with generalization.
【衍】 psychology 心理学；psychological（*adj.*）

quotation [kwəuˈteiʃən]
【释】 *n.* 引用语，语录（from）
【例】 From her general reading came *quotations* that she found striking or insightful.
【近】 citation，quote，excerpt

rattle [ˈrætl]
【释】 *n.* 格格地响的东西
【例】 The dancers shook *rattles* or pounded hand-held drums to underscore their footbeats.
【衍】 rattlesnake（*n.*）响尾蛇
【近】 clatter（*n.*）

recording [riˈkɔːdiŋ]
【释】 *n.* 唱片；录了音的磁带

【例】 Ella Fitzgerald taught herself the sentimental music so popular in the 1930's and her ***recordings*** became best-sellers.

【衍】 record（*v. & n.*）；recorder（*n.*）录音机；recorded（*adj.*）

【近】 tape，CD

regional ['riːdʒənəl]

【释】 ***adj.*** 地方(性)的；地方主义的；区域(性)的；局部的

【例】 Local music store owners pioneered their own local recording industry since national record companies had abandoned ***regional*** traditional styles.

【衍】 region（*n.*）；regionalism（*n.*）；regionally（*adv.*）

【近】 local，provincial

renaissance [ri'neisəns]

【释】 ***n.*** 复兴；新生；文艺复兴(期)

【例】 A hundred years after the invention of the steel skeleton made it possible，the skyscraper is undergoing a ***renaissance***.

【近】 rebirth，revival，recovery

resemble [ri'zembl]

【释】 ***v.*** 像，类似，相似

【例】 When disturbed，a sea anemone retracts its tentacles and shortens its body so that it ***resembles*** a lump on a rock.

【衍】 resemblance（*n.*）相似（to；between；of）；相似性

【近】 look like，be similar to

retreat [ri'triːt]

【释】 ***v. & n.*** 后退，撤退，退缩，凹进

【例】 The rise and fall of the lakes were undoubtedly linked to the advances and ***retreats*** of the great ice sheets that covered much of the northern part of the North American continent during those times.

【衍】 retreater（*n.*）

【近】 move back，withdraw

rival ['raivəl]

【释】 ***v.*** 相匹敌；对抗，竞争

【例】 No other colonial artisans ***rivaled*** the silversmiths' prestige.

【衍】 rivalrous（*adj.*）；rivalry（*n.*）

【近】	match，resemble，be similar to
rush	[rʌʃ]
【释】	① *v. & n.* 向前猛进，冲，突进
【例】	If windows are open in the building，some of the inside air will *rush* out through them.
【衍】	rushed（*adj.*）
【近】	hurry，sprint，dash
【释】	② *n.* 蜂拥而至；激增，猛长；繁忙
【例】	In some areas，local governments are encouraging companies to start telecommuting programs in order to reduce *rush*-hour congestion and improve air quality.
【近】	blast，current
scent	[sent]
【释】	*n.* 气味 *v.* 发出气味，闻出气味
【例】	Bloodhounds apparently have denser concentrations of receptor sites tuned to human *scents*.
【衍】	scented（*adj.*）；scentless（*adj.*）
【近】	smell，odor，perfume
secure	[si'kjuə]
【释】	① *v.* 搞到；把…拿到手；得到；获得
【例】	Here，in the popular rising against a "tyrannical" government，the fruits were more than the *securing* of a freer constitution.
【近】	obtain，acquire，get
【释】	② *v.* 招致；促成
【例】	The Louisiana Purchase doubled the size of the United States，pushed back the frontier，and *secured* the Mississippi River as a highway for Western trade.
【释】	③ *v.* 使安全；防护；保卫；妥善保管
【例】	Customers generally *secured* the silver for the silver objects they ordered.
【衍】	security（*n.*）
shade	[ʃeid]
【释】	① *n.* 朦胧色；浓淡；色调
【例】	The sea anemone is formed quite like the flower forwhich it is named，with a body like a stem and tentacles like

petals in brilliant *shades* of blue，green，pink，and red.

【近】 hue，tinge，tint

【释】 ② *n.* 荫；阴处；树阴

【例】 Men gossiped and exchanged rumors while whittling bits of wood or while squatting in the *shade* to get acquainted with strangers.

【衍】 shadeless（*adj.*）没有阴影的

【近】 shadow，dimness，canopy

shut [ʃʌt]

【释】 *v.* 关闭；把…关在门外，封闭

【例】 This will balance the pressure inside and outside the building，but if the windows are *shut* tightly，the enormous inside pressure may cause the building to burst.

【衍】 shutdown（*n.*）停工，停业；shutter（*n.*）百叶窗，护窗板

【近】 close up，fasten，lock up

slip [slip]

【释】 ① *v.* 滑动；滑脱；滑落

【例】 Occasionally the knives *slip* and leave scratches on the users' teeth.

【衍】 slipper（*n.*）拖鞋

【近】 slide，glide，slither

【释】 ② *n.* 润滑性

【例】 Often a wet clay solution，known as a *slip*，was applied to the smooth surface.

sort [sɔːt]

【释】 ① *n.* 种类，类别，品种；种

【例】 Their clothes and their homes act as a *sort* of "miniature climate" that can be taken with them everywhere.

【近】 kind，class，species，variety

【释】 ② *v.* 分类；整顿，整理

【例】 To measure soil texture，the sand，silt，and clay particles are *sorted* out by size and weight.

【衍】 sortable（*adj.*）；sorter（*n.*）

【近】 classify，rank，separate

— 62 —

spine ［spain］

【释】 ① *n.* 脊骨，脊柱

【例】 The prohibited items are brain，*spine*，thymus，tonsils，spleen and intestine.

【衍】 spinal（*adj.*）；spinal cord（*n.*）脊髓

【近】 vertebrate

【释】 ② *n.* 棘状突起，刺，针

【例】 Some of the tropical species are adorned with *spines* or ridges，imitating the thorny bushes or trees in which they live.

【近】 spike，need，thorn，bristle

stabilize ［'steibilaiz］

【释】 *v.* （使）稳定；（使）固定

【例】 In Japan and elsewhere，the trees are planted to *stabilize* soil on steep mountain slopes.

【衍】 stability（*n.*）；stable（*adj.*）

【近】 steady，become constant

stem ［stem］

【释】 ① *n.* 茎，干，梗；叶柄，花梗，果柄

【例】 More specifically，the sea anemone is formed quite like the flower for which it is named，with a body like a *stem* and tentacles like petals in brilliant shades of blue，green，pink，and red.

【衍】 stemmed（*adj.*）有茎的；去掉茎的；stemming（*n.*）堵塞物；stemless（*adj.*）无茎(柄、梗)的

【近】 stalk，trunk，twig，limb

【释】 ② *v.* 起源于，起因于，（由…）发生，来自

【例】 Her dance *stemmed* from her soul and spirit.

【释】 ③ *n.* 种族，血统，家系

【例】 Her seclusion was the result of renunciation through which she carried on an argument with the Puritan fathers，attacking their *stem* patriarchal God and their rigid notions of "true womanhood."

【衍】 stemmata（*n.*）家谱，血统

strategy ［'strætidʒi］

【释】 *n.* 战略(学)；策略，作战方针

【例】 Another *strategy* of large desert animals is to tolerate the loss of body water to a point that would be fatal for nonadapted animals.

【衍】 stratagem（*n.*）策略，谋略；strategist（*n.*）战略家

【近】 approach，tactic，stratagem

subsequent ['sʌbsikwənt]

【释】 *adj.* 其后的，其次的；作为结果而发生的（[*opp.*] **preceding**）

【例】 John Olmsted did the investigation and *subsequent* report on Seattle's parks.

【衍】 subsequently（*adv.*）

【近】 following，succeeding，consequent

superb [sjuːˈpəːb]

【释】 *adj.* 极好的，超等的，宏伟的，壮丽的

【例】 The city had a *superb* natural harbor, as well as excellent rail connections.

【衍】 superbly（*adv.*）；superbness（*n.*）

【近】 excellent，outstanding，wonderful

swallow ['swɔləu]

【释】 ① *v.* 吞，咽

【例】 Beginning with such decisions as whether to *swallow* something or spit it out, the negation mechanism became, in time, able to distinguish what is real and what is not.

【衍】 swallowable（*adj.*）可吞食的；swallower（*n.*）

【近】 ingest，consume，gulp down

【释】 ② *v.* 淹没(**up**)

【例】 ... another of Alaska's large peninsulas in Seward, in which a number of smaller eastern states could be *swallowed* up.

tale [teil]

【释】 *n.* 故事，传说

【例】 Critics and historians have remarked more than once that *tale*-telling is a regional trait of the South.

【近】 fiction，legend，romance

temperate ['tempərit]

【释】 *adj.* (气候等)温和的

【例】 Perhaps the aspect of butterfly diversity that has received the most attention over the past century is the striking difference in species richness between tropical and *temperate* regions.

【衍】 temperature （*n.*）温度，气温；temper（*n.*）中和剂；调和剂

【近】 moderate，mild，pleasant

thereafter [ðɛərˈɑːftə]

【释】 *adv.* 此后

【例】 Indeed，for many years *thereafter*，the United States had two groups from which to chose—either the local craftspeople or the imported talent of Europeans sculptors.

【衍】 thereinafter（*adv.*）在下文；以下

【近】 afterward，subsequently，later

till [til]

【释】 ① *conj.* 直到…为止

【例】 "I think real hard *till* I think of something real pretty，and then I paint it," she said.

【释】 ② *n.* 冰碛土（物）

【例】 Because most glacial *till* has a fairly high water content，ice forms beneath fieldstones when they freeze，and the expansion of this ice forces them upward.

tow [təu]

【释】 *v.* 拖着走，拉着走

【例】 But even if the icebergs lost half of their volume in *towing*，the water they could provide would be far cheaper than that produced by desalination，or removing salt from water.

【衍】 towage（*n.*）牵引；拖船；拖船费

【近】 pull，drag，draw

trap [træp]

【释】 *v.* 设陷阱捕捉，诱捕；使受限制　*n.* 陷阱

【例】 In the countryside farmers therefore relieved the burden of the daily routine with such double purpose relaxations as hunting，fishing，and *trapping*.

【衍】 trapper（*n.*）；trapping（*n.*）；trapped（*adj.*）

【近】 ensnare，entrap，ambush

troupe [truːp]

【释】 ① *n.* 剧团，戏班子；马戏团

【例】 Durang continued his remarkable career for the next 20 years，performing in theaters and circuses and even managing his own dramatic touring *troupe* for nine consecutive summers.

【衍】 trouper（*n.*）演员

【释】 ② *n.* 一团，一班，一伙

【例】 Boucicault claims to have initiated it around 1860 when he sent out a *troupe* with Colleen Bawn，but a book published in 1859 speaks of combination companies as already established.

【近】 group，company，band

underlie [ˌʌndəˈlai]

【释】 *v.* (-lay; -lain; -lying) 位于…下面；成为…的基础

【例】 This principle，which *underlay* the whole later development of the continental United States，was generally accepted by this time and cannot be properly credited to any single man.

utter [ˈʌtə]

【释】 ① *v.* 发出(声音等)；讲，说

【例】 The words I *utter* and you hear as vibrations in the air are certainly human changes in the material world and may be of great historical significance.

【衍】 utterance（*n.*）

【近】 say，pronounce，articulate

【释】 ② *adj.* 完全的，十足的

【例】 A look of *utter* confusion swept across his handsome face.

【衍】 utterly（*adv.*）

【近】 complete，absolute，sheer

verse [vəːs]

【释】 *n.* 韵文([*opp.*] prose)；诗

【例】 Her productivity since then has been prodigious，accumulating in less than two decades to nearly thirty titles，including novels，collections of short stories and *verse*, plays and literary criticism.

【近】 poetry, rhyme

vivid ['vivid]

【释】 *adj*. (光、色)鲜明的；生动的

【例】 Meteorologists and computer scientists now work together to design computer programs and video equipment capable of transforming raw weather data into words, symbols, and *vivid* graphic displays that forecasters can interpret easily and quickly.

【衍】 vividly (*adv*.)

weary ['wiəri]

【释】 *adj*. 疲倦的；感到厌倦的(of)

【例】 Food, drink, and celebration after the group work provided relaxation and soothed *weary* muscles.

【衍】 wearily (*adv*.); weariness (*n*.)

【近】 exhausted, fatigued

witness ['witnis]

【释】 *v*. 目击，目睹　　*n*. 证人，证据

【例】 Since surpluses of food could also be bartered for other commodities, the Neolithic era *witnessed* the beginnings of large-scale exchange of goods.

Exercise of Unit 3

左列单词在右列中有一个同义词，请找出并在相应的位置写上正确答案。

Exercise 1：

（A）tow _____ revision
（B）amendment _____ poetry
（C）verse _____ shadow
（D）embody _____ pull
（E）shade _____ eagerness
（F）enthusiasm _____ include

Exercise 2：

（A）abnormal _____ rebirth
（B）candidate _____ water
（C）renaissance _____ disorder
（D）chaos _____ forerunner
（E）aquatic _____ atypical
（F）precursor _____ nominee

Exercise 3：

（A）converse _____ opposite
（B）stabilize _____ steady
（C）inclination _____ worsen
（D）earnest _____ tendency
（E）awkward _____ clumsy
（F）deteriorate _____ serious

Exercise 4：

（A）utter _____ bare
（B）immediate _____ instant
（C）basic _____ splendid
（D）fundamental _____ essential
（E）grand _____ say
（F）expose _____ basic

Exercise 5：

（A）sort _____ essential
（B）integral _____ infuse
（C）inject _____ border
（D）boundary _____ classify
（E）sort _____ kind
（F）scent _____ smell

Exercise 6：

（A）fashion _____ make
（B）conservation _____ protection
（C）genuine _____ evaluate
（D）regional _____ ridicule
（E）mock _____ local
（F）assess _____ real

Exercise 7:

(A) quotation _____ citation
(B) utter _____ complete
(C) troupe _____ look like
(D) conclusive ____ prehistoric
(E) resemble _____ decisive
(F) primitive _____ group

Exercise 8:

(A) heritage _____ beacon
(B) rush _____ stalk
(C) forge _____ abundant
(D) lighthouse _____ inheritance
(E) plentiful _____ build
(F) stem _____ hurry

Exercise 9:

(A) strategy _____ meadow
(B) definite _____ obtain
(C) secure _____ disappointment
(D) rival _____ specific
(E) pasture _____ approach
(F) dismay _____ match

Exercise 10:

(A) swallow _____ moderate
(B) temperate _____ volatilize
(C) notable _____ strange
(D) odd _____ excellent
(E) evaporate _____ ingest
(F) superb _____ distinguished

ANSWERS:

1	B C E A F D
2	C E D F A B
3	A B F C E D
4	F B E C A D
5	B C D A E F
6	A B F E D C
7	A B E F D C
8	D F E A C B
9	E C F B A D
10	B E D F A C

Unit 4

abroad	embrace	motif	shaft
acoustic(al)	entity	nectar	shuttle
affair	evenly	notice	slope
amid	expressive	odor	soul
arbitrary	fatal	organic	spiral
assign	flattering	oyster	staff
axe	formation	patch	stereotype
basin	fungus	percussion	streamline
bison	genus	physicist	subsidize
bow	granite	plot	superficial
bunch	hardness	portray	swamp
canoe	hesitate	predator	talent
caterpillar	humidity	principal	temple
chapel	immigrant	pronounced	thereby
clay	incongruous	publication	timber
commerce	injury	race	towel
concrete	integrate	raven	treasure
conservative	investigate	recover	trumpet
convert	Jupiter	regular	undermine
crater	launch	render	vacant
cylinder	limb	reserve	version
degrade	longing	retrieve	vocal
determine	majestic	roam	weather
disperse	maximum	rust	wonder
domain	meticulously	schedule	
earthenware	mode	sediment	

abroad [ə'brɔːd]

【释】① *adv.* 到国外，在海外

【例】She aided artists in numerous other ways—sending them *abroad* to study，paying their hospital bills and studio rents，and most important，purchasing their works.

【近】overseas（*adj.*，*adv.*）

【释】② *n.* 国外，海外

【例】Travelers from *abroad* were mildly shocked by this high social position.

acoustic(al) [ə'kuːstik(əl)]

【释】*adj.* 听觉的；声学的

【例】The ability to modulate a chemical signal is limited，compared with communication by visual or *acoustic* means.

【衍】acoustics（*n.*）声学；acoustically（*adv.*）

affair [ə'fɛə]

【释】*n.* 事情，事件；（常[*pl.*]）事务；事态

【例】The village chief dealt with land disputes and religious *affairs*.

【近】matter，issue，event

amid [ə'mid]

【释】*prep.* 在…的当中；在…的包围中

【例】… *amid* enemies（dangers）

【衍】amidst（*prep.*）

【近】among，in the middle of，in the midst of

arbitrary ['ɑːbitrəri]

【释】*adj.* 任意的；强词夺理的

【例】In documenting geographical variation in butterfly diversity，some *arbitrary*，practical decisions are made.

【衍】arbitrarily（*adv.*）

【近】subjective，capricious

assign [ə'sain]

【释】① *v.* 指定，选定

【例】Throughout a country，children arrive at school at approximately the same time. Take *assigned* seats，are taught by an adult，use similar textbooks，do homework，take exams，and so on.

【衍】 assignation （*n*.）

【近】 allot，allocate，designate，dispense

【释】 ② *v*. 把…归因于

【例】 Since he believed the unconscious consist solely of desire, he *assigned* the ability to say "no" to the conscious and the ego.

【近】 ascribe to，attribute to，blame on

axe　[æks]

【释】 *n*. (＝ax) ([*pl*.] axes) 斧

【例】 Stone Age hand *axes* and hatchets were made from stones that were carefully chipped away to form sharp cutting edges.

【近】 blade，machete

basin　['beisn]

【释】 *n*. 脸盆，水盆；盆地，流域

【例】 There seem to have been several periods within the last tens of thousands of years when water accumulated in these *basins*.

bison　['baisn]

【释】 *n*. ([*pl*.] bison)【动】(欧洲种和美洲种)野牛

【例】 Several different *bison* species have lived on the North American continent since the Ice Age，today only two exist.

bow　[bəu]

【释】 *n*. 弓；弓形物，琴弓

【例】 While drawing the *bow* to and fro with the right arm—ten entirely different movements.

【衍】 bowed (*adj*.)

【近】 bend，stoop

bunch　[bʌntʃ]

【释】 *n*. 球，束，朵，串

【例】 But in the polar regions，the magnetic lines of force of the Earth and of the solar wind *bunch* together.

【近】 group，gathering，gang，cluster

canoe　[kə'nuː]

【释】 *n*. 独木舟

【例】 Even Lewis and Clark in their journey up the Missouri sometimes met the descending *canoes* of trappers and hunters, loaded with furs, on their way to St. Louis, the center of the fur trade.

【近】 boat, vessel, craft

caterpillar [ˈkætəpilə]

【释】 *n.* 鳞翅目幼虫，毛虫

【例】 Every parent knows the propensity of small children to bring home *caterpillars*, grasshoppers, toads, and other small living things.

【近】 worm, larva

chapel [ˈtʃæpəl]

【释】 *n.* （常附属于大教堂的）小教堂

【例】 Post *chapels* provided a setting for religious services and boosted morale.

clay [klei]

【释】 *n.* 黏土；泥土

【例】 Caves have preserved the bones of many animals that died in them and were subsequently buried under a blanket of *clay* or a cover of dripstone.

【近】 mud, dirt, soil, earth, terracotta

commerce [ˈkɔməːs]

【释】 *n.* 商业；商务，贸易

【例】 The National Marine Sanctuaries Program is administered by the National Oceanic and Atmospheric Administration, a branch of the United States Department of *Commerce*.

【衍】 commercial（*adj.*）；commercially（*adv.*）

concrete [ˈkɔnkriːt]

【释】 ① *n.* 混凝土

【例】 These hominids walked across a stretch of moist volcanic ash, which was subsequently tamed to mud by rain, and which then set like *concrete*.

【衍】 concretion（*n.*）

【释】 ② *adj.* 具体的，实在的

【例】 This is true even if the protester's ultimate goal is to alter radically the legal system; an act of civil disobedience must be directed against one *concrete* example of that system's inequities.

【衍】 concretely（*adv.*）

【近】 real，tangible

conservative ［kən'sə:vətiv］

【释】 *adj.* 保守的，守旧的

【例】 A folk culture is small，isolated，cohesive，*conservative*，nearly self-sufficient group that is homogeneous in custom and race，with a strong family or clan structure and highly developed rituals.

【衍】 conservatism（*n.*）

【近】 traditional，conventional

convert ［kən'və:t］

【释】 *v.* 转换，转化

【例】 In fact，nuclear reactions that *convert* hydrogen to helium are responsible for most of the energy that stars produce.

【衍】 conversion（*n.*）

【近】 transform，change

crater ［'kreitə］

【释】 *n.* 火山口；（月球上的）环形山；（炸成的）弹坑；陨石坑

【例】 Snow accumulating yearly in Rainier's summit *craters* is compacted and compressed into a dense form of ice.

【衍】 craterlet（*n.*）小火山口

【近】 cave，chamber，cavity

cylinder ［'silində］

【释】 *n.* 圆筒；【数】柱（面），柱体；汽缸

【例】 Steam was accumulated in a large，double-acting vertical *cylinder*，but the steam reached only a few pounds of pressure per square inch.

【衍】 cylindrical（*adj.*）

degrade ［di'greid］

【释】 *v.* 降低；堕落；【生】（使）退化；（使）剥蚀

【例】 … enzymes that *degrade* cell walls.

【衍】 degradation（*n.*）

【近】 disgrace，corrupt，humiliate

determine ［di'tə:min］

【释】 *v.* 决心，决意；测定

【例】　No one had ever isolated it and experimentally *determined* its properties.

【衍】　determination（*n.*）决心，决意；determinant（*n.*）决定因素；determined（*adj.*）坚决的；毅然的；确定的；determinedly（*adv.*）

【近】　decide，resolve

disperse　[dis'pəːs]

【释】　*v.* 使疏散，使散开；驱散(云、雾等)

【例】　Even a trail that has been *dispersed* by breezes may still seem rich to a bloodhound.

【衍】　disperser（*n.*）；dispersal/dispersion（*n.*）分散，散开；离散

【近】　scatter，diffuse

domain　[dəu'mein]

【释】　*n.* 领土；(学问、活动等的)领域，范围

【例】　They are great experimenters in the *domain* of art.

【近】　area，field，realm

earthenware　['əːθənwɛə]

【释】　*n.* 瓦器，陶器

【例】　In a relatively brief period the archaeological record is reduced to mere scraps of stone，bone，glass，metal，and *earthenware*.

【近】　stoneware，pottery

embrace　[im'breis]

【释】　*v.* 拥抱，抱；参加

【例】　These new urbanites eagerly *embraced* the progressive reforms that promised to bring order out of the chaos of the city.

【衍】　embracement（*n.*）

【近】　hug，cuddle

entity　['entiti]

【释】　*n.* 实体；统一体

【例】　But none of the shapes on this list describes the largest single *entities* in the universe.

evenly　['iːvənli]

【释】　*adj.* 一致的；均匀的

【例】　As it burned，the ashes would fall around the pots and

bake them *evenly* over a few hours.

【衍】 unevenly（*adj.*）；evenness（*n.*）

【近】 proportional，symmetrical

expressive [ik'spresiv]

【释】 *adj.* 富于表情的；意味深长的

【例】 Taking a walnut plank，the sculptor carved the *expressive*，stylized design.

【衍】 expressiveness（*n.*）

【近】 animated，meaningful，emotional，vivid

fatal ['feitəl]

【释】 *adj.* 致命的；命中注定的

【例】 Another strategy of large desert animals is to tolerate the loss of body water to a point that would be *fatal* for nonadapted animals.

【衍】 fate（*n.*）；fatalism（*n.*）宿命论

【近】 lethal，deadly

flattering ['flætəriŋ]

【释】 *adj.* 谄媚的，讨好的，奉承的

【例】 While it was not intended as *flattering*，it was hardly inappropriate.

【衍】 unflattering（*adj.*）；flatteringly（*adv.*）；flatter（*v.*）奉承，谄媚，阿谀；flatterer（*n.*）

【近】 pleasing，obsequious，toadying，sycophantic，fawning

formation [fɔː'meiʃən]

【释】 *n.* 组织，构造

【例】 The additional material consisted of some 14 layered *formations* of rock.

【近】 configuration，structure，pattern，shape

fungus ['fʌŋgəs]

【释】 *n.* （[*pl.*] funguses，fungi）真菌（包括霉菌、酵母菌和伞菌等）

【例】 Certain *fungi* and even some kinds of bacteria secrete substances known as antibiotics into their external environment.

【衍】 fungal/fungous（*adj.*）如真菌的；真菌状的；因真菌引起的；fungicide（*n.*）杀真菌剂

genus ['dʒiːnəs]

【释】 *n.* 种类，类，属

【例】 The koala lives in trees，specifically some 35 of the more than 600 species of the *genus* Eucalyptus that grow in Australia.

granite ['grænit]

【释】 *n.* 花岗岩，花岗石

【例】 Magma flows onto the surface and is quickly cooled by the atmosphere，and the resulting rock will appear different from *granite*.

hardness ['hɑːdnis]

【释】 *n.* 坚固，冷酷无情，苛刻，困难

【例】 In the mineral table of *hardness*，it has a rating of 8，which means that a knife cannot cut it.

【近】 rigidity, stiffness

hesitate ['heziteit]

【释】 *v.* 犹豫，踌躇；不愿，含糊，支吾

【例】 All cars *hesitate* in the streets because there are no traffic lights to guide them.

【衍】 hesitation（*n.*）；hesitating（*adj.*）；hesitatingly（*adv.*）

humidity [hjuː'midəti]

【释】 *n.* 湿气；湿度

【例】 When parrots incubate their eggs in the wild，the temperature and *humidity* of the nest are controlled naturally.

【衍】 humid（*adj.*）；humidly（*adv.*）；humidness（*n.*）

【近】 moisture, wetness, dampness

immigrant ['imigrənt]

【释】 *n. & adj.* （来自外国的）移民（的）

【例】 Matching the influx of foreign *immigrants* into the larger cities of the United States during the late nineteenth century was a domestic migration.

【衍】 immigration（*n.*）

【近】 settler, migrant, colonist

incongruous [in'kɔŋgruəs]

【释】 *adj.* 不调和的，不相称的

【例】 With spontaneous irreverence，satire rearranges perspectives， scrambles familiar objects into *incongruous* juxtaposition，and speaks in a personal idiom instead of abstract platitude.

【衍】 incongruously (*adv.*)；incongruity (*n.*)

【近】 absurd，odd，strange，bizarre

---

injury ['indʒəri]

【释】 *n.* 损害，毁坏，伤害

【例】 Trees cannot heal: they make no repairs. Instead，they defend themselves from the consequences of *injury* and infection by walling off the damage.

【衍】 injured (*adj.*)；injure (*v.*)

【近】 wound，damage

---

integrate ['intigreit]

【释】 *v.* 使成整体，使并入，使一体化，使结合起来

【例】 At that point in time，medical schools started to become more interested in having their curricula *integrate* nutritional concepts into the basic sciences.

【衍】 reintegrate (*v.*)；disintegrate (*v.*)；integration (*n.*)；integrity (*n.*) 诚实，正直

【近】 incorporate

---

investigate [in'vestigeit]

【释】 *v.* 研究，调查；审查

【例】 The more thoroughly scientists *investigate* the universe，the more clearly its simplicity shines through.

【衍】 investigation (*n.*)；investigator (*n.*)

【近】 examine，scrutinize

Jupiter ['dʒuːpitə]

【释】 *n.* 木星；【罗神】（主神）朱庇特

【例】 *Jupiter* rotates very fast，once every 9.8 hours.

---

launch [lɑːntʃ]

【释】 ① *v.* 发射；投出；提出，发出

【例】 Synchronous satellites are *launched* to an altitude of 22,300 miles.

【衍】 launcher (*n.*) 发射者，发射装置

【近】 send off，discharge，dispatch

【释】 ② *v.* 开办，创办；发动，发起；开展

【例】 The WAOAW was *launched* in 1971 by artists Gloria Bilotta and Millie Graham.

【近】 introduce，present，start on

limb ［lim］

【释】 ① *n.* 肢，手足；翼，翅膀

【例】 Its fur is thick and woolly，its *limbs* are long，and its toes are strongly clawed.

【衍】 limbed（*adj.*）有…肢（分枝、翼）的；limbless（*adj.*）无肢的，无翼的，无枝叉的

【近】 extremity，appendage

【释】 ② *n.* 大树枝

【例】 A macaque or gibbon can hurl itself farther than a mouse can：it can achieve a running start，and it can more effectively use a branch as a springboard，even bouncing on a *limb* several times before jumping.

【近】 branch，bough

longing ［'lɔŋiŋ］

【释】 *adj.* 渴望的，热望的　　*n.* 渴望

【例】 While tulip bulbs were traveling from Europe to the United States to satisfy the nostalgic *longings* of homesick English and Dutch settlers，North American Plants were traveling in the opposite direction.

【衍】 longingly（*adv.*）

【近】 desire，wish，yearning

majestic ［mə'dʒestik］

【释】 *adj.* 有威严的，威风凛凛的

【例】 In this period her walls became more ambitious in scale，achieving a serene and *majestic* presence.

【衍】 majestically（*adv.*）

【近】 royal，grand，magnificent

maximum ［'mæksiməm］

【释】 *n.* & *adj.* 极点(的)，最高额(的)，最大值(的)；最高点(的)

【例】 In 1938 the Fair Labor Standards Act mandated a weekly *maximum* of 40 hours to begin in 1940，and since that time the 8-hour day，5-day workweek has been the standard in the United States.

【近】 utmost, most, greatest

meticulously [mə'tikjuləsli]

【释】 *adv.* 小心翼翼地，细致地

【例】 The successive layering of these *meticulously* applied paints produced the final, translucent colors.

【衍】 meticulous (*adj.*)

【近】 carefully, scrupulously, fastidiously

mode [məud]

【释】 *n.* 方式；模式；样式，习惯

【例】 The older painters practiced in a *mode* often self-taught and monopolized by landscape subject matter and were securely established in and fostered by the reigning American art organization.

【衍】 modal (*adj.*) 方式上的；model (*n.* & *adj.*)；modeling (*n.*) 制造模型的方法，造型(术)

【近】 form, style, type

motif [məu'ti:f]

【释】 *n.* (图案的)基本花纹，基本色彩；(艺术作品的)主题，动机，主旨

【例】 After O'Keeffe's trip around the world by plane, the sky "paved with clouds" as seen from an airplane also became one of her favorite *motifs* and the subject of her largest work, a 24-foot mural.

【近】 design, theme, pattern

nectar ['nektə]

【释】 *n.* 花蜜

【例】 For example, a worker honeybee that has found a rich source of *nectar* and pollen flies rapidly home to the hive to report.

notice ['nəutis]

【释】 *v.* & *n.* 注意；认识

【例】 Thousands of tons were extracted before 1875, when it was first *noticed* that the tar contained fossil remains.

【衍】 noticeable (*adj.*) 引人注意的，显著的；noticeably (*adv.*)

【近】 become aware of, perceive, note

odor [ˈəudə]

【释】 *n.* 气味；香，香气；臭气

【例】 The process by which the nose recognizes an *odor* is not fully understood，but there are apparently specific receptor sites for specific odors.

【衍】 odorless（*adj.*）没有香气(气味)的；odorant（*n.*）有气味的物质；odoriferous（*adj.*）有气味(臭味)的；odorous（*adj.*）；有气味(臭味)的

【近】 smell，scent，aroma

organic [ɔːˈgænik]

【释】 *adj.* 器官的；有机体的；有机的([*opp.*] inorganic)

【例】 Although they were entombed in the rocks for hundreds of millions of years，many of the fossils consist of the *organic* remains of the organism.

【衍】 organ（*n.*）器官；organically（*adv.*）有机地；organism（*n.*）有机体，有机组织(社会等)；organize（*v.*）组织起来，成立组织；organization（*n.*）组织，构成，编制；organizational（*adj.*）组织的

【近】 natural

oyster [ˈɔistə]

【释】 *n.* 蚝，牡蛎

【例】 In the past *oysters* were raised in much the same way as dirt farmers raised tomatoes—by transplanting them.

【衍】 oystercatcher（*n.*）【动】蛎鹬

patch [pætʃ]

【释】 *n.* 碎片；碎屑；斑点，斑纹；斑

【例】 Like pines, ash trees have *patches* of secondary cork cambium.

【近】 scrap，bit，piece

percussion [pəˈkʌʃən]

【释】 *n.* 敲打，打击；(乐队的)打击乐器组

【例】 In the music of the Western world, the greatest expansion and experimentation have involved *percussion* instruments.

【衍】 percussive（*adj.*）

【近】 drumming，beating，hitting，striking

physicist [ˈfizisist]

【释】 *n.* 物理学家

【例】 Studies of auroras have given *physicists* new information about the behavior of plasmas.

【衍】 physics (*n.*) 物理学

plot [plɒt]

【释】 *n. & v.* 密谋，图谋；策划

【例】 All that we really need to *plot* out the future of our universe are a few good measurements.

【近】 plan，design，conspire，scheme

portray [pɔːˈtrei]

【释】 *v.* 画(人物、风景)，画(肖像)，描绘；描写；描述

【例】 Another realist, Bret Harte, achieved fame with stories that *portrayed* local life in the California mining camps.

【衍】 portrayal (*n.*) 描写，描画；portrayer 肖像画家

【近】 depict，describe

predator [ˈpredətə]

【释】 *n.* 捕食其他动物的动物，食肉动物

【例】 There is some evidence that the two types of sleep, dreaming and dreamless, depend on the life-style of the animal, and that *predators* are statistically much more likely to dream than prey, which are in turn much more likely to experience dreamless sleep.

【衍】 predatory (*adj.*)

principal [ˈprinsəpəl]

【释】 *adj.* 主要的，首要的，最重要的；第一的

【例】 The Earth comprises three *principal* layers.

【衍】 principally (*adv.*)

【近】 main，major，chief，primary

pronounced [prəuˈnaunst]

【释】 *adj.* 决然的，断然的，强硬的

【例】 Relationships tend to be impersonal, and a *pronounced* division of labor exists.

【衍】 pronounce (*v.*); pronouncement (*n.*)

【近】 marked，distinct，definite，obvious

publication [ˌpʌbliˈkeiʃən]

【释】 *n.* 发行物，出版物，刊物

【例】 Magazines as they are known today began *publication* around 1882.

【近】 journal, magazine, newspaper

race [reis]

【释】 ① *n. & v.* 竞赛

【例】 Her first novel dealt with stock car racing, though she had never seen a *race*.

【衍】 racing (*n.*); raced (*adj.*)

【近】 competition, contest, compete

【释】 ② *n.* 种族

【例】 It is being considered quite seriously by many nations, especially since scientists have warned that the human *race* will outgrow its fresh water supply faster than in runs out of food.

【近】 ethnic group, nation

raven [ˈreivən]

【释】 *n.* 大乌鸦

【例】 Young *ravens*, for example, first attempt to build with sticks of quite unsuitable size, while a jackdaw's first nest includes virtually any movable object.

recover [riˈkʌvə]

【释】 ① *v.* 重新获得(找到)(失传的技术等)([*opp.*] lose)

【例】 The finely crafted ornaments and tools *recovered* at Cahokia, as this center of Mississippi culture is called, include one funeral blanket fashioned from 12,000 shell beads.

【衍】 recoverable (*adj.*); recover (*v.*) 重新盖；改装(更换)封面；recovery (*n.*)

【近】 get back, regain, retrieve, rehabilitate

【释】 ②*v.* 恢复；痊愈 (from; of)；清醒([*opp.*] deteriorate)

【例】 The patient *recovered* and was soon back at his activities as if he had never been stabbed.

【衍】 recovery (*n.*); recoverability (*n.*)

【近】 restore your health, get well, recuperate

— 83 —

【释】 ③ *v.* 赔偿(损失等)；取得(损害赔偿等)

【例】 In North America，potash making quickly became an adjunct to the clearing of land for agriculture，for it was estimated that as much as half the cost of clearing land could be ***recovered*** by the sale of potash.

【近】 recoup

regular ['regjulə]

【释】 ① *adj*. 有规律的；有秩序的；正规的，正式的

【例】 When you first drift off into slumber，your eyes will roll about a bit，your temperature will drop slightly，your muscles will relax，and your breathing will slow and become quite ***regular***.

【衍】 regularly（*adv.*）；regularity（*n.*）；regularize（*v.*）；regularization（*n.*）

【近】 normal，standard

【释】 ② *adj*. 定期的，定时的，常例的，习惯的

【例】 Without ***regular*** supplies of some hormones our capacity to behave would be seriously impaired：without others we would soon die.

【衍】 regularly（*adv.*）

【近】 customary，habitual，usual

render ['rendə]

【释】 ① *v.* 致使…；使变成…

【例】 Passive plant defense comprises physical and chemical barriers that prevent entry of pathogens，such as bacteria，or ***render*** tissues unpalatable or toxic to the invader.

【近】 make，cause to be

【释】 ② *n.* 表现，描写

【例】 Researchers have found that thirteen spots of light on each hand and one spot on the nose—to show head motion and provide a reference point to hand position—are sufficient for intelligible ***rendering*** of American Sign Language.

【近】 depicting，interpreting

reserve [ri'zə:v]

【释】 *n.* 贮藏物，贮藏量；保留地，贮藏所　*v.* 保留，储备（以备后用等）

【例】 They saved the best to the harvest for seeds or for trade, with the remainder eaten right away or stored for later use in underground *reserves*.

【衍】 reservation（*n.*）（印第安人）居留地；reserved（*adj.*）

【近】 preserve，store，keep

retrieve [ri'tri:v]

【释】 *v.* 找回；取回

【例】 Often formed to individual specifications, they always carried the silversmith's distinctive markings and consequently could be traced and *retrieved*.

【衍】 retrievable（*adj.*）；retrieval（*n.*）；retrievement（*n.*）

【近】 get back，recover，regain

roam [rəum]

【释】 *n. & v.* 漫游，游历，游荡，漫步

【例】 At one time, they had been forced to *roam* the forests and plains of the Earth in search of wild game and edible plants.

【衍】 roamer（*n.*）

【近】 wander，travel，rove

rust [rʌst]

【释】 *v.* 生锈　*n.* 锈；铁锈

【例】 Copper nails are better than iron nails because the iron *rusts*.

【衍】 rustproof（*adj.*）抗锈的，防锈的，不锈的；rustler（*n.*）活跃分子

【近】 corrosion，oxidation

schedule ['skedʒul]

【释】 ① *v.* 将…列入程序表（计划表，进度表）　*n.* 排定，安排

【例】 For management, telecommuting allows periods of solitude for high-concentration tasks, and provides *scheduling* flexibility.

【衍】 scheduling（*n.*）行程、时序安排；scheduled（*adj.*）预定的，排定的

【近】 agenda，timetable，calendar

【释】 ② *n.* 表（格）；清单，明细表

【例】 Colonial artisans tried to keep their shops as efficient as possible and to regularize their *schedules* and methods of production for the best return on their investment in time, tools, and materials.

【近】 list, scheme, diary

sediment ['sedimənt]

【释】 *n.* 沉淀物

【例】 The rapidly accumulating *sediments* in flood plains, deltas, and stream channels buried freshwater organisms, along with other plants and animals that happened to fall into the water.

【衍】 sedimentation (*n.*) 沉淀作用；sedimentary (*adj.*) 沉淀性的，沉淀(沉积)成的

shaft [ʃɑːft]

【释】 ① *n.* 光线；电光

【例】 Droplets and ice crystals behave somewhat like dust in the air made visible in a *shaft* of sunlight.

【近】 ray, beam

【释】 ② *n.* 隧道，管道

【例】 Three one-way *shafts* beneath the Hudson and two under the Harlem River were already holed through; three more Hudson tubes were being built.

【近】 duct, tube, pipe

shuttle ['ʃʌtl]

【释】 *v.* 穿梭般来回；短程来回运输　　*n.*【宇航】太空穿梭机

【例】 Equally important to everyday life was the morning and evening commuter locals *shuttling* back ions and urban terminals.

【衍】 shuttlecock (*n.*) 羽毛球

【近】 ferry, transport, transfer

slope [sləup]

【释】 *n.* 坡，斜坡，斜面；倾斜，坡度

【例】 In Japan and elsewhere, the trees are planted to stabilize soil on steep mountain *slopes*.

【衍】 sloping (*adj.*) 倾斜的，成斜坡的；sloper (*n.*) 整坡机

【近】 incline, gradient, slant

soul	[səul]
【释】	*n.* 灵魂，心灵；精神
【例】	Her dance stemmed from her *soul* and spirit.
【衍】	souled（*adj.*）有灵魂的，有感情的；soulful（*adj.*）充满激情的；精神（灵魂）上的；soulless（*adj.*）没有灵魂的，卑鄙的
【近】	spirit，essence，heart
spiral	['spaiərəl]
【释】	*adj.* 螺旋形的　　*v.* 盘旋
【例】	On such a scale the nearest giant *spiral* galaxy, the Andromeda galaxy, is two million light years away.
【衍】	spirally（*adv.*）
【近】	twisting，coiled，corkscrew
staff	[stɑːf]
【释】	*n.*（全体）工作人员
【例】	The Palace was more than a home：it contained offices for the president and some of his *staff* and advisors.
【衍】	staffer（*n.*）职员，工作人员；staffing（*n.*）安置职工
【近】	employees，personnel，workforce
stereotype	['stiəriətaip]
【释】	*n.* 旧框框；陈规老套，旧习，成规，定型
【例】	Certain Americans had included persons of African descent in their paintings as serious studies rather than as trivial or sentimental *stereotypes*.
【衍】	stereotyped（*adj.*）；stereophotograph（*n.*）立体摄影
【近】	label，pigeonhole
streamline	['striːmlain]
【释】	*v.* 把…做成流线型；调整(机构等)使现代化或提高效率
【例】	If a satellite had to get into orbit by itself，it would have to be *streamlined* to push its way through the Earth's atmosphere.
【衍】	streamlined（*adj.*）流线型的；streaming（*n.*）流动；streambed（*n.*）河床
【近】	modernize，rationalize，update
subsidize	['sʌbsidaiz]
【释】	*v.* 给…补助金，给…津贴，向…发放奖金

【例】In New York City，except for government-*subsidized* construction，the only rental units being built are luxury units，which are exempt from controls.

【衍】subsidy（*n.*）补助金，津贴，奖金；subsidiary（*adj.*）辅助的，补足的

【近】finance，fund，sponsor

superficial [ˌsjuːpəˈfiʃəl]

【释】*adj.* 表面的；肤浅的，浅薄的，一知半解的（[*opp.*] **profound**）

【例】This record exhibits certain peculiarities the consequences of which produce a rather *superficial* contrast between archaeological history and the more familiar kind based upon written records.

【衍】superficially（*adv.*）

【近】surface，shallow，trivial

swamp [swɔmp]

【释】*n.* 沼泽，沼地，湿地

【例】The distance was more than 350 miles，and there were ridges to cross and a wilderness of woods and *swamps* to penetrate.

【衍】swampland（*n.*）沼泽地；swampy（*adj.*）沼泽的，多沼泽的，潮湿的

【近】marsh，bog，quagmire

talent [ˈtælənt]

【释】*n.* 天资；才能；才干；本事

【例】The main reservoir of mathematical *talent* in any society is thus possessed by children who are about two years old.

【衍】talented（*adj.*）有才能的；talentless（*adj.*）

【近】aptitude，gift，bent

temple [ˈtempl]

【释】*n.* 庙，寺，圣堂，神殿

【例】Many of these buildings were shaped in the ziggurat form，a design resembling an ancient Mesopotamian *temple* tower that recedes in progressively smaller stages to the summit.

【近】holy place，shrine，sanctuary

thereby [ˌðɛəˈbai]

【释】*adv.* 因此，所以

【例】	Television brought candidates into voters' living rooms, *thereby* antiquating some of the communication and education functions of party workers.
【衍】	therefore (*adv.*) 因此; therefrom (*adv.*) 从那里
【近】	thus, so, by this means

timber ['timbə]

【释】	***n.*** 原木, 木材, 木料; (可做木材的)树木; 森林; 林场
【例】	Along the North Fork of the Flathead River, the park also borders about 17,000 acres of private lands that are currently used for ranching, *timber*, and agriculture.
【衍】	timbered (*adj.*) 森林的; 木制的; timbering (*n.*) 木材
【近】	wood, lumber

towel ['tauəl]

【释】	***n.*** 毛巾; 手巾 ***v.*** 用毛巾擦
【例】	The novelist John Steinbeck recorded the contents of a young osprey nest built in his garden, which included three shirts, a bath *towel*, and one arrow.
【衍】	towelette (*n.*) 小毛巾; toweling (*n.*) 毛巾料; towelling (*n.*) 毛巾布

treasure ['treʒə]

【释】	***n.*** 财富, 金银财宝, 珍宝; 珍藏, 宝藏
【例】	The pioneer farmer could still find an abundance of good land east of the river, and the mineral *treasures* of the mountains in the distant West were as yet undisclosed.
【衍】	treasurer (*n.*) 司库, 财务员; treasury (*n.*) 宝库; 财政部; 国库
【近】	wealth, fortune, riches

trumpet ['trʌmpit]

【释】	***n.*** 喇叭; 小号
【例】	The *trumpet* family is much more than a group of related instruments that can stir one with their sound, or narrow tubes of metal capable of producing a variety of musical sounds.
【衍】	trumpeter (*n.*) 喇叭手, 号手

undermine ['ʌndəmain]

【释】	***v.*** 掘…的下面, 削弱…的基础
【例】	By about A.D. 500 the Mound Builder culture was declining, perhaps because of attacks from other tribes

or perhaps because of severe climatic changes that *undermined* agriculture.

【近】 weaken, demoralize

vacant ['veikənt]

【释】 *n.* (房子等)空着的，没人住的；(位置等)空缺的

【例】 Of course, many were never occupied; there was always a huge surplus of subdivided, but *vacant*, land around Chicago and other cities.

【衍】 vacancy (*n.*)

【近】 available, unoccupied, empty

version ['vəːʃən]

【释】 *n.* 版本；形式

【例】 In her *versions* the figures became more stylized and the landscapes less naturalistic.

【近】 edition, form

vocal ['vəukəl]

【释】 *adj.* 声的，(关于)声音的　*n.*【语音】元音

【例】 Then, perhaps later, an assortment of *vocal* sounds was developed as a word tally against the number of objects in a small group.

【衍】 vocally (*adv.*)

【近】 verbal, oral

weather ['weðə]

【释】 *v.* 使风化

【例】 The tiny, delicate skeletons are usually scattered by scavengers or destroyed by *weathering* before they can be fossilized.

【近】 season

wonder ['wʌndə]

【释】 ① *adj.* 非凡的，奇妙的

【例】 Almost daily the public is besieged by claims for "no-aging" diets, new vitamins, and other *wonder* foods.

【释】 ② *v.* (对…)觉得奇怪

【例】 The experiment called for familiarizing the animal with the mirror and then marking individual, it might *wonder* about the curious red spot and might even touch the mirror.

Exercise of Unit 4

左列单词在右列中有一个同义词，请找出并在相应的位置写上正确答案。

Exercise 1:

(A) expressive _____ subjective
(B) assign _____ allot
(C) arbitrary _____ traditional
(D) longing _____ extremity
(E) limb _____ desire
(F) conservative _____ animated

Exercise 2:

(A) spiral _____ introduce
(B) earthenware _____ stoneware
(C) version _____ edition
(D) regular _____ weaken
(E) undermine _____ normal
(F) launch _____ twisting

Exercise 3:

(A) crater _____ scatter
(B) principal _____ settler
(C) fatal _____ lethal
(D) disperse _____ cave
(E) immigrant _____ mud
(F) clay _____ main

Exercise 4:

(A) embrace _____ preserve
(B) treasure _____ wealth
(C) integrate _____ incorporate
(D) incongruous _____ available
(E) vacant _____ absurd
(F) reserve _____ hug

Exercise 5:

(A) investigate _____ bend
(B) evenly _____ royal
(C) plot _____ proportional
(D) injury _____ wound
(E) bow _____ examine
(F) majestic _____ plan

Exercise 6:

(A) slope _____ form
(B) mode _____ marked
(C) talent _____ aptitude
(D) amid _____ transform
(E) convert _____ incline
(F) pronounced _____ among

Exercise 7:
(A) timber _____ decide
(B) determine _____ wood
(C) schedule _____ list
(D) percussion _____ disgrace
(E) portray _____ depict
(F) degrade _____ drumming

Exercise 8:
(A) race _____ utmost
(B) motif _____ competition
(C) humidity _____ design
(D) superficial _____ surface
(E) regular _____ moisture
(F) maximum _____ customary

Exercise 9:
(A) stereotype _____ label
(B) roam _____ smell
(C) odor _____ make
(D) render _____ wander
(E) staff _____ matter
(F) affair _____ employees

Exercise 10:
(A) rust _____ corrosion
(B) schedule _____ area
(C) concrete _____ real
(D) domain _____ depicting
(E) render _____ branch
(F) limb _____ agenda

ANSWERS:
1 C B F E D A
2 F B C E D A
3 D E C A F B
4 F B C E D A
5 E F B D A C
6 B F C E A D
7 B A C F E D
8 F A B D C E
9 A C D B F E
10 A D C E F B

Unit 5

abrupt	embryo	motivation	shake
acquaint	entrance	needlework	sieve
agent	evoke	notion	sloth
ample	extend	offensive	soup
arch	fatigue	orientation	spirit
assume	flavor	pace	in spite of
axis	formidable	patent	stagecoach
battery	funnel	performance	sterile
bite	geographic	pianist	strength
boycott	grasp	plow	subsist
burden	hardship	positive	superheat
canopy	hexagon	predict	swarm
cathedral	humorous	prior	tame
charcoal	immobilize	propel	temporarily
clerk	incorporate	publicize	thermodynamics
commission	inland	radar	tin
condense	intense	raw	tower
consist	inviting	recreation	treat
convey	jurisdiction	regulate	trunk
credit	lava	renew	underscore
dairy	limestone	reservoir	vaccinate
deity	loom	revere	vertebrate
devastate	makeup	roar	vocation
disposal	meager	saber	weave
domestic	metropolis	scheme	wool
eccentric	modem	seemingly	

abrupt [əˈbrʌpt]

【释】 *adj*. 突然的；生硬的

【例】 Most paleontologists suspect that *abrupt* changes in climate led to the mass extinctions.

【衍】 abruptly（*adv.*）；abruptness（*n.*）突然；abruption（*n.*）突然分离，分裂，断裂

【近】 sudden, rushed, unexpected

acquaint [əˈkweint]

【释】 *v.* 使熟悉，了解［多用被动语态］

【例】 Men gossiped and exchanged rumors to get *acquainted* with strangers.

【衍】 acquaintance（*n.*）熟人

agent [ˈeidʒənt]

【释】 *n.* 作用物；成分

【例】 Hazen methodically screened and cultured scores of soil samples, isolated and purified active *agents*...

【衍】 agency（*n.*）作用；媒介；机构

【近】 constituent, ingredient, component, element

ample [ˈæmpl]

【释】 *adj*. 丰富的，充足的，富裕的

【例】 Located on heap land along water—power sites in the midst of a farming region that could supply *ample* labor, they were satellites in the fullest sense of the term.

【衍】 amplify（*v.*）扩大，放大；amplification（*n.*）扩大；扩充；amplitude（*n.*）广阔，广大

【近】 plenty, sufficient, plentiful, abundant

arch [ɑːtʃ]

【释】 *n.* 拱门；弓形门 *v.* 把…做成拱形；使弯成弓形

【例】 Previously the poor quality of the iron had restricted its use in architecture to items such as chains and tie bars for supporting *arches*, vaults, and walls.

【近】 arc, arcade, curve, vault

assume [əˈsjuːm]

【释】 ① *v.* 假定，想象，设想；以…为先决条件

【例】 Newton's laws of motion *assume* that the total amount of spin of a body cannot change unless an external torque speeds it up or slows it down.

【衍】 assumable（*adj.*）；assumption（*n.*）

【近】 suppose，presume

【释】 ② *v.* 承担，担任

【例】 As the years passed，"Harlem" *assumed* an even larger meaning.

axis ['æksis]

【释】 *n.* 轴，轴线

【例】 Satellite completes one orbit during the same length of time that the Earth makes one rotation on its *axis*.

battery ['bætəri]

【释】 *n.*【电】电池(组)

【例】 The electric eel is an amazing storage *battery*.

bite [bait]

【释】 *v.* 咬，叮，螫；紧咬 *n.* 一小口(食物)，少量(食物)

【例】 The impostors do not pick parasites instead，they take *bites* from the soft tissue of the unsuspecting fish.

【衍】 biter（*n.*）咬人的动物；骗子

boycott ['bɔikət]

【释】 *n.* 联合抵制；联合拒绝购买(使用、销售等)

【例】 In 1955 Martin Luther King，Jr. gained national recognition for his nonviolent methods used in a bus *boycott* in Montgomery.

【近】 refuse，embargo，reject，shun

burden ['bəːdən]

【释】 *n.* 担子，负担，包袱

【例】 Cattle have served humanity since prehistoric days as beasts of *burden* and as suppliers of leather，meat，and milk.

【衍】 burdensome（*adj.*）

【近】 load，weight，lumber，saddle

canopy ['kænəpi]

【释】 *n.* (树)冠；冠层

【例】 Growing tightly packed together and collectively weaving a dense *canopy* of branches，a stand of red alder trees can totally dominate a site to the exclusion of almost everything else.

【近】 shade，tree crown

cathedral [kə'θiːdrəl]

【释】 *n.* 大教堂

【例】 Designers of the railroad stations of the new age explored the potential of iron，covering huge areas with spans that surpassed the great vaults of medieval churches and *cathedrals*.

【近】 church，chapel

charcoal ['tʃɑːkəul]

【释】 *n.* (木)炭

【例】 Iron production was revolutionized in the early eighteenth century when coke was first used instead of *charcoal* for refining iron ore.

clerk [kləːk]

【释】 *n.* 办事员，职员；(商店的)店员

【例】 She leaves the little town for Washington，D. C. where she works as a government *clerk*.

commission [kə'miʃən]

【释】 *v. & n.* 委托

【例】 Once again an original portrait became a luxury，*commissioned* by the wealthy and executed by the professional.

【衍】 commissioner (*n.*) 督察(官)

condense [kən'dens]

【释】 *v.* 压缩；使浓缩

【例】 At the core of every ice crystal is a minuscule nucleus，a solid particle of matter around which moisture *condenses* and freezes.

【衍】 condensation (*n.*)

【近】 compact

consist [kən'sist]

【释】 *v.* 由…组成(of)；存在于(in)；并存，并立(with)

【例】 As their name suggests，the iron meteorites *consist* almost entirely of metal.

【近】 compose，comprise

convey [kən'vei]

【释】 *v.* 表达（意义）；输送；搬运

【例】 A person *conveys* thoughts and ideas through choice of words.

【近】 express

credit ['kredit]

【释】 ① *v.* 归（功于某人）

【例】 Another leading musician was Joseph "King" Oliver，who is also *credited* with having discovered Armstrong，when they were both in New Orleans.

【近】 tribute，ascribe to

【释】 ② *n.* 名誉，名望，声望

【例】 Three decades later，people still argue about who deserves the *credit* for the concept of the laser.

【近】 reputation，prestige

dairy ['dɛəri]

【释】 *n.* 牛奶场

【例】 *Dairy* cattle produce more than fifteen and one-half billion gallons of milk every year.

【衍】 dairying（*n.*）奶品制造业

【近】 pasture，meadow，grazing land

deity ['diːiti]

【释】 *n.* 神；神性；神的身份

【例】 According to Cherokee doctrine，east was associated with the color red because it was the direction of the Sun，the greatest *deity* of all.

【衍】 deist（*n.*）自然神论者

devastate ['devəsteit]

【释】 *v.* 蹂躏，破坏；使荒废

【例】 About a million and a half soldiers from both sides had to be demobilized，readjusted to civilian life，and reabsorbed by the *devastated* economy.

【衍】 devastation（*n.*）

【近】 demolish，ruin，ravage

disposal [dis'pəuzəl]

【释】 *n.* 处置，处理

【例】 All his life Carver battled against the *disposal* of waste materials.

【衍】 dispose（*v.*）

【近】 removal, discarding, dumping

domestic [dəˈmestik]

【释】 *adj.* 家里的；国内的，本国的

【例】 Electric power was available for lamps, sewing machines, irons, and even vacuum cleaners. No *domestic* task was unaffected.

【衍】 domesticate（*v.*）（动物等）驯化

【近】 family, national, local

eccentric [ikˈsentrik]

【释】 *adj.* 异常的，反常的

【例】 She was as exciting and *eccentric* in her personal life as in her dance.

【衍】 eccentrically（*adj.*）；eccentricity（*n.*）

【近】 peculiar, weird, odd

embryo [ˈembriəu]

【释】 *n.*（[*pl.*] embryos）& *adj.* 胚胎(的)，胚(的)

【例】 The *embryos* are quite advanced in their physical development.

【衍】 embryology（*n.*）胚胎学，发生学；embryonic（*adj.*）萌芽期的，初期的，未发达的

entrance [ˈentrəns]

【释】 *n.* 入口，大门

【例】 Whoever controlled the St. Lawrence and its *entrance* also controlled Canada.

【近】 entry, access, gate, door

evoke [iˈvəuk]

【释】 *v.* 唤起；引起，招致

【例】 An unpleasant stimulus was paired with the sight of the animal（perhaps the person was knocked down by an exuberant dog）and the subsequent sight of dogs *evokes* the earlier response—fear.

【近】 educe, obtain

extend [ikˈstend]

【释】 *v.* 扩充，扩大，扩展；发挥(力量)；延续

【例】 Kindergartens, vocation schools, extracurricular activities, and vocational education and counseling *extended* the influence of public schools over the lives of students.

【衍】 extension (*n.*); extensive (*adj.*) 广阔的，广大的；extensively (*adv.*)

【近】 broaden, widen, expand, lengthen

fatigue [fəˈtiːg]

【释】 *n.* 疲乏，劳累

【例】 People who suffer sleep deprivation experience *fatigue*, irritability, and loss of concentration.

【近】 weariness, exhaustion, tiredness

flavor [ˈfleivə]

【释】 *n.* 风味

【例】 But the total result is a pervasive pattern that continues to give New England its distinctive *flavor*.

【衍】 flavoring (*n.*) 调味品，佐料；flavorless (*adj.*) 无味的；无风趣的；flavorous (*adj.*) 味浓的；有香味的；有风趣的

【近】 savor, zest

formidable [ˈfɔːmidəbl]

【释】 *adj.* 可怕的，可畏的；庞大的

【例】 Hubbard's surge closed off Russell Fiord with a *formidable* ice dam, some 2,500 feet wide and up to 800 feet high, whose caged waters threatened the town of Yakutat to the south.

【近】 awesome, astounding

funnel [ˈfʌnəl]

【释】 *n.* 漏斗，漏斗形物

【例】 But suppose a tornado *funnel* passes over a small building that measures 20 by 10 by 10 feet.

【近】 cone

geographic [ˌdʒiəˈgræfik]

【释】 *adj.* 地理学的，地理的

【例】 As the natural *geographic* center of this region, Chicago became the crossroads of a vast transportation network.

【衍】 geographer （*n.*）; geographical （*adj.*）; geographically （*adv.*）

grasp ［grɑːsp］

【释】 *v.* 抓住，握紧，抱住；领会，理解

【例】 The stick caterpillar walks by arching its body，then stretching out and ***grasping*** the branch with its front feet.

【衍】 grasping （*adj.*）; graspingly （*adv.*）

【近】 clutch，grab，grip，seize

hardship ［ˈhɑːdˌʃip］

【释】 *n.* 艰难，困苦

【例】 These writers，called naturalists，often focused on economic ***hardship***.

【近】 privation，adversity

hexagon ［ˈheksəɡən］

【释】 *n.* 六角形，六边形

【例】 Three classes of convex ***hexagons*** were uncovered by the end of the First World War.

【衍】 hexagonal （*adj.*）

humorous ［ˈhjuːmərəs］

【释】 *adj.* 有幽默感的，诙谐的，可笑的

【例】 Mark Twain was the country's most outstanding realist author，observing life around him with a ***humorous*** and skeptical eye.

【衍】 humorously （*adv.*）; humor （*n.*）

【近】 funny，amusing，jokey，entertaining

immobilize ［iˈməubilaiz］

【释】 *v.* 使不动，使固定

【例】 In dream sleep the animal is powerfully ***immobilized*** and remarkably unresponsive to external stimuli.

【近】 anaesthetize

incorporate ［inˈkɔːpəreit］

【释】 *v.* 使混合；使加入

【例】 When hypotheses are confirmed，they are ***incorporated*** into theories.

【衍】 incorporation （*n.*）结合，合并

【近】 integrate

inland	[ˈinlənd]
【释】	*adj.* 内地的，内陆的
【例】	Chicago was already established as the focal point of the largest system of *inland* waterways in the world and the hub of a rail network that extended to the Atlantic，Gulf and Pacific coasts.
【近】	domestic，interior
intense	[inˈtens]
【释】	*adj.* 激烈的，强烈的；紧张的
【例】	Deep-ocean sediments are largely isolated from the mechanical erosion and the *intense* chemical and biological activity that rapidly destroy much land-based evidence of past climates.
【衍】	intensely（*adj.*）；intensify（*v.*）；intensive（*adj.*）
【近】	strong，powerful，passionate
inviting	[inˈvaitiŋ]
【释】	*adj.* 引人注目的，吸引人的
【例】	In spite of Hunt's *inviting* facade，the living space was awkwardly arranged.
【衍】	invitingly（*adj.*）；invitingness（*n.*）
【近】	attractive，appealing，tempting
jurisdiction	[ˌdʒuərisˈdikʃən]
【释】	*n.* 裁判权，司法权；管辖权，管辖范围，权限
【例】	Unfortunately these seldom coincide with the legal *jurisdiction* of country and state boundaries.
【衍】	jurisdictional（*adj.*）
【近】	power，command，rule
lava	[ˈlɑːvə]
【释】	*n.* 熔岩；火山岩
【例】	Although most of the cave ice in the United States is found in *lava* caves，there are a number of limestone ice caves as well.
【近】	magma
limestone	[ˈlaimstəun]
【释】	*n.* 石灰石
【例】	Although most of the cave ice in the United States is found in lava caves，there are a number of *limestone*

ice caves as well.

【衍】 lime（n.）石灰

loom ［luːm］

【释】 ① n. 织布机

【例】 The flow of industry has passed and left idle the **loom** in the attic，the soap kettle in the shed.

【释】 ② v. 朦胧出现；（危险、忧虑等）阴森森地逼近

【例】 Now，marine scientists have at last begun to study this possibility，especially as the sea's resources **loom** even more important as a means of feeding an expanding world population.

【衍】 looming（n.）上现蜃景

【近】 appear，emerge，be about to happen

makeup ［'meikʌp］

【释】 n. 组成，结构

【例】 As the population grew，its **makeup** also changed.

【近】 structure，composition，framework

meager ［'miːgə］

【释】 *adj.* 瘦的；（土地）不毛的；思想贫乏的

【例】 Prior to this report，Seattle's park development was very limited and funding **meager**.

【衍】 meagerly（*adv.*）粗陋地；meagerness（*n.*）

【近】 scanty，insufficient，inadequate

metropolis ［me'trɔpəlis］

【释】 n. 首都，主要都市；（产业、艺术等的）中心

【例】 Los Angeles was a decentralized **metropolis**，sprawling across the desert landscape over an area of 400 square miles.

【衍】 metropolitan（*adj.*）

【近】 city，capital，conurbation

modem ［'məudəm］

【释】 n. 调制解调器　　v. 用调制解调器联通

【例】 An accountant stays home to care for her sick child；she hooks up her telephone **modem** connections and does office work between calls to the doctor.

motivation ［ˌməuti'veiʃən］

【释】 *n.* 动机；动机因素；动力

【例】 The *motivation* derived from the text in combination with the performer's skills，personality，and ability to create empathy will determine the success of artistic，political，or pedagogic communication.

【衍】 motivational（*adj.*）动机的，有关动机的

【近】 incentive，drive，impetus

needlework ['niːdlwəːk]

【释】 *n.* 针线活，女红；刺绣，缝纫

【例】 Her painting was preceded by the production of landscapes in *needlework*，and it was only the onset of arthritis that forced the change of medium.

【衍】 needlelike（*adj.*）针状的；needlepoint（*n.*）针尖；针绣花边

【近】 sewing，embroidery，tapestry，needlepoint

notion ['nəuʃən]

【释】 *n.* 意见，见解，想法，看法，观点；学说

【例】 Subsequent reforms have made these *notions* seem quite out-of-date.

【衍】 notional（*adj.*）概念上的；想象中的；[语法] 表意的；notionally（*adv.*）；notionalist（*n.*）理论家

【近】 idea，concept，opinion

offensive [ə'fensiv]

【释】 *n.* 进攻，攻势

【例】 However Britain anticipated Napoleon's imminent invasion and decided that its only hope was to take the *offensive* immediately.

【衍】 offend（*v.*）冒犯，触犯；使不舒服；offending（*adj.*）不愉快的，厌恶的；offender（*n.*）罪犯，冒犯者

orientation [ˌɔːrien'teiʃən]

【释】 *n.* 方向；定向；取向

【例】 The explanation was that while nobody can acquire spin without torque，a flexible one can readily change its *orientation*，or phase.

【衍】 orient（*v.*）定…的方位，定向

【近】 direction，course

pace [peis]

【释】 *n.* 步，步调；速度，进度

【例】 This system of production eroded workers' control over the *pace* and conditions of labor.

【近】 speed，rapidity，swiftness

patent ['pætənt]

【释】 *n.* 专利(权)；专利品；特权

【例】 Elijah McCoy was a Canadian inventor who was awarded over fifty-seven *patents*.

【近】 copyright，rights

performance [pə'fɔːməns]

【释】 *n.* 执行，实行；演奏；演出

【例】 In her *performances* she used the symphonies of great masters, including Beethoven and Wagner.

【衍】 performer (*n.*)

【近】 act，show，presentation

pianist ['piənist]

【释】 *n.* 钢琴家；钢琴师

【例】 At seventeen she went to New York to study music at Juilliard with the idea of becoming a concert *pianist*.

【衍】 piano (*n.*)

plow [plau]

【释】 *n.* 犁；犁形器具

【例】 The most important of the early inventions was the iron *plow*.

【衍】 plowable (*adj.*)

positive ['pɔzətiv]

【释】 *adj.* 明确的；积极的；建设性的；肯定的([*opp.*] **negative**)

【例】 For example studies of brain activity in ten-month-olds show that the right frontal regions are more active during *positive* emotions.

【衍】 positiveness (*n.*)；positively (*adv.*)

【近】 optimistic，helpful，constructive，encouraging

predict [pri'dikt]

【释】 *v.* 预言，预告，预报，预示

【例】 The cities *predicted* the future.

【衍】 prediction (*n.*)

【近】	guess，foresee，foretell
prior	[ˈpraiə]
【释】	*adj*. 在前的；优先的（to）（[*opp.*]posterior）
【例】	It would be composed of the children who were born during the period of the high birth rate *prior* to 1957.
【衍】	priority（*n.*）
【近】	previous，preceding，former，earlier
propel	[prəˈpel]
【释】	*v.* 推，推进；驱使
【例】	In 1908 she organized her motley teenagers into an act and *propelled* them onto the vaudeville stage.
【衍】	propeller（*n.*）；propellant（*adj.*）
【近】	push，drive，force，impel
publicize	[ˈpʌblisaiz]
【释】	*v.* 发表，公布；宣传，为…做广告
【例】	After a theory has been *publicized*，scientists design experiments to test the theory.
【近】	broadcast，announce，expose，advertise
radar	[ˈreidɑː]
【释】	*n.* 雷达，无线电探测器
【例】	Besides being of critical importance to pilots，*radar* is essential for air traffic control，tracking ships at sea，and tracking weather systems and storms.
raw	[rɔː]
【释】	*adj*. 未加工的，粗的
【例】	Meteorologists and computer scientists work together to design computer programs and video equipment capable of transforming *raw* weather data into words，symbols，and vivid graphic displays.
【衍】	rawly（*adv.*）；rawness（*n.*）；rawhide（*n.*）生牛皮
【近】	unprocessed，crude
recreation	[ˌrekriˈeiʃən]
【释】	*n.* 休养；娱乐，消遣
【例】	Favored *recreations* included fishing，hunting，skating and swimming.
【衍】	recreate（*v.*）

【近】	leisure，amusement

regulate ['regjuleit]

【释】 *v.* 调节(温度、速度等)；管制，控制

【例】 For centuries it has been recognized that mammals and birds differ from other animals in the way they *regulate* body temperature.

【衍】 regulator (*n.*)；regulation (*n.*)；regulatory (*n.*)

【近】 control，adjust，order

renew [ri'njuː]

【释】 *v.* 重新开始，重订，更改(契约等)

【例】 Under New York's controls，a landlord generally cannot raise rents on apartments as long as the tenants continue to *renew* their leases.

【衍】 renewable (*adj.*)；renewal (*n.*) 恢复，更新；(票据等的)更换

【近】 renovate，refurbish，restore

reservoir ['rezəvwaː]

【释】 ① *n.* 贮水池，水库

【例】 Three-quarters of the Earth's fresh water supply is still tied up in glacial ice，a *reservoir* of untapped fresh water so immense that it could sustain all the rivers of the world for 1,000 years.

【近】 tank，pool，lake

【释】 ② *n.* (知识、精力等的)贮藏，蓄积

【例】 The main *reservoir* of mathematical talent in any society is thus possessed by children who are about two years old.

【近】 repertory

revere [ri'viə]

【释】 *v.* 尊敬，崇敬

【例】 Founded in the late nineteenth century by British social critics John Ruskin and William Morris，the movement *revered* craft as a form of art.

【衍】 revered (*adj.*) 受尊敬的；reverend (*adj.*) 应受尊敬的；reverently (*adv.*) 尊敬地

【近】 respect，look up to，venerate

roar [rɔː]

【释】 *n.* 轰鸣，吼(声)　*v.* 咆哮

【例】	The ***roar*** of gunfire，the massed movements of uniformed men，the shrill of bugles，and the drama of hand-to-hand combat have fascinated students of warfare for a century.
【衍】	roaring（*adj*.）；roaringly（*adv*.）
【近】	howl，growl，snarl

saber [ˈseibə]

【释】	***n*. 军刀，马刀**
【例】	Direct competition may have brought about the demise of large carnivores such as the ***saber***-toothed cats.
【衍】	saber-toothed（*adj*.）有军刀形的；上犬齿的

scheme [skiːm]

【释】	① ***n*. 系统；配合；组织**
【例】	In this localized region，human output may be dominant and may temporarily overload the natural purification ***scheme*** of the cycles.
【衍】	schematize（*v*.）
【近】	system，format
【释】	② ***n*. 计划；方案；路线；设计**
【例】	Almost immediately a number of ***schemes*** were proposed for sending pictures by wire (it was，of course，before radio).
【衍】	schemer（*n*.）计划者
【近】	design，idea，proposal

seemingly [ˈsiːmiŋli]

【释】	***adv*. 表面上地**
【例】	Dr. King never forgot the racial prejudice that was a ***seemingly*** insurmountable barrier that kept black Atlantans from mingling with whites.
【衍】	seem（*v*.）；seeming（*adj*. & *n*.）表面的，表面，外表
【近】	outwardly，ostensibly，on the face of it

shake [ʃeik]

【释】	***v*. 摇；摇动；摇撼**
【例】	The dancers ***shook*** rattles or pounded hand-held drums to underscore their footbeats.
【衍】	shaker（*n*.）摇动者，振荡器；shakedown（*n*.）摇落；临时地铺；shakeout（*n*.）股票暴跌；轻度经济衰退

【近】	quiver，vibrate，quake

sieve ［siv］

【释】 *n.*（细眼）筛，过滤网 *v.* 筛，筛选

【例】 Another method of determining soil texture involves the use of devices called sediment *sieves*，screens built with a specified mesh size.

【衍】 sieving（*n.*）筛选，筛分法

【近】 strainer，sifter，screen

sloth ［sləuθ］

【释】 *n.*【动】树懒

【例】 It feeds on only one kind of leaf，Cecropia，which happily for the *sloth* grows in quantity and is easily found.

soup ［su:p］

【释】 *n.*（浓）汤；浓汤般的东西

【例】 After drying the fish，the women pounded some of them into fish meal，which was an easily transported food used in *soups*，stews，or other dishes.

【衍】 soupy（*adj.*）

【近】 broth，potage，gumbo

spirit ［'spirit］

【释】 *n.* 精神，心灵，灵魂

【例】 Her dance stemmed from her soul and *spirit*.

【衍】 spiritual（*adj.* & *n.*）精神（上）的，心灵的；（黑人的）圣歌

【近】 courage，strength of mind，soul

in spite of ［in 'spait əv］

【释】 不管，不顾

【例】 Deeper still，the pressure is even more intense，preventing the rock from melting *in spite of* a higher temperature.

stagecoach ［'steidʒkəutʃ］

【释】 *n.* 公共马车，驿站马车

【例】 They offered the traveler reliable transportation in comfortable facilities—a welcome alternative to *stagecoach* travel，which at the best of times could only be described as wretched.

| 【衍】 | stage（*n.* & *v.*） |
| 【近】 | carriage，cart，wagon |

sterile [ˈsterəl]

【释】 *adj.* 贫瘠的，无生殖力的，毫无结果的

【例】 Were it not for these algae，the seas would still be completely *sterile* and the land uninhabited.

【衍】 sterilely（*adv.*）；sterility（*n.*）；sterilize（*v.*）

【近】 barren，unproductive，infertile，arid

strength [streŋθ]

【释】 *n.* 力量，体力；强度，浓度；长处（[*opp.*] weakness）

【例】 As many as four-fifths of all the cells in the electric eel's body are specialized for generating electricity，and the *strength* of the shock it can deliver corresponds roughly to the length of its body.

【衍】 strengthen（*v.*）增强；变强

【近】 potency，forte，asset

subsist [səbˈsist]

【释】 *v.* 生存；活下去，维持生命，维持生活

【例】 For some fifty million years，despite all its eccentricities，the sea cucumber has *subsisted* on its diet of mud.

【衍】 subsistence（*n.*）

【近】 survive，live

superheat [ˌsjuːpəˈhiːt]

【释】 *v.* 使过（度加）热

【例】 Therefore，if the Earth began as a *superheated* sphere in space，all the rocks making up its crust may well have been igneous and thus the ancestors of all other rocks.

【衍】 superheater（*n.*）过热器

swarm [swɔːm]

【释】 ① *n.* (昆虫的)群，蜂群；大群；大堆

【例】 From as far north as Canada，*swarms* of butterflies begin gathering from their homes in the fields，clinging to trees and bushes by the thousands.

【近】 group，crowd，flock

【释】 ② *v.* 蜂拥而至，涌往；挤满；充满

【例】 Northerners *swarmed* over the South journalists，agents of

Unit 5

prospective investors，speculators mitt plant for railroads，waters anxious to expose themselves to a new environment.

【近】 flock，crowd，throng

tame 〔teim〕

【释】 *v.* 驯服，制服 *adj.* 驯服的，温顺的

【例】 These hominids walked across a stretch of moist volcanic ash，which was subsequently *tamed* to mud by rain，and which then set like concrete.

【衍】 tameable（*adj.*）；tameless（*adv.*）难驯养的；野性的；暴烈的

【近】 domesticate，cultivate，discipline

temporarily 〔ˌtempə'reərili〕

【释】 *adv.* 一时地，暂时地，临时地

【例】 Their play，and ours，appears to serve no other purpose than to give pleasure to the players，and apparently，to remove us *temporarily* from the anguish of life in earnest.

【衍】 temporary（*adj.*）；temporariness（*n.*）

【近】 provisionally，for the time being，for the interim

**thermody-
namics** 〔ˌθəːməudai'næmiks〕

【释】 *n.* 热力学

【例】 Nitinol appears to be breaking the laws of *thermodynamics* by springing back into shape with greater force than was used to deform it in the first place.

【衍】 thermal（*adj.*）热的，热量的；thermoplastic（*n.*）热塑性物质；thermoset（*n.* & *adj.*）热固性（的），热硬性（的）；thermosetting（*n.* & *adj.*）热固（的），热硬性（的）

tin 〔tin〕

【释】 *n.* 锡器；罐头

【例】 Overshadowed by all this was Beach's substantial contribution to engineering，his method of tunnel construction：a hydraulic shield that looked something like an open-ended *tin* can.

【衍】 tinplate（*n.*）镀锡铁皮

【近】 container，can，flask

tower ['tauə]

【释】① *n.* 塔，楼塔；城堡

【例】Since most stations in the Northeast were built on rocky eminences, enormous *towers* were not the rule.

【衍】towered（*adj.*）高耸云霄的；有塔的

【释】② *v.* 高耸；胜过；(鹰等)翱翔

【例】On mountain slopes that receive plentiful rainfall, huge Douglas firs rise in *towering* columns.

【衍】towering（*adj.*）高耸的，屹立的；突出的；高傲的；激烈的

【近】surpass, exceed, soar

treat [triːt]

【释】① *v.* 对待，待遇；处置；处理

【例】Not militant, she nevertheless urged men to educate their daughters and to *treat* their wives as equals.

【衍】treatment（*n.*）待遇；处理；论述；治疗；疗法；消毒（处理）

【近】behave toward, regard, deal with

【释】② *v. & n.* 探讨，论述

【例】This *treat* was dramatized by a cavity one—eighth of an inch in a diameter created in a window of a United States space shuttle in 1983.

【衍】treaty（*n.*）(国家间的)条约，(个人间的)约定；协商，谈判，交涉

trunk [trʌŋk]

【释】*n.* 树干；躯干

【例】The most obvious results of the process are growth rings, which are visible on the cross section of a *trunk*, a root, or a branch.

【衍】trunkful（*n.*）满箱；许多

【近】stem, stalk, shaft

underscore ['ʌndəskɔː]

【释】*v.* 在…下面划线；强调

【例】This last requirement strengthens the act's effect on public opinion, since it serves to *underscore* the injustice of the protest's target.

【近】	underline，highlight，emphasize
vaccinate	['væksineit]
【释】	*v.* (给…)接种(疫苗)
【例】	For example，a school superintendent wishes to determine the proportion of children in a large school system who come to school without breakfast，have been *vaccinated* for flu，or whatever.
【衍】	vaccination (*n.*)
【近】	immunize
vertebrate	['vəːtibrit]
【释】	*n. & adj.* 脊椎动物(的)
【例】	Since then，over 100 tons of fossils，1.5 million from *vertebrates*，2.5 million from invertebrates，have been recovered，often tit densely concentrated tangled masses.
【衍】	invertebrate (*n.*) 无脊椎动物
vocation	[vəu'keiʃən]
【释】	*n.* 职业，行业
【例】	Nursing is not a job—it's a *vocation*.
【衍】	vocational (*adj.*)
【近】	profession，craft，career，occupation
weave	[wiːv]
【释】	*v.* (wove, woven/weaved) 织；编制
【例】	Moreover，Pomo people made use of more *weaving* techniques than did their neighbors.
【衍】	weaver (*n.*)
wool	[wul]
【释】	*n.* 羊毛；绒线
【例】	Sometimes artisans transformed material provided by the customer：wove cloth of yam spun at the farm from the *wool* of the family sheep.
【衍】	woolen (*adj.*)；woolly (*adj.*)
【近】	fleece

Exercise of Unit 5

左列单词在右列中有一个同义词，请找出并在相应的位置写上正确
答案。

Exercise 1:

(A) abrupt _____ magma
(B) tin _____ entry
(C) ample _____ sudden
(D) lava _____ container
(E) entrance _____ unprocessed
(F) raw _____ plenty

Exercise 2:

(A) fatigue _____ compact
(B) cathedral _____ weariness
(C) condense _____ survive
(D) vaccinate _____ church
(E) spirit _____ immunize
(F) subsist _____ courage

Exercise 3:

(A) devastate _____ optimistic
(B) immobilize _____ domestic
(C) positive _____ demolish
(D) incorporate _____ integrate
(E) inland _____ group
(F) swarm _____ anaesthetize

Exercise 4:

(A) intense _____ act
(B) extend _____ scanty
(C) seemingly _____ broaden
(D) meager _____ strong
(E) publicize _____ broadcast
(F) performance _____ outwardly

Exercise 5:

(A) vocation _____ attractive
(B) eccentric _____ profession
(C) underscore _____ educe
(D) evoke _____ underline
(E) reservoir _____ peculiar
(F) inviting _____ repertory

Exercise 6:

(A) convey _____ appear
(B) arch _____ idea
(C) loom _____ express
(D) notion _____ guess
(E) strength _____ arc
(F) predict _____ potency

— 113 —

Exercise 7:

(A) motivation _____ renovate
(B) tower _____ surpass
(C) orientation _____ copyright
(D) assume _____ suppose
(E) renew _____ direction
(F) patent _____ incentive

Exercise 8:

(A) dairy _____ pasture
(B) agent _____ design
(C) metropolis _____ awesome
(D) revere _____ constituent
(E) scheme _____ respect
(F) formidable _____ city

Exercise 9:

(A) sieve _____ leisure
(B) recreation _____ screen
(C) swarm _____ power
(D) sterile _____ flock
(E) jurisdiction _____ refuse
(F) boycott _____ barren

Exercise 10:

(A) credit _____ carriage
(B) makeup _____ previous
(C) reservoir _____ load
(D) burden _____ tank
(E) prior _____ structure
(F) stagecoach _____ tribute

ANSWERS:

1 D E A B F C
2 C A F B D E
3 C E A D F B
4 F D B A E C
5 F A D C B E
6 C D A F B E
7 E B F D C A
8 A E F B D C
9 B A E C F D
10 F E D C B A

Unit 6

absent	emerge	mud	shale
acquire	entrepreneur	needy	sight
aggregate	evolve	notwithstanding	smell
analogy	extent	official	spacious
archaeology	feasible	origin	splendid
asteroid	flaw	pack	stagnant
baboon	formulate	patience	stew
battle	fur	periodic	stress
bizarre	geologic	pigeon	subspecies
brass	grasshopper	pluck	superintendent
burgeon	hardware	possess	sweat
canyon	hibernate	predominant	tan
cautious	hunger	prison	tenant
chest	immortal	propensity	thickness
cliff	incredible	puddle	tip
commodity	inner	radiate	toxic
condor	intent	react	tremendous
consistent	involve	recruit	truth
convict	jury	rehabilitate	understand
crisscross	lavish	renounce	vacuum
dam	limitation	reshape	vertical
deliberate	loosely	reverse	volatile
devoid	mammalian	rocky	weed
dispute	meander	sack	worm
dominate	microbe	scholar	
echo	moderate	seep	

absent ['æbsənt]
【释】 *adj.* 不在的，缺席的
【例】 Lacking the right to vote and *absent* from the seats of power, women were not considered an important force in history.
【衍】 absence （*n.*）；absenteeism （*n.*）旷课，旷工；absentee （*n.*）缺席者，缺勤者；absentee ballot 缺席选举人票
【近】 lacking, deficient

acquire [ə'kwaiə]
【释】 *v.* 获得
【例】 They *acquired* Benjamin's book and began to pattern their construction work on his plans.
【衍】 acquisition （*n.*）取得，获得；习得
【近】 attain, obtain

aggregate ['ægrigeit]
【释】 *n. & adj.* 聚集(的)，集合(的)；总计(的)，共计(的)
【例】 Marine mammals have the misfortune to be swimming *aggregates* of commodities that humans want: fur, oil, and meat.
【衍】 aggregation （*n.*）聚合，集合；【植】【动】族聚；群聚
【近】 collection, total, whole, entire sum

analogy [ə'nælədʒi]
【释】 *n.* 类比，相似
【例】 The *analogy* was a clever one, but on closer inspection looked mainly like a clever way to put a preposterously brave face on the Tories' troubles.
【衍】 analogous （*adj.*）；analogously （*adv.*）
【近】 similarity, comparison, likeliness

archaeology [ˌɑːki'ɔlədʒi]
【释】 *n.* 考古学，古物学
【例】 *Archaeology* is a source of history, not just a humble auxiliary discipline.
【衍】 archaeological （*adj.*）；archaeologist （*n.*）

asteroid ['æstərɔid]
【释】 *adj.* 星状的 *n.* 小行星
【例】 ... by an astronomer who was searching the sky for *asteroids*.

【近】	planetoid
baboon	[bə'buːn]
【释】	*n.* 狒狒
【例】	Chimpanzees are more human than *baboons*.
battle	['bætl]
【释】	*n.* 战，战斗(行动)，交战
【例】	Mercy Warren joined her husband in political *battle*.
【衍】	battlefield（*n.*）战场，沙场
【近】	fight，combat，clash，conflict
bizarre	[bi'zɑː]
【释】	*adj.* 稀奇古怪的，不同寻常的
【例】	What else can be said about a *bizarre* animal.
【近】	odd，weird，absurd，peculiar
brass	[brɑːs]
【释】	*n.* （主 [*pl.*]）黄铜制品；铜管乐器
【例】	They also mixed it with zinc to make *brass* for maritime and scientific instruments.
burgeon	['bəːdʒən]
【释】	*v.* 发芽，（突然）发展，急速成长
【例】	The vigor of this *burgeoning* science is apparent in the meetings of the society.
【近】	mushroom，multiply，prosper
canyon	['kænjən]
【释】	*n.* 峡(谷)
【例】	At least a dozen large stone houses took shape below the bluffs of Chiaco *Canyon* in northwest New Mexico.
【近】	gorge，valley，rift
cautious	['kɔːʃəs]
【释】	*adj.* 谨慎的，小心的
【例】	Because of the space crunch, the Art Museum has become increasingly *cautious* in considering acquisitions and donations of art, in some cases passing up opportunities to strengthen its collections.
【衍】	cautiously（*adv.*）；incautious（*adj.*）

【近】 careful，precautious，vigilant

chest [tʃest]

【释】 ① *n.* 箱，柜，匣

【例】 This kind of construction was used for making everything from housed to *chests*.

【近】 box，coffer

【释】 ② *n.* 胸部，胸腔

【例】 He went into shock，indicating that the stub in the *chest* had penetrated to his heart.

cliff [klif]

【释】 *n.* 峭壁，断崖

【例】 These buildings were usually put up against *cliffs*，both to make construction easier and for defense against enemies.

【近】 precipice，crag

commodity [kə'mɔdəti]

【释】 *n.* 日用品；商品

【例】 With collections expanding，with the needs and functions of museums changing，empty space has become a very precious *commodity*.

【近】 product，goods

condor ['kɔndɔ:]

【释】 *n.* 秃鹰

【例】 All birds living today，from the great *condors* of the Andes to the tiniest wrens，trace their origin back to the Mesozoic dinosaurs.

【近】 falcon，kestrel，hawk，eagle

consistent [kən'sistənt]

【释】 *adj.* 一致的，不矛盾的

【例】 Although leaders are often thought to be people with unusual personal ability，decades of research have failed to produce *consistent* evidence that there is any category of "natural leaders."

【衍】 consistently（*adv.*）；inconsistent（*adj.*）；self-consistent（*adj.*）自相一致的；能自圆其说的；consistency（*n.*）

【近】 reliable，constant

convict ['kɔnvikt]

【释】 *v.* 证明…有罪，宣告…有罪，定…的罪

【例】 Most cases go no further than the trial court: for example, the criminal defendant is *convicted*（by a trial or a guilty plea）and sentenced by the court and the case ends.

【衍】 conviction（*n.*）

crisscross ['kriskrɔs]

【释】 *v. & n. & adj.* 十字交叉(的)

【例】 They also helped build the vast network of canals and railroads that *crisscrossed* the continent and linked important trade centers essential to industrial growth.

【近】 interweave, interlace, network

dam [dæm]

【释】 *n.* 水闸，坝，堰

【例】 Well established by A. D. 500，the Anasazi built *dams* and irrigation canals to water the corn，squash，and beans.

deliberate [di'libəreit]

【释】 *adj.* 深思熟虑的，盘算周到的

【例】 Every step in the process was slow and *deliberate*.

【衍】 deliberately（*adv.*）；deliberative（*adj.*）考虑过的，慎重的；deliberation（*n.*）深思熟虑

【近】 prudent, cautious, careful

devoid [di'vɔid]

【释】 *adj.* 无一的，缺…的(of)

【例】 A well *devoid* of water is useless.

【近】 lacking, deficient

dispute [dis'pjuːt]

【释】 *v. & n.* 辩论，争论；争吵；争端

【例】 The village chief dealt with land *disputes* and religious affairs.

【近】 disagree, quarrel, debate

dominate ['dɔmineit]

【释】 *v.* 操纵，支配

【例】 Although the states *dominated* economic activity during this period，the federal government was not inactive.

Unit 6

【衍】	dominating（*adj.*）；dominant（*n.*）主因，要素，主要的人（物）；domination（*n.*）支配，统治；优势
【近】	dictate，control
echo	[ˈekəu]
【释】	*n.* 回声，反响　*v.* 共鸣
【例】	The *echo* of the sounds against the walls helps a person determine the size of the cave.
【近】	resonance，ricochet
emerge	[iˈməːdʒ]
【释】	*v.* 出现；发生
【例】	The key concepts *emerged* about 1957.
【衍】	emergence（*n.*）；emergency（*n.*）突然事件；紧急情况，非常时期
【近】	appear，arise，turn up，occur
entrepreneur	[ˌɔntrəprəˈnəː]
【释】	*n.* 企业家；创业人
【例】	Forts also served as bases where enterprising *entrepreneurs* could bring commerce to the West.
【衍】	entrepreneurial（*adj.*）；entrepreneurship（*n.*）
【近】	industrialist
evolve	[iˈvɔlv]
【释】	*v.* 发展；进化
【例】	Until the coming of the Industrial Revolution，science and technology *evolved* for the most part independently of each other.
【衍】	evolution（*n.*）；evolutionary（*adj.*）
【近】	develop，change
extent	[ikˈstent]
【释】	*n.* 程度；广度
【例】	Humans，even in prehistoric times，had some number sense，at least to the *extent* of recognizing the concepts of more and less when some objects were added to or taken away from a small group.
【近】	degree，level，scope，amount
feasible	[ˈfiːzəbl]
【释】	*adj.* 可实行的，行得通的

【例】 It mushroomed in the 1870's, as the rapid expansion of the railway system made it increasingly *feasible* to transport full productions.

【衍】 feasibly (*adv.*) 有理地，适宜地；feasibility (*n.*) 现实性，可行性

【近】 possible, practicable, viable

flaw [flɔː]

【释】 *n.* 瑕疵，缺点

【例】 However there is a *flaw* in the argument that the evolution of wheeled animals was thwarted by the insoluble joint problem.

【衍】 flawed (*adj.*)；flawless (*adj.*)

【近】 defect, blemish, mistake

formulate ['fɔːmjuleit]

【释】 *v.* 把…做成公式，用公式表示

【例】 The professor was impressed by the way he could *formulate* his ideas.

【衍】 formula (*n.*) 公式，程式；formulation (*n.*)

fur [fəː]

【释】 *n.* 毛皮；[*pl.*] 兽皮，皮货

【例】 Missouri sometimes met the descending canoes of trappers and hunters, loaded with furs, on their way to St. Louis, the center of the *fur* trade.

【近】 hair, down, hide

geologic [dʒiə'lɔdʒik]

【释】 *adj.* 地质学的，地质的

【例】 Recently, however, paleontologists have been taking a closer look at the sediments below this Silurian-Devonian *geological* boundary.

【衍】 geology (*n.*)；geological (*adj.*)；geologically (*adv.*)；geologist (*n.*)

grasshopper ['grɑːsˌhɔpə]

【释】 *n.* 蚱蜢，蝗虫

【例】 Every parent knows the propensity of small children to bring home caterpillars, *grasshoppers*.

hardware ['hɑːdweə]

【释】 *n.* 五金器具；金属制品，零件，部件；硬件

【例】 Relatively little *hardware* was used during this period.

hibernate [ˈhaibəneit]

【释】 *v.* 冬眠；蛰居；越冬

【例】 The fertilized young queens *hibernate* and found their own nests the next spring.

【衍】 hibernation（*n.*）

【近】 overwinter，lie dormant

hunger [ˈhʌŋgə]

【释】 *n.* 饥，饥饿

【例】 The unfortunate beasts would die of exhaustion and *hunger*.

【衍】 hungered（*adj.*）

【近】 starvation，appetite

immortal [iˈmɔːtəl]

【释】 *adj. & n.* 不死的(人、物)

【例】 For the last 82 years, Sweden's Nobel Academy has decided who will receive the Nobel Prize in Literature, thereby determining who will be elevated from the great and the near great to the *immortal*.

【衍】 immortality（*n.*）

【近】 eternal，perpetual，everlasting

incredible [inˈkredəbl]

【释】 *adj.* 不可思议的；惊人的

【例】 The technical skill evident in these blankets is *incredible*, considering the complexity of the design.

【近】 amazing，remarkable

inner [ˈinə]

【释】 *adj.* (最高级为：innermost; inmost)内部的([opp.] outer)

【例】 Some scientists believe that the *innermost* core of Jupiter might be rocky, or metallic like the core of Earth.

【近】 interior，internal，inside

intent [inˈtent]

【释】 *n.* 意图；目的

【例】 The *intent* of this legislation was to provide protection to selected coastal habitats similar to that existing for land areas designated as national parks.

【衍】 intention（*n.*）意图，目的

【近】 purpose，objective

---

involve [inˈvɔlv]

【释】 *v.* 包括，涉及

【例】 People who lived in the cities and were not directly *involved* in trade often participated in small cottage industries making handcrafted goods.

【衍】 involvement（*n.*）

---

jury [ˈdʒuəri]

【释】 *n.* 陪审团，(展览会、竞赛等的)全体评审员，评奖人

【例】 Annual exhibitions gave members a rare opportunity to present their work to the public without first submitting it to a *jury*.

---

lavish [ˈlæviʃ]

【释】 *adj.* 过分大方的；过于丰富的；过度的；浪费的

【例】 Skyscraper are also *lavish* consumers，and wasters，of electric power.

【衍】 lavishly（*adv.*）；lavishment（*n.*）；lavishness（*n.*）

【近】 plentiful，extravagant，profligate

---

limitation [ˌlimiˈteiʃən]

【释】 *n.* 限制；界限；极限；限制因素

【例】 Much of the early work on plastics was on thermosets，and it may have been this *limitation* that prevented them from becoming highly acceptable materials.

【衍】 limit（*n.* & *v.*）限制，限定；limited（*adj.*）有限的，有限制的；limiting（*adj.*）限制(性)的，有限制力的，起限定作用的

【近】 restraint，constraint，restriction

---

loosely [ˈluːsli]

【释】 *adv.* 宽松地，松散地

【例】 In its early history，the violin had a dull and rather quiet tone resulting from the fact that the strings were thick and were attached to the body of the instrument very *loosely*.

【衍】 loose（*adj.*）；looseness（*n.*）

【近】 insecurely，with a loose knot，slackly

mammalian [mæˈmeiljən]

【释】 *n. & adj.* 哺乳动物(的)

【例】 The most successful *mammalian* species would have been those that developed efficient hormonal systems for maintaining the needed sodium concentrations.

【衍】 mammal (*n.*) 哺乳纲动物

meander [miˈændə]

【释】 *v.* 曲曲折折地流；蜿蜒，弯曲

【例】 Rather than bringing in the bulldozers, San Antonio's leaders rehabilitated existing structures, while simultaneously cleaning up the San Antonio River, which *meanders* through the business district.

【衍】 meandering (*adj. & n.*) 曲折的，弯弯曲曲的；meanderingly (*adv.*)

【近】 wind, zigzag, snake

microbe [ˈmaikrəub]

【释】 *n.* 微生物；(尤指引起疾病的)细菌

【例】 *Microbes*, one-celled organisms that cause the decay of dead plants and animals, are decomposers.

【衍】 microcosm (*n.*) 微观世界；缩影；microbiologist (*n.*) 微生物学者；microfossil (*n.*) 微体化石；microorganism (*n.*) 微生物

【近】 germ, bacteria, virus

moderate [ˈmɔdərət]

【释】 *adj.* 中等的；适度的；有节制的

【例】 Desert-adapted mammals have the further ability to feed normally when extremely dehydrated: it is a common experience in people that appetite is lost even under conditions of *moderate* thirst.

【衍】 moderately (*adv.*) 适度地；普通地；moderateness (*n.*)

【近】 reasonable, modest, temperate

mud [mʌd]

【释】 *n.* 泥；泥浆；淤泥

【例】 The nest is a deep cup, made of *mud* or seaweed, to hold the eggs safely, compared with the shallow scrape of other gulls, and the chicks are remarkably immobile until fully grown.

【近】	mire，sludge，muck
needy	[ˈniːdi]
【释】	*adj*．贫穷的，贫困的
【例】	Two distinguished（and financially ***needy***）writers would receive enough money so they could devote themselves entirely to "prose literature".
【衍】	need（*n*. & *v*.）；needful（*adj*.）；needless（*adj*.）
【近】	disadvantaged，poor，deprived
notwith-standing	[ˌnɔtwiθˈstændiŋ]
【释】	*prep*. & *adv*. & *conj*．虽然，尽管…仍…
【例】	*Notwithstanding* preening and constant care，the marvelously intricate structure of a bird's feather inevitably wears out.
【近】	despite，in spite of，although
official	[əˈfiʃəl]
【释】	① *adj*．官方的，正式的
【例】	The Lewis and Clark expedition，sponsored by President Jefferson，was the most important ***official*** examination of the high plains and the Northwest before the War of 1812.
【衍】	officially（*adv*.）职务上地；正式地；officialism（*n*.）拖拉作风，官僚主义
【近】	authorized，certified，sanctioned
【释】	② *n*. 官员，高级职员
【例】	Meetings between park ***officials*** and landowners have led to a dramatically improved understanding of all concerns.
【近】	administrator，officer，executive
origin	[ˈɔridʒin]
【释】	*n*. 根源，起因，由来；出身，来历
【例】	Another theory traces the theater's ***origin*** from the human interest in story telling.
【衍】	original（*adj*. & *n*.）最初的；原物，原作；originally（*adv*.）；originality（*n*.）独创性，新颖；originate（*v*.）开始，发生，起始于，发起，创办，创设
【近】	source，derivation，foundation

pack [pæk]

【释】 *v.* 包，把…打包，包装

【例】 Beekeepers remove honey from the hives and *pack* it in bottles or jars.

【衍】 package（*n.*）

【近】 set，bundle，bunch，group

patience [ˈpeiʃəns]

【释】 *n.* 忍耐，容忍，忍受；耐心，耐性

【例】 When the digging or excavation does finally begin，the archaeologist needs great *patience*.

【衍】 patient（*adj.*）；impatient（*adj.*）；patiently（*adv.*）；impatiently（*adv.*）

【近】 endurance，tolerance

periodic [ˌpiəriˈɔdik]

【释】 *adj.* 周期的，定期的，定时的

【例】 Even with its size and complexity，the contemporary Congress has undergone *periodic* waves of change or reformism.

【衍】 periodical（*adj.*）；periodically（*adv.*）

【近】 intermittent，interrupted

pigeon [ˈpidʒin]

【释】 *n.* 鸽子

【例】 Homing *pigeons* are placed in a training program from about the time they are twenty-eight days of age.

pluck [plʌk]

【释】 *v.* 拔，扯(羽毛等)；采，摘(花、果实)

【例】 A pianist may reach inside the piano to *pluck* a string and then run a metal blade along it.

possess [pəˈzes]

【释】 *v.* 具有(能力、性质等)；掌握(知识等)

【例】 Generally，in order to be preserved in the fossil record，organisms must *possess* hard body parts such as shells or bones.

【衍】 possession（*n.*）；possessed（*adj.*）着魔的，疯狂的

【近】 have，own，hold，take

predominant [priˈdɔminənt]

【释】 *adj.* 掌握主权的；有力的，有效的

【例】 France was *predominant* on land，Britain at sea.

【衍】 predominate（*v.*）

【近】 main，major，chief，prime，preponderant

prison ['prizən]

【释】 *n.* 监狱，拘留所；监禁，禁闭

【例】 In the United States today there are more than half a million criminals serving time in *prison*.

【衍】 prisoner（*n.*）

【近】 jail，penitentiary

propensity [prə'pensəti]

【释】 *n.* 倾向，癖好

【例】 Every parent knows the *propensity* of small children to bring home caterpillars.

【近】 tendency，inclination，partiality，predilection

puddle ['pʌdl]

【释】 *n.* (路上的)水坑，污水坑

【例】 Crabs and shrimp swim upstream from the bays, and their freshwater cousins, the crayfish, live in almost every pond and *puddle*.

【近】 pond，lake

radiate ['reidieit]

【释】 *v.* 辐射；向周围扩展

【例】 Its center was beneath present-day St. Louis, and it *radiated* out to encompass most of the Mississippi watershed，from Wisconsin to Louisiana and from Oklahoma to Tennessee.

【衍】 radiated（*adj.*）；radiating（*adj.*）

【近】 spread out，emit，give out

react [ri'ækt]

【释】 *v.* 反应；发生反作用；反抗

【例】 Its principal function is that of providing safety from predators, partly because if one bird *reacts* to danger, the whole flock is warned.

【衍】 reaction（*n.*）；reactive（*adj.*）

【近】 act in response，respond，reply

recruit [ri'kruːt]

【释】 *v.* 招募(新兵)，召集

【例】 One suspects that the oratorio audience is *recruited* largely from friends and families of the singers.

【衍】 recruitment (*n.*)；recruiter (*n.*)

【近】 conscript，enlist

rehabilitate [ˌriː(h)ə'biliteit]

【释】 *v.* 改善；复兴；使复原

【例】 In other cases valued buildings have been *rehabilitated* and returned to economic productivity.

【衍】 rehabilitation (*n.*)；rehabilitative (*adj.*)；rehabilitant (*n.*) 康复者

【近】 recover，restore

renounce [ri'nauns]

【释】 *v.* 抛弃，放弃，背弃

【例】 She completely *renounced* the styles of her student and commercial art days.

【衍】 renouncement (*n.*)

【近】 give up，abandon，relinquish

reshape [ˌriː'ʃeip]

【释】 *v.* 给…以新形态(新方针)；改造

【例】 Railroads *reshaped* the North American environment and reoriented North American behavior.

【衍】 reshaper (*n.*) 整形器

【近】 reform，redesign，change the format

reverse [ri'vəːs]

【释】 *n. & v.* 颠倒，倒转，倒退；逆转

【例】 For the universe，the *reverse* seems to be the case：bigger is simpler.

【衍】 reversal (*n.*)

【近】 overturn，turn around

rocky ['rɔki]

【释】 *adj.* 岩石的；岩石重叠的，岩石多的

【例】 Some scientists believe that the innermost core of Jupiter might be *rocky*，or metallic like the core of Earth.

【近】	stony，gravel
sack	[sæk]
【释】	***n.*** 袋，包；麻袋；硬纸袋
【例】	Bees draw this nectar into the honey *sacks* of their bodies, and enzymes in their bodies turn the nectar into honey.
【衍】	sackcloth（*n.*）麻布；麻袋布
【近】	bag，pack，rucksack
scholar	['skɔlə]
【释】	***n.*** 学者，有文化的人
【例】	The military aspect of the United States Civil War has always attracted the most attention from *scholars*.
【衍】	scholarly（*adj.*）有学问的，博学的；scholarship（*n.*）奖学金
【近】	researcher，intellectual，academic
seep	[siːp]
【释】	***v.*** 渗出；漏出；（观念等）渗入
【例】	They believe that cold water sinks down through cracks into these caves until the temperature is chilly enough to freeze the water that *seeps* in.
【衍】	seepage（*n.*）渗流，渗出（现象）；seepy（*adj.*）排水不良的；湿气很重的
【近】	leak，ooze，dribble
shale	[ʃeil]
【释】	***n.*** 页岩
【例】	The beautifully preserved fossil fish from the Green River oil *shale* of Wyoming in the western United States lived in a vast shallow lake.
sight	[sait]
【释】	***n.*** 壮观；奇观；风景
【例】	Its beautiful rays are a sensational *sight* during an eclipse.
【衍】	sightly（*adj.*）好看的；sightsee（*n.*）游览，参观
【近】	view，spectacle，prospect
smell	[smel]
【释】	***n.*** 气味；嗅觉
【例】	Much of the forebrain deals only with *smell*.

【近】	odor，aroma，scent，perfume
spacious	['speiʃəs]
【释】	***adj.*** 广阔的，宽敞的([*opp.*] cramped)
【例】	It housed about 1,000 people in a vast structure of 800 ***spacious*** rooms stretching over 3 acres.
【衍】	space (*n.*)；spaciously (*adv.*)；spaciousness (*n.*)
【近】	roomy，large，open
splendid	['splendid]
【释】	***adj.*** 杰出的，显著的，伟大的，名声赫赫的
【例】	The house has got a ***splendid*** view across towards the Cotswolds.
【衍】	splendor (*n.*) 光彩；壮观；杰出
【近】	grand，superb，marvelous
stagnant	['stægnənt]
【释】	***adj.*** 停滞的，不流动的；萧条的，不景气的
【例】	Appalled by the ***stagnant*** life of the town，and failing to become adjusted to it，she tries a number of cultural ideas.
【衍】	staggering (*adj.*) 令人吃惊的
【近】	sluggish，dull，inert
stew	[stjuː]
【释】	***n.*** 炖煮的菜肴 ***v.*** 用文火慢慢煨炖
【例】	After drying the fish，the women pounded some of them into fish meal，which was an easily transported food used in soups，***stews***，or other dishes.
【衍】	stewpot (*n.*)（有盖的）炖锅
【近】	simmer，cook
stress	[stres]
【释】	① ***n.*** 压力，压迫，紧迫，紧张
【例】	Generally，molt occurs at the time of least ***stress*** on the bird.
【衍】	stressful (*adj.*)；stressless (*adj.*)
【近】	pressure，strain，tension
【释】	② ***v.*** 着重，强调，加重语气说
【例】	Freud did not ***stress*** that the ability to negate is directly connected to the development of the self.
【近】	emphasize，address，accentuate

Unit 6

subspecies ['sʌbspiːʃiːz]

【释】 ([*sing.*], [*pl.*]) *n.* 【生】亚种

【例】 The bills of different crossbill species and *subspecies* vary... some are stout and deep, others more slender and shallow.

【衍】 subspecific (*adj.*)

【近】 breed, species, sort

superintendent [ˌsjuːpərinˈtendənt]

【释】 *n.* 管理人，监督人，指挥人;(某一部门的)主管，负责人

【例】 For example, a school *superintendent* wishes to determine the proportion of children in a large school system who come to school without breakfast, have been vaccinated for flu, or whatever.

【衍】 superintend (*v.*); superintendence (*n.*) 管理;监督(权); superintendency (*n.*) 监督者的地位

【近】 manager, supervisor, administrator

sweat [swet]

【释】 *n.* 汗;出汗

【例】 The body also produces about 31 to 40 ounces of *sweat* a day.

【衍】 sweatshop (*n.*) 血汗工厂; sweaty (*adj.*) 流汗的，辛苦的，吃力的

tan [tæn]

【释】 *v.* 鞣(革)，硝(皮);使晒成棕褐色

【例】 Sometimes artisans transformed material provided by the customer such as produced shoes or leather breeches from cow, deer, or sheepskin *tanned* on the farm.

【衍】 tanne (*n.*) 制革工人; tannin (*n.*) 鞣质

tenant ['tenənt]

【释】 *n.* 租屋人，房客

【例】 Rent control is the system whereby the local government tells building owners how much they can charge their *tenants* in rent.

【近】 renter, occupant

thickness ['θiknis]

【释】 *n.* 厚度;密度;稠密

【例】 When new snow layer upon layer and were of such great *thickness* that the weight of the upper layers compressed the lower ones.

【衍】	thick（*adj.*）；thickly（*adv.*）；thicken（*v.*）
【近】	width，breadth
tip	［tip］
【释】	① *n.*（塔、手指、尾巴等的）尖，尖端，末端
【例】	Kiwis smell out earthworms thanks to nostrils located at the *tip* of their beaks.
【近】	apex，top，point
【释】	② *v.* 倾斜；翻倒；翻
【例】	All but two of the Mysticeti reach 40 feet or more at maturity，with the blue whale running up to 100 feet and *tipping* the scales at up to 130 tons.
【近】	tilt，lean，incline
toxic	［'tɔksik］
【释】	*adj.* 有毒的；中毒的
【例】	Scientists had been feverishly searching for an antibiotic *toxic* enough to kill the fungi but safe enough for human use.
【衍】	toxically（*adv.*）；toxication（*n.*）；intoxication（*n.*）陶醉
【近】	poisonous，deadly，lethal
tremendous	［tri'mendəs］
【释】	*adj.* 可怕的，惊人的；巨大的；非常的；＜俚＞极好的
【例】	One of the reasons Philadelphia's merchants generally prospered was because the surrounding area was undergoing *tremendous* economic and demographic growth.
【衍】	tremendously（*adv.*）；tremendousness（*n.*）
【近】	marvelous，incredible，fabulous
truth	［truθ］
【释】	*n.* 真理；真实；真相，事实
【例】	Dreiser thought that writers should tell the *truth* about human affairs，not fabricate romance.
【衍】	truthful（*adj.*）；truthfulness（*n.*）
【近】	reality，genuineness，certainty
understand	［ˌʌndə'stænd］
【释】	*v.* 听说，获悉
【例】	Most colonists have *understood* that the federal law had been changed.

【近】	hear, know, learn
vacuum	['vækjuəm]
【释】	*n.* 真空
【例】	Electric power was available for lamps, sewing machines, irons, and even *vacuum* cleaners.
vertical	['və:tikəl]
【释】	*adj.* 垂直的，直立的，竖立的，纵的([*opp.*]horizontal)
【例】	Most groups made all their basketwork by twining—the twisting of a flexible horizontal material, called a weft, around stiflfer *vertical* strands of material, the warp.
【近】	perpendicular, upright, plumb
volatile	['vɔlətail]
【释】	*adj.* 挥发(性)的
【例】	These bacteria release *volatile* substances that usually strike the bloodhound's nose as an entire constellation of distinctive scents.
【衍】	volatility (*n.*); volatilize (*v.*); volatilization (*n.*)
weed	[wi:d]
【释】	*n.* 杂草
【例】	The farmers, however, were not interested in it, claming that the iron poisoned the soil and made the *weeds* grow.
【近】	wild plant, grass
worm	[wə:m]
【释】	*n.* 蠕虫；虫，蛆
【例】	This *worm* is found mainly in sheepdogs that eat infected sheep carcasses.
【衍】	earthworm (*n.*) 蚯蚓；flatworm (*n.*) 扁平无环节的寄生虫
【近】	larva

Unit 6

Exercise of Unit 6

左列单词在右列中有一个同义词，请找出并在相应的位置写上正确答案。

Exercise 1:
　(A) inner ＿＿＿＿　resonance
　(B) reshape ＿＿＿　interior
　(C) devoid ＿＿＿＿　reform
　(D) echo ＿＿＿＿　degree
　(E) extent ＿＿＿＿　lacking
　(F) renounce ＿＿＿　abandon

Exercise 2:
　(A) pack ＿＿＿＿　researcher
　(B) battle ＿＿＿＿　product
　(C) spacious ＿＿＿　fight
　(D) seep ＿＿＿＿　roomy
　(E) scholar ＿＿＿＿　leak
　(F) commodity ＿＿＿　set

Exercise 3:
　(A) sight ＿＿＿＿　view
　(B) splendid ＿＿＿　wind
　(C) meander ＿＿＿　attain
　(D) acquire ＿＿＿　jail
　(E) intent ＿＿＿＿　purpose
　(F) prison ＿＿＿＿　grand

Exercise 4:
　(A) dispute ＿＿＿＿　principal
　(B) hunger ＿＿＿＿　manager
　(C) superintendent ＿＿　disagree
　(D) fur ＿＿＿＿　starvation
　(E) predominant ＿＿＿　apex
　(F) tip ＿＿＿＿　hair

Exercise 5:
　(A) evolve ＿＿＿＿　pressure
　(B) flaw ＿＿＿＿　respond
　(C) stress ＿＿＿＿　dictate
　(D) react ＿＿＿＿　breed
　(E) dominate ＿＿＿＿　develop
　(F) subspecies ＿＿＿　defect

Exercise 6:
　(A) cautious ＿＿＿＿　marvelous
　(B) tremendous ＿＿＿　falcon
　(C) consistent ＿＿＿　careful
　(D) condor ＿＿＿＿　reality
　(E) truth ＿＿＿＿　overturn
　(F) reverse ＿＿＿＿　reliable

Exercise 7:
(A) notwithstanding __ planetoid
(B) asteroid _____ odor
(C) puddle _____ despite
(D) official _____ industrialist
(E) entrepreneur ___ pond
(F) smell _____ administrator

Exercise 8:
(A) immortal _____ mushroom
(B) possess _____ mire
(C) burgeon _____ appear
(D) emerge _____ have
(E) mud _____ eternal
(F) tip _____ tilt

Exercise 9:
(A) analogy _____ similarity
(B) recruit _____ perpendicular
(C) microbe _____ hear
(D) chest _____ conscript
(E) understand _____ box
(F) vertical _____ germ

Exercise 10:
(A) rehabilitate _____ bag
(B) sack _____ restraint
(C) aggregate _____ recover
(D) patience _____ endurance
(E) cliff _____ precipice
(F) limitation _____ collection

ANSWERS:
1   D A B E C F
2   E F B C D A
3   A C D F E B
4   E C A B F D
5   C D E F A B
6   B D A E F C
7   B F A E C D
8   C E D B A F
9   A F E B D C
10 B F A D E C

Unit 7

absorb	emit	multiple	shallow
acre	entry	negate	signature
aggressive	exaggerate	nourishing	smoke
analyze	external	offshore	span
architecture	feat	ornament	staircase
astonishing	flax	paddle	stick
backbone	fossil	patriot	stretch
bay	furnace	peripheral	substantial
blade	geomagnetic	pigment	superior
breach	gravity	plummet	sweep
burial	harm	postage	tank
cap	hide	pregnant	tendency
cavity	hurl	private	thin
chief	immune	proper	tire
cling	incubate	pueblo	tract
commonsense	innocent	radiation	trench
conduct	interact	ready	tube
constant	involved	rectangular	undertake
convince	keen	reheating	vague
critic	lawn	rent	vessel
damp	limner	reside	volcano
delicate	loyal	review	weird
devour	mammoth	rod	wrap
disrepute	mechanism	saddle	
dot	microscopic	score	
eclipse	modest	segment	

absorb [əb'sɔːb]
- 【释】 *v.* 吸收
- 【例】 Healthy chlorophyll *absorbs* light of colors other than green, which is reflected.
- 【衍】 absorbed (*adj.*); reabsorb (*v.*)
- 【近】 take in, soak up

acre ['eikə]
- 【释】 ① *n.* 英亩
- 【例】 It housed about 1,000 people in a vast structure of 800 spacious rooms stretching over 3 *acres*.
- 【衍】 acreage (*n.*) 英亩数；面积
- 【释】 ② *n.* 地产，土地，耕地
- 【例】 The plantations maintained their independence because the *acre* located on navigable streams, each had a wharf accessible to the small shipping of that day.

aggressive [ə'gresiv]
- 【释】 *adj.* 好斗的；敢做敢为的；有进取心的，行动积极的
- 【例】 *Aggressive* behavior is a sign of emotional distress.
- 【衍】 aggress (*v.*) 攻击；侵略；aggression (*n.*) 攻击；侵略，侵犯；aggressively (*adv.*); aggressiveness (*n.*)
- 【近】 belligerent

analyze ['ænəlaiz]
- 【释】 *v.* 分析
- 【例】 Craver's first step was to *analyze* plant parts to find out what they were made of.
- 【衍】 analysis (*n.* [*pl.*] -ses); analytic(al) (*adj.*); analytically (*adv.*)
- 【近】 examine, investigate, scrutinize

architecture ['ɑːkitektʃə]
- 【释】 *n.* 建筑学；建筑(样式、风格)；建筑物
- 【例】 It was not the first book on *architecture* printed in the United States, but it was the first genuinely American treatment of the subject.
- 【衍】 architectural (*adj.*); architect (*n.*) 建筑师

astonishing [əs'tɔniʃiŋ]
- 【释】 *adj.* 令人惊讶的

Unit 7

【例】 Inventories of colonial libraries show an *astonishing* number of these handbooks for builders，and the houses erected during the eighteenth century show their influence.

【衍】 astonish（*v.*）；astonished（*adj.*）；astonishingly（*adv.*）；astonishment（*n.*）

【近】 amazing，surprising，astounding，shocking

backbone ['bækbəun]

【释】 *n.* 脊骨，脊椎；骨干，主力

【例】 But like most animals without a *backbone*，flatworms act mostly by instinct and reflex.

【衍】 backboned（*adj.*）

【近】 spine，vertebra

bay [bei]

【释】 *n.* 湾，海湾；(山中的)凹地

【例】 Crabs and shrimp swim upstream from the *bays*.

【衍】 bayou（*n.*）小海湾；支流；河口

【近】 inlet，cove

blade [bleid]

【释】 *n.* (壳、草等的)叶片，叶身；刀片；刀口，刃

【例】 The pianist may reach inside the piano to pluck a string and then run a metal *blade* along it.

【衍】 bladed（*adj.*）

breach [bri:tʃ]

【释】 *v.* (对法律、义务等的)破坏；违背，不履行

【例】 If the physical barriers of the plant are *breached*，then preformed chemicals may inhibit or kill the intruder.

【近】 abuse，neglect，violate

burial ['beriəl]

【释】 *n.* 埋葬；葬礼；墓地

【例】 The beds of ancient lakes were also excellent sites for rapid *burial* of skeletal remains of freshwater organisms.

【衍】 bury（*v.*）

【近】 interment，funeral，entombment

cap [kæp]

【释】 *n.* 盖，罩子

【例】	Squirrels pry off the *caps* of acorns, bite through the shells to get at the nutritious inner kernels, and then discard them half-eaten.
【近】	coat, crown

cavity ['kævəti]

【释】	*n.* 穴，腔，空腔
【例】	Solitary roosters shelter in dense vegetation or enter a *cavity*.
【近】	cave, chamber, hole, crater

chief [tʃiːf]

【释】	① *adj.* 主要的
【例】	In any vertebrate two *chief* parts of the nervous system may be distinguished.
【衍】	chiefly (*adv.*)
【近】	principal, paramount
【释】	② *n.* 酋长
【例】	Each village had two *chiefs*.
【近】	leader, ruler, head

cling [kliŋ]

【释】	*v.* 缠住，绕住
【例】	Clams and snails burrow along the bottom or *cling* to water plants.
【衍】	clinger (*n.*); clingy (*adj.*)
【近】	adhere

common-sense [ˌkɔmən'sens]

【释】	*n. & adj.* 常识（的）
【例】	The *commonsense* notion that the best icebox was one that prevented the ice from melting was of course mistaken, for it was the melting of the ice that performed the cooling.

conduct [kən'dʌkt]

【释】	① *v.* 实行；进行
【例】	In preparing to *conduct* a survey, sociologists must exercise great care in the wording of questions.
【近】	carry out, perform
【释】	② *v.* 传导，传（热、电等）
【例】	Water *conducts* heat faster than air.

【衍】 conductor（n.）；conductive（adj.）；conductivity（n.）

constant ['kɔnstənt]

【释】 ① adj. 稳定的，恒久的

【例】 Desert mammals also depart from the normal mammalian practice of maintaining a *constant* body temperature.

【近】 steady，even

【释】 ② adj. 继续不断的

【例】 Notwithstanding preening and *constant* care，the marvelously intricate structure of a bird's feather inevitably wears out.

【衍】 constantly（adv.）

【近】 continuous，continual，perpetual

convince [kən'vins]

【释】 v. 使确信，说服，使承认

【例】 The waste disposal industry is finding it difficult to *convince* the public that its operations are safe.

【衍】 convincing（adj.）有说服力的

【近】 persuade

critic ['kritik]

【释】 n. 批评家

【例】 *Critics* ignorant of western conditions often attacked it as wasteful and dangerous.

【衍】 criticism（n.）；criticize（v.）

damp [dæmp]

【释】 n. 湿气，潮湿 adj. 有湿气的，潮湿的 v. 弄湿，打湿

【例】 Cold *damp* air brought in the new year under a blanket of fog.

【衍】 damper（n.）使人扫兴的人（事）；【音】制止（琴弦的）音；dampen（v.）使潮湿；使沮丧；dampness（n.）

【近】 moist，humid

delicate ['delikit]

【释】 adj. 精巧的，精致的；（仪器）灵敏的

【例】 A fresh snowfall is a fluffy mass of loosely packed snowflakes，small *delicate* ice crystals grown in the atmosphere.

【衍】 delicately（adv.）；delicacy（n.）微妙

【近】 subtle，ingenious，exquisite，fine

devour [di'vauə]

【释】 *v.* 狼吞虎咽地吃；挥霍

【例】 If it were not for this faculty, they would *devour* all the food available in a short time and would probably starve themselves out of existence.

【近】 consume

disrepute [ˌdisri'pjuːt]

【释】 *n.* 坏名声，声名狼藉

【例】 In the early 1950's to mid 1960's, vitamin therapy began to fall into *disrepute*.

【衍】 disreputable（*adj.*）声名狼藉的；破烂不堪的

【近】 disgrace

dot [dɔt]

【释】 *v.* (-tt-)点缀

【例】 In the closing decades of the nineteenth century, large apartment houses began *dotting* the developed portions of New York City.

eclipse [i'klips]

【释】 *n.* (日、月)食 *v.* 使失色；超越；盖过

【例】 This is the only part of the Sun that can be seen during an *eclipse* such as the one in February 1979.

emit [i'mit]

【释】 *v.* (-tt-)出(声)，发、放(光等)，发射，放射(热等)

【例】 Stimulated emission is different because it occurs when an atom or molecule holding onto excess energy has been stimulated to *emit* it as light.

【衍】 emission（*n.*）; emissive（*adj.*）发射的，放射(性)的

【近】 release, emanate, erupt, issue

entry ['entri]

【释】 *n.* 入口；门口；登录

【例】 Many of the *entry*-level management jobs are going to students graduating with Master of Arts degrees in English and the humanities as well as those holding MBA degrees.

【衍】 entry-level（*n.*）最低级

【近】 admission, entrance

Unit 7

exaggerate [ɪɡˈzædʒəreɪt]
【释】 *v.* 夸张，夸大
【例】 Adults make it as easy as they can for babies to pick up a language by *exaggerating* such cues.
【衍】 exaggeration（*n.*）
【近】 overstate，amplify

external [ɪkˈstɜːnəl]
【释】 *adj.* 外部的，外面的（[*opp.*] interior）；表面上的（[*opp.*] intrinsic）
【例】 Certain fungi and even some kinds of bacteria secrete substances known as antibiotics into their *external* environment.
【衍】 externally（*adv.*）；exterior（*adj.* & *n.*）外部(的)，外面(的)，表面(的)
【近】 exterior，peripheral

feat [fiːt]
【释】 *n.* 卓绝的手艺；技术；本领
【例】 According to this view，tales（about the hunt，war，or other *feats*）are gradually elaborated at first through the use of impersonation，action，and dialogue by a narrator and then through the assumption of each of the roles by a different person.
【近】 skill，achievement

flax [flæks]
【释】 *n.* 亚麻；亚麻皮；亚麻纤维
【例】 It is these cellulose-destroying enzymes that enable fungi to attack anything made from wood，wood pulp，cotton，*flax*，or other plant material.
【衍】 flaxen（*adj.*）亚麻的，亚麻制的；亚麻(淡黄)色的

fossil [ˈfɒsəl]
【释】 *n.* 化石
【例】 Most of the *fossils* date to between 40,000 and 10,000 years ago.
【衍】 fossilize（*v.*）；fossilization（*n.*）

furnace [ˈfɜːnɪs]
【释】 *n.* 炉子；熔炉 *v.* 在炉中烧热(金属)

142

【例】 As the air shot through the *furnace*，the bubbling metal would erupt in showers of sparks.

【近】 oven，kiln

geomagnetic ［ˌdʒiːəumæɡˈnetik］

【释】 *adj.* 地磁的

【例】 Ferromagnetic minerals in the magma become magneti zed in the direction of the *geomagnetic* field.

【衍】 geomagnetism（*n.*）

gravity ［ˈɡrævəti］

【释】 *n.* 重力，引力

【例】 The effect of *gravity* on the droplets or ice is minute.

【衍】 gravitation（*n.*）（万有）引力；gravitational（*adj.*）

harm ［haːm］

【释】 *n.* 损害；伤害；危害

【例】 The camel can lose up to 30 percent of its body weight without *harm* to itself.

【衍】 harmful（*adj.*）；harmfully（*adv.*）

【近】 damage，hurt，injury

hide ［haid］

【释】 *n.* 兽皮；皮革

【例】 He also collected animal *hides* and horns.

【衍】 hiding（*n.*）

hurl ［həːl］

【释】 *v. & n.* 猛投，猛掷

【例】 A macaque or gibbon can *hurl* itself farther than a mouse can.

【衍】 hurler（*n.*）

【近】 throw，fling，toss，chuck

immune ［iˈmjuːn］

【释】 *adj.* 免疫(性)的

【例】 Active plant defense mechanisms are comparable to the *immune* system of vertebrate animals.

【衍】 immunity（*n.*）

incubate ［ˈinkjubeit］

【释】 *v.* 孵卵；孵化

【例】 When parrots *incubate* their eggs in the wild，the temperature and humidity of the nest are controlled naturally.

【衍】 incubation（*n.*）

【近】 hatch，nurture

innocent ['inəsənt]

【释】 *adj.* 天真无邪的；单纯的

【例】 Although her art has an *innocent* earnestness and folkloric affinity，Lomas Garza's expression is neither naive nor instinctive.

interact [,intər'ækt]

【释】 *v.* 相互作用，相互影响

【例】 Attachment behaviors of babies，such as smiling，babbling，grasping，and crying，are built-in social signals that encourage the parents to approach，care for，and *interact* with the baby.

【衍】 interactive（*adj.*）；interaction（*n.*）

【近】 interrelate

involved [in'vɔlvd]

【释】 *adj.* 复杂的

【例】 Molting is one of the most *involved* processes of a bird's annual life cycle.

【近】 complicated，intricate，elaborated，complex

keen [kiːn]

【释】 *adj.* 敏锐的，敏捷的

【例】 *Keen* observers and quick learners，crows are astute about the intentions of other creatures，including researchers，and adept at avoiding them.

【近】 sharp，acute

lawn [lɔːn]

【释】 *n.* 草地，草坪，草场

【例】 Elijah McCoy invented twenty-three lubricators for different kinds of equipment as well as inventing an ironing table，a *lawn* sprinkler and other useful devices.

【衍】 lawny（*adj.*）

【近】 grass，turf，sod

limner ['limnə]

【释】 *n.* 画师，画匠；描述者

【例】 But in the heyday of portrait painting—from the late eighteenth century until the 1850's—anyone with a modicum of artistic ability could become a *limner*, as such a portraitist was called.

【衍】 limn (*v.*) 描画，勾画；描写；生动地叙述

loyal ['lɔiəl]

【释】 *adj.* 忠诚的；忠实的

【例】 She used her influence to keep the western tribes of Iroquois *loyal* to the English king, George III.

【衍】 loyalist (*n.*) 忠诚的人；反对独立者

【近】 faithful, devoted, reliable

mammoth ['mæməθ]

【释】 ① *n.* 猛犸(象)(古生代的巨象)

【例】 Amid rumors that there were prehistoric *mammoths* wandering around the unknown region and that somewhere in its wilds was a mountain of rock salt 80 by 45 miles in extent, the two captains set out.

【释】 ② *n. & adj.* 巨物(的)，庞然大物(的)；巨大(的)

【例】 Under such a liberal proposition, the transfer of the land was soon made, and the construction of the *mammoth* hotel began.

【近】 enormous, huge, massive

mechanism ['mekənizəm]

【释】 *n.* 机制，机能；(机械)结构；机械装置(作用)

【例】 Active plant defense *mechanisms* are comparable to the immune system of vertebrate animals, although the cellular and molecular bases are fundamentally different.

【衍】 mechanic (*n.*) 机工，技工；mechanics (*n.*) 力学，机械学；mechanical (*adj.*) 机械的，机械(地工作)的；无意识的，自动的；mechanically (*adv.*)；mechanization (*n.*) 机械化，机能化；mechanize (*v.*) 使机械化

【近】 system, procedure, means

microscopic [ˌmaikrə'skɔpik]

【释】 *adj.* 用显微镜可见的；微观的；极微的([*opp.*] macroscopic)

Unit 7

【例】 The mineral particles found in soil range in size from *microscopic* clay particles to large boulders.

【衍】 microscope（*n.*）显微镜；microscopically（*adv.*）；microscopy（*n.*）显微镜学；显微镜使用术

【近】 tiny，minute，infinitesimal

modest ['mɔdist]

【释】 *adj.* 有节制的，适度的，适中的；谨慎的，谦虚的

【例】 Of their major discovery，Brown said lightly that it simply illustrated "how unpredictable consequences can come from rather *modest* beginnings."

【衍】 modestly（*adv.*）

【近】 moderate，unpretentious，unassuming

multiple ['mʌltipl]

【释】 ① *adj.* 多重的；复合的，复式的；多数的，多样的

【例】 Glass can be decorated in *multiple* ways and its optical properties are exceptional.

【衍】 multiplicity（*n.*）多样性；multiply（*adv.*）多样地；多倍地；multiply（*v.*）增殖，繁殖；（成倍）增加；【数】乘；multitude（*n.*）许多，大量；群众

【近】 numerous，various，compound

【释】 ② *n.*【数】倍数

【例】 One microbiologist estimates the resident bacteria population of a clean square centimeter of skin on the human shoulder at "*multiples* of a million."

negate [ni'geit]

【释】 *v.* 否定，否认；取消，使无效

【例】 Freud did not stress that the ability to *negate* is directly connected to the development of the self.

【衍】 negation（*n.*）；negative（*adj.* & *n.*）；negatively（*adv.*）

【近】 cancel out，deny，exclude

nourishing ['nʌriʃiŋ]

【释】 *adj.* 有营养的

【例】 When they dried in this way，they remained naturally sweet and *nourishing* through the winter.

【衍】 nourish（*v.*）滋养，使健壮；怀有；nourishment（*n.*）营养品；食物

【近】 nutritious，beneficial，healthful

offshore [ˈɔ(ː)fˈʃɔː]

【释】 *adj. & adv.* 向海面吹的(地)；离岸的(地)；海面上的(地)

【例】 Other oceans，such as the Pacific，are shrinking as seafloor descends under their fringing coastlines or *offshore* arcs of islands.

ornament [ˈɔːnəmənt]

【释】 *n.* 装饰，修饰；装饰物(品)　　*v.* 装饰，修饰；美化

【例】 Wandering tradespeople began to spin glass fibers at fairs，making decorations and *ornaments* as novelties for collectors，but this material was of little practical use.

【衍】 ornamental（*adj.*）装饰的，作装饰用的；ornamentation（*n.*）装饰，装饰术，饰品；ornate（*adj.*）装饰的，华美的；ostentatious（*adj.*）讲排场的，虚饰的，浮华的

【近】 decoration，adornment，embellishment

paddle [ˈpædl]

【释】 *n.* 桨，桨状物；(轮船等的)蹼，桨板

【例】 Their *paddles* are already well formed.

【近】 scull

patriot [ˈpeitriət]

【释】 *n.* 爱国者；爱国主义者

【例】 Both Mercy Warren and Abigail Adams admired Catharine Macaulay，who supported the cause of the American *patriots*.

【衍】 patriotic（*adj.*）

【近】 partisan，nationalist

peripheral [pəˈrifərəl]

【释】 *adj.* 周围的，外围的；(神经)末梢区域的

【例】 The term "autonomic nervous system" refers to the parts of the central and *peripheral* systems.

【衍】 periphery（*n.*）；peripherally（*adv.*）

【近】 marginal，fringe

pigment [ˈpigmənt]

【释】 *n.* 颜料，色料；色素

【例】 The *pigment* will leave the smooth surface and stick to the paper.

【衍】 pigmentary（*adj.*）

【近】 color，dye，tint

plummet ['plʌmit]

【释】 *v.* 笔直掉下；骤然跌落

【例】 Ice expands when it initially forms，but as the tempera-ture *plummets*，the ice contracts.

【近】 fall，dive，drop

postage ['pəustidʒ]

【释】 *n.* 邮费

【例】 In 1847 the United States Post Office Department adopted the idea of a *postage* stamp.

【衍】 postal（*adj.*）；poster（*n.*）海报，招贴

pregnant ['pregnənt]

【释】 *adj.* 怀孕的，有孕的，怀胎的

【例】 Why are there so many *pregnant* females and young at Holzmaden when they are so rare elsewhere?

【衍】 pregnancy（*n.*）

private ['praivit]

【释】 *adj.* 私的，私人的；秘密的；保密的

【例】 The government postal service lost volume to *private* competition.

【衍】 privately（*adv.*）

【近】 confidential，personal，secret

proper ['prɔpə]

【释】 *adj.* 适当的，相当的；正当的

【例】 The *proper* message is not transmitted.

【衍】 properly（*adv.*）

【近】 good，correct，suitable，right

pueblo ['pwebləu]

【释】 *n.* （[*pl.*] pueblos）印第安人的村庄

【例】 Each *pueblo* represented an astonishing amount of well-organized labor.

radiation [ˌreidi'eiʃən]

【释】 *n.* 发光，放热；辐射线(热，能)

【例】 The nuclear energy is released at the Sun's center as high-energy gamma *radiation*，a form of electromagnetic radiation like light and radio waves，only of very much shorter wavelength.

【衍】 radiational（*adj.*）；radiationless（*adj.*）；radiative（*adj.*）

【近】 emission，rays，waves

ready ['redi]

【释】 ① *adj.* 已做好准备(预备)的

【例】 Once fired，the pots were allowed to cool slowly，and small cracks were repaired before they were *ready* for use.

【衍】 readiness（*n.*）

【近】 prepared

【释】 ② *adj.* 现成的，现有的

【例】 The broken valleys of the Great Basin provided *ready* receptacles for this moisture.

【衍】 readily（*adv.*）容易地；毫不勉强地

【近】 set

rectangular [rek'tæŋgjulə]

【释】 *adj.* 矩形的，长方形的；成直角的

【例】 That lot was a *rectangular* area 25 feet wide by 100 feet deep—a shape perfectly suited for a row house.

【衍】 rectangle（*n.*）

reheating [riːˈhiːtiŋ]

【释】 *n.* 重新加热

【例】 The thermosets are materials that，once heated，take on a permanent form that cannot be changed by *reheating*.

【衍】 reheat（*v.*）

rent [rent]

【释】 *n.* 裂缝，缝隙；(意见等的)分裂，分歧

【例】 The intimacy of marriage that was common in earlier periods was *rent*，and a gulf that at times seemed unbridgeable was created between husbands and wives.

【近】 gulf，gap

reside [riˈzaid]

【释】 *v.* 居住；留驻；停留；存在

Unit 7

【例】 Two species of these finches, *reside* in the evergreen forests of North America and feed on the seeds held within the cones of coniferous trees.

【衍】 residence (*n.*); residency (*n.*); resident (*adj. & n.*) 住户; residential (*adj.*)

【近】 inhabit, dwell, live in

review [ri'vjuː]

【释】 *n. & v.* 回顾; 评论; 再验查; 检查

【例】 However, the truth of the matter is that the *reviews* for these early shows were nearly all favorable.

【衍】 reviewable (*adj.*); reviewer (*n.*)

【近】 evaluation, assessment, examination

rod [rɔd]

【释】 *n.* 棍棒; 杆

【例】 *Rod*-shaped bacteria are usually from two to four microns long, while rounded ones are generally one micron in diameter.

【近】 bar, pole, stick

saddle ['sædl]

【释】 *n.* 马鞍; 鞍

【例】 There vaqueros invented almost all the tools of the cowhand's trade, from the broad-brimmed felt hat and the rope lariat to the special western *saddle*.

【衍】 saddlebag (*n.*) 鞍囊

【近】 burden

score [skɔː]

【释】 ① *n.* 刻痕; 裂缝; 记号

【例】 The tar pits were found to contain the remains of *scores* of species of animals from the last 30,000 years of the Ice Age.

【近】 notch, mark, cut

【释】 ② *n.* 总谱, 乐谱; (电影歌舞等的)配乐

【例】 Because standard music notation makes no provision for many of these innovations, recent music *scores* may contain new note shapes and novel ways of arranging notation on the page.

segment ['segmənt]

【释】 *n.* 部分，节，段　　 *v.* 分割，分裂

【例】 Their attitudes toward themselves changed，and，to some extent，other *segments* of American society began to change their attitudes toward them.

【衍】 segmented（*adj.*）

【近】 section，part，piece，fraction

shallow ['∫æləu]

【释】 *adj.*（水、器物等）浅的；薄的（[*opp.*] deep）

【例】 The beautifully preserved fossil fish from the Green River oil shale of Wyoming in the western United States lived in a vast *shallow* lake.

【近】 low，thin，superficial

signature ['signət∫ə]

【释】 *n.* 签名，盖章

【例】 Below are some Sioux *signatures*.

【衍】 sign（*n.* & *v.*）；signal（*n.*）信号；signed（*adj.*）有符号的

【近】 name，autograph，mark

smoke [sməuk]

【释】 *n.* 烟，烟尘　　 *v.* 用烟熏，熏制

【例】 It was made like a small，secondary fireplace with a flue leading into the main chimney to draw out *smoke*.

【衍】 smokehouse（*n.*）熏制室；smokable（*adj.*）可吸的，可抽的

【近】 burn，be on fire，smolder

span [spæn]

【释】 ① *n.* 一段时间；很小的间隔；片刻，顷刻

【例】 It refers to a limited times *span* during which the child is biologically prepared to acquire certain adaptive behaviors but needs the support of suitably stimulating environment.

【释】 ② *v.* 横跨，跨越　　 *n.* 跨度，跨距，范围

【例】 Apart form its low cost，the appeal of iron as a building material lay in its strength，its resistance to fire，and its potential to *span* vast areas.

【近】 width，cross，cover

【释】 ③ *v.* 达到，及

【例】 As with many folk artists, her career as a painter started late in life, at the age of 67, but she continued painting until her death at the age of 101, so her active painting life still *spanned* over 34 years.

staircase ['stɛəkeis]

【释】 *n.* 楼梯；楼梯间(室)

【例】 Many of these buildings were shaped in the ziggurat form, a design that recedes in progressively smaller stages to the summit, creating a *staircase*-like effect.

【衍】 stair (*n.*); stairway (*n.*) 楼梯；stairwell (*n.*) 楼梯井

stick [stik]

【释】 ① *n.* 棒，棍；枝条；柴

【例】 Young ravens, for example, first attempt to build with *sticks* of quite unsuitable size, while a jackdaw's first nest includes virtually any movable object.

【衍】 stickpin (*n.*) 领带别针

【近】 twig, pole, rod

【释】 ② *v.* 粘住；贴；使固着；安置

【例】 If a drawing is made with a greasy substance, nonabsorbent's surface and a piece of soft paper is then pressed down on it, the pigment will leave the smooth surface and *stick* to the paper.

【衍】 sticky (*adj.*) 胶黏的，黏性的；sticking (*adj.*) 黏的

【近】 glue, fasten, paste

stretch [stretʃ]

【释】 *v.* 伸展，伸出；展

【例】 It housed about 1,000 people in a vast structure of 800 spacious rooms *stretching* over 3 acres.

【近】 extend

substantial [səb'stænʃəl]

【释】 *adj.* 实质的，真正的

【例】 Only Harvard's MBA School showed a *substantial* increase in enrollment in the 1993 school year.

【衍】 substantially (*adv.*); substantiate (*v.*) 证实，证明某事有根据；substantive (*adj.*) 真实的，实质的，本质的

superior [sjuːˈpiəriə]

【释】 *adj.* 较高的，上级的，有优势的，出众的（[*opp.*] **inferior**）

【例】 Their distrust was caused, in part, by a national ideology that proclaimed farming the greatest occupation and rural living *superior* to urban living.

【衍】 superiority（*n.*）优越（性），优势；傲慢

【近】 better, finer, advanced

sweep [swiːp]

【释】 *n.* 扫除，打扫　　*v.* 扫过，擦过，掠过；吹去，刮去

【例】 Their stalks and branches also act as screens to keep the wind from *sweeping* great drifts of sand along the surface.

【衍】 sweeper（*n.*）清道夫

【近】 brush, remove, clean

tank [tæŋk]

【释】 ① *n.* 【军】战车，坦克

【例】 The same metal that makes kitchen foil serves as armor for battlefield *tanks*.

【衍】 tanker（*n.*）油轮

【释】 ② *n.* 贮水池，池塘

【例】 The water *tanks* provide a total capacity of 400 liters.

【近】 reservoir, container

tendency [ˈtendənsi]

【释】 ① *n.* 倾向，趋势

【例】 The general practice is best described as "easy come, easy go," although there are certain group-forming *tendencies*.

【衍】 tendentious（*adj.*）有倾向性的

【近】 propensity, bent, inclination

【释】 ② *n.* 性情，偏好

【例】 Kittiwakes defecate over the edge of the nest, which keeps it clean, but this practice, as well as their *tendency* to leave the nest littered with eggshells, makes its location very conspicuous.

【近】 bias, penchant, trend

thin [θin]

【释】 *adj.* 薄瘦的，细小的，稀疏的　　*v.* 使薄瘦，使稀疏

【例】 The rays of gas *thin* out as they reach the space around the planets.

【衍】 thinly (*adv.*); thinner (*n.*) 稀释剂

【近】 slim, slender, skeletal

tire ['taiə]

【释】 *v.* 疲倦，使疲倦；使厌倦

【例】 Interest and demand were especially strong after the Second World War among returning soldiers, *tired* of foreign wars, who wanted only to get back to the comfort and security of their own culture.

【衍】 tired (*adj.*); tireless (*adj.*); tiredness (*n.*)

【近】 exhaust, tire out, fatigue

tract [trækt]

【释】 ① *n.* 广阔的地面；(一大片)土地(森林)；地带

【例】 Not much to anyone's surprise but to the disappointment of many, he chose a *tract* of land on the banks of the Potomac River.

【近】 territory, zone, region

【释】 ② *n.* (政治、宗教的)短文；小册子；传单

【例】 In addition to broadsides, books and pamphlets, consisting mainly of political *tracts*, catechisms, primers, and chapbooks were relatively inexpensive to print and to buy.

【近】 leaflet, pamphlet, article

trench [trentʃ]

【释】 *n.* 沟，渠　*v.* 掘沟

【例】 The new river then began to carve out the 277-mile-long *trench* that eventually became the Grand Canyon.

【近】 ditch, channel, drain

tube ['tjuːb]

【释】 *n.* 管，管道；管状地下隧道

【例】 The trumpet family is much more than a group of related instruments that can stir one with their sound, or narrow *tubes* of metal capable of producing a variety of musical sounds.

【衍】 tubelike (*adj.*) 管状的

【近】 pipe, hose, cylinder

undertake [ˌʌndə'teik]

【释】 *v.* 承担；承办；着手，从事

【例】 The Erie Canal，begun in 1817 and completed in 1825，was by far the greatest construction job that Americans had ever ***undertaken***.

【近】 assume

vague ［veig］

【释】 *adj*. 含糊的；笼统的

【例】 In fact，if awakened from slow-wave sleep，a person can often remember *vague* thoughts that occurred during that period of sleep.

【衍】 vaguely（*adv*.）；vagueness（*n*.）

【近】 unclear，blurred

vessel ［'vesəl］

【释】 ① 船，舰；飞船

【例】 In shallow western rivers the weight of *vessel* and engine was important.

【近】 craft，ship，yacht

【释】 ② 脉管，血管；导管

【例】 Living cells in an animal's body are connected to the heart by blood *vessels*，and to the brain by nerves.

volcano ［vɔl'keinəu］

【释】 *n*. 火山

【例】 *Volcanoes* often provide environments favorable to fossil preservation.

【衍】 volcanic（*adj*.）；volcanism（*n*.）火山作用

weird ［wiəd］

【释】 *adj*. 离奇的，古怪的

【例】 Surrounding the column are three sepals and three petals，sometimes easily recognizable as such，often distorted into gorgeous，*weird*，but always functional shapes.

【近】 odd，bizarre，peculiar

wrap ［ræp］

【释】 *v*. 卷，缠(绕)，包裹

【例】 Viewed from outer space，auroras can be seen as dimly glowing belts *wrapped* around each of the Earth's magnetic poles.

【近】 enclose，swathe

Unit 7

Exercise of Unit 7

左列单词在右列中有一个同义词，请找出并在相应的位置写上正确答案。

Exercise 1:

(A) interact _____ numerous
(B) undertake _____ slim
(C) loyal _____ faithful
(D) mammoth _____ assume
(E) thin _____ interrelate
(F) multiple _____ enormous

Exercise 2:

(A) vessel _____ interment
(B) burial _____ gulf
(C) lawn _____ better
(D) chief _____ principle
(E) rent _____ craft
(F) superior _____ grass

Exercise 3:

(A) constant _____ spine
(B) span _____ belligerent
(C) damp _____ width
(D) backbone _____ moist
(E) chief _____ continuous
(F) aggressive _____ leader

Exercise 4:

(A) exaggerate _____ propensity
(B) rod _____ notch
(C) tendency _____ bar
(D) score _____ throw
(E) cavity _____ overstate
(F) hurl _____ cave

Exercise 5:

(A) harm _____ oven
(B) furnace _____ damage
(C) tube _____ brush
(D) stick _____ glue
(E) tire _____ exhaust
(F) sweep _____ pipe

Exercise 6:

(A) analyze _____ inhabit
(B) shallow _____ examine
(C) peripheral _____ prepared
(D) ready _____ leaflet
(E) reside _____ marginal
(F) tract _____ low

Exercise 7:
(A) stick _____ unclear
(B) pigment _____ twig
(C) cling _____ fall
(D) plummet _____ adhere
(E) vague _____ disgrace
(F) disrepute _____ color

Exercise 8:
(A) radiation _____ consume
(B) devour _____ emission
(C) involved _____ decoration
(D) ready _____ set
(E) ornament _____ moderate
(F) modest _____ complicated

Exercise 9:
(A) entry _____ evaluation
(B) nourishing _____ subtle
(C) delicate _____ steady
(D) constant _____ nutritious
(E) review _____ admission
(F) emit _____ release

Exercise 10:
(A) segment _____ reservoir
(B) incubate _____ exterior
(C) external _____ section
(D) tank _____ bias
(E) tendency _____ ditch
(F) trench _____ hatch

ANSWERS:
1   F E C B A D
2   B E F D A C
3   D F B C A E
4   C D B F A E
5   B A F D E C
6   E A D F C B
7   E A D C F B
8   B A E D F C
9   E C D B A F
10   D C A E F B

Unit 8

abstract	emphasize	mundane	sharp
acronym	enzyme	neglect	significance
agitation	excavate	novelty	smooth
ancestor	extinct	offspring	spare
arctic	federal	outbreak	split
astronomy	flee	painstaking	stake
background	foster	patron	stiff
beacon	furnish	perishable	strict
blast	geometric	pile	substitute
breakdown	graze	plunge	supernatural
burrow	harmonious	potash	swift
capable	hierarchy	prejudice	tap
cease	hydrogen	probe	tenement
chill	impact	proponent	thorny
clip	indispensable	pull	tissue
commute	innovation	radical	traditionally
cone	interfere	realism	trend
constituent	ion	recycle	tumble
coordinate	kernel	reign	uniform
critical	layout	rental	valid
daring	linear	residue	vestige
delta	lubrication	revise	volt
dictate	mandate	rodent	welfare
disseminate	medicine	sail	wreck
down	midair	scout	
ecology	modify	segregate	

abstract ['æbstrækt]

【释】 *n. & adj.* 抽象(的)

【例】 Although many painters began working in the *abstract* style Georgia O'Keeffe followed no one.

【衍】 abstracted (*adj.*)；abstraction (*n.*)；abstractism (*n.*)

【近】 intangible，elusive

acronym ['ækrənim]

【释】 *n.* 首字母缩略词

【例】 The word laser was coined as an *acronym* for Light Amplification by the Stimulated Emission of Radiation.

【衍】 antonym (*n.*) 反义词；synonym (*n.*) 同义词

【近】 abbreviation，ellipsis

agitation [ˌædʒi'teiʃən]

【释】 *n.* (民众的)骚动，兴奋

【例】 Such organizational tie-ups often cause *agitation* for change or reform.

【衍】 agitate (*v.*) 搅动；煽动；热烈讨论

【近】 disturbance，stir

ancestor ['ænsestə]

【释】 *n.* 祖先；先祖，原种

【例】 Although it looks nothing like its *ancestors*，there are many similarities.

【衍】 ancestress (*n.*)；ancestral (*adj.*)；ancestry (*n.*)(集合名词)祖先

【近】 antecedent，forebear，precursor，predecessor

arctic ['ɑːktik]

【释】 *n. & adj.* 北极(的)；寒带(的) ([*opp.*] antarctic)

【例】 The Alaska pipeline starts at the frozen edge of the *Arctic* ocean.

astronomy [ə'strɔnəmi]

【释】 *n.* 天文学

【例】 An alternative would be sodium lights，which emit no ultraviolet waves and free the ultraviolet band that is essential to spectral *astronomy*.

【衍】 astronomical (*adj.*)；astronomer (*n.*) 天文学家；astronauts (*n.*) 宇(宙)航(行)员

background [ˈbækɡraund]
【释】 *n.* 后景，背景；基本情况；衬托音乐，伴音
【例】 That model may be an unrelated species，such as the *background* against which an organism spends most of its time.
【衍】 backgrounder（*n.*）背景情况介绍会
【近】 backdrop，setting，surroundings，conditions

beacon [ˈbiːkən]
【释】 *n.* (作为信号的)烽火，灯塔
【例】 Paid for and maintained by "light dues" levied on ships，the original *beacon* was blown up in 1776.
【近】 bonfire，flare，inspiration，signal

blast [blɑːst]
【释】 *v.* 使爆炸，爆破，炸掉；摧毁
【例】 McAdoo's men were forced to *blast* when they ran into a unexpected ledge of rock.
【衍】 blasted（*adj.*）枯萎的；被害的
【近】 explode，discharge，blow up

breakdown [ˈbreikdaun]
【释】 *n.* 崩溃，倒塌；故障
【例】 They obtain their supplies either from the *breakdown* of dead organic matter or from other living organisms.
【近】 fail，collapse，crash

burrow [ˈbʌrəu]
【释】 *v.* 打(地洞)，掘(穴)；掘成
【例】 Clams and snails *burrow* along the bottom or cling to water plants.
【近】 dig，delve，grub

capable [ˈkeipəbl]
【释】 ① *adj.* 有技能的；有资格的(for)
【例】 The tight arrangement enabled the Mandans to protect themselves more easily from the attacks of others who might seek to obtain some of the food these highly *capable* farmers stored from one years to the next.
【衍】 capability（*n.*）
【近】 competent，proficient，skilled

【释】 ② *adj*. 可以…的；能…的；易…的(of)

【例】 Radar systems，automated weather instruments，and satellites are all *capable* of making detailed，nearly continuous observation over large regions at a relatively low cost.

cease ［siːs］

【释】 *v. & n.* 停，终止

【例】 By the time the universe was a few minutes old，helium production had effectively *ceased*.

【衍】 ceaseless（*adj.*）；ceaselessly（*adv.*）；cease-fire（*n.*）停火

【近】 stop，end

chill ［tʃil］

【释】 *n. & adj.* 寒冷(的)　　*v.* 使冷，变冷

【例】 If eggs rest against the wooden bottom in extremely cold weather conditions，they can become *chilled* to point where the embryo can no longer survive.

【衍】 chilly（*adj.*）寒冷的；怕冷的

【近】 cool，freeze

clip ［klip］

【释】 *n.* 剪去，剪短，修剪

【例】 When a neighbor needed help，families rallied from miles around to assist in building a house or barn，husking corn，shearing sheep，or *clipping* wood.

【衍】 clipping（*n.*）（报纸等的)剪辑

【近】 shear，cut，snip

commute ［kəˈmjuːt］

【释】 *v.* 使用长期票经常旅行(来往)，通勤来往(between)

【例】 McLaren began *commuting* between Paris and London.

【衍】 commuter（*n.*）

【近】 travel

cone ［kəun］

【释】 *n.* 圆锥；圆锥形火山；(松树的)球果

【例】 As a rule，large-billed crossbills are better at securing seeds from large *cones*，while small-billed crossbills are more deft at removing the seeds from small，thin scaled *cones*.

constituent [kənˈstitjuənt]

【释】 *n.* 成分；构成

【例】 Water is, meteorologically, the most important *constituent* of the atmosphere of the Earth.

【近】 component, agent, ingredient

coordinate [kəuˈɔːdineit]

【释】 *adj.* 同等的，同位的

【例】 It was carried out by thousands of small investors who paid little attention to *coordinated* land use or to future land users.

【衍】 coordinate（*v.*）；coordination（*n.*）

【近】 corresponding

critical [ˈkritikəl]

【释】 ① *adj.* （在某方面）有鉴定力的（in）

【例】 Their writings were celebratory in nature, and they were *critical* in their selection and use of sources.

【衍】 critically（*adv.*）；uncritical（*adj.*）不加鉴别的

【近】 analytical, judicious

【释】 ② *adj.* 决定性的，重大的

【例】 Biological diversity has become widely recognized as a *critical* conservation issue only in the past two decades.

【近】 significant, vital, crucial, essential, important

daring [ˈdɛəriŋ]

【释】 *adj.* 胆大的，勇敢的

【例】 The establishment of these posts opened new roads and provided for the protection of *daring* adventurers and expeditions as well as established settlers.

【衍】 daringly（*adv.*）；daringness（*n.*）

【近】 bold, brave, audacious

delta [ˈdeltə]

【释】 *n.* （河流的）三角洲；三角形物

【例】 The rapidly accumulating sediments in flood plains, *deltas*, and stream channels buried freshwater organisms, along with other plants and animals that happened to fall into the water.

dictate ['dikteit]

【释】 *v.* 口述，听写；命令，支配，摆布

【例】 For the past two decades chemists have been striving for the ultimate in control—to *dictate* the course of a reaction by putting energy directly into the bonds that join atoms to make up a molecule.

【衍】 dictation（*n.*）；dictator（*n.*）发号施令者，（特指）独裁者；dictatorial（*adj.*）专政的，独裁的

【近】 order，command，mandate

disseminate [di'semineit]

【释】 *v.* 传播，散布，普及

【例】 Television has transformed politics in the United States by changing the way in which information is *disseminated*.

【衍】 disseminator（*n.*）播种者，撒种者；dissemination（*n.*）

【近】 distribute，spread

down [daun]

【释】 *n.* （装被、褥等用的）鸭绒，绒毛；（鸟的）绒羽；柔毛，汗毛，毳毛；（男孩脸上初生的）细软短须；（蒲公英等的）冠毛

【例】 The whole plant is covered with fine *down*.

ecology [i:'kɔlədʒi]

【释】 *n.* 生态学；任何均衡的系统（制度等）

【例】 These off-road vehicles can cause damage to desert landscapes that has long-range effects on the entire *ecology*，both plant and animal.

【衍】 ecologic（*adj.*）；ecologically（*adv.*）；ecologist（*n.*）

【近】 ecosystem

emphasize ['emfəsaiz]

【释】 *v.* 强调，着重

【例】 Instrumental leadership is leadership that *emphasizes* the completion of tasks by a social group.

【衍】 emphasis（*n.*）

【近】 accentuate，address

enzyme ['enzaim]

【释】 *n.* 酶

Unit 8

【例】 *Enzyme* systems of mammals and birds are most efficient only within a narrow range around 37 ℃.

【衍】 enzymatic（*adj.*）；enzymology（*n.*）酶(化)学

excavate [ˈekskəveit]

【释】 *v.* 掘出，发掘

【例】 ... Pit 9, the deepest bone-bearing deposit, which was *excavated* in 1914.

【衍】 excavation（*n.*）出土文物，发掘物；发掘；挖掘

【近】 dig, unearth, exhume

extinct [ikˈstiŋkt]

【释】 *adj.*（生物)已绝种的，已灭绝的

【例】 Fortunately, as far back as the early 1900's marine biologists realized that if new measures were not taken, oysters would become *extinct* or at best a luxury food.

【衍】 extinction（*n.*）(生物等的)灭绝

【近】 died out, vanished

federal [ˈfedərəl]

【释】 *adj.*（美国)联邦政府的，中央政府的

【例】 In the United States in the early 1880's, individual state governments had more effect on the economy than did the *federal* government.

flee [fliː]

【释】 *v.*（fled; fled）逃走（from; before）；逃避，逃出（from）

【例】 The Home Secretary wants to protect the rights of refugees *fleeing* persecution or torture.

【近】 run away, escape

foster [ˈfɔstə]

【释】 *v.* 助长，鼓励，促进

【例】 The sole purpose of the American Academy and Institute of Arts and Letters is to "*foster*, assist and sustain an interest" in literature, music, and art.

【衍】 fosterage（*n.*）

【近】 promote, cultivate

furnish [ˈfəːniʃ]

【释】 *v.* 供给，供应，提供

【例】 ... the region that supplies goods to the city and to which the city *furnishes* services and other goods.

【近】 supply，provide

geometric [ˌdʒiəˈmetrik]

【释】 *adj*. 有几何图形的

【例】 In Cubism，natural forms were broken down analytically into *geometric* shapes.

【衍】 geometry（*n*.）；geometrical（*adj*.）

graze [greiz]

【释】 *v*. 喂草，放牧；吃草

【例】 Cloth pays such little attention to its personal hygiene that communities of a parasitic moth live in the depths of its coat producing caterpillars which *graze* on its mouldy hair.

【衍】 grazing（*n*.）；grazer（*n*.）吃草的动物

【近】 browse

harmonious [haːˈməunjəs]

【释】 *adj*. 悦耳的；和谐的；融洽的；和睦的

【例】 The importance now placed on attractive and *harmonious* home decoration can also be traced in the nineteenth century.

【衍】 harmony（*n*.）；harmonize（*v*.）

【近】 melodious

hierarchy [ˈhaiəˌraːki]

【释】 *n*. 层次

【例】 Beyond the galaxies，in the *hierarchy* of the cosmos，there are clusters of galaxies.

【衍】 hierarchical（*adj*.）

hydrogen [ˈhaidrəudʒən]

【释】 *n*. 氢

【例】 Around the coma there is often an even larger invisible envelope of *hydrogen* gas.

impact [ˈimpækt]

【释】 ① *n*. 碰撞

【例】 The *impact* caused an explosion clearly visible from Earth.

【近】 crash

【释】 ② *n. & v.* 影响

【例】 One *impact* of the new household technology was to draw sharp dividing lines between women of different classes and regions.

【近】 influence，effect

indispensable [ˌindisˈpensəbl]

【释】 *adj.* 不可缺少的，必需的，重要的

【例】 From the very beginning，music was regarded as an *indispensable* accompaniment.

【衍】 indispensability（*n.*）

【近】 crucial，vital，essential

innovation [ˌinəuˈveiʃən]

【释】 *n.* 创新，革新；改革

【例】 They were responsible for many fundamental inventions and *innovations* that the modern world takes for granted.

【衍】 innovative（*adj.*）；innovate（*v.*）；innovator（*n.*）

【近】 advance，improvement

interfere [ˌintəˈfiə]

【释】 *v.* 妨碍，打扰

【例】 Skyscrapers also *interfere* with television reception，block bird flyways，and obstruct air traffic.

【衍】 interference（*n.*）

【近】 hinder，obstruct，impede

ion [ˈaiən]

【释】 *n.* 离子

【例】 Soluble *ions* such as calcium，sodium，potassium，and some magnesium are dissolved and transported.

【衍】 ionize（*v.*）（使）电离，使电离成离子

kernel [ˈkəːnəl]

【释】 *n.* （果实的）核，仁

【例】 Using the combined action of the bill and tongue，the bird cracks open and discards the woody seed covering and swallows the nutritious inner *kernel*.

【近】 core

layout [ˈleiˌaut]

【释】 *n.* 规划设计，布局图，版面设计

【例】 In 1903 the members of the governing board of the University of Washington engaged a firm of landscape architects to advise them on an appropriate *layout* for the university grounds.

【近】 outline，design，blueprint

linear [ˈliniə]

【释】 *adj.* 线的，直线的

【例】 It was，therefore，an ideal technique for emphasizing the hard *linear* edges and pure，fine areas of color that were so much a part of the overall aesthetic of the time.

【衍】 line（*n.* & *v.*）；lined（*adj.*）具线纹的，排列成…的；liner（*n.*）班机；linen（*n.*）亚麻布，亚麻线；lineage（*n.*）血统，世系，门第

lubrication [ˌluːbriˈkeiʃən]

【释】 *n.* 润滑，油润，上油；润滑作用

【例】 With this invention，it was no longer necessary to stop or shut down large machinery in order to apply the needed *lubrication*.

【衍】 lubricant（*n.*）润滑剂，润滑油；lubricator（*n.*）润滑剂；注油器

mandate [ˈmændeit]

【释】 ① *n.* & *v.* 命令，指令

【例】 In 1938 the Fair Labor Standards Act *mandated* a weekly maximum of 40 hours to begin in 1940，and since that time the 8-hour day，5-day workweek has been the standard in the United States.

【衍】 mandator（*n.*）命令者；mandatory（*adj.*）命令的，训令的

【近】 command，instruct，order，dictate

【释】 ② *n.*【法】财产委托；(国际上的)委托管理

【例】 Whitney announced in January 1930 that she would establish her own museum with a new and dramatically different *mandate*—to support artists from the United States.

【衍】 mandated（*adj.*）委托管理的；mandatory（*adj.*）委任的，委托的

【近】 permission，authorization，consent

medicine ［'medisin］

【释】 *n.* 医药；内服药；医学，医术；内科（治疗）（［*opp.*］ surgery）

【例】 In addition，fungi are the source of many of the most potent antibiotics used in clinical ***medicine***，including penicillin.

【衍】 medicinal（*adj.*）医学的，医药的，药用的；medicinally（*adv.*）；medical（*adj.*）医学的，医术的，医疗的，医师的

【近】 drug，medication，remedy

midair ［ˌmid'ɛə］

【释】 *n.* 半空中

【例】 The ability of falling cats to right themselves in ***midair*** and land on their feet has been a source of wonder for ages.

【衍】 middle（*adj. & n.*）；midst（*n.*）中间，中央

【近】 aerial，airborne，above ground

modify ［'mɔdifai］

【释】 *v.* 变更；修改；调节

【例】 Tiny amounts of some hormones can ***modify*** our moods and our actions，our inclination to eat or drink，our aggressiveness or submissiveness，and our reproductive and parental behavior.

【衍】 modified（*adj.*）改良的，改进的；modification（*n.*）

【近】 adapt，adjust，alter，modulate

mundane ［ˌmʌn'dein］

【释】 *adj.* 世俗的；平凡的

【例】 The thinker or philosopher stood apart from this ***mundane*** world，where the practical arts appeared to lack any intellectual content or interest.

【衍】 mundanely（*adv.*）

【近】 routine，ordinary，everyday

neglect ［ni'glekt］

【释】 *n. & v.* 疏忽；忽略；玩忽，轻忽；轻视，忽视

【例】 Central Park，emerging from a period of abuse and ***neglect***，remains one of the most popular attractions in New York City.

【衍】	negligible（*adj.*）无足轻重的，微不足道的；negligibly（*adv.*）
【近】	disregard，ignore，abandon
novelty	['nɔvəlti]
【释】	*n.* 新奇，奇异；新奇的东西(事情)
【例】	Wandering tradespeople began to spin glass fibers at fairs，making decorations and ornaments as *novelties* for collectors，but this material was of little practical use.
【衍】	novel（*adj. & n.*）新颖的，新奇的，珍奇的；小说；novelist（*n.*）小说家；novice（*n.*）新手，初学者
【近】	originality，newness，freshness
offspring	['ɔfspriŋ]
【释】	*n.* 子女；子孙，后代；产物
【例】	Its fitness，measured as the number of *offspring* produced that survive into the next generation，must be increased as the result of deception.
【近】	progeny，children，litter
outbreak	['autbreik]
【释】	*n.* 突然发生；爆发；暴动；骚扰；反抗
【例】	In the fifteen years prior to the *outbreak* of the War for Independence in 1775，more than 200,000 immigrants arrived on North American shores.
【衍】	outcry（*n.*）大声疾呼
【近】	eruption，outburst，occurrence
painstaking	['peinsteikiŋ]
【释】	*adj.* (不辞)劳苦的，费力的
【例】	Panel painting，common in thirteenth- and fourteenth-century Europe，involved a *painstaking*，laborious process.
patron	['peitrən]
【释】	*n.* 赞助人；主顾
【例】	She remains the greatest *patron* of art of the twentieth century.
【衍】	patronage（*n.*）赞助
【近】	supporter，benefactor
perishable	['periʃəbl]
【释】	*adj.* 易腐败的；脆弱的

Unit 8

【例】 What is perhaps worse, most organic materials are *perishable*.

【近】 unpreserved

pile [pail]

【释】 *v.* 堆（up on）；积蓄（up）；堆积

【例】 She patiently rips up plants and other vegetation and *piles* it in layers until satisfied.

【衍】 piled（*adj.*）有细毛的

【近】 mound, heap, stack

plunge [plʌndʒ]

【释】 *v.* 跳进，掉进，钻进（into）

【例】 With the continued rise in sea level, more ice would *plunge* into the ocean, causing sea levels to rise even higher.

【近】 force, throw, push, fall

potash ['pɒtæʃ]

【释】 *n.* 碳酸钾

【例】 In North America, *potash* making quickly became an adjunct to the clearing of land for agriculture.

prejudice ['predʒudis]

【释】 *n.* 偏见，成见；歧视

【例】 Dr. King never forgot the community spirit he had known as a child, nor did he forget the racial *prejudice*.

【衍】 prejudiced（*adj.*）

【近】 unfairness, injustice, discrimination

probe [prəub]

【释】 *v.* (用探针)探查；探索

【例】 Hummingbirds have stiletto like bills to *probe* the deepest nectar-bearing flowers.

【近】 search, explore, investigate

proponent [prə'pəunənt]

【释】 *n.* 支持者；主张者；辩护者（[*opp.*] opponent）

【例】 Charles Lindbergh visited the Soviet Union in 1938 with his wife, Anne—herself a pilot and gifted *proponent* of aviation.

【近】 advocator, supporter, fan, promoter

pull	[pul]
【释】	***v.* 拉，拖，牵，拽（[*opp.*] push)**
【例】	By the start of the nineteenth century, glassmakers learned how to make longer, stronger fibers by ***pulling*** them from molten glass with a hot glass tube.
【近】	drag, draw, haul
radical	['rædikəl]
【释】	① ***adj.* 激烈的；彻底的**
【例】	The American Revolution was not a revolution in the sense of a ***radical*** or total change.
【衍】	radically (*adv.*)
【近】	fundamental, essential, major
【释】	② ***adj.* 激进的**
【例】	Understandably she is ***radical*** in her views about her country, but I get on fine with her, especially as I can talk to her in her own language.
【衍】	radicalism (*n.*); radically (*adv.*); radicalize (*v.*); radicalness (*n.*)
【近】	extreme, revolutionary
realism	['riəlizəm]
【释】	***n.* 现实主义，现实性**
【例】	The economic depression in the late-nineteenth-century United States contributed significantly to a growing movement in literature toward ***realism*** and naturalism.
【衍】	realist (*n.*); reality (*n.*) 真实，现实；realistic (*adj.*); realistically (*adv.*)
【近】	pragmatism
recycle	[riː'saikl]
【释】	***v. & n.* (使)再循环；(使废物回收后)反复利用**
【例】	For the most part, the remains of organisms are ***recycled*** in the earth, which is fortunate because otherwise soil and water would soon become depleted of essential nutrients.
【衍】	recycling (*adj.*); recyclable (*adj.*)
【近】	reprocess, reuse
reign	[rein]
【释】	***n. & v.* 统治，支配**

【例】 During this time the colonial style developed, based on the architecture of the *reigns* of Queen Anne in England, and in the case of churches, on the styles of Wren and James Gibbs.

【衍】 reigning（*adj.*）统治的，起支配作用的

【近】 rule, govern, administrate

rental ['rentəl]

【释】 *adj.* 租用的　*n.* 租费

【例】 One result of rent control is a decrease in the construction of new *rental* units.

【衍】 rent（*n.*）；rentable（*adj.*）；renter（*n.*）

【近】 rental fee

residue ['rezidju:]

【释】 *n.* 残余，残渣

【例】 The *residues* from these explosions left huge black marks on the face of Jupiter, some of which have stretched out to form dark ribbons.

【衍】 residual（*adj.*）；residuum（[*pl.*] residua）

【近】 remainder, remains, scum

revise [ri'vaiz]

【释】 *v.* 修订，校订；修正；改变(意见等)

【例】 There may be a fault in the experiment, or the theory may have to be *revised* or rejected.

【衍】 revision（*n.*）；revisal（*n.*）

【近】 amend, modify, alter

rodent ['rəudənt]

【释】 *n.* 啮齿动物　*adj.* 咬的，嚼的

【例】 The beaver is North America's largest *rodent*.

sail [seil]

【释】 ① *v. & n.* 扬帆行驶，航行；滑行，滑翔

【例】 The picture gives us a sense of the pleasure and independence of *sailing*.

【衍】 sailboard（*n.*）帆板；sailboat（*n.*）帆船；sailing（*n.*）；sailor（*n.*）

【近】 navigate, cruise, float

【释】 ② *n.* 帆，帆形物

【例】 They can have *sails*, wings, umbrellas, flaps, hoops, scoops, legs, paddles, or whatever attachments they need to do their job in orbit.

【衍】 sailcloth (*n.*) 帆布

scout [skaut]

【释】 *n.* 侦察员；侦察；守望

【例】 A naturalist has discovered that the bee *scout* delivers her report through a complicated dance in the hive.

【近】 explore, reconnoiter, survey

segregate ['segrigeit]

【释】 *v.* 分开；分离；隔开（[*opp.*] **integrate**）

【例】 Since clays settle so slowly, they are easily *segregated* from sand and silt.

【衍】 segregation (*n.*); segregative (*adj.*)

【近】 separate, isolate, set apart

sharp [ʃɑ:p]

【释】 ① *adj.* 清晰的；轮廓鲜明的；明显的

【例】 One impact of the new household technology was to draw *sharp* dividing lines between women of different classes and regions.

【近】 well-defined, distinct, clear-cut

【释】 ② *adj.* 急剧的；激烈的；强烈的

【例】 The *sharp* postwar reactions to the style and conventions of the preceding decades created an entirely new public taste which caused Art Nouveau types of glass to fall out of favor.

【衍】 sharply (*adv.*)

【近】 severe, intense, acute

significance [sig'nifikəns]

【释】 *n.* 意义，重要(性)

【例】 The high rate of species extinctions in these environments is jolting, but it is important to recognize the *significance* of biological diversity in all ecosystems.

【衍】 significant (*adj.*); significantly (*adv.*); signify (*v.*) 表示，意味

【近】 meaning, importance, implication

smooth ［smuːð］

【释】 ① v. 把…弄平滑（光滑）；使流利，使流畅　*adj.* 平滑的，流畅的

【例】 Since surface finishes provided a pleasing appearance and also improved the durability in day-to-day use，the potter *smoothed* the exterior surface of the pot with wet hands.

【衍】 smoothen（v.）；smoothly（*adv.*）平稳地；smoothness（*n.*）；smoothy（*n.*）举止优雅的人

【近】 flat，glossy，silky

【释】 ② v. 使容易；消除（障碍等）

【例】 The ability of agriculture to *smooth* out the seasonal scarcities of wild foodstuffs had major consequences for the sizes of Native American populations in New England.

spare ［spɛə］

【释】 ① v. 使某人免遭（麻烦等）

【例】 Pianists are *spared* by this particular anxiety，for the notes are already there，waiting for them，and it is the piano tuner's responsibility to tune the instrument for them.

【近】 release，do without，free

【释】 ② *adj.* 粗陋的；俭朴的

【例】 The clear，*spare*，and energetic lyrics of H. D. 's early poems，with their classical images，later became fuller，freer，and more "open" philosophic explorations of the world.

【衍】 sparely（*adv.*）；spareness（*n.*）；sparingly（*adv.*）节俭地；保守地

【近】 stark，frugal

split ［split］

【释】 v. 裂开，劈开；分离，分开　*adj.* 裂开的；分离的，分裂的

【例】 The composition of bands may change a number of times during the course of a day as individuals wander off and groups *split* or combine with other groups.

【近】 tear，rip，gash

stake ［steik］

【释】 *n.* 利害关系；风险

【例】 Holding a large *stake* in the community，they exercised power to make it prosper.

【近】	venture，bet
stiff	[stif]
【释】	*adj*. 硬的，挺的；紧绷绷的
【例】	Walking or leaping species of a similar size access the outer twigs either by snapping off and retrieving the whole branch or by clutching *stiff* branches with the feet or tail and plucking food with their hands.
【衍】	stiffen（*v.*）；stiffly（*adv.*）；stiffness（*n.*）
【近】	rigid，inflexible，taut
strict	[strikt]
【释】	*adj*. 严格的；严谨的；严密的
【例】	Unlike bacteria，they are not living agents in the *strictest* sense.
【衍】	strictly（*adv.*）；strictness（*n.*）
【近】	severe，exacting，precise，stringent
substitute	['sʌbstitjuːt]
【释】	*v*. 代替，取代 *n*. 代替品，代用品
【例】	All his life Carver battled against the disposal of waste materials，and warned of the growing need to develop *substitutes* for the natural substances being used up by humans.
【衍】	substitution（*n.*）；substitutive（*adj.*）
【近】	alternate，replacement，surrogate
supernatural	[ˌsjuːpə'nætʃərəl]
【释】	*adj*. 超自然的；不可思议的；怪异的
【例】	Or the belief in the *supernatural* powers of a stone or tree may cause a sculptor to be sensitive to that material.
【衍】	supernaturalism（*n.*）超自然力，超自然主义；supernaturalist（*n.*）；supernaturally（*adv.*）
【近】	paranormal，weird，bizarre
swift	[swift]
【释】	*adj*. 飞快的，迅速的，敏捷的（[*opp.*] slow）
【例】	The White House was *swift* to deny the rumors.
【衍】	swiftly（*adv.*）；swiftness（*n.*）
【近】	speedy，fast，rapid
tap	[tæp]
【释】	① *v*. 开辟，开发

【例】 Canada's river and lakes allowed and, indeed, invited venturesome pioneers to explore the interior of the continent and, in spite of natural barriers, to *tap* its great wealth.

【衍】 taproot (*n.*) 直根；主根

【近】 exploit，mine

【释】 ② *v.* 轻打，轻敲

【例】 String players may *tap* or scrape their instruments.

【近】 knock，strike，hit

tenement ['tenimənt]

【释】 *n.* (几户合住的低级)公共住宅

【例】 Urban slums often had no sewers, garbage collection, or gas or electric lines; and *tenements* lacked both running water and central heating.

【近】 apartment building，residence，dwelling

thorny ['θɔːni]

【释】 *adj.* 多刺的，有针的；像刺的；刺丛繁茂的

【例】 Some of the tropical species are adorned with spines or ridges, imitating the *thorny* bushes or trees in which they live.

【近】 prickly，barbed，spiky

tissue ['tiʃjuː]

【释】 *n.* 组织

【例】 The nervous system is composed of many millions of nerve and glial cells, together with blood vessels and a small amount of connective *tissue*.

traditionally [trə'diʃənəli]

【释】 *adv.* 传统上，照惯例

【例】 In taking up a new life across the Atlantic, the early European settlers of the United States did not abandon the diversions with which their ancestors had *traditionally* relieved the tedium of life.

【衍】 tradition (*n.*)；traditional (*adj.*)

【近】 conventionally，customarily，habitually

trend [trend]

【释】 *n. & v.* 倾向，趋势

【例】 This may well be true, but critics respond that this very distance may also be responsible for the Academy's inability to perceive accurately authentic *trends* in the literary world.

【衍】	trendy（*adj.*）最流行的，合乎潮流的；trendiness（*n.*）
【近】	tendency，inclination，vogue
tumble	［ˈtʌmbl］
【释】	***v. & n.* 打滚，翻滚**
【例】	In the speed of its execution，the righting of a *tumbling* cat resembles a magician's trick.
【衍】	tumbledown（*adj.*）摇摇欲坠的
uniform	［ˈjuːnifɔːm］
【释】	① *adj.* 一致的，相同的
【例】	The way that seismic waves travel shows that the Earth's interior is far from *uniform*.
【衍】	uniformly（*adv.*）；uniformity（*n.*）
【近】	consistent，homogeneous，identical
【释】	② *n.* 制服
【例】	Denied Southern cotton，textile mills turned to wool for blankets and *uniforms*.
【近】	costume，garb，attire，dress
valid	［ˈvælid］
【释】	***adj.* (理由、证据等)有确实根据的，确凿的；正确的**
【例】	This definition is，of course，*valid* as far as it goes.
【衍】	validly（*adv.*）；validity（*n.*）
【近】	sound，reasonable，legitimate
vestige	［ˈvestidʒ］
【释】	***n.* 痕迹，遗迹；证据**
【例】	Most scientists believe that the great majority of craters are the ancient *vestiges* of meteorites.
【衍】	vestigial（*adj.*）发育不全的；退化的
【近】	trace，evidence，remnant
volt	［vəult］
【释】	***n.*【电】伏(特)**
【例】	The electric eel is an amazing storage battery. It can send a jolt of as much as eight hundred *volts* of electricity through the water in which it lives.
welfare	［ˈwelfɛə］
【释】	***n.* 福利(事业)；繁荣，兴隆**

【例】 Students were also trained as economists, architects, agriculturalists, social *welfare* workers, and teachers.

wreck [rek]

【释】 *n.* 失事船；残骸　　*v.* 使(船只)遇险(失事)

【例】 In 1977 a group of marine archaeologists excavating a 900-year-old *wreck* recovered engraved glassware, Greek coins, bronze kettles, and amazingly, even a plate with chicken bones.

【衍】 wreckage (*n.*)

Exercise of Unit 8

左列单词在右列中有一个同义词，请找出并在相应的位置写上正确答案。

Exercise 1:

(A) uniform	_____	release
(B) novelty	_____	originality
(C) acronym	_____	dig
(D) spare	_____	abbreviation
(E) burrow	_____	rule
(F) reign	_____	costume

Exercise 2:

(A) radical	_____	fundamental
(B) clip	_____	distribute
(C) disseminate	_____	remainder
(D) breakdown	_____	shear
(E) residue	_____	fail
(F) medicine	_____	drug

Exercise 3:

(A) commute	_____	order
(B) dictate	_____	drag
(C) kernel	_____	core
(D) innovation	_____	advance
(E) offspring	_____	travel
(F) pull	_____	progeny

Exercise 4:

(A) extinct	_____	browse
(B) layout	_____	consistent
(C) plunge	_____	outline
(D) perishable	_____	force
(E) graze	_____	died out
(F) uniform	_____	unpreserved

Exercise 5:

(A) proponent	_____	crucial
(B) trend	_____	alternate
(C) indispensable	_____	significant
(D) impact	_____	advocator
(E) critical	_____	crash
(F) substitute	_____	tendency

Exercise 6:

(A) mandate	_____	command
(B) valid	_____	navigate
(C) sail	_____	reprocess
(D) ecology	_____	prickly
(E) recycle	_____	ecosystem
(F) thorny	_____	sound

Exercise 7:
(A) excavate _____ hinder
(B) pile _____ influence
(C) coordinate _____ mound
(D) impact _____ supply
(E) interfere _____ corresponding
(F) furnish _____ dig

Exercise 8:
(A) mandate _____ promote
(B) foster _____ severe
(C) strict _____ knock
(D) probe _____ separate
(E) tap _____ permission
(F) segregate _____ search

Exercise 9:
(A) radical _____ extreme
(B) capable _____ exploit
(C) constituent _____ supporter
(D) patron _____ competent
(E) tap _____ pragmatism
(F) realism _____ component

Exercise 10:
(A) harmonious _____ antecedent
(B) ancestor _____ rigid
(C) emphasize _____ disregard
(D) neglect _____ melodious
(E) agitation _____ accentuate
(F) stiff _____ disturbance

ANSWERS:
1   D B E C F A
2   A C E B D F
3   B F C D A E
4   E F B C A D
5   C F E A D B
6   A C E F D B
7   E D B F C A
8   B C E F A D
9   A E D B F C
10   B F D A C E

Unit 9

absurd	enclose	municipal	shed
acute	episode	negotiate	silence
akin	exclusive	noxious	smug
angle	extol	olfactory	spark
arid	felt	outermost	spoil
astute	fleeting	pale	stalk
backward	fountain	payment	stimulus
beak	furniture	permanent	strikingly
blazing	giant	pilot	subterranean
breathe	guarantee	poet	supervise
burst	harness	potassium	swing
capture	highlight	preponderance	tape
cedar	hypersensitive	procedure	tension
chimpanzee	impair	proportion	thoroughly
clue	induce	pulse	title
compact	innumerable	radius	traffic
confederacy	interior	realize	trial
constitute	irony	reddish	tundra
cope	kerosene	reinforce	union
crop	lean	repair	vanish
dawn	linguistic	resin	veteran
democrat	lucrative	revival	volume
differentiate	maneuver	roll	well
dissolve	medieval	sale	wren
draft	migrate	scramble	
edge	modulate	seldom	

absurd	[əbˈsəːd]
【释】	*adj*. 不合理的；荒谬的
【例】	Don Quixote makes chivalry seem *absurd*.
【衍】	absurdly（*adv*.）；absurdity（*n*.）；absurdness（*n*.）
【近】	odd，weird，peculiar，ridiculous，silly
acute	[əˈkjuːt]
【释】	*adj*. 尖锐的；敏锐的；剧烈的
【例】	With the acceleration of industrial growth came *acute* urban crowding and accompanying social stress.
【衍】	acutely（*adv*.）；acuteness（*n*.）
【近】	sharp，severe，intense
akin	[əˈkin]
【释】	*adj*. 同样的，类似的（**be akin to...**）
【例】	Her fictive world remains strikingly *akin* to that real one reflected in the daily newspapers，the television news and talk shows，and the popular magazines of our day.
【近】	analogous，parallel，similar
angle	[ˈæŋgl]
【释】	*n*. 角
【例】	The *angles*，and sides of a polygon are equal.
【衍】	angular（*adj*.）；triangle（*n*.）三角形；rectangle（*n*.）长方形
【近】	slant，tilt，slope
arid	[ˈærid]
【释】	*adj*. 干旱的；贫瘠的，荒芜的
【例】	But the Great Basin has not always been so *arid*.
【衍】	aridity（*n*.）；aridness（*n*.）
【近】	dry，barren，infertile，sterile
astute	[əˈstjuːt]
【释】	*adj*. 机敏的，伶俐的，狡猾的
【例】	The electorate is *astute* enough to vote tactically against the Government.
【衍】	astutely（*adv*.）；astuteness（*n*.）
【近】	shrewd
backward	[ˈbækwəd]
【释】	*adv*. & *adj*. 向后地(的)，相反地(的)

【例】 Pushing slowly *backward* into the plateau, the side canyons expose new rocks, and the pattern of erosion continues.

【近】 rearward, back

beak [biːk]

【释】 *n.* (猛禽等的)嘴，喙

【例】 Kiwis smell out earthworms thanks to nostrils located at the tip of their *beaks*.

【衍】 beaked (*adj.*)

【近】 bill, mouth

blazing [ˈbleiziŋ]

【释】 *adj.* 炽烈燃烧的；灿烂的；明显的，显著的

【例】 Place far enough away, even the *blazing* Sun would become a dim point of light.

【衍】 blaze (*n.*)

【近】 burning, glowing, shining

breathe [briːð]

【释】 *v.* 呼吸；活着，生存

【例】 Nitrogen, which composes 80 percent of the air we *breathe*, usually causes a balmy feeling of well-being at this pressure.

【衍】 breath (*n.*)；breathing (*adj.*)

【近】 respire, inhale, exhale

burst [bəːst]

【释】 *v.* 破裂，迸裂；爆炸；爆发出；喷出

【例】 If the windows are shut tightly, the enormous inside pressure may cause the building to *burst*.

【近】 rupture, fracture, disintegrate

capture [ˈkæptʃə]

【释】 *v. & n.* 俘获，捕获

【例】 They can move slowly, but more often they attach the lower part of their mouth surrounded by tentacles that the animal uses to *capture* its food.

【近】 detain, arrest

cedar [ˈsiːdə]

【释】 *n.* 【植】雪松；雪松木

【例】 By 1745，New Market was opened on Second Street between Pine and *Cedar*.

chimpanzee [ˈtʃimpənˈziː]

【释】 *n.* 黑猩猩

【例】 The most striking single fact about *chimpanzees* is the flexibility of other social life，the lack of any rigid form of organization.

【近】 ape，chimp，monkey，gorilla，orangutan，primate

clue [kluː]

【释】 *n.* 线索

【例】 There are only a few *clues* in the rock record about climate in the Proterozoic era.

【近】 sign，trace，evidence

compact [ˈkɔmpækt，kəmˈpækt]

【释】 ① *adj.* 密集的；紧密的；（文体等）紧凑的，简洁的

【例】 But city dwellers also developed other pleasures，which only *compact* communities made possible.

【近】 dense，compressed

【释】 ② *v.* 把…弄紧密，把…弄结实，压实

【例】 Snow accumulating yearly in Rainier's summit craters is *compacted* and compressed into a dense form of ice called firm，a substance midway between ordinary ice and the denser crystalline ice that makes up glaciers.

【衍】 compaction（*n.*）紧密；压缩

【近】 squeeze，press

confederacy [kənˈfedərəsi]

【释】 *n.* 联盟，联邦

【衍】 The six states holding no claim to the transmontane region doubted whether a *confederacy* in which territory was so unevenly apportioned would truly prove what it claimed to be，a union of equals.

【衍】 the Confederacy（*n.*）（南北战争时的）南部同盟，南部联邦；confederate（*n.*）同盟者

【近】 federation

constitute [ˈkɔnstitjuːt]

【释】 *v.* 构成，组成

【例】	What *constitutes* an act of civil disobedience?
【近】	comprise，compose
cope	[kəup]
【释】	*v.* 善于对付；克服（困难等）（**with**）
【例】	Under certain circumstances，the human body must *cope* with gases at greater-than-normal atmospheric pressure.
crop	[krɔp]
【释】	*n.* 农作物，庄稼
【例】	River boats carried to New Orleans the corn and other *crops* of northwestern farmers，the cotton and tobacco of southwestern planters.
【近】	harvest，produce
dawn	[dɔ:n]
【释】	*n.* 黎明，拂晓；开端，发端（[*opp.*] dusk）
【例】	Perhaps the human species was driving others to extinction long before the *dawn* of history.
【衍】	dawning（*n.*）曙光
democrat	['deməkræt]
【释】	*n.* (D-)(美国)民主党党员
【例】	Both *Democrats* and Republicans maintained potent local political organizations in many cities and states.
【衍】	democratic（*adj.*）民主主义的
differentiate	[ˌdifə'renʃieit]
【释】	*v.* 使有差别，区别；划分，区分
【例】	Export merchants became *differentiated* from their importing counterparts.
【衍】	differentiation（*n.*）
【近】	distinguish，discriminate，discern，tell apart
dissolve	[di'zɔlv]
【释】	*v.* 使溶解；使分解；使分离
【例】	When seawater is frozen，the *dissolved* materials are left behind.
【衍】	dissolvable（*adj.*）；dissolvent/solvent（*n.*）溶剂
draft	[drɑ:ft]
【释】	① *adj.* (马等)拉车用的；供役使的
【例】	… *draft* animals.

【释】 ② *v.* 起草，拟(方案)；画(草图、轮廓)；为…打样；设计　　*adj.* 正在起草的

【例】 A *draft* plan has been prepared.

edge [edʒ]

【释】 *n.* 边缘，边界

【例】 The *edge* of the Pacific Ocean has been called the "Ring of Fire" because so many volcanic eruptions and earthquakes happen there.

【近】 rim, periphery, boundary

enclose [in'kləuz]

【释】 *v.* (用篱、墙等)围起，圈起，包围，围绕

【例】 Each lock is a stretch of water *enclosed* by gates at each end.

【衍】 enclosure (*n.*)

【近】 surround, encircle, encompass

episode ['episəud]

【释】 *n.* (一系列事件中的)一个事件

【例】 visual *episodes* within an unfolding epic tale of cultural coherence to Chicano identity

【近】 affair, event, occurence

exclusive [ik'sklu:siv]

【释】 *adj.* 独有的，唯一的；专有的

【例】 Such studies, as well as studies of tool use, indicate that right or left-sided dominance is not *exclusive* to modern Homo sapiens.

【衍】 exclusively (*adv.*); exclude (*v.*) 排除

extol [ik'stɔl]

【释】 *v.* (-ll-) 赞美，称赞，颂扬；吹捧

【例】 In the United States as well as in Great Britain, reformers *extolled* the virtues of handcrafted objects.

【衍】 extolment (*n.*)

【近】 praise, commend, exaggerate

felt [felt]

【释】 *n.* 毛毡；毛布；毡制品；油毛毡

【例】 Its (the piano) strings were struck by a recoiling hammer with a *felt*-padded head.

fleeting [ˈfliːtiŋ]
- 【释】 *adj*. 飞逝的；短暂的；飞跑的
- 【例】 They would not, by nature, be highly topical or political, as such publications would prove of *fleeting* interest.
- 【衍】 fleetingly (*adv*.)；fleetingness (*n*.)
- 【近】 momentary, passing, ephemeral

fountain [ˈfauntin]
- 【释】 *n*. 喷泉；人造喷泉
- 【例】 A sunken plaza, complete with gardens and *fountains*, was designed to provide access to these shops.

furniture [ˈfəːnitʃə]
- 【释】 *n*. 家具，器具
- 【例】 The *furniture* makers in those early decades of the 1600's were known as "joiners".

giant [ˈdʒaiənt]
- 【释】 *adj*. 巨大的 *n*. 巨人；巨兽
- 【例】 The largest of the *giant* gas planets, Jupiter, with a volume 1,300 times greater than Earth's, contains more than twice the mass of all the other planets combined.
- 【近】 huge, massive, gigantic, enormous

guarantee [ˌgærənˈtiː]
- 【释】 *n. & v.* 保证，担保
- 【例】 Public regulation would insure widespread access to these utilities and *guarantee* a fair price.
- 【衍】 guaranty (*n*.) 担保物；guarantor (*n*.) 保证人
- 【近】 assurance, promise, warranty

harness [ˈhɑːnis]
- 【释】 ① *n*. 马具，挽具
- 【例】 Hides by the hundreds of thousands were turned into shoes and *harness* and saddles.
- 【释】 ② *v*. 利用自然力使产生动力
- 【例】 Some scientists are working hard at how tide can be *harnessed* to produce electricity.

highlight [ˈhailait]
- 【释】 *v*. 在…上投上强光；强调，使显著

【例】 The exciting interior timber structure of the building was *highlighted* by cutting light courts through the interior.

【衍】 highlighted (*adj.*)；highlights (*n.*) 集锦（精彩会议文献）

【近】 emphasize，underline

hypersensitive [ˌhaipəˈsensitiv]

【释】 *adj.* 过敏的，过敏性的

【例】 In the *hypersensitive* response，cells undergo rapid necrosis.

【衍】 hypersensitiveness (*n.*)

【近】 touchy，oversensitive

impair [imˈpɛə]

【释】 *v.* 损害，损伤

【例】 If children are deprived of adequate food or physical and social stimulation during the early years of life，will their intelligence be permanently *impaired*?

【衍】 impairment (*n.*)

【近】 damage，harm，spoil

induce [inˈdjuːs]

【释】 *v.* 引导，导致

【例】 Its focus on decorative arts helped to *induce* United States museums and private collectors to begin collecting furniture，glass，ceramics，metalwork，and textiles in the late nineteenth and early twentieth centuries.

【衍】 inducible (*adj.*)；inducement (*n.*)

【近】 cause，bring about

innumerable [iˈnjuːmərəbl]

【释】 *adj.* 无数的，数不清的

【例】 Official documents from many regions contained *innumerable* reports of sickness that virtually incapacitated entire garrisons.

【衍】 innumerably (*adv.*)

【近】 countless，numerous，inestimable，infinite，incalculable

interior [inˈtiəriə]

【释】 *n. & adj.* 内(的)；内部(的) ([*opp.*] **exterior**)

【例】	Merchandizing establishments were，accordingly，advantageously located to port cities from which goods could be readily distributed to *interior*，settlements.
【近】	domestic，inner，inland，internal
irony	['aiərəni]
【释】	*n.* 讽刺，讥讽
【例】	The *irony* is that many officials in Washington agree in private that their policy is inconsistent.
【衍】	ironical（*adj.*）令人啼笑皆非的；ironically（*adv.*）
【近】	satire，sarcasm，paradox
kerosene	['kerəsi:n]
【释】	*n.* 煤油，火油
【例】	Crude oil could be refined into many products. For some years *kerosene* continued to be the principal one.
【近】	oil，petrol，gasoline
lean	[li:n]
【释】	*v.* (使)倾斜
【例】	Such was the dwelling on the Georgia Sea Island that sidled and *leaned* in Jupiter Lights with one of its roofless wings failing into the cellar.
【近】	bend，incline，tilt
linguistic	[liŋ'gwistik]
【释】	*adj.* 语言的；语言学的
【例】	This relationship is especially evident in *linguistic* ties.
【衍】	linguist（*n.*）语言学家；linguistics（*n.*）语言学
【近】	linguistical
lucrative	['lju:krətiv]
【释】	*adj.* 有利的，赚钱的，合算的
【例】	Contemporary Western American art has been a very popular and *lucrative* part of the art marketplace.
【衍】	lucratively（*adv.*）；lucrativeness（*n.*）
【近】	profitable，rewarding，worthwhile
maneuver	[mə'nu:və]
【释】	*v.* 调动，部署；用策略使…，用计使… *n.* 调动，部署；策动；谋略

【例】 The crossed mandibles enable the bird to exert a powerful biting force at the bill tips, which is critical for *maneuvering* them between the scales and spreading the scales apart.

【衍】 maneuverable (*adj.*) 容易操作的，有机动性的；maneuverability (*n.*) 可操作性，机动性

【近】 manipulate

medieval [ˌmediˈiːvəl]

【释】 *adj.* 中世纪的，仿中世纪的，老式的

【例】 An examination of the art of the Middle Ages tells us something about the *medieval* preoccupation with the theological doctrine.

【衍】 medievalism (*n.*) 中世纪性质，中世纪精神；medievalist (*n.*) 中世纪研究家

migrate [ˈmaigreit]

【释】 *v.* 迁移；移居（尤指移居海外）；（鸟）定期移栖；（鱼）洄游

【例】 Researchers have found that *migrating* animals use a variety of inner compasses to help them navigate.

【衍】 migrant (*n.*) 候鸟；移栖动物；移居者；migration (*n.*)；migratory (*adj.*)

【近】 transfer, travel, journey

modulate [ˈmɔdjuleit]

【释】 *v.* 调节，调整；缓和，减轻

【例】 These chemicals *modulate* the effect of potassium.

【衍】 modulation (*n.*)；module (*n.*) 组件，模块；（太空船上各个独立的）舱；modus (*n.*) 方法，方式

【近】 adapt, adjust, alter, modify

municipal [mjuːˈnisipəl]

【释】 *adj.* 市政的；地方性的；市营的

【例】 Water and sewerage systems were usually operated by *municipal* governments, but the gas and electric networks were privately owned.

【衍】 municipalism (*n.*) 市自治主义；municipalist (*n.*) 市自治主义者；市政当局；municipality (*n.*) 自治市，自治区；市政府，市政当局

Unit 9

【近】 civic, community, urban

negotiate [nɪˈɡəʊʃieɪt]
【释】 ① v. 协议，谈判，交涉
【例】 In April 1803 Napoleon Bonaparte *negotiated* the sale of the Louisiana Territory with the envoys of President Thomas Jefferson.
【衍】 negotiation (n.); negotiable (adj.) 可协商的，可谈的
【近】 discuss, confer, consult
【释】 ② v. 通过，跳过(障碍)；克服(困难等)；处理；处置
【例】 With that design they can move remarkably rapidly through the trees, swinging from branch to branch with a sureness and smoothness, often *negotiating* gaps of ten feet or more.
【近】 get past, navigate, traverse
【释】 ③ v. 使(证券、票据等)流通，转让，兑现；卖(让)与
【例】 Of the tens of thousands of ships on the ocean bottom, only a handful, less than 1 percent, contain *negotiable* treasure, such as gold and jewels.
【衍】 negotiable (adj.) 可转让的，可流通的；negotiability (n.) 流通性，可转移性，流通能力

noxious [ˈnɒkʃəs]
【释】 adj. 有害的，有毒的
【例】 The result is an increased concentration of *noxious* chemicals in the air.
【衍】 noxiously (adv.); noxiousness (n.)
【近】 harmful, toxic, poisonous

olfactory [ɒlˈfæktəri]
【释】 adj. 嗅觉器官的，嗅觉的
【例】 Armadillos are the most primitive of the edentates; their neocortex is quite small, but the *olfactory* brain is well developed and provides a keen sense of smell.
【衍】 olfaction (n.) 嗅觉作用；嗅觉

outermost [ˈaʊtəməʊst]
【释】 adj. 最外面的，最远的(普通级: outer)
【例】 The Sun's *outermost* layer begins about 10,000 miles above the visible surface and goes outward for millions of miles.

【衍】	outer（*adj.*）外的，外部的，外侧的；outdoor（*adj.*）户外的；outdoors（*adv.* & *n.*）
【近】	furthest，remotest，outmost
pale	［peil］
【释】	*adj.* 灰白的，(脸色等)苍白的；(颜色等)淡的；微暗的
【例】	The *pale*，smooth desert plain provides a perfect backdrop for spotting meteorites.
【衍】	palely（*adv.*）；paleness（*n.*）
【近】	light，soft
payment	［'peimənt］
【释】	*n.* 支付；缴纳，报偿；补偿
【例】	There would be no agonizing wait with large amounts of capital tied up，and creditors impatient for *payment*.
【近】	sum，expense，recompense
permanent	［'pəːmənənt］
【释】	*adj.* 永久的，不变的
【例】	They developed *permanent* squints from peering into the glaring sunlight of the treeless plains.
【衍】	permanently（*adv.*）
【近】	enduring，lasting，stable，unending
pilot	［'pailət］
【释】	*n.* 飞行员；领航员
【例】	A *pilot* cannot fly a plane by sight alone.
poet	［'pəuit］
【释】	*n.* 诗人
【例】	From that time on her poetry has been read with interest by succeeding generations of *poets* and readers.
【衍】	poem（*n.*）诗；poetry（*n.*）；poetic（*adj.*）
potassium	［pə'tæsjəm］
【释】	*n.* 钾
【例】	Potash (the old name for *potassium* carbonate) is one of the two.
preponder-ance	［pri'pɔndərəns］
【释】	*n.* (数量、重量、力量、影响、重要性上的)优势；优越

【例】 The New World butterflies make up the ***preponderance*** of examples because they are the most familiar species.

【近】 prevalence，predominance

procedure [prə'siːdʒə]

【释】 ***n.*** 工序，过程，步骤

【例】 Proponents of the worksheet ***procedure*** believe that it will yield optimal，that is，the best decisions.

【近】 process，practice，method

proportion [prə'pɔːʃən]

【释】 ***n.*** 比，比率；【数】比例

【例】 They generally take high ***proportions*** of each year's crop of young.

【衍】 proportioned（*adj.*）

【近】 amount，part，share，section

pulse [pʌls]

【释】 ***n.*** 脉搏；有节奏的跳动，拍子，节拍

【例】 All living cells sent out tiny ***pulses*** of electricity.

【衍】 pulser（*n.*）脉冲发生器

【近】 beat，throb，rhythm，pulsate

radius ['reidjəs]

【释】 ***n.*** 半径；半径范围

【例】 In 1850，the borders of Boston lay scarcely two miles from the old business district；by the turn of the century the ***radius*** extended ten miles.

realize ['riəlaiz]

【释】 ① ***v.*** 领悟，了解，体会

【例】 Abigail Adams welcomed every advance for women and foresaw more than could be ***realized*** in her lifetime.

【衍】 realizable（*adj.*）；realization（*n.*）；realized（*adj.*）

【近】 understand，comprehend，apprehend

【释】 ② ***v.*** 实现，实行(希望、计划等)

【例】 Proponents believed that if simple design，high-quality materials，and honest construction were ***realized*** in the home and its appointment，then the occupants would enjoy moral and therapeutic effects.

【衍】 realizable（*adj.*）；realization（*n.*）；realized（*adj.*）

Unit 9

【近】 fulfill，accomplish，carry out

reddish ['rediʃ]

【释】 *adj*. 带红色的，淡红的，微红的

【例】 Because of their pink color，they often appear as a solid *reddish* mass when viewed from a ship or from the air.

【衍】 reddishness（*n.*）

【近】 ruddy，rosy

reinforce [ˌriːin'fɔːs]

【释】 *v.* 增强，加固；补充，增加

【例】 This first phase of mass-scale suburbanization was *reinforced* by the simultaneous emergence of the urban Middle class.

【衍】 reinforcement（*n.*）

【近】 strengthen，support

repair [ri'pɛə]

【释】 ① *v. & n.* 修理，修补

【例】 Once fired，the pots were allowed to cool slowly，and small cracks were *repaired* before they were ready for use.

【衍】 repairable

【近】 mend，revamp

【释】 ② *n.*（健康等的）恢复

【例】 Trees cannot heal：they make no *repairs*.

【近】 recover

resin ['rezin]

【释】 *n.* 树脂；松脂；树脂状沉淀物

【例】 The first synthetic plastic was a thermosetting *resin* called ebonite，patented in 1843.

【衍】 resinate（*v.*）；resinoid（*adj. & n.*）树脂状的；树脂状物质；resinous（*adj.*）含树脂的

revival [ri'vaivəl]

【释】 *n.* 苏醒；更生，复活；复兴

【例】 The Hispanic crafts *revival* was confined to a much shorter period of time，less than 20 years.

【衍】 revivalism（*n.*）；revive（*v.*）；revivify（*v.*）

【近】 revitalization，renewal，restoration

roll	[rəul]
【释】	① *v.* 滚转，旋转
【例】	When you first drift off into slumber，your eyes will ***roll*** about a bit.
【衍】	roller（*n.*）滚转物；滚筒
【近】	rotate，turn round，revolve
【释】	② *v.* 包卷，卷拢，卷捆，卷起
【例】	Later the food passes into the second stomach or reticulum where it is ***rolled*** into little balls or cuds.
【释】	③ *v.* 波动，起伏
【例】	In 1979 Santa Monica's municipal government ordered landlords to ***roll*** back their rents to the levels charged in 1978.
sale	[seil]
【释】	*n.* 卖，出售；销量，销售额
【例】	Now a stage full of happy and earnest oratorio singers must represent considerable potential ticket ***sales***，and if this is true，it does not make much difference what work the singers select to perform.
【衍】	saleable（*adj.*）适于销售的；salesperson（*n.*）售货员，推销员
【近】	transaction，trade，retailing
scramble	['skræmbl]
【释】	① *v. & n.* 爬上去，攀登；攀缘
【例】	Small size makes it easy to ***scramble*** among twigs and branches in the canopy for insects，flowers，or fruit.
【衍】	scrambler（*n.*）爬行者；攀缘者
【近】	climb，clamber，crawl
【释】	② *v.* 拼凑
【例】	With spontaneous irreverence，satire rearranges perspectives，***scrambles*** familiar objects into incongruous juxtaposition，and speaks in a personal idiom instead of abstract platitude.
【衍】	scrambler（*n.*）扰频器；scrambling（*n.*）不规则性
【近】	mess up，jumble，mix up
seldom	['seldəm]
【释】	*adv. & adj.* 不常(的)；很少(的)；难得(的)（[*opp.*] **often**）

【例】 The speed of most small migrating birds *seldom* exceeds 30 miles per hour.

【近】 rarely，infrequently，hardly ever

shed [ʃed]

【释】 ① *v.* 脱落；脱换；脱毛

【例】 The human body，which consists of about 60 trillion living cells，*sheds* exposed skin at a rate of 50 million cells a day.

【衍】 shedder（*n.*）脱落者；脱壳期的虾（蟹）；shedding （*n.*）脱落，蜕落

【近】 discard，get rid of，cast

【释】 ② *n.* 小屋；棚屋；堆房；库房

【例】 "The flow of industry has passed and left idle the loom in the attic，the soap kettle in the *shed*，" Ellen Richards wrote in 1908.

【近】 hut，shack，tool shed

silence ['sailəns]

【释】 *n.* 沉默，无言；无表示；无声，沉静，肃静，寂静

【例】 With such techniques，including the use of thin pain and clear colors to emphasize a feeling of mystical *silence* and space，she achieved an abstract simplicity in her paintings.

【衍】 silent（*adj.*）

【近】 quiet，stillness，hush

smug [smʌg]

【释】 *adj.* 沾沾自喜的，自以为是的

【例】 Gopher Prairie is a town of 3,000 inhabitants，*smug*，dull people whose one idea is to get on materially.

【衍】 smugly（*adv.*）；smugness（*n.*）；smuggle（*v.*）走私，夹带，偷偷拿

【近】 self-satisfied，arrogant，conceited

spark [spɑːk]

【释】 ① *n.* 火花；火星

【例】 As the air shot through the furnace，the bubbling metal would erupt in showers of *sparks*.

【衍】 sparkle（*v.*）发火花，闪耀；sparkly（*adj.*）闪耀的；sparking（*n.*）打火花

【近】　flash，flicker，glimmer

【释】　② *v.* 鼓舞，激励

【例】　However，much of this interest has been *sparked* by sweeping claims that the food supply is a unsafe or inadequate in meeting nutritional needs.

【衍】　sparkplug（*v.*）倡导；激励

【近】　generate，inspire，trigger

spoil ［spɔil］

【释】　*v.* 损坏，弄坏，糟蹋；变坏，腐败

【例】　When there is a power failure，people grope about in flickering candlelight，cars hesitate in the streets because there are no traffic lights to guide them，and food *spoils* in silent refrigerator.

【衍】　spoilage（*n.*）；spoiler（*n.*）；spoiling（*n.*）

【近】　ruin，blight，decay

stalk ［stɔːk］

【释】　*n.* 茎，柄，秆，轴

【例】　Their *stalks* and branches also act as screens to keep the wind from sweeping great drifts of sand along the surface.

【衍】　stalky（*adj.*）有茎的，似茎的

【近】　stem，trunk，twig

stimulus ［'stimjuləs］

【释】　*n.* 刺激；刺激物；促进因素

【例】　Satire has lived because readers appreciated refreshing *stimulus*，an irreverent reminder that they live in a world of platitudinous thinking，cheap moralizing，and foolish philosophy.

【衍】　stimulate（*v.*）；stimulation（*n.*）；stimuli（*n.* stimulus 的复数形式）

【近】　incentive，spur，motivation

strikingly ［'straikiŋli］

【释】　*adv.* 显著地，明显地；触目地，惊人地

【例】　A complete lichen is *strikingly* different from its separated partners in both appearance and biochemistry.

【衍】　striking（*adj.*）

【近】　markedly，conspicuously，outstandingly

subterranean [ˌsʌbtəˈreiniən]
【释】 *adj.* 地下的，地中的
【例】 Separate *subterranean* rooms in these pueblos—known as kivas or chapels—w· set aside for religious ceremonials.
【衍】 subterraneanly（*adv.*
【近】 underground，cavernous

supervise [ˈsjuːpəvaiz]
【释】 *v.* 监督；管理
【例】 For nearly 20 years，Julia Morgan *supervised* virtually every detail of erecting and furnishing Hearst's 144 room pleasure park.
【衍】 supervisor（*n.*）监督人，管理人；supervisorship（*n.*）管理人的职位
【近】 manage，run，take charge of

swing [swiŋ]
【释】 ① *v. & n.* 摇摆，摇动，(往复)摇荡
【例】 They move by brachiation，by *swinging* like pendulums from branch to branch.
【衍】 swinger（*n.*）
【近】 move backward and forward，sway，dangle
【释】 ② *n.* 摇摆舞音乐
【例】 However，by the late 1940's，commercially recorded Cajun music had begun to lose its individual character in favor of new sounds heavily influenced by hillbilly music and western *swing*.

tape [teip]
【释】 *n.* 磁带；狭带
【例】 The oceanic crust thus serves as a magnetic *tape* recording of the history of the geomagnetic field that can be dated independently: the width of the stripes indicates the rate of the sea-floor spreading.
【近】 ribbon，record，cassette

tension [ˈtenʃən]
【释】 ① *n.* 张力，拉力，牵力
【例】 The same forces that create surface *tension* in any sample of water rare responsible for the maintenance of these

unbroken columns of water.

【衍】 tensional（*adj.*）；tensionless（*adj.*）

【近】 tightness，tautness，stiffness

【释】 ② *n.*（精神、局势等）紧张（［*opp.*］relief）

【例】 Expressive leaders are less concerned with the overall goals of the group than with providing emotional support to group members and attempting to minimize *tension* and conflict among them.

【衍】 tensional（*adj.*）；tensionless（*adj.*）

【近】 friction，stress，strain

thoroughly ［'θʌrəli］

【释】 *adv.* 彻底地，全面地

【例】 Great artists are those who are so *thoroughly* at home in the language of music that they can enjoy performing works written in any century.

【衍】 thorough（*adj.*）；thoroughness（*n.*）

【近】 comprehensively，completely，absolutely

title ［'taitl］

【释】 ① *n.* 标题，题目，题；篇名，书名

【例】 Her productivity since then has been prodigious, accumulating in less than two decades to nearly thirty *titles*, including novels，collections of short stories and verse，plays and literary criticism.

【衍】 titled（*adj.*）有爵位的，有贵族头衔的；entitle（*v.*）给…定名；subtitle（*n.*）副题；说明对白的字幕

【近】 heading，name

【释】 ② *n.*【律】土地财产所有权；地契

【例】 It permitted access to public western lands on increasingly easy terms，culminating in the Homestead Act of 1862，by which *title* to land could be claimed on the basis of residence alone.

【衍】 entitle（*v.*）使…有资格（做某事）；给予…权利（资格）

【近】 ownership，entitlement，deed

traffic ［'træfik］

【释】 *n.* 交通，运输；交往；交流

【例】 Skyscrapers also interfere with television reception，block bird flyways，and obstruct air *traffic*.

【衍】 trafficable（*adj.*）可通行的
【近】 transfer，interchange，passage

trial ['traiəl]
【释】 ① *n.* 考验；磨难
【例】 This community becomes a testing ground of personality, a place where the raw material of experience is shaped by imagination and where the joys and *trials* of being human are both sung and judged.
【近】 ordeal，hardship，suffering
【释】 ② *n.* 试验；(人或物的)试用；试车
【例】 All but one member of each group had been instructed to agree upon a wrong answer for a majority of the *trials*.
【近】 experiment，tryout，testing
【释】 ③ *n.* 审问；审判
【例】 Thus，the typical court case begins in a *trial* court—a court of general jurisdiction—in the state or federal system.
【近】 tribunal，judgment，court case

tundra ['tʌndrə]
【释】 *n.* 冻土带，寒漠
【例】 The woolly mammoth，a long-haired rhinoceros，and other mammals have been periodically exposed in the *tundra* of Siberia，the hair and red flesh still frozen in cold storage.

union ['juːnjən]
【释】 *n.* 工会
【例】 Classes for adult immigrants were sponsored by public schools，corporations，*unions*，churches，settlement houses，and other agencies.

vanish ['væniʃ]
【释】 *v.* 消失不见
【例】 If too much volcanic heat is discharged，the crater's ice pack will melt away entirely and the caves will *vanish* along with the snows of yesteryear.
【近】 disappear，fade away，peter out

veteran ['vetərən]
【释】 *n.* 复员军人，退役军人

【例】	They included Civil War *veterans* and freed slaves，Irish and German immigrants，Mormons and atheists，and Chinese.
volume	['vɔljuːm]
【释】	*n.* 体积；容积
【例】	During ascent from a depth of 10 meters，the *volume* of air in the lungs will double because the air pressure at the surface is only half of what it was at 10 meters.
【近】	capacity
well	[wel]
【释】	① *v.* (使)涌出，(使)喷出，(使)流出
【例】	Periodically，molten material *wells* out of the Earth's interior to invade the surface layers or to flow onto the surface itself.
【衍】	well (*n.*) 泉水；源头，来源
【近】	emit，erupt，surge，issue
【释】	② *n.* 井；油井
【例】	Farm women had to haul large quantities of water into the house from *wells* or pumps for every purpose.
wren	[ren]
【释】	*n.* 鹪鹩(北美地区褐色的小鸟)
【例】	When we were just about to get the last tree stump out，we discovered that a *wren* had started nesting in it，and that held us up for another six weeks.
【近】	sparrow

Exercise of Unit 9

左列单词在右列中有一个同义词，请找出并在相应的位置写上正确答案。

Exercise 1:

(A) well _____ ruin
(B) spoil _____ rim
(C) angle _____ slant
(D) akin _____ emit
(E) edge _____ analogous
(F) backward _____ rearward

Exercise 2:

(A) supervise _____ manage
(B) beak _____ surround
(C) procedure _____ bill
(D) breathe _____ process
(E) enclose _____ amount
(F) proportion _____ respire

Exercise 3:

(A) permanent _____ profitable
(B) vanish _____ disappear
(C) lucrative _____ quiet
(D) astute _____ stem
(E) silence _____ shrewd
(F) stalk _____ enduring

Exercise 4:

(A) chimpanzee _____ sharp
(B) thoroughly _____ momentary
(C) compact _____ ape
(D) induce _____ comprehensivel
(E) fleeting _____ squeeze
(F) acute _____ cause

Exercise 5:

(A) spark _____ climb
(B) burst _____ oil
(C) outermost _____ hut
(D) scramble _____ furthest
(E) shed _____ rupture
(F) kerosene _____ flash

Exercise 6:

(A) episode _____ distinguish
(B) innumerable _____ countless
(C) scramble _____ mess up
(D) seldom _____ rarely
(E) irony _____ satire
(F) differentiate _____ affair

Exercise 7:

(A) maneuver _____ prevalence
(B) reddish _____ civic
(C) highlight _____ emphasize
(D) compact _____ ruddy
(E) preponderance _____ manipulate
(F) municipal _____ dense

Exercise 8:

(A) reinforce _____ strengthen
(B) shed _____ discard
(C) migrate _____ transfer
(D) giant _____ underground
(E) subterranean _____ ribbon
(F) tape _____ huge

Exercise 9:

(A) tension _____ domestic
(B) extol _____ detain
(C) interior _____ friction
(D) volume _____ praise
(E) arid _____ dry
(F) capture _____ capacity

Exercise 10:

(A) negotiate _____ assurance
(B) stimulus _____ odd
(C) guarantee _____ adapt
(D) modulate _____ comprise
(E) constitute _____ discuss
(F) absurd _____ incentive

ANSWERS:

1	B E C A D F
2	A E B C F D
3	C B E F D A
4	F E A B C D
5	D F E C B A
6	F B C D E A
7	E F C B A D
8	A B C E F D
9	C F A B E D
10	C F D E A B

Unit 10

abundant	encompass	mural	sheer
adapt	epoch	neighbor	silica
alarm	execute	nuclear	snake
anonymous	extract	onset	sparse
arise	fertile	outgoing	sponge
atheist	flexible	pamphlet	stamp
bacteria	fraction	peak	sting
beam	fuse	perpetuate	stringent
bleak	gibbon	pine	subtle
breed	gulf	poison	supplant
bust	harsh	potent	switch
carbon	hinge	prerequisite	target
ceiling	hypothesis	proceed	tentacle
chip	impart	propose	thought
clumsy	inevitable	pump	toad
comparative	insert	raft	tragedy
confer	interpret	realm	triangle
constitution	irresistible	reduction	tune
copper	kettle	reject	unique
crouch	leap	repeat	vantage
dazzling	lip	resist	via
demolish	lumber	revolutionary	vulnerable
diffuse	manifestation	romance	whale
distant	medium	salinity	wrought
drain	mild	scrape	
edible	moisture	select	

abundant [əˈbʌndənt]
【释】 *adj*. 丰富的，大量的
【例】 Women also specialized in the gathering of the *abundant* shellfish that lived closer to shore.
【衍】 abundantly（*adv*.）；abundance（*n*.）
【近】 ample，plentiful，sufficient，adequate

adapt [əˈdæpt]
【释】 *v*. 使适应，使适合
【例】 Bloodhounds are biologically *adapted* to trailing their prey.
【衍】 adaptable（*adj*.）；adaptability（*n*.）；adaptive（*adj*.）；adaptation（*n*.）
【近】 accommodate，acclimatize

alarm [əˈlɑːm]
【释】 *n*. 警报；恐慌
【例】 Fire ants also make use of an *alarm* pheromone to alert workers to an emergency.
【衍】 alarming（*adj*.）；alarmingly（*adv*.）；alarmism（*n*.）危言耸听；谎报军情

anonymous [əˈnɒniməs]
【释】 *adj*. 匿名的；无名的
【例】 The terminology by which artists were described at the time suggests their status: "limner" was actually applied to the *anonymous* portrait painter up to the 1760's: "winter" characterized anyone who could paint a flat surface.
【衍】 anonym（*n*.）匿名（作）者；anonymity（*n*.）匿名；无名；anonymously（*adv*.）
【近】 indistinctive，undistinguished，uncharacterized

arise [əˈraiz]
【释】 *v*. 出现；发生
【例】 The difficulty *arises* in other technical matters.
【近】 occur，emerge

atheist [ˈeiθiist]
【释】 *n*. 无神论者；不信神的人
【衍】 atheistic(al)（*adj*.）

bacteria [bæk'tiəriə]
【释】 *n.* [*pl.*] ([*sing.*] bacterium) 细菌
【例】 Soft，fleshy structures are quickly destroyed by predators decayed by *bacteria*.
【衍】 bacterial (*adj.*)
【近】 germs，microbes，microorganisms

beam [biːm]
【释】 *n.* (光线的)束，道，柱；波束，射束
【例】 In one second a *beam* of light travels 1,860,000 miles, nearly 300,000 kilometers, or seven times around the Earth.
【衍】 beaming (*adj.*)
【近】 ray

bleak [bliːk]
【释】 *adj.* 风吹雨打的，无遮蔽的
【例】 The Aleutian Islands pursue their *bleak* and windswept course in a long arc that encloses the Bering Sea.
【近】 unsheltered，windswept

breed [briːd]
【释】 *v.* 繁殖；育种
【例】 Insects' lives are very short and they have many enemies，but they must survive long enough to *breed* and perpetuate their kind.
【衍】 breeder (*n.*)
【近】 raise，rear

bust [bʌst]
【释】 *n.* 半身像，胸像
【例】 A few marble memorials with carved *busts*, urns, or other decorations were produced in England.

carbon ['kɑːbən]
【释】 *n.* 碳
【例】 Many of the more important air pollutants，such as sulfur oxides，*carbon* monoxide，and nitrogen oxides，are found in nature.
【衍】 carbonate (*n.*) 使碳化；carbohydrate (*n.*) 碳水化合物；carbonaceous (*adj.*) 碳质的，含碳的

ceiling	[ˈsiːliŋ]
【释】	*n.* 天花板，顶板
【例】	Sometimes, as the writhing, twisting funnel passes over a house, the walls and *ceiling* burst apart as if a bomb had gone off inside.
chip	[tʃip]
【释】	*v.* 削，凿，刻
【例】	Stone Age hand axes and hatchets were made from stones that were carefully *chipped* away to form sharp cutting edges.
【近】	carve, cut, whittle, hew
clumsy	[ˈklʌmzi]
【释】	*adj.* 笨拙的；愚笨的
【例】	The phlogiston theory, always *clumsy*, became suspect, eventually fell into scientific disrepute, and was replaced by new ideas.
【衍】	clumsily (*adv.*); clumsiness (*n.*)
【近】	awkward, inept
comparative	[kəmˈpærətiv]
【释】	*adj.* 相当的，还可以的
【例】	Still modern archaeology, by applying appropriate techniques and *comparative* methods, aided by a few lucky finds from peat bogs, deserts, and frozen soils, is able to fill up a good deal of the gap.
【衍】	comparatively (*adv.*)
【近】	relative, relevant
confer	[kənˈfəː]
【释】	*v.* 授予，颁予(称号、学位等)
【例】	In the family, traditional cultural patterns *confer* leadership on one or both of the parents.
【近】	bestow, grand
constitution	[ˌkɔnstiˈtjuːʃən]
【释】	*n.* 宪法；政体
【例】	The king was forced to adopt a new *constitution* which reduced his powers.
【衍】	constitutional (*adj.*)

copper [ˈkɔpə]

【释】 *n.* 铜

【例】 In addition，depending on the locality，other resources may be accessible: shells，horns，gold，*copper*，and silver.

crouch [ˈkrautʃ]

【释】 *v. & n.* 蹲下；蜷着

【例】 They walked in a *crouch*，each bent over close to the ground.

【近】 squat，duck，bend

dazzling [ˈdæzliŋ]

【释】 *adj.* 晃眼睛的，灿烂的

【例】 He gave Alberg a *dazzling* smile.

【衍】 dazzle（*v.*）；dazzlingly（*adv.*）

【近】 dizzying，stunning，shining

demolish [diˈmɔliʃ]

【释】 *v.* 拆毁(建筑物等)；毁坏，破坏(组织等)

【例】 Eruptions at glaciated volcanoes typically destroy ice fields，as they did in 1980 when 70 percent of Mount Saint Helens ice cover was *demolished*.

【衍】 demolishment（*n.*）

【近】 annihilate，destroy，ruin

diffuse [diˈfjuːz]

【释】 *v.* 扩散；渗出

【例】 A gas forms no free surface but tends to *diffuse* throughout the space available.

【衍】 diffused（*adj.*）；diffusedly（*adv.*）；diffuseness（*n.*）

【近】 disperse，spread

distant [ˈdistənt]

【释】 *adj.* 远的，远方的，远离的

【例】 The most *distant* luminous objects seen by telescopes are probably ten thousand million light years away.

【衍】 distantly（*adj.*）；distance（*n.*）

【近】 remote

drain [drein]

【释】 *v.* 排去(水等液体) *n.* 排水渠

【例】	After a boat enters the lock，water is let in or ***drained*** out until it reaches approximately the same level as the water ahead.
【衍】	drainage（*n.*）下水道；排水设备，排水系统
【近】	ditch，sewerage

edible ['edibl]

【释】	***adj.*** 适合食用的，可以吃的（[*opp.*] poisonous）
【例】	At one time，they had been forced to roam the forests and plains of the Earth in search of wild game and ***edible*** plants.
【衍】	edibility（*n.*）

encompass [in'kʌmpəs]

【释】	***v.*** 包含
【例】	The term "art deco" has come to ***encompass*** three distinct but related design trends of the 1920's and 1930's.
【近】	include，enclose，cover

epoch ['epək,'i:pɔk]

【释】	***n.*** 纪元，时代；时期
【例】	The year 1850 may be considered the beginning of a new ***epoch*** in American art.
【衍】	epochal（*adj.*）
【近】	era，period，eon

execute ['eksikju:t]

【释】	***v.*** 执行；履行；贯彻，完成
【例】	Once again an original portrait became a luxury, commissioned by the wealthy and ***executed*** by the professional.
【衍】	executive（*n.* & *adj.*）行政官（的）；总经理（的）；execution（*n.*）实行，履行
【近】	carry out，perform，implement，accomplish

extract [ik'strækt]

【释】	***v.*** 分离出，提取
【例】	Thousands of tons were ***extracted*** before 1875，when it was first noticed that the tar contained fossil remains.
【衍】	extractable（*adj.*）；extraction（*n.*）
【近】	remove，get，obtain

fertile ['fəːtil]

【释】① *adj*. 肥沃的，丰饶的；多产的，丰富的（of；in）（[*opp*.] sterile）

【例】New York and Philadelphia，by contrast，served a rich and *fertile* hinterland laced with navigable watercourses.

【近】productive，fruitful，prolific

【释】② *adj*. 能生育的，有繁殖力的；已受孕(受精)的

【例】Sterilization is only suitable for the woman who is certain that she will not want to have another child since the operation cannot be reversed to make her *fertile* again.

【衍】fertilize（*v*.）使受孕（受精）；fertilizer（*n*.）肥料（特指化学肥料）

flexible ['fleksəbl]

【释】*adj*. 灵活的

【例】Perhaps most important，the Sumerians adapted writing into a *flexible* tool of communication.

【衍】flex（*n*. & *v*.）弯曲，折曲；flexibly（*adv*.）；flexibility（*n*.）机动性，灵活性

【近】adaptable，accommodating

fraction ['frækʃən]

【释】*n*. 小部分；碎片；片断

【例】Only a small *fraction* of all the organisms that have ever lived are preserved as fossils.

【衍】fractional（*adj*.）

【近】part，portion

fuse [fjuːz]

【释】*v*. 熔合

【例】The resulting mass was further heated to *fuse* the mass into what was called potash.

【衍】fusion（*n*.）

【近】blend，combine，mingle

gibbon ['gibən]

【释】*n*. 长臂猿

【例】There are five kinds of apes in the world today. Two of them—*gibbons* and siamangs are true swingers.

gulf [gʌlf]

【释】 *n.* 鸿沟；分歧，隔阂

【例】 The intimacy of marriage that was common in earlier periods was rent, and a *gulf* that at times seemed unbridgeable was created between husbands and wives.

【近】 gap, rent

harsh [hɑːʃ]

【释】 *adj.* 粗糙的；荒芜的，不毛的

【例】 In the *harsh* conditions of the tundra, lichens and a few flowering plants all hug the ground for shelter from icy winds.

【衍】 harshness (*n.*); harshly (*adv.*)

hinge [hindʒ]

【释】 *v.* 看…而定，以…为转移（on; upon）

【例】 Industrial growth *hinged* on several economic factors.

【近】 depend

hypothesis [hai'pɔθisis]

【释】 *n.* ([*pl.*] -ses) 假设；假说，【逻】前提

【例】 In a way, any *hypothesis* is a leap into the unknown.

【衍】 hypothesize (*v.*) 假定，猜测

【近】 theory, premise, assumption

impart [im'pɑːt]

【释】 *v.* 告诉，通知（to）；给予，把…分给，传授（to）

【例】 But parents rarely encourage this instinctive attraction by *imparting* a knowledge of nature to their children.

【衍】 impartation (*n.*)

【近】 convey, inform, tell

inevitable [in'evitəbl]

【释】 *adj.* 不可避免的，不可逃避的；必然的

【例】 The defeat had *inevitable* consequences for British policy.

【衍】 inevitably (*adv.*)

【近】 unavoidable

insert [in'səːt]

【释】 *v.* 插进，夹入

【例】 If we were randomly *inserted* into the cosmos, the chance that we would find ourselves on or near a planet would be less than one in a billion trillion trillion.

【衍】 insertion（n.）

interpret [inˈtəːprit]

【释】 **v. 理解，解释；翻译**

【例】 These criteria were *interpreted* in a variety of styles，ranging from rational and geometric to romantic or naturalistic.

【衍】 interpretation（n.）

【近】 understand，construe

irresistible [ˌiriˈzistəbl]

【释】 **adj. 不可抗拒的**

【例】 At the same time they（orchards）have made themselves *irresistible* to collectors.

【衍】 resist（v.）

【近】 appealing，inviting，attractive

kettle [ˈketl]

【释】 **n.（烧水用的）水壶，水锅**

【例】 The solution draining from the bawl was boiled down in iron *kettles*.

【近】 pot，flask，jug

leap [liːp]

【释】 **n. & v. 跳跃；飞跃，跃进；跳跃（的高度[距离]）**

【例】 In a way，any hypothesis is a *leap* into the unknown.

【衍】 leaper（n.）；leaping（adj. & n.）；leapfrog（n.）跳背游戏；蛙跳（游戏）

【近】 jump，bound，hurdle

lip [lip]

【释】 **n. 嘴唇；唇状物**

【例】 And they all use the player's *lips* to produce the basic sound.

【近】 rim，edge，brim

lumber [ˈlʌmbə]

【释】 **n. 木材，木料，方料；（英国）原木**

【例】 More *lumber* is produced from these trees than from any other kind of tree in North America.

【衍】 lumberer（n.）伐木人；lumbering（n.）木材业；lumberyard（n.）木材堆置场

【近】 wood，timber

manifestation [ˌmænifes'teiʃən]

【释】 *n.* 表现，表示；显现

【例】 The railroad could be and was a despoiler of nature；furthermore，in its *manifestation* of speed and noise，it might be a despoiler of human nature as well.

【衍】 manifesto（*n.*）（[*pl.*] manifesto(e)s)宣言，声明；告示，布告

【近】 demonstration，expression，appearance

medium ['miːdjəm]

【释】 *n.* 媒介；（常作 [*pl.*]）宣传工具；传播媒介；手段，方法

【例】 Traditionally，television has been a *medium* of the masses.

【衍】 media（*n.*）媒体，传播媒介(指报刊、广播、电视等)

【近】 vehicle，means，channel

mild [maild]

【释】 *adj.* 温和的，温良的，轻微的；适当的

【例】 The southwestern coastal region has a humid *mild* marine climate.

【衍】 mildly（*adv.*）适度地，温和地，柔和地

【近】 gentle，kind，pleasant

moisture ['mɔistʃə]

【释】 *n.* 湿气，水分，潮湿；湿度；（空气中的)水蒸气；泪

【例】 Some cacti，like the saguaro，grow to tree size，but true trees need more *moisture* than most desert environments can supply，so they are scarce on deserts.

【衍】 moist（*adj.*）润湿的，潮湿的；多雨的

【近】 damp，wetness，humidity

mural ['mjuərəl]

【释】 *n.* 壁画；壁饰 *adj.* 墙壁(上)的；墙壁似的

【例】 After O'Keeffe's trip around the world by plane，the sky "paved with clouds" as seen from an airplane also became one of her favorite motifs and the subject of her largest work，a 24-foot *mural*.

【衍】 muralist（*n.*）壁画家；壁饰家

【近】 wall painting，fresco

Unit 10

neighbor [ˈneibə]

【释】 *n.* 邻人，邻居，邻近的人；邻国(人)

【例】 In towns and cities, the nuclear family was more dependent on its immediate *neighbors* than on kinfolk.

【衍】 neighborhood (*n.*) 附近，周围；街道；地区；neighboring (*adj.*) 邻近的

【近】 fellow citizen

nuclear [ˈnjuːkliə]

【释】 *adj.* 核的；核心的；原子能的；核动力的

【例】 In towns and cities, the *nuclear* family was more dependent on its immediate neighbors than on kinfolk.

【衍】 nucleus (*n.*) 核；核心；细胞核；原子核；nuclei ([*pl.*] nucleus)；nucleic (*adj.*) 核的

onset [ˈɔnset]

【释】 *n.* 开始，动手；攻击，突击

【例】 Her painting was preceded by the production of landscapes in needlework, and it was only the *onset* of arthritis that forced the change of medium.

【近】 start, commencement, inception

outgoing [ˈautɡəuiŋ]

【释】 *adj.* 对人友好的；开朗的

【例】 Self-image can be indicated by a tone of voice that is confident, pretentious, shy, aggressive, *outgoing*, or exuberant, to name only a few personality traits.

【近】 sociable, friendly, extrovert

pamphlet [ˈpæmflit]

【释】 *n.* 小册子；(时事问题等的)小册子刊物

【例】 She wrote other farces, as well as anti-Federalist *pamphlet*.

【近】 brochure, booklet, guide

peak [piːk]

【释】 *n.* 山顶，最高点

【例】 After the *peak* year of 1957, the birth rate in Canada began to decline.

【衍】 peaked (*adj.*) 尖的

【近】 climax, crest

perpetuate	[pə'petjueit]
【释】	*v.* 使永久存在(继续)；使不朽，使不灭
【例】	Insects' lives are very short and they have many enemies，but they must survive long enough to breed and *perpetuate* their kind.
【衍】	perpetuation（*n.*）；perpetually（*adv.*）
【近】	achieve，carry on，continue
pine	[pain]
【释】	*n.*【植】松树；松木
【例】	Roof beams of *pine* or fir had to be carried from logging areas in the mountain forests many kilometers away.
poison	['pɔizn]
【释】	*n.* 毒；毒药
【例】	The term "virus" is derived from the Latin word for *poison*，or slime.
【衍】	poisonous（*adj.*）
【近】	venom，toxin
potent	['pəutənt]
【释】	*adj.* 强有力的；有势力的，有效力的；烈性的
【例】	In addition，fungi are the source of many of the most *potent* antibiotics used in clinical medicine，including penicillin.
【衍】	potential（*adj.*）；potentially（*adv.*）
【近】	strong，powerful，effective
prerequisite	[ˌpriː'rekwizit]
【释】	*n.* 先决条件　*adj.* 必须先具备的，必要的；先决条件的（to）
【例】	It is certainly a *prerequisite* for knowledge.
【近】	precondition，qualification，requirement
proceed	[prə'siːd]
【释】	*v.* 前进；进行
【例】	Real estate subdivision there *proceeded* much faster than population growth.
【近】	go on，continue，keep
propose	[prə'pəuz]
【释】	*v.* 申请；提议，建议，提出

【例】 Initially, 70 sites were ***proposed*** as candidates for sanctuary status.

【衍】 proposal（*n.*）; proposer（*n.*）申请人，提案人

【近】 suggest, advise, plan, offer

pump ［pʌmp］

【释】 *n.* 泵，抽(水)机

【例】 Farm women had to haul large quantities of water into the house from wells or ***pumps*** for every purpose.

【近】 force, drive, impel, push

raft ［rɑːft］

【释】 *n.* 筏

【例】 Some small local canals, which are able to float only 100 to 300 ton boats or small ***rafts*** of timber, may be only 3 feet deep.

realm ［relm］

【释】 *n.* 领域，区域，范围

【例】 For the most part, the literature in which the railroad plays an important role belong to popular culture rather than to the ***realm*** of serious art.

【近】 domain, area, field

reduction ［riˈdʌkʃən］

【释】 ① *n.* 简化，约简

【例】 Large masses of data must generally undergo a process of summarization or ***reduction*** before they are comprehensible.

【衍】 reductionist（*n.*）; reduce（*v.*）; reductive（*adj.*）; reductional（*adj.*）

【释】 ② *n.* 缩小，减少；降级，降位

【例】 Many companies have announced dramatic ***reductions*** in staff.

【衍】 reduce（*v.*）; reductive（*adj.*）; reductional（*adj.*）

【近】 decrease, decline, diminution

reject ［riˈdʒekt］

【释】 *v.* 拒绝，抵制，驳回，否决（［*opp.*］accept）

【例】 There may be a fault in the experiment, or the theory may have to be revised or ***rejected***.

【衍】	rejection (*n.*)；rejective (*adj.*)；rejecter (*n.*)；rejectee (*n.*) 被拒绝者
【近】	refuse，rebuff，deny
repeat	[ri'pi:t]
【释】	*v.* 反复，复述
【例】	This whole process takes but a few seconds and is *repeated* hundreds of times a day.
【衍】	repeatedly (*adv.*)；repeating (*adj.*)；repeated (*adj.*)
【近】	reiterate，replicate，recur
resist	[ri'zist]
【释】	*v.* 抵抗，反对；忍耐(艰苦等)；抵制(疾病等)
【例】	Copper's ability to conduct heat efficiently and to *resist* corrosion contributed to its attractiveness.
【衍】	resistant (*adj.*)；resistance (*n.*)；resistible (*adj.*)
【近】	oppose，forbear，withstand，survive
revolutionary	[ˌrevə'lu:ʃənəri]
【释】	*adj.* 革命的，大变革的，革命性的
【例】	Yet even the political overturn was not so *revolutionary* as one might suppose.
【衍】	revolution (*n.*)；revolutionized (*adj.*)
【近】	radical，innovative，innovatory
romance	['rəumæns]
【释】	*n.* 浪漫，浪漫史
【例】	Dreiser thought that writers should tell the truth about human affairs，not fabricate *romance*.
【衍】	romantic (*adj.*)；romantically (*adv.*)；romanticism (*n.*) 浪漫主义；romanticize (*v.*)
【近】	story，fiction，legend
salinity	[sə'linəti]
【释】	*n.* 盐分；盐浓度，咸度；含盐量
【例】	If the *salinity* of ocean waters is analyzed，it is found to vary only slightly from place to place.
【衍】	salt (*n. & v.*) 盐；加盐；salty (*adj.*)；saltless (*adj.*)
scrape	[skreip]
【释】	① *v.* 挖成 *n.* 挖成的坑

【例】 The most thoroughly studied cases of deception strategies employed by ground-nesting birds involve plovers，their nests merely *scrape* in the sand or earth.

【近】 scratch

【释】 ② *v.* 摩擦，打磨　*n.* 刮痕，擦伤

【例】 Wind and string players may tap or *scrape* their instruments.

【衍】 scrap（*n.*）碎屑；废料；scraping（*n.*）刮削

【近】 rub，abrade，chafe

select ［si'lekt］

【释】 *v.* 选择；挑选；选拔

【例】 Most speakers of English will，during appropriate situations，*select* and use all three types of expressions.

【衍】 selected（*adj.*）经过挑选的，挑选的；selection（*n.*）

【近】 choose，pick，decide on

sheer ［ʃiə］

【释】 ① *adj.* 险峻的；陡峭的；垂直的

【例】 The advantage of nesting on cliffs is the immunity it gives from foxes，which cannot scale the *sheer* rocks.

【近】 vertical，perpendicular，steep

【释】 ② *adj.* 绝对的；十足的；全然的

【例】 Objects of *sheerest* beauty，Icebergs have been called.

【衍】 sheerly（*adv.*）

【近】 pure，absolute，utter

silica ［'silikə］

【释】 *n.* 硅石；硅土

【例】 For the first time in the Earth's long history，very large quantities of *silica* skeletons，which would eventually harden into rock，began to pile up in parts of the deep sea.

【衍】 silicon（*n.*）硅元素；silicate（*n.*）硅盐酸；siliceous（*adj.*）硅酸的；硅土的

snake ［sneik］

【释】 *v.* 扭弯；扭转；迂回前进

【例】 Next，the crossbill *snakes* its long tongue into the gap and draws out the seed.

【近】	bend，twist，meander
sparse	[spɑːs]
【释】	***adj.*** 稀疏的；稀缺的；瘦小的（[*opp.*] **dense**)
【例】	Along the rare watercourses，cottonwoods and willows eke out a ***sparse*** existence.
【衍】	sparsely（*adv.*）；sparsity（*n.*）；sparseness（*n.*）
【近】	thin，bare，scarce
sponge	[spʌndʒ]
【释】	***n.*** 海绵；海绵动物；海绵状的东西
【例】	Every spoonful of ocean water contains life，including larvae of organisms ranging from ***sponges*** and corals to starfish and clams and much more.
【衍】	spongy（*adj.*）
stamp	[stæmp]
【释】	① ***n.*** 邮票，印花(税)
【例】	Besides，the ***stamp*** covered only delivery to the post office and did not include carrying it to a private address.
【衍】	stamped（*adj.*）有邮戳的
【释】	② ***v.*** 印刷，压印
【例】	Some pots were adorned with incised or ***stamped*** decorations.
【衍】	stamping（*v.* & *n.*）冲压；stamper（*n.*）盖章人；打印器；压模；冲压工
【近】	engrave，impress，imprint
sting	[stiŋ]
【释】	***n.***【昆】螫针 ***v.*** 螫，刺；叮
【例】	The bee's barbed ***sting*** is used only once and is made more effective by the fact that it is left behind in the victim.
【衍】	stinger（*n.*）；stingy（*adj.*）有刺的；吝啬的；stingless（*adj.*）无刺的；stinging（*adj.*）刺一样的；刺人的
【近】	tingle，hurt，smart
stringent	['strindʒənt]
【释】	***adj.*** 严格的，严重的，严厉的；紧急的，迫切的
【例】	When the group was originally formed，requirements for membership were not ***stringent*** and involved a willingness to participate and a membership fee.

Unit 10

【衍】　stringently（*adv*.）；stringentness（*n*.）

【近】　severe，strict，rigorous

subtle　['sʌtl]

【释】　① *adj*. 微妙的，难于捉摸的，难解的（［*opp*.］ obvious）

【例】　This interdependence is sometimes *subtle*，sometimes obvious.

【衍】　subtleness（*n*.）

【近】　slight，faint，delicate

【释】　② *adj*. 敏感的，敏锐的；精细的；巧妙的，精巧的

【例】　Miss Woolson was a highly conscious writer，careful，skillful，*subtle* with a sensitive clairvoyant footing for human nature with the gift of discriminating observation.

【衍】　subtleness（*n*.）

【近】　ingenious，clever，cunning

supplant　［sə'plɑːnt]

【释】　*v*. 排挤掉，代替

【例】　Within a short time the trading company had *supplanted* the individual promoter of colonization.

【衍】　supplantation（*n*.）；supplanter（*n*.）

【近】　displace，replace，supersede

switch　［switʃ]

【释】　*v. & n.* 转换，转变；调配

【例】　Some use the Sun as their guide during the day，and then *switch* to star navigation by night.

【衍】　switching（*n*.）；switchyard（*n*.）（铁路的）调车场，编组站

【近】　change，alter，substitute

target　['tɑːgit]

【释】　*n*. 靶子，目标；对象　　*v*. 把…作为目标，瞄准

【例】　And for the very first time，most of humanity came to fully appreciate the fact that we ourselves live on a similar *target*，a world subject to catastrophe by random assaults from celestial bodies.

【衍】　targetable（*adj*.）可命中目标的

【近】 faim，goal，objective

tentacle [ˈtentəkl]

【释】 *n.* 触须，触角；触丝，触毛

【例】 Stinging cells in the *tentacles* throw out tiny poison threads that paralyze other small sea animals.

【衍】 tentacled（*adj.*）有触器的；tentacular（*adj.*）触手（状）的

【近】 feeler，trichome

thought [θɔːt]

【释】 *n.* 思想，想法，意图，观念

【例】 A person conveys *thoughts* and ideas through choice of words，by a tone of voice that is pleasant or unpleasant，gentle or harsh，by the rhythm that is inherent within the language itself.

【衍】 thoughtful（*adj.*）；thoughtless（*adj.*）；thoughtway（*n.*）思想方法

【近】 consideration，deliberation，notion

toad [təud]

【释】 *n.* 蟾蜍，癞蛤蟆

【例】 Every parent knows the propensity of small children to bring home caterpillars，grasshoppers，*toads*，and other small living things.

tragedy [ˈtrædʒidi]

【释】 *n.* 悲剧；惨剧，悲惨事件

【例】 Play is release from the tedious battles against scarcity and decline which are the incessant，and inevitable，*tragedies* of life.

【衍】 tragedian（*n.*）悲剧演员；悲剧作者

【近】 disaster，catastrophe，misfortune

triangle [ˈtraiæŋgl]

【释】 *n.* 三角形；三角形的东西；三角板

【例】 Equilateral *triangles* are also a fairly clear-cut case.

【衍】 triangular（*adj.*）

tune [tjuːn]

【释】 ① *n.* 曲调，调子

【例】 Singers and instrumentalists have to be able to get every note perfectly in *tune*.

【近】 melody，song

【释】 ② *n.* 和谐，调谐，调和

【例】 At birth it weighs 8 gram its manifestations of life are wholly out of *tune* with its quest to achieve a weight of 8 to 9 grams as quickly as possible the latter being the weight of an adult treecreeper.

【衍】 tuneful（*adj.*）；tuneless（*adj.*）

【近】 harmony

【释】 ③ *v.* 校准(乐器的)音调；调整，使调和

【例】 Pianists are spared this particular anxiety，for the notes are already there，waiting for them，and it is the piano tuner's responsibility to *tune* the instrument for them.

【衍】 tuner（*n.*）调音师；调音器

【近】 adjust，alter，regulate

unique [juːˈniːk]

【释】 *adj.* 独特的；唯一的

【例】 The Native American peoples of the north Pacific Coast created a highly complex maritime culture as they invented modes of production *unique* to their special environment.

【衍】 uniquely（*adv.*）；uniqueness（*n.*）

【近】 sole，distinctive

vantage [ˈvɑːntidʒ]

【释】 *n.* 优势；优越的地位

【例】 The Cubists abandoned the conventional single *vantage* point of the viewer，and objects depicted from multiple view points were shown，at the same time.

【衍】 advantage（*n.*）；disadvantage（*n.*）

【近】 superiority，preponderance

via [ˈvaiə]

【释】 *prep.* 凭借，以…为媒介，通过(某种手段)

【例】 The modulation of chemical signals occurs *via* the elaboration of the number of exocrine glands that produce pheromones.

【近】 through，by

vulnerable	['vʌlnərəbl]
【释】	*adj*. 脆弱的；易受责难(攻击、损坏)的
【例】	Few predators fail to pursue such obviously *vulnerable* prey.
【衍】	vulnerably (*adv*.)；vulnerability (*n*.)
【近】	weak，fragile，defenseless
whale	[(h)weil]
【释】	*n*. 鲸；庞然大物
【例】	Kerosene was used to light lamps. It was a cheap substitute for *whale* oil，which was becoming harder to get.
wrought	[rɔːt]
【释】	*adj*. 制造的；锻炼的
【例】	Although social changes in the United Stated were being *wrought* throughout most of the nineteenth century, public awareness of the changes increased to new levels in the 1890's.
【近】	shaped，fashioned，created

Exercise of Unit 10

左列单词在右列中有一个同义词，请找出并在相应的位置写上正确答案。

Exercise 1:

(A) crouch _____ include

(B) encompass _____ accommodate

(C) demolish _____ suggest

(D) adapt _____ annihilate

(E) bleak _____ unsheltered

(F) propose _____ squat

Exercise 2:

(A) extract _____ demonstration

(B) potent _____ strong

(C) drain _____ ditch

(D) manifestation _____ thin

(E) snake _____ bend

(F) sparse _____ remove

Exercise 3:

(A) select _____ productive

(B) revolutionary _____ relative

(C) chip _____ radical

(D) fertile _____ carve

(E) leap _____ choose

(F) comparative _____ jump

Exercise 4:

(A) perpetuate _____ ray

(B) repeat _____ venom

(C) poison _____ reiterate

(D) beam _____ feeler

(E) dazzling _____ dizzying

(F) tentacle _____ achieve

Exercise 5:

(A) tune _____ convey

(B) distant _____ decrease

(C) impart _____ germs

(D) interpret _____ adjust

(E) bacteria _____ understand

(F) reduction _____ remote

Exercise 6:

(A) diffuse _____ disperse

(B) onset _____ part

(C) prerequisite _____ start

(D) inevitable _____ precondition

(E) fraction _____ adaptable

(F) flexible _____ unavoidable

Exercise 7:

(A) vulnerable _____ climax

(B) lumber _____ melody

(C) fuse _____ oppose

(D) tune _____ blend

(E) resist _____ weak

(F) peak _____ wood

Exercise 8:

(A) clumsy _____ domain

(B) tragedy _____ disaster

(C) pamphlet _____ awkward

(D) anonymous _____ indistinctive

(E) sheer _____ brochure

(F) realm _____ pure

Exercise 9:

(A) hinge _____ depend

(B) reject _____ pot

(C) kettle _____ ample

(D) breed _____ era

(E) abundant _____ raise

(F) epoch _____ refuse

Exercise 10:

(A) switch _____ tingle

(B) moisture _____ severe

(C) scrape _____ change

(D) sting _____ displace

(E) stringent _____ damp

(F) supplant _____ rub

ANSWERS:

1	B D F C E A
2	D B C F E A
3	D F B C A E
4	D C B F E A
5	C F E A D B
6	A E B C F D
7	F D E C A B
8	F B A D C E
9	A C E F D B
10	D E A F B C

Unit 11

abuse	encounter	mushroom	sheet
address	equator	neoclassical	silt
algae	exemplify	numerical	snap
antagonize	extraordinary	ooze	spatial
armor	fiber	outgrow	sponsor
attach	float	pancreas	staple
balance	fracture	pearl	stipulate
beast	gallery	perplexing	strip
blend	gifted	pinhead	subtractive
breeze	habitat	polar	supplement
butterfly	hatch	potter	symbiosis
career	hinterland	presence	tariff
celebrated	iceberg	proclaim	term
chisel	impediment	proposition	in terms of
cluster	infant	purchase	thousandfold
compass	insight	rage	tobacco
configuration	interrupt	reap	trail
consume	irreverent	reef	tribe
coral	kiln	relax	turbulent
crow	lease	repel	unity
dealer	lipid	resolution	vapor
dense	luminous	reward	viable
dilemma	manipulate	roof	wage
distinct	melancholy	sanctuary	wheat
drama	military	scratch	yarn
eject	mold	sensational	

abuse [əˈbjuːz]

【释】 *v. & n.* 滥用，乱用

【例】 Central Park, emerging from a period of *abuse* and neglect, remains one of the most popular attractions in New York City.

【衍】 abusive (*adj.*); abusively (*adv.*)

【近】 mistreatment, neglect, violate

address [əˈdres]

【释】 *v.* 应付，处理(问题)

【例】 The Democrats have more prepared to use government to *address* economic problems.

【近】 tackle

algae [ˈældʒiː]

【释】 *n.* [*pl.*] 藻；藻类([*sing.*] alga)

【例】 The food supply for fish is made by *algae*.

antagonize [ænˈtægənaiz]

【释】 *v.* 反抗，对抗；引起⋯的对抗

【例】 His speech *antagonized* many voters.

【衍】 antagonist (*n.*) 反对者，对抗者；antagonistic(al) (*adj.*) 对抗（性）的，敌对的；相反的，不相容的；antagonistically (*adv.*)；antagonism (*n.*) 敌对，对立；相克作用，对抗(作用)，对抗性

【近】 provoke, irritate, annoy

armor [ˈɑːmə]

【释】 *n.* 甲胄，盔甲

【例】 The name armadillo means "little *armored* one," referring to the platelike shell covering that is unique among mammals.

【衍】 armory (*n.*) (武器)军械库(= arsenals)

【近】 shell, shield

attach [əˈtætʃ]

【释】 *v.* 贴上，系上

【例】 The larvae drifted until they *attached* themselves to the clean shells on the bottom.

【衍】 attached (*adj.*); attachment (*n.*)

【近】 affix, append

balance ['bæləns]
【释】 *n. & v.* 平衡，均衡，对称
【例】 The midbrain handles vision，the hindbrain *balances*.
【衍】 balanced（*adj.*）
【近】 poise，stability，steadiness

beast [biːst]
【释】 *n.* 动物，牛马，家畜
【例】 Cattle have served humanity since prehistoric days as *beasts* of burden and as suppliers of leather，meat，and milk.
【衍】 beastly（*adj.*）
【近】 creature，animal，monster

blend [blend]
【释】 *v.* 混合，搀合，混杂，掺杂
【例】 The picture *blends* elements of two European styles cubism.
【衍】 blender（*n.*）搅拌机
【近】 merge，combine，unify，mix

breeze [briːz]
【释】 *n.* 微风；柔风，和风
【例】 Then，on just the right *breeze*，they rise in a red cloud and head south.
【衍】 breezy（*adj.*）；breezily（*adv.*）
【近】 waft，gust，wind

butterfly ['bʌtəflai]
【释】 *n.* 蝴蝶；蝶式，蝶形
【例】 One of the most remarkable of migrations is that taken each fall by the North American monarch *butterfly*.

career [kə'riə]
【释】 *n.* 职业；前途
【例】 Her *career* blossomed at a time when the American art world had embraced Modernism and found a new beauty in technology.
【衍】 careerist（*n.*）投机分子；careerism（*n.*）野心；追求名利
【近】 vocation，occupation，profession

celebrated ['selibreitid]
【释】 *adj.* 驰名的，有名的，大名鼎鼎的

【例】 France produced a number of outstanding exponents of the Art Nouveau style: among the most *celebrated* was Emile Galle (1846—1901).

【衍】 celebrity (*n.*)

【近】 famous, eminent, distinguished

chisel ['tʃizəl]

【释】 *n.* 凿子

【例】 Craftsmen who could use knife and *chisel* skillfully were still in demand.

cluster ['klʌstə]

【释】 *n.* (一大)丛，群，片　*v.* (使)成群；(使)群集

【例】 The process can be very rapid, quickly creating sizable ice crystals, some of which adhere to each other to create a *cluster* of ice crystals or a snowflake.

【近】 bunch, mass

compass ['kʌmpəs]

【释】 *n.* 罗盘，指南针

【例】 The very tools that the first New England furniture makers used were, after all, not much different from those used for centuries—even millennia: basic hammers, saws, chisels, planes, augers, *compasses*, and measures.

configuration [kənˌfigjuˈreiʃən]

【释】 *n.* 结构；外形

【例】 Very often, the human eye and brain can recognize familiar *configurations* even if all but a few significant data points are left out.

【衍】 configure (*v.*) 使成形

【近】 appearance, profile

consume [kənˈsjuːm]

【释】 *v.* 消费，消耗

【例】 Bacteria in the asphalt mould have *consumed* some of the tissues other than bones.

【衍】 consumer (*n.*)；consumption (*n.*)

【近】 use, devour, eat

coral ['kɔrəl]

【释】 *n.* 珊瑚；珊瑚虫

【例】 Every spoonful of ocean water contains life，including larvae of organisms ranging from sponges and *corals* to starfish and clams and much more.

crow ［krəu］

【释】 *n.* 鸦(包含 raven, rook, jackdaw, chough)

【例】 On the other hand，when it comes to substantive—particularly behavioral—information，*crows* are less well known than many comparably common species.

dealer ［'di:lə］

【释】 *n.* 商人，…商

【例】 In 1905 he was sent to Paris as an apprentice to an art *dealer*.

【衍】 dealership（*n.*）商品经销特许权；商品特许经销商

【近】 trader，merchant，broker

dense ［dens］

【释】 *adj.* 密集的，(物质等)密度大的，(人口等)稠密的

【例】 Due to their *dense* structure，iron meteorites have the best chance of surviving an impact，and most are found by farmers plowing their fields.

【衍】 densely（*adv.*）；denseness（*n.*）；density（*n.*）浓度；密度；比重

【近】 thick，crowded

dilemma ［di'lemə］

【释】 *n.* 窘境，困境，进退两难

【例】 In fact，even before independence from Britain was won，it became clear that resolving the *dilemmas* surrounding the public domain prove necessary to preserve the Union itself.

【衍】 dilemmatic（*adj.*）左右为难的

【近】 predicament，Catch-22，quandary

distinct ［dis'tiŋkt］

【释】 *adj.* 独特的；清楚的，明显的；明确的；显著的

【例】 Soon a *distinct* aesthetic code evolved: form should be simple，surfaces plain，and any ornament should be based on geometric relationships.

【衍】	distinctive（*adj*.）独特的；有特色的；distinction（*n*.）区别；特性
【近】	dissimilar，diverse，definitive
drama	[ˈdrɑːmə]
【释】	*n*. 戏剧
【例】	There are many theories about the beginning of *drama* in ancient Greece.
【衍】	dramatize（*v*.）；dramatization（*n*.）；dramatized（*adj*.）
【近】	performance，comedy
eject	[iˈdʒekt]
【释】	*v*. 喷出，吐出（烟等）；发射，喷射
【例】	Why should a galaxy *eject* matter at such tremendous speeds in two narrow jets?
【衍】	ejective（*adj*.）；ejection（*n*.）
【近】	emit，expel，issue，erupt
encounter	[inˈkauntə]
【释】	*n*. 遇见，碰见　*v*. 邂逅（友人等）
【例】	Environmental problems they found in Poland were among the worst they *encountered*.
【近】	come into，meet
equator	[iˈkweitə]
【释】	*n*. 赤道
【例】	Because they melt more slowly than smaller pieces of ice，icebergs have been known to drift as far north as 35 degrees south of the *equator* in the Atlantic Ocean.
exemplify	[igˈzemplifai]
【释】	*v*. (-fied)举例证明（解释）；示范；做…的范例
【例】	The basic principle of radar is *exemplified* by what happens when one shouts in a cave.
【衍】	exemplification（*n*.）
【近】	demonstrate，represent，illustrate
extraordinary	[ikˈstrɔːdənəri]
【释】	*adj*. 非凡的，卓绝的
【例】	It is *extraordinary* enough for a first novel，but is prodigious for an author of twenty-two.

Unit 11

【近】	amazing，astonishing，remarkable，wonderful
fiber	['faibə]
【释】	***n.*** 纤维，纤维质
【例】	The nerve ***fibers*** in the brain insulate themselves in such a way that the baby begins to hear sounds very precisely.
【衍】	fibered（*adj.*）含纤维的，纤维质的
【近】	thread，strand，yarn，string，filament，twine
float	[fləut]
【释】	***v. & n.*** 漂浮，浮起
【例】	The additional sea ice ***floating*** toward the tropics would increase.
【近】	drift，hover，glide
fracture	['fræktʃə]
【释】	***v. & n.*** （使）破裂；（使）折断；（使）断裂
【例】	***Fractured*** or wear patterns on tools also indicate that a majority of ancient people were right-handed.
【近】	break，rupture
gallery	['gæləri]
【释】	***n.*** 美术馆，美术品陈列室，画廊；回廊，走廊
【例】	In 1914 Whitney converted a townhouse into a small ***gallery*** known as the Whitney Studio.
【衍】	galleried（*adj.*）；galleries（*n.*）图表种类
【近】	balcony，porch，corridor
gifted	['giftid]
【释】	***adj.*** 有天才的，天赋的
【例】	Some homing pigeon experts claim that this bird is ***gifted*** with a form of built-in radar.
【衍】	gift（*n.*）
【近】	talented
habitat	['hæbitæt]
【释】	***n.*** （动、植物生长的）自然环境（地区）；住所，居住地
【例】	Watching the behaviors of diverse animal species in their natural ***habitats***, Lorenz and Tinbergen observed behavior patterns that promote survival.
【衍】	habitant（*n.*）居住者，居民；inhabit（*v.*）居住，栖息；

habitation（*n.*）聚居地

hatch [hætʃ]
【释】 *v.* 孵化，孵；创造；使发生
【例】 Most gulls keep the nest area clear of droppings，and remove empty eggshells after the chicks have ***hatched***.
【衍】 hatcher（*n.*）孵卵器；hatchable（*adj.*）
【近】 produce

hinterland [ˈhintəlænd]
【释】 *n.* 内地，偏僻地区
【例】 The quality of the ***hinterland*** dictated the pace of growth of the cities.

iceberg [ˈaisbəg]
【释】 *n.* 冰山
【例】 The concept of obtaining fresh water from ***icebergs*** that are towed to populated areas and arid regions of the world was once treated as a joke more appropriate to cartoons than real life.

impediment [imˈpedimənt]
【释】 *n.* 妨碍，阻碍(to)；障碍物
【例】 Napoleon never lost sight of his goal，because Britain represented the last substantial ***impediment*** to his control of Europe.
【近】 obstacle，barrier

infant [ˈinfənt]
【释】 *n.* & *adj.* 婴儿(的)，幼儿(的)
【例】 At birth，the ***infant*** has only the most elementary emotional life.
【近】 baby，tot

insight [ˈinsait]
【释】 *n.* 顿悟；洞察力；见识
【例】 Nevertheless，the basic arrangements are similar in all vertebrates，and the study of lower animals gives ***insight*** into the form and structure of the nervous system of higher animals.
【衍】 insightful（*adj.*）有眼光的；显出洞察力的

interrupt [ˌintəˈrʌpt]
【释】 *v.* 打断(别人的话等)；中断
【例】 Nevertheless，it has been said that today children ***interrupt*** their education to go to school.

【衍】	interruption (*n.*)
【近】	disrupt, suspend

irreverent [i'revərənt]

【释】	*adj.* 无礼的
【例】	Satire has lived because readers appreciated refreshing stimulus, an *irreverent* reminder that they live in a world of platitudinous thinking, cheap moralizing, and foolish philosophy.
【衍】	irreverently (*adv.*); irreverence (*n.*)
【近】	disrespectful

kiln [kiln]

【释】	*n.* 窑
【例】	More and more large *kilns* were built to create the high-fired stoneware.
【近】	oven, furnace

lease [li:s]

【释】	*n.* 租契，租约；租借权；租借物；租借期限
【例】	Under New York's controls, a landlord generally cannot raise rents on apartments as long as the tenants continue to renew their *leases*.
【衍】	leasehold (*adj.*) 租赁的；(*n.*) 租得物，租借期；leaseholder (*n.*) 租借人
【近】	rent, let, charter

lipid ['lipid]

【释】	*n.* 脂类
【例】	Some viruses also contain carbohydrates and *lipids*.
【衍】	lipide (*n.*) 脂质，油脂；lipidic (*adj.*)

luminous ['lju:minəs]

【释】	*adj.* 发光的；明亮的；照耀着的；辉耀的
【例】	It can happen that a star which is really very *luminous* can appear faint simply because it's far away.
【衍】	luminosity (*n.*) 发光度；luminously (*adv.*); luminousness (*n.*)
【近】	glowing, shining, brilliant

manipulate [mə'nipjuleit]

【释】	*v.* 巧妙地处理，巧妙地使用

【例】 Environmental sounds, such as thunder, and electronically generated hisses and blips can be recorded, *manipulated*, and then incorporated into a musical composition.

【衍】 manipulation (*n.*)（熟练的）操作，操纵，控制；manipulative (*adj.*)；manipulator (*n.*) 巧于处理的人，操纵者；manipulatory (*adj.*)

【近】 maneuver

melancholy ['melənkəli]

【释】 *n.* 忧郁；忧郁症　*adj.* 令人伤感的；意气消沉的

【例】 The blues, a predominately *melancholy* type of jazz popular in New Orleans, may be a folk song.

【衍】 melancholia (*n.*) 忧郁病；melancholic (*adj. & n.*) 患忧郁病的(人)

【近】 depressed, miserable, dejection

military ['militəri]

【释】 *adj.* 军人的；军队的；军事的；军用的　*n.* 军方

【例】 A variation of barbed wire is also used for *military* purposes.

【衍】 militarily (*adv.*) 在军事上，从军事角度；militant (*adj.*) 好战的；斗志昂扬的；富于战斗性的

【近】 armed, martial, armed forces

mold [məuld]

【释】 ① *n.* 模子，铸型　*v.* 浇铸，塑造

【例】 They had invented bronze, an alloy that could be cast in *molds*, out of which they made tools and weapons.

【衍】 moldable (*adj.*) 可模压的，适于模压的

【近】 cast, shape, pattern

【释】 ② *n.* 霉；霉菌，霉病(又作：**mould**)

【例】 Fungi, including yeasts and other single-celled organisms as well as the common *molds* and mushrooms, were formerly classified as members of the plant kingdom.

mushroom ['mʌʃrum]

【释】 ① *n.* (主指食用)蘑菇；蘑菇状物；蘑菇状烟云

【例】 Fungi, including yeasts and other single-celled organisms as well as the common molds and *mushrooms*, were formerly classified as members of the plant kingdom.

— 235 —

【释】	② v. 迅速增长
【例】	It *mushroomed* in the 1870's，as the rapid expansion of the railway system made it increasingly feasible to transport full productions.
【衍】	mushrooming（n.）迅速增长，迅速生长
【近】	expand，flourish，thrive

neoclassical ['ni:əuklæsikəl]

【释】	adj. 新古典主义的
【例】	*Neoclassical* sculptors seldom held a mallet or chisel in their own hands，readily conceding that the assistants they employed were far better than they were at carving the finished marble.

numerical [nju:'merikəl]

【释】	adj. 数字的；数值的；用数字表示的
【例】	Next，the pertinent considerations that will be affected by each decision are listed，and the relative importance of each consideration is assigned a *numerical* value to reflect its relative importance.
【衍】	numerically（adv.）用数字；在数字上；numerous（adj.）众多的；number（n.）
【近】	statistical，arithmetical，mathematical

ooze [u:z]

【释】	① v. 渗出，徐徐流出；滴出；分泌
【例】	This newly made honey *oozes* from the underside of the bees and is stored in cells in the hive to be used as food during the winter months.
【近】	seep，leak，trickle，secrete
【释】	② n.（海底、河底的）淤泥；沼地；分泌物
【例】	Crude oil，or petroleum—a dark，thick *ooze* from the earth—had been known for hundreds of years.
【衍】	oozy（adj.）（有）淤泥的；渗出的，滴出的，漏出的；oozily（adv.）

outgrow [aut'grəu]

【释】	v. 长得比…快（大）；发展得比…快；过大而不适于
【例】	But now it is being considered quite seriously by many nations，especially since scientists have warned that the human race will *outgrow* its fresh water supply faster than it runs out of food.

【衍】 outgrowth（n.）（自然的）结果；overgrown（adj.）长得太大的，畸形发展的；outlast（v.）较…经久，比…命长

pancreas ['pæŋkriəs]

【释】 *n.* 胰（腺）

【例】 This substance travels through the bloodstream and stimulates the *pancreas* to liberate pancreatic juice.

【衍】 pancreatic（adj.）

pearl [pəːl]

【释】 *n.* 珍珠；珍品；［pl.］珍珠项链

【例】 This cometary train, glistening like a string of *pearls*, had been first glimpsed only a few months before its fateful impact with Jupiter.

【衍】 pearly（adj.）

perplexing [pə'pleksiŋ]

【释】 *adj.* 使人困惑的；使人为难的；麻烦的，复杂的

【例】 A simple alloy of nickel and titanium, nitinol has some *perplexing* properties.

【衍】 perplex（v.）；perplexity（n.）

【近】 confusing, difficult, puzzling

pinhead ['pinhed]

【释】 *n.* 针头；小东西；无聊的东西；傻子，笨人

【例】 One micron is a thousandth of a millimeter: a *pinhead* is about millimeter across.

polar ['pəulə]

【释】 *adj.* （南、北）极的，地极的

【例】 The *polar* bears of Hudson Bay are a distinct population thriving at the southern end of their range.

【衍】 polarity（n.）极性；polarize（v.）

potter ['pɔtə]

【释】 *n.* 陶工；［英方］陶器小贩

【例】 By careful kneading, the *potter* removed the air bubbles and made the clay as plastic as possible.

【衍】 pottery（n.）陶器

presence ['prezəns]

【释】 *n.* 存在，实在；出席，列席，到场

【例】 Quite literally, they find each others, *presence* repulsive.

【衍】 present (*adj.* & *v.*); presentation (*n.*)

【近】 attendance, company

proclaim [prə'kleim]

【释】 *v.* 宣布，公布，宣告，声明；表示

【例】 Advocates of organic foods frequently *proclaim* that such products are safer and more nutritious than others.

【近】 announce, declare, state

proposition [ˌprɔpə'ziʃən]

【释】 *n.* 提议，建议；主张

【例】 Under such a liberal *proposition*, the transfer of the land was soon made, and the construction of the mammoth hotel began.

【衍】 propositional (*adj.*)

【近】 proposal, plan, scheme, suggestion

purchase ['pəːtʃəs]

【释】 *v.* 买，购买；努力取得，（付出代价）赢得

【例】 He *purchased* and prepared land for residential purposes, particularly land near or outside city.

【衍】 purchaser (*n.*)

【近】 get, buy, obtain

rage [reidʒ]

【释】 ① *n.* [口] 时兴的东西

【例】 By the 1930's, big dance bands were the *rage*. Large numbers of people went to ballrooms to dance to jazz music played by big bands.

【近】 fashion, trend

【释】 ② *v.* (战争)猛烈进行

【例】 In the late eighteenth century, battles *raged* almost every corner of Europe, as well as in the Middle East, South Africa, the West Indies, and Latin America.

reap [riːp]

【释】 ① *v.* 收割，采收

【例】 These ponderous machines—sometimes pulled by as many as 40 horses—*reaped* the grain, threshed it, and bagged it, all in one simultaneous operation.

【衍】	reaper（*n.*）
【近】	harvest，collect
【释】	② *v.* 得到，获得
【例】	The urban poor，similarly，*reaped* few benefits from household improvements.
【近】	obtain，acquire

reef ［riːf］

【释】	*n.* 暗礁，礁脉
【例】	Relatively little has been said，however，about diversity of life in the sea even though coral *reef* systems are comparable to rain forests in terms of richness of life.

relax ［ri'læks］

【释】	*v.* 松弛，放松；休养，休息
【例】	When one set is working，the other set is usually *relaxed*.
【衍】	relaxed（*adj.*）；relaxation（*n.*）
【近】	loosen up，have a break，slacken

repel ［ri'pel］

【释】	*v.* 排斥，拒绝
【例】	The agent gives the surfaces of the oil droplets identical electrical charges：since like charges *repel* each other，the droplets *repel* each other.
【衍】	repellency（*n.*）；repellent（*adj.*）
【近】	repulse，revolt

resolution ［ˌrezə'luːʃən］

【释】	① *n.* 解决
【例】	The new X-ray microscopes considerably improve on the *resolution* provided by optical microscopes.
【衍】	resolve（*v.*）解决（问题等）；resolute（*adj.*）坚决的，坚定的
【释】	② *n.*【自】分辨（力）
【例】	With the advent of high-*resolution* radio interferometers during the late 1970's，part of the answer became clear...

reward ［ri'wɔːd］

【释】	*v.* 报答，酬劳，奖赏　*n.* 酬金，报酬
【例】	If for no other reason，the prize will continue to be desirable for the financial *rewards* that accompany it.

Unit 11

【衍】 rewarding（*adj.*）有价值的，有益的；rewardless（*adj.*）徒劳的

【近】 prize，recompense，remuneration

roof [ruːf]

【释】 *n.* 屋顶；最高部，顶部

【例】 Because of its location in the shelter's *roof*, a beam of sunlight can pass through this second hole and cast a spot onto the shelter's wall and floor.

【衍】 rooftop（*n.*）；roofless（*adj.*）

【近】 top，covering

sanctuary ['sæŋktjuəri]

【释】 ① *n.* 圣所，圣堂；礼拜堂；神殿

【例】 They functioned as *sanctuaries* where the elders met to plan festivals, perform ritual dances, settle pueblo affairs, and impart tribal lore to the younger generation.

【衍】 sanctimonious（*adj.*）假装神圣（虔诚）的；伪善的；sanctity（*n.*）神圣，圣洁；sanctum（*n.*）圣所；密室

【释】 ② *n.* 禁猎期，禁猎区

【例】 The designation of an area a marine *sanctuary* indicates that it is a protected area, just as a national park is.

【近】 preserves

scratch [skrætʃ]

【释】 ① *n.* 抓痕；搔痕；抓伤（破）；刮坏

【例】 Even *scratches* found on fossil human teeth offer clues.

【近】 scrape，cut，score

【释】 ② *v.* 潦草地写；涂写；乱画；打草稿

【例】 Stoneware grew increasingly ornate throughout the nineteenth century, and in addition to the earlier *scratched* and drawn designs, three-dimensional molded relief decoration became popular.

【衍】 scratched（*adj.*）

【近】 draw

sensational [sen'seiʃənəl]

【释】 *adj.* 耸人听闻的；令人激动的

【例】 Its beautiful rays are a *sensational* sight during an eclipse.

【衍】 sensationalize（*v.*）；sensationalism（*n.*）感觉论；追求轰动效应

【近】	amazing，astounding，exciting
sheet	[ʃiːt]
【释】	① *n.* （一）片；（一）块；（一）层；薄片；薄板
【例】	Muscle tissue covers the body in *sheets* and bands that lie between the skin and the skeleton.
【近】	piece，page，leaf
【释】	② *n.* （水、雪、冰、火、颜色等的）一片
【例】	The rise and fall of the lakes were undoubtedly linked to the advances and retreats of the great ice *sheets* that covered much of the northern part of the North American continent.
【近】	expanse，mass，area
【释】	③ *n.* 单子；表格；图表
【例】	The suggestions became more explicit，and so emerged the musical cue *sheet* containing indications of mood，the titles of suitable pieces of music.
silt	[silt]
【释】	*n.* 泥沙，淤泥（沉积处）
【例】	Although sieves work well for *silt*，sand，and larger particles，they are not appropriate for clay particles.
【衍】	siltation（*n.*）沉积作用；淤积
【近】	deposit，mud，sludge
snap	[snæp]
【释】	① *v.* 猛扑
【例】	Walking or leaping species of a similar size access the outer twigs either by *snapping* off and retrieving the whole branch or by clutching stiff branches with the feet or tail and plucking food with their hands.
【衍】	snappy（*adj.*）活泼的；敏捷的；snappish（*adj.*）暴躁的；爱骂人的；snapshoot（*v.*）快镜拍摄
【释】	② *v.* 突然折断
【例】	Before barbed wire came into general use，fencing was often made from serrated wire，which was unsatisfactory because it broke easily when under strain，and could *snap* in cold weather due to contraction.
【近】	break，crack，shatter

Unit 11

spatial ['speiʃəl]

【释】 *adj.* 空间的

【例】 Los Angeles was a product of the auto age in another sense as well; its distinctive *spatial* organization depended on widespread private ownership of automobiles.

【衍】 spatially（*adv.*）; spatiality（*n.*）空间性

sponsor ['spɔnsə]

【释】 *v.* 资助

【例】 The exhibit was *sponsored* by an independent group called The Artists Fund Society.

【衍】 sponsorship（*n.*）

【近】 support, subsidize, fund

staple ['steipl]

【释】 *n.* 主要产物（商品）

【例】 The women planted another *staple*, squash, about the first of June, and harvested it near the time of the green corn harvest.

stipulate ['stipjuleit]

【释】 *v.* 约定; 规定; 保证

【例】 The founders *stipulated* that senators be designated by their respective state legislatures rather than by the voter themselves.

【衍】 stipulation（*n.*）合同, 契约; 约定条件, 条款; stipulator（*n.*）立约人

【近】 specify, insist on, require

strip [strip]

【释】 ① *n.* 条带; 长条; 条板; 带状地带

【例】 It is often dramatically marked as an unmistakable landing *strip* to attract the specific insect the orchid has chosen as its pollinator.

【衍】 stripe（*n.*）条纹; 条子

【近】 band, sliver, ribbon

【释】 ② *v.* 剥光; 除去; 剥夺

【例】 She *stripped* away everything, and then built again for herself slowly and over a period of time.

【衍】 strippable（*adj.*）可剥夺的

【近】	undress，remove clothes
subtractive	[səbˈtræktiv]
【释】	***adj.*** 减少的
【例】	But the ***subtractive*** method，while requiring complex chemical techniques，has turned out to be more practical and is the basis of all modern color films.
【衍】	subtract（*v.*）减去，扣除；subtraction（*n.*）
supplement	[ˈsʌplimənt]
【释】	***v. & n.*** 补足，增补
【例】	Hunting is at best a precarious way of procuring food，even when the diet is ***supplemented*** with seeds and fruits.
【衍】	supplementation（*n.*）；supplementary（*adj.*）
【近】	complement
symbiosis	[ˌsimbaiˈəusis]
【释】	***n.*** 共生(现象)，共栖
【例】	This union by which two dissimilar organisms live together is called "***symbiosis***".
【衍】	symbiotic（*adj.*）
tariff	[ˈtærif]
【释】	***n.*** 关税(表)，税率(表)，税则
【例】	Finally，it set up a system of ***tariffs*** that was basically protectionist in effect，although maneuvering for position by various regional interests produced frequent changes in ***tariff*** rates.
【近】	import tax，export tax
term	[təːm]
【释】	***n.*** 词语；术语，专门名词
【例】	The ***term*** "art deco" has come to encompass three distinct but related design trends of the 1920's and 1930's.
【衍】	terminology（*n.*）术语；术语学
【近】	concept，phrase
in terms of	
【释】	***adv.*** 根据，按照，用…的话说；在…方面
【例】	Accordingly，a higher standard of performance was achieved，***in terms of*** both facility and interpretation.

Unit 11

thousandfold [ˈθauzəndˈfəuld]

【释】 *adj*. & *adv*. & *n*. 成千倍(的、地);千倍(的、地)

【例】 Cats know this instinctively, but scientists could not be sure how it happened until they increased the speed of their perceptions a *thousandfold*.

【衍】 thousand (*n*. & *adj*.); thousandth (*adj*. & *n*.) 千分之一(的)

tobacco [təˈbækəu]

【释】 *n*. 烟草;烟叶;烟丝,卷烟

【例】 River boats carried to New Orleans the corn and other crops of northwestern farmers, the cotton and *tobacco* of southwestern planters.

【衍】 tobacconist (*n*.) 烟草商(店);香烟(烟丝)制造人

trail [treil]

【释】 ① *n*. 痕迹,足迹,线索

【例】 Critics and historians have remarked more than once that taletelling is a regional *trail* of the South.

【近】 path, track, trace

【释】 ② *v*. 跟踪追赶

【例】 Bloodhounds are biologically adapted to *trailing* their prey.

【衍】 trailer (*n*.)

【近】 follow, track, tail

tribe [traib]

【释】 *n*. 部落,部族;家族

【例】 When the colonists won the war, she and her *tribe* had to abandon their lands and retreat to Canada.

【衍】 tribesman (*n*.) 部族(男)成员,同族人;tribal (*adj*.)

【近】 ethnic group, clan, family

turbulent [ˈtə:bjulənt]

【释】 *adj*. 骚乱的;动荡的

【例】 Small mammals, being warm blooded, suffer hardship in the exposed and *turbulent* environment of the uppermost trees.

【衍】 turbulence (*n*.)

【近】 disorderly, chaotic, fluctuate, changing

unity	[ˈjuːniti]

【释】 *n.* 统一

【例】 The use of home bases is a fundamental component of human social behavior; the common meal served at a common hearth is a powerful symbol, a mark of social *unity*.

【近】 harmony, concord

vapor	[ˈveipə]

【释】 *n.* 汽，蒸汽

【例】 Evaporated from the oceans; water *vapor* forms clouds, some of which are transported by wind over the continents.

【衍】 vaporish（*adj.*）像蒸汽的；evaporate（*v.*）使蒸发；evaporation（*n.*）

【近】 steam, spray

viable	[ˈvaiəbl]

【释】 *adj.* 能养活的，能成活的

【例】 During the nineteenth century further advances were made, notably Bessemer's process for converting iron into steel, which made the material more commercially *viable*.

【衍】 viability（*n.*）（尤指胎儿或婴儿的)生存能力

wage	[weidʒ]

【释】 *v.* 进行，发动(战争等)

【例】 The government, along with the three factions that had been *waging* a civil war, signed a peace agreement.

【近】 carry on, pursue, fight

wheat	[(h)wiːt]

【释】 *n.* 小麦

【例】 In contrast, *wheat* and wheat flour composed only 6 percent of the value of American exports in that year.

yarn	[jɑːn]

【释】 *n.* 纱，纱线，毛线

【例】 Inventors wound the cooling end of the thread around a *yarn* reel, then turned the reel rapidly to pull more fiber from the molten glass.

【近】 thread, fiber, wool

Unit 11

Exercise of Unit 11

左列单词在右列中有一个同义词，请找出并在相应的位置写上正确答案。

Exercise 1:

(A) blend _____ thick
(B) interrupt _____ merge
(C) career _____ deposit
(D) breeze _____ disrupt
(E) dense _____ waft
(F) silt _____ vocation

Exercise 4:

(A) mold _____ talented
(B) perplexing _____ confusing
(C) gifted _____ baby
(D) hatch _____ tackle
(E) address _____ produce
(F) infant _____ cast

Exercise 2:

(A) repel _____ use
(B) term _____ harvest
(C) consume _____ concept
(D) reap _____ thread
(E) manipulate _____ repulse
(F) fiber _____ maneuver

Exercise 5:

(A) armor _____ mistreatment
(B) irreverent _____ shell
(C) lease _____ drift
(D) float _____ rent
(E) abuse _____ depressed
(F) melancholy _____ disrespectful

Exercise 3:

(A) fracture _____ complement
(B) luminous _____ glowing
(C) eject _____ break
(D) dealer _____ trader
(E) scratch _____ emit
(F) supplement _____ scrape

Exercise 6:

(A) unity _____ affix
(B) proposition _____ obstacle
(C) mushroom _____ proposal
(D) attach _____ harmony
(E) stipulate _____ expand
(F) impediment _____ specify

Exercise 7:

(A) celebrated _____ get
(B) ooze _____ support
(C) balance _____ poise
(D) purchase _____ seep
(E) distinct _____ dissimilar
(F) sponsor _____ famous

Exercise 8:

(A) roof _____ amazing
(B) sanctuary _____ preserves
(C) sheet _____ attendance
(D) numerical _____ statistical
(E) presence _____ top
(F) extraordinary ___ piece

Exercise 9:

(A) cluster _____ demonstrate
(B) kiln _____ predicament
(C) scratch _____ prize
(D) exemplify _____ draw
(E) dilemma _____ bunch
(F) reward _____ oven

Exercise 10:

(A) antagonize _____ provoke
(B) proclaim _____ announce
(C) snap _____ follow
(D) trail _____ path
(E) strip _____ undress
(F) trail _____ break

ANSWERS:

1	E A F B D C
2	C D B F A E
3	F B A D C E
4	C B F E D A
5	E A D C F B
6	D F B A C E
7	D F C B E A
8	F B E D A C
9	D E F C A B
10	A B F D E C

Unit 12

academy	endangered	mutual	shelf
adjacent	equilibrium	net	silver
alien	exempt	nurse	snowflake
Antarctica	exuberant	opera	spawn
array	fiction	outline	spontaneous
attain	flock	panel	startling
balcony	fragile	pebble	stir
beaver	gallon	persist	strive
blossom	gigantic	pitch	suburb
brick	hail	pole	suppose
cabinet	haul	poverty	symbol
cargo	hive	preservation	taste
celestial	ichthyosaur	prodigious	terminal
chlorophyll	imperative	prose	thread
coach	infect	pure	toe
compile	inspect	ragged	trait
confine	interstellar	rear	tributary
contact	irreversible	reel	turnpike
cord	kinetic	release	universal
crowd	leather	repertoire	variable
debate	listless	resonance	vibrant
depict	lump	rhetoric	wagon
dilute	mansion	rope	whereas
distinguish	melody	sandy	yearn
dramatic	mill	screen	
elaborate	molecular	sensitive	

academy	[əˈkædəmi]
【释】	**n. 学会，研究院**
【例】	The experiment was described in a paper presented to the Paris *Academy* in 1894.
【衍】	academic（*adj.*）学院的；理论的；academically（*adv.*）学术上；academicals（*n.*）大学礼服；academician（*n.*）学会会员，院士
【近】	college，school，institute

adjacent	[əˈdʒeisənt]
【释】	**adj. 毗邻的，邻近的**
【例】	A few houses in New England were built of stone，but only in Pennsylvania and *adjacent* areas was stone widely used in dwellings.
【衍】	adjacently（*adv.*）；adjacency（*n.*）
【近】	adjoining，contiguous，neighboring

alien	[ˈeiljən]
【释】	**n. & adj. 外来(的)；异己(的)；不熟悉(的)**
【例】	The conditions in the Earth's core make it far more *alien* world than space.
【近】	strange，unknown，foreign，unfamiliar，exotic

Antarctica	[æntˈɑːktikə]
【释】	**n. 南极洲**
【例】	The southern one—which included the modern continents of South America，Africa，Australia，and *Antarctica*—is called Gondwanaland.
【衍】	Antarctic（*adj.*）

array	[əˈrei]
【释】	**n. 一大批，一大群，一连串**
【例】	The urban middle class was now able to buy a wide *array* of food products and clothing—baked goods，canned goods，suits，shirts，shoes，and dresses.
【近】	range，assortment，variety

attain	[əˈtein]
【释】	**v. 达到，获得**
【例】	The Native American peoples also *attained* one of the most complex social organizations in the world.

【衍】	attainable（*adj.*）；attainment（*n.*）
【近】	achieve，accomplish，reach
balcony	['bælkəni]
【释】	*n.* 露台，阳台；(剧场二楼)楼座
【例】	Loud speakers may be placed at opposite ends of the stage，in the *balcony*，or at the back and sides of the auditorium.
【衍】	balconied（*adj.*）
【近】	circle，gallery，veranda，terrace
beaver	['biːvə]
【释】	*n.* 海狸，海獭
【例】	Some mammals，such as *beavers*，are largely aquatic and spend most of their time in the bayou.
blossom	['blɔsəm]
【释】	*n.* 花(特指果树花)；群花，开花时期；(发育的)初期
【例】	Orchids are unique in having the most highly developed of all *blossoms*.
【衍】	blossomy（*adj.*）
【近】	bloom，flower
brick	[brik]
【释】	*n.* 砖；砖块
【例】	Whether the material was wood，stone，or *bricks* is unknown.
【衍】	bricklaying（*n.*）砌砖，砌砖工作
cabinet	['kæbinit]
【释】	① *n.* 柜，箱
【例】	To be sure，there were still small workshops，where skilled craftspeople manufactured products ranging from newspapers to *cabinets* to plumbing fixtures.
【衍】	cabinet-maker（*n.*）
【释】	② *n.* 陈列室；(矿物、生物、古钱币等)陈列品
【例】	Hence my writing is，if not a *cabinet* of fossils，a kind of collection of life in amber.
cargo	['kɑːgəu]
【释】	*n.* (船上的)货；负荷
【例】	From New Orleans，ships took the *cargoes* on to eastern seaports.

【近】	freight，load，goods
celestial	[si'lestjəl]
【释】	*adj.* 天上的；天体的([*opp.*] **terrestrial**)
【例】	Stars may be spheres，but not every *celestial* object is spherical.
【近】	space，extraterrestrial
chlorophyll	['klɔːrəfil]
【释】	*n.* 叶绿素
【例】	Healthy *chlorophyll* absorbs light of colors other than green，which is reflected.
coach	[kəutʃ]
【释】	① *n.* 轿式马车
【例】	Wagon freighters continued operating throughout the 1870's and 1880's and into the 1890's although over constantly shrinking routes，and *coaches* and wagons continued to crisscross the West wherever the rails had not yet been laid.
【衍】	stagecoach（*n.*）公共马车
【近】	cart，carriage，wagon
【释】	② *n.* 教练 *v.* 训练
【例】	Tony Woodcock has joined German amateur team SC Brueck as *coach*.
【近】	trainer，teacher，instructor
compile	[kəm'pail]
【释】	*v.* 汇集，编辑
【例】	Communications satellites can transmit data around the world cheaply and instantaneously，and modern computers can quickly *compile* and analyze this large volume of weather information.
【衍】	compilation（*n.*）
【近】	assemble，create，compose
confine	['kɔnfain]
【释】	*v.* 限制(**to**；**within**)
【例】	When water is *confined* in tubes of very small bore，the forces of cohesion(the attraction between water molecules)are so great that the strength of a column of water compares with the strength of a steel wire of the same diameter.

【衍】 confinement（n.）
【近】 restrict

contact ['kɔntækt]
【释】 *n.* 接触；联系
【例】 It can only evolve in species with sense organs that are well enough developed so that continuous sensory *contact* can be maintained.

cord [kɔːd]
【释】 *n.* 绳子，索子
【例】 The movement itself is caused by the pull of sheets and *cords* of very tough tissue called muscle.
【近】 string, thread

crowd [kraud]
【释】 *n. & v.* 拥挤
【例】 Market days saw the crowded city even more *crowded*，as farmers from within a radius of 24 or. more kilometers brought their sheep，cows，pig，vegetables，cider，and other products for direct sale to the townspeople.
【衍】 crowded（*adj.*）；crowdedness（*n.*）

debate [di'beit]
【释】 *n. & v.* 辩论；讨论
【例】 Sound bites in news and answers to questions in *debates* increasingly sound like advertisements.
【衍】 debatable（*adj.*）
【近】 discuss, argue, dispute, contest

depict [di'pikt]
【释】 *v.* 画，刻画，描写；叙述
【例】 In ancient Egyptian artwork，for examples，the right hand is *depicted* as the dominant one in about 90 percent of the example.
【衍】 depiction（*n.*）
【近】 portray, describe

dilute [di'ljuːt,dai'ljuːt]
【释】 *v. & adj.* 冲淡(的)，搀淡(的)，稀释(的)
【例】 Here the ocean is being *diluted* so that the salinity is decreased.

— 252 —

【衍】	diluted（adj.）；dilution（n.）
【近】	water down，adulterate

distinguish ［disˈtiŋgwiʃ］

【释】	v. 区别；辨别，识别，判别
【例】	But two characteristics *distinguish* jazz from other dance music.
【衍】	distinguishable（adj.）；distinguished（adj.）卓越的，卓著的
【近】	differentiate，discriminate，discern

dramatic ［drəˈmætik］

【释】	*adj.* 戏剧性的；激动人心的；引人注目的
【例】	war set the stage for the most *dramatic* events in marketing the western crop.
【衍】	dramatically（adv.）
【近】	radical，drastic，severe

elaborate ［iˈlæbəreit，-rət］

【释】	① v. 精心制作；详尽阐述
【例】	According to this view，tales（about the hunt，war，or other feats）are gradually *elaborated* at first through the use of impersonation，action，and dialogue by a narrator and then through the assumption of each of the roles by a different person.
【衍】	elaboration（n.）
【释】	② adj. 精巧的，精细的，精益求精的；详尽的
【例】	Although nest-building is an instinctive ability，there is considerable adaptability in both site selection and use of materials，especially with those species which build quite *elaborate* constructions.
【衍】	elaborative（adj.）认真做的；精练的；细致的；elaborately（adv.）
【近】	complicated，intricate，involved，complex

endangered ［inˈdeindʒəd］

【释】	adj. 濒临灭绝的
【例】	... such *endangered* animals in China as red crown crane，Chinese tiger and Chinese alligator.
【近】	rare，scarce，in danger of extinction

Unit 12

equilibrium [ˌiːkwiˈlibriəm]

【释】 *n.* 平衡，均衡

【例】 For the economy to be in *equilibrium*，income must equal expenditure.

【近】 balance，symmetry

exempt [igˈzempt]

【释】 *v. & adj.* 被免除(的)，被豁免(的)(**from**)

【例】 … these commodities *exempt* from taxes.

【衍】 exemption (*n.*)

【近】 excuse，release

exuberant [igˈzjuːbərənt]

【释】 *adj.* (感情等)充溢的；(活力)充沛的，(精神)旺盛的

【例】 An unpleasant stimulus was paired with the sight of the animal (perhaps the person was knocked down by an *exuberant* dog) and the subsequent sight of dogs evokes the earlier response—fear.

【衍】 exuberantly (*adv.*)；exuberance (*n.*)

【近】 excited，enthusiastic，energetic，vigorous

fiction [ˈfikʃən]

【释】 *n.* 小说；编造，想象，虚构

【例】 There is even an award for a very good work of *fiction* that failed commercially.

【衍】 fictive (*adj.*) 虚构的

flock [flɔk]

【释】 *n.* (禽、畜等的)群，羊群

【例】 Among mammals，such behavior is very rare in rodents，which almost never move in *flocks* or herds.

【近】 herd，drove，flight，group

fragile [ˈfrædʒil]

【释】 *adj.* 脆的，易碎的

【例】 The models are kept in locked cases as they are too valuable and *fragile* for classroom use.

【衍】 fragility (*n.*)

【近】 delicate，brittle，flimsy

gallon [ˈgælən]

【释】 *n.* 加仑

【例】 Dairy cattle produce more than fifteen and one-half billion *gallons* of milk every year.

【衍】 gallonage（*n*.）加仑数，加仑量

gigantic [dʒaiˈɡæntik]

【释】 *adj.* 巨大的；庞大的；巨人似的

【例】 Scientists speculate it might be a *gigantic* hurricane, which because of its large size, lasts for hundreds of years.

【衍】 gigantism（*n*.）巨人症

【近】 huge，giant，massive，enormous

hail [heil]

【释】 ① *n.* 雹，冰雹

【例】 In the two latter states, it comprises visible precipitation—rain, *hail*, sleet, snow.

【衍】 hailstone（*n*.）（一粒）冰雹

【近】 sleet

【释】 ② *v.* 向…高呼，为…欢呼

【例】 Telecommuting—substituting the computer for the trip to the job—has been *hailed* as a solution to all kinds of problems related to office work.

【近】 acclaim，uphold

haul [hɔːl]

【释】 *v.* （用力）拽，牵，拖，拖运

【例】 Farm women had to *haul* large quantities of water into the house form wells or pumps for every purpose.

【衍】 hauler（*n*.）运输业者，搬运工

【近】 drag，pull

hive [haiv]

【释】 *n.* 蜂巢，蜂房，蜂箱

【例】 Bees live in groups in a *hive* and every bee does certain work that helps the other members of the group.

【衍】 hives（*n*.）麻疹；假膜性喉头炎

ichthyosaur [ˈikθiəsɔː]

【释】 （[*pl*.] ichthyosauria）【古生】鱼龙

【例】 Some areas have become a treasury of well-preserved *ichthyosaur* fossils.

imperative [im'perətiv]

【释】 *adj.* 绝对必要的；迫切的，紧急的

【例】 With the gradual evolution of society, simple counting became *imperative*.

【近】 crucial, urgent, necessary

infect [in'fekt]

【释】 *v.* 传染；感染

【例】 A single mosquito can *infect* a large number of people.

【衍】 infection (*n.*)

【近】 contaminate

inspect [in'spekt]

【释】 *v.* 询问，查问

【例】 So popular did his lubrication system becomes that persons *inspecting* new equipment generally inquired if it contained the "real McCoy".

【衍】 inspection (*n.*)

【近】 check, examine, scrutinize

interstellar ['intə'stelə]

【释】 *adj.* 星际的

【例】 Spiral galaxies are well supplied with the *interstellar* gas in which new stars form.

irreversible [,iri'vəːsəbl]

【释】 *adj.* 不可逆的

【例】 In terrestrial ecosystems and in fringe marine ecosystems, the most common problem is habitat destruction. In most situations, the result is *irreversible*.

【衍】 irreversibly (*adv.*); irreversibility (*n.*)

【近】 irrevocable, irretrievable, permanent

kinetic [kai'netik]

【释】 *n.* 动力(学)的；运动的

【例】 When each fragment slammed at 60 kilometers per second into the dense atmosphere, its immense *kinetic* energy was transformed into heat, producing a super-heat.

leather ['leðə]

【释】 *n.* 皮，皮革

【例】 Cattle have served humanity since prehistoric days as beasts of burden and as suppliers of *leather*，meat，and milk.

【衍】 leathery（*adj.*）似革的，革质的；强韧的；leathern（*adj.*）皮革的，似皮革的；leatherette（*n.*）人造革

【近】 pelt，fur，rawhide

listless ［'listlis］

【释】 *adj.* 冷淡的；懒洋洋的，无精打采的，倦怠的

【例】 It is not surprising that a bird in heavy molt often seems *listless* and unwell.

【衍】 listlessly（*adv.*）；listlessness（*n.*）

【近】 languid，lethargic，indolent

lump ［lʌmp］

【释】 *n.* 块，团　*v.* 使成块，使成团

【例】 When disturbed，a sea anemone retracts its tentacles and shortens its body so that it resembles a *lump* on a rock.

【衍】 lumpy（*adj.*）多团块的，结成块的，满是疙瘩的

【近】 bump，protuberance，knob

mansion ［'mænʃən］

【释】 *n.* 宅第，公馆；大楼，公寓

【例】 So while the city's newly emerging social leadership commissioned their *mansions* apartment houses and hotels began to sprout on multiple lots，thus breaking the initial space constraints.

【近】 house，manor，hall

melody ［'melədi］

【释】 *n.* 旋律，曲调；好听的声音；歌曲

【例】 Unlike string and wind instruments，the piano is completely self-sufficient，as it is able to play both the *melody* and its accompanying harmony at the same time.

【衍】 melodic（*adj.*）旋律的，调子美妙的；melodrama（*n.*）情节剧

【近】 tune，song，piece of music

mill ［mil］

【释】 *n.* 磨坊；厂，工场

【例】 Subsequently, manufacturers made use of new improved stationary steam engines to power their *mills*.

【衍】 miller (*n.*) 磨坊主；工厂经营人

molecular [məu'lekjulə]

【释】 *adj.* 分子的，由分子形成的

【例】 Active plant defense mechanisms are comparable to the immune system of vertebrate animals, although the cellular and *molecular* bases are fundamentally different.

【衍】 molecule (*n.*) 分子；微小颗粒

mutual ['mju:tʃuəl]

【释】 *adj.* 相互的，共有的，共同的

【例】 The association for *mutual* benefit goes so far that when a wrasse nudges at a grouper's gill covers, the grouper obliges by extending them to give the picker access to the delicate breathing organs underneath.

【衍】 mutually (*adv.*)

【近】 joint, shared, common

net [net]

【释】 ① *n.* 网，网状物，网状组织，网状系统

【例】 As the trunk expands, the fibers pull apart, creating a *net* of diamond-shaped furrows, but the bark does not flake off in scales.

【衍】 network (*n.*) 网眼织物，网状系统，网路，电路，电脑网络

【近】 mesh, web

【释】 ② *adj.* 净的，纯的；基本的；最后的 ([*opp.*] gross)

【例】 Air currents move and lift droplets so that the *net* downward displacement is zero, even though the droplets are in constant motion.

【近】 remaining, after deductions

nurse [nə:s]

【释】 *n.* 护士，看护 *v.* 护理，照料

【例】 Professional *nursing*, in short, emerged neither from medical discoveries nor from a program of hospital reform initiated by physicians; outsiders saw the need first.

【衍】 nursing (*n.*) 看护；养育

【近】 care for，tend，nurture

opera [ˈɔpərə]

【释】 *n.* 歌剧；［口］歌剧院

【例】 Its importance as an instrument in its own right dates from the early 1600's，when it first became standard in Italian *opera* orchestras.

【衍】 operatic（*adj.*）歌剧的，歌剧式的，歌剧体的

outline [ˈautlain]

【释】 ① *n.* 外形，轮廓 *v.* 画轮廓；打草图，描略图

【例】 The new taste demanded dramatic effects of contrast stark *outline* and complex textural surfaces.

【衍】 outlet（*n.*）出口，出路；outlook（*n.*）展望，前景

【近】 shape，figure，sketch

【释】 ② *v.* 概括地论述，略述 *n.*［常 *pl.*］梗概，大纲；草稿；要点

【例】 This does not mean that we can sit down today and *outline* the future course of the universe with anything like certainty.

【近】 summarize，sketch out，framework

panel [ˈpænəl]

【释】 *n.* 面，板；【建】四分板；门窗材；幅板，板条

【例】 The carpenter's shop probably provided the frame and perhaps supplied the *panel*.

【近】 board，pane，sheet

pebble [ˈpebl]

【释】 *n.* 砾，卵石，石子

【例】 Rattles were made of gourds or of turtle shells filled with *pebbles* or seeds.

【近】 stone，rubble，cobble

persist [pəˈsist]

【释】 *v.* 坚持，固执(in)；继续存在，存留

【例】 As time passed some rituals were abandoned，but the stories，later called myths，*persisted* and provided material for art and drama.

【衍】 persistent（*adj.*）；persistency（*n.*）

【近】 persevere，continue，keep on

pitch [pitʃ]

【释】① *n.* 音高；音高标准

【例】None-Western music typically divides and interval between two *pitches* more finely than Western music does.

【衍】pitcher（*n.*）（带柄和倾口的）大水罐；（棒球）投手

【释】② *n.* 沥青

【例】Touch *pitch*，and you will be defiled.（You can't touch pitch without being defiled.）近墨者黑。

【近】tar，asphalt

pole [pəul]

【释】*n.* 极，极点，顶点

【例】The corona's rays flash out in a brilliant fan that has wispy spikelike rays near the sun's north and south *poles*.

【衍】polestar（*n.*）

poverty ['pɔvəti]

【释】*n.* 贫穷；缺乏，缺少，贫乏

【例】These writers，called naturalists，often focused on economic hardship，studying people struggling with *poverty*.

【近】lack，shortage

preservation [ˌprezə'veiʃən]

【释】*n.* 保存；储藏；防腐

【例】The *preservation* of embryos and juveniles is a rare occurrence in the fossil record.

【衍】preserve（*v.*）；preservative（*n.*）防腐剂

【近】conservation，protection

prodigious [prə'didʒəs]

【释】*adj.* 巨大的，庞大的，奇妙的

【例】It is extraordinary enough for a first novel，but is *prodigious* for an author of twenty-two.

【衍】prodigy（*n.*）

【近】abnormal，extraordinary，unusual，remarkable

prose [prəuz]

【释】*n.* 散文（[*opp.*] verse）；平凡，单调，普通

【例】Mercy Otis Warren produced a variety of poetry and *prose*.

【近】style，text

pure	[pjuə]
【释】	*adj*. 纯的，纯粹的；清一色的([*opp*.] mixed)
【例】	In theory, the upward movement of fieldstones should result in *pure* soil.
【衍】	purely (*adv*.)
【近】	clean, unpolluted, uncontaminated
ragged	['rægid]
【释】	*adj*. 粗糙的
【例】	All adult birds molt their feathers at least once a year, and upon close observation, one can recognize the frayed, *ragged* appearance of feathers that are nearing the end of their useful life.
【衍】	raggedly (*adv*.); raggedness (*n*.)
【近】	worn out, frayed
rear	[riə]
【释】	① *n*. & *adj*. 后部(的)，背面(的)；屁股([*opp*.] front)
【例】	Eohippus had four toes on its front feet, three on the *rear*, and teeth adapted to a forest diet of soft leaves.
【近】	back, stern
【释】	② *v*. 抚养，教养
【例】	Some kinds of seabirds use the windswept cliffs of the Atlantic coast of Canada in the summer to mate, lay eggs, and *rear* their young.
【近】	bring up, raise, nurture
reel	[riːl]
【释】	*n*. (棉纱、电线等的)卷轴
【例】	This process continues automatically, and the finished barbed wire is wound onto *reels*.
【近】	roll, spool
release	[riˈliːs]
【释】	① *v*. 释放；吐出；放出
【例】	The nuclear energy is *released* at the Sun's center as high-energy gamma radiation, a form of electromagnetic radiation like light and radio waves, only of very much shorter wavelength.
【近】	discharge, liberate

Unit 12

【释】 ② *v.* 发表；发行
【例】 The most famous of these early special scores was that composed and arranged for D. W. Griffith's film *Birth of a Nation*，which was *released* in 1915.
【近】 publish，issue

repertoire [ˈrepətwɑː]
【释】 ① *n.* （排好待演的）常备剧目；演奏节目；保留节目
【例】 In both urban and rural communities，a rich and varied *repertoire* of ballads，tales，and poetic forms is preserved in memory and passed from generation to generation.
【近】 catalog，inventory，selection
【释】 ② *n.* 全部技能；所有组成部分
【例】 Plovers also have an effective *repertoire* of tricks for distracting potential nest predators from their exposed and defenseless eggs or chicks.

resonance [ˈrezənəns]
【释】 *n.* 回声，反响；共鸣
【例】 During the twenties，Martha Graham and her colleagues had rescued art-dance from vaudeville and movies and musical comedy and all the *resonances* of the idyllic mode in the United States.
【衍】 resonator（*n.*）共鸣器；resonant（*adj.*）
【近】 reverberation，timbre

rhetoric [ˈretərik]
【释】 *n.* 修辞学；辩论法
【例】 At the same time，the new university greatly expanded in size and course offerings，breaking completely out of the old，constricted curriculum of mathematics，classics，*rhetoric*，and music.
【衍】 rhetorical（*adj.*）；rhetorician（*n.*）修辞学者；雄辩家
【近】 oratory，expression，speech-making

rope [rəup]
【释】 *n.* 绳索，麻索，索子
【例】 There vaqueros invented almost all the tools of the cowhand's trade，from the broad-brimmed felt hat and the *rope* lariat to the special western saddle.
【衍】 ropewalker（*n.*）走钢索的演员

【近】	cord，line，twine
sandy	['sændi]
【释】	*adj*. 沙的，沙质的，多沙的
【例】	The particles in a *sandy* soil are comparatively large permitting water to enter the soil and to pass through it so quickly that it often carries nutrients with it and dries out very rapidly.
【衍】	sand（*n*.）；sandstone（*n*.）砂岩；sandals（*n*.）凉鞋；便鞋
screen	[skriːn]
【释】	① *n. & v.* 粗筛；筛选(煤炭等)；甄别
【例】	Another method of determining soil texture involves the use of devices called sediment sieves，*screens* built with a specified mesh size.
【衍】	screened（*adj.*）筛过的；screening（*n*.）审查；甄别
【近】	partition，select，weed out
【释】	② *n.* 屏风；围屏
【例】	Their stalks and branches also act as *screens* to keep the wind from sweeping great drifts of sand along the surface.
【近】	conceal，partition，divider
sensitive	['sensitiv]
【释】	*adj*. 敏感的，感觉灵敏的
【例】	The electric currents generated by most living cells are extremely small—often so small that *sensitive* instruments are needed to record them.
【衍】	sensitivity（*n*.）灵敏性；sensibility（*n*.）敏感(性)；感受性
【近】	responsive，susceptible，hypersensitive
shelf	[ʃelf]
【释】	① *n.* 架子
【例】	His laboratory at Menlo Park，New Jersey，was equipped with a rich variety of scientific instruments，and its library *shelves* included the latest scientific books as well as periodicals.
【衍】	shelfful（*n*.）可装一架的量，一个架所装之量

— 263 —

【近】ledge，bookshelf，sill
【释】② *n.* 大陆架
【例】If enough surge glaciers reach the ocean and raise sea levels，West Antarctic ice *shelves* could rise off the seafloor and become adrift.

silver [ˈsilvə]
【释】*n.* 银；银器　*adj.* 银的
【例】Their products，primarily *silver* plates and bowls，reflected their exalted status and testified to their customers' prominence.
【衍】silversmith（*n.*）银（器）匠；silvered（*adj.*）镀银的；silvering（*n.*）镀银，包银；silverly（*adv.*）像银一样地；silvery（*adj.*）含银的

snowflake [ˈsnəufleik]
【释】*n.* 雪花
【例】Icebergs afloat today are made of *snowflakes* that have fallen over long ages of time.
【衍】snowfall（*n.*）降雪；降雪量；snowstorm（*n.*）雪暴，暴风雪
【近】snow

spawn [spɔːn]
【释】① *v.* (使)产卵，大量生育　*n.* (鱼等的)卵，子
【例】The marine biologists discovered that by raising the temperature of the water，they could induce oysters to *spawn* not only in the summer but also in the fall，winter，and spring.
【衍】spawner（*n.*）产卵鱼，已成熟的雌鱼
【近】offspring，eggs，seed
【释】② *v.* 引起，酿成
【例】Significantly，the use of exposed iron occurred mainly in the new building types *spawned* by the Industrial Revolution.
【近】generate，produce，initiate

spontaneous [spɔnˈteiniəs]
【释】*adj.* 自发的，自动的；非勉强的
【例】The notion that an artist could or would dash off an idea in a fit of *spontaneous* inspiration was completely alien to these

deliberately produced works.

【衍】 spontaneously (*adv*.)；spontaneity (*n*.)

【近】 unprompted，natural，unstructured

startling ['stɑːtliŋ]

【释】 *adj*. 令人吃惊的

【例】 For Julia Morgan，however，San Simeon was a *startling* incon—gruity in a brilliant 46-year career.

【衍】 starting (*n*.) 出发，开始

【近】 astonishing，amazing，astounding

stir [stəː]

【释】 *v*. 搅动，搅拌；使混淆

【例】 Steel was made by a slow and expensive process of heating，*stirring*，and reheating iron ore.

【近】 whisk，swirl，mix

strive [straiv]

【释】 *v*. 力求，努力；竞争，斗争；反抗

【例】 Like all artists，jazz musicians *strive* for an individual style，and the improvised or paraphrased solo is a jazz musician's main opportunity to display his or her individuality.

【衍】 striver (*n*.) 努力者，奋斗者；竞争者

【近】 struggle，endeavor，attempt

suburb ['sʌbəːb]

【释】 *n*. 郊区，城郊，市郊，近郊

【例】 Some visitors from the east coast were dismayed at the endless urban sprawl and dismissed Los Angeles as a mere collection of *suburbs* in search of a city.

【衍】 suburban (*adj*.)；suburbanization (*n*.) 市郊化

【近】 neighborhood，community，town

suppose [sə'pəuz]

【释】 *v*. 设想，推测；假定

【例】 Yet even the political overturn was not so revolutionary as one might *suppose*.

【衍】 supposed (*adj*.)；supposedly (*adv*.)

【近】 presume，assume，expect

symbol ['simbəl]

【释】 *n*. 记号，符号；象征，表征

【例】 No wonder these trees became *symbols* of strength, fruitfulness, and everlasting life.

【衍】 symbolic（*adj.*）; symbolize（*v.*）

【近】 representation, mark, character

---

taste ［teist］

【释】 ① *n.* 滋味；味觉　*v.* 品(尝)味道

【例】 Newborns show an expression of disgust, for example, in response to strong *tastes*, and show surprise in reaction to sudden changes.

【衍】 tasty（*adj.*）美味的

【近】 flavor, savor, tang

【释】 ② *n.* 风味，风格；兴趣；品味；审美力，鉴别力，欣赏力

【例】 Citizens of prosperous, essentially middle-class republics, have always shown a marked *taste* for portraiture.

【衍】 tasteful（*adj.*）; taster（*n.*）鉴赏师

【近】 tastefulness, style, preference

---

terminal ［'təːminəl］

【释】 ① *n.* 终点(站)

【例】 Passenger *terminals*, like the luxury express trains that hurled people over spots, spotlight the romance of railroading.

【衍】 terminate（*v.*）使结束，使终止; termination（*n.*）

【近】 station, passenger terminal, depot

【释】 ② *adj.* 终端的，终点的，结尾的

【例】 The weight of a gibbon(a small ape) hanging below a branch arches the *terminal* leaves down so that fruit-bearing foliage drops toward the gibbon's face.

【衍】 terminally（*adv.*）

---

thread ［θred］

【释】 ① *n.* 细线，细流

【例】 Stinging cells in the tentacles throw out tiny poison *threads* that paralyze other small sea animals.

【衍】 threadlike（*adj.*）细长的; thready（*adj.*）线状的，丝状的

【近】 yarn, fiber, string

【释】	② *n.* (议论等的)思路；条理；线索；情节
【例】	Throughout all of these works, moreover, runs the ***thread*** of freedom(equal treatment)for women.
【近】	storyline, plot

toe [təu]

【释】	*n.* 脚趾，脚尖
【例】	Recently, we have waded a little out to sea, enough to dampen our ***toes*** or, at most, wet our ankles.
【衍】	toed (*adj.*) 有(若干)趾的

trait [treit]

【释】	*n.* 特色，特点，特征；性格；脾气；容貌
【例】	Mimetic ***traits*** may include morphological structures, color patterns, behaviors or other attributes of the mimic that promote its resemblance to a model.
【近】	peculiarity, attribute, characteristic

tributary ['tribjutəri]

【释】	*n. & adj.* 纳贡(的)；从属(的)，附庸的(国等)；支流 (的)
【例】	He had no desire to break from the British Empire simply to establish an American one—in which the newer region should be subsidiary and ***tributary*** to the old.
【衍】	tribute (*n.*) 贡品；纳贡义务(地位)；勒索款；赠品
【近】	branch, stream, offshoot

turnpike [təːn'paik]

【释】	*n.* 收税高速公路，收费公路
【例】	Despite the road improvements of the ***turnpike*** era (1790—1830), Americans continued as in colonial times to depend wherever possible on water routes for travel and transportation.

universal [ˌjuːni'vəːsəl]

【释】	① *adj.* 一般的，普遍的
【例】	The poetry of Gwendolyn Brooks has been praised for deepening the significance of personal and social experiences so that these experiences become ***universal*** in their implication.

【衍】 universally（*adv.*）；universality（*n.*）
【近】 widespread，general
【释】 ② *adj.* 宇宙的
【例】 The only typical place is within the vast，cold *universal* vacuum，the everlasting night of intergalactic space.
【近】 cosmic，extraterrestrial，celestial

variable [ˈvɛəriəbl]
【释】 ① *n.*【数】变量
【例】 One of the benefits of a pencil and paper decision-making procedure is that it permits people to deal with more *variables* than their minds can generally comprehend and remember.
【释】 ② *adj.* 易变的，可变的
【例】 The acting is of *variable* quality.
【衍】 invariable（*adj.*）；variant（*n.*）变体，变形；variation（*n.*）变化，变动；variance（*n.*）变化，变动
【近】 changeable，uneven，capricious

vibrant [ˈvaibrənt]
【释】 *adj.* 生气勃勃的
【例】 Orlando itself is *vibrant*，full of affordable accommodation and great places to eat.
【衍】 vibrancy（*n.*）
【近】 vivacious，energetic

wagon [ˈwægən]
【释】 (二马以上的四轮)运货马车
【例】 At that point the trains turned their height，mail，and passengers over to steamboats，*wagons*，and stage-coaches.
【衍】 wagonette（*n.*）(坐六人或八人的)四轮游览轻便马车
【近】 cart，carriage

whereas [(h)wɛərˈæz]
【释】 *conj.* 而，却
【例】 The camel can lose up to 30 percent of its body weight as water without harm to itself，*whereas* human beings die after losing only 12 to 13 percent of their body weight.
【近】 while，but

yearn [jə:n]

【释】 *v.* 想念，怀念，向往

【例】 And now those who *yearn* for the good old days of the untamed frontier，when men were men and wolves were literally at the wagon door，can tick off the top 100 adventures still left in America.

【衍】 yearning（*n.* & *adj.*）思慕(的)，想念(的)

【近】 long，hanker

Exercise of Unit 12

左列单词在右列中有一个同义词，请找出并在相应的位置写上正确答案。

Exercise 1:

(A) academy ＿＿＿＿　college
(B) release ＿＿＿＿　struggle
(C) distinguish ＿＿＿＿　discuss
(D) strive ＿＿＿＿　publish
(E) vibrant ＿＿＿＿　differentiate
(F) debate ＿＿＿＿　vivacious

Exercise 2:

(A) haul ＿＿＿＿　huge
(B) alien ＿＿＿＿　drag
(C) gigantic ＿＿＿＿　strange
(D) compile ＿＿＿＿　assemble
(E) taste ＿＿＿＿　tastefulness
(F) pebble ＿＿＿＿　stone

Exercise 3:

(A) dilute ＿＿＿＿　water down
(B) sensitive ＿＿＿＿　flavor
(C) celestial ＿＿＿＿　space
(D) spawn ＿＿＿＿　offspring
(E) spawn ＿＿＿＿　responsive
(F) taste ＿＿＿＿　generate

Exercise 4:

(A) terminal ＿＿＿＿　style
(B) prose ＿＿＿＿　while
(C) exempt ＿＿＿＿　irrevocable
(D) irreversible ＿＿＿＿　excuse
(E) reel ＿＿＿＿　station
(F) whereas ＿＿＿＿　roll

Exercise 5:

(A) array ＿＿＿＿　delicate
(B) flock ＿＿＿＿　check
(C) elaborate ＿＿＿＿　neighborhood
(D) suburb ＿＿＿＿　range
(E) fragile ＿＿＿＿　herd
(F) inspect ＿＿＿＿　complicated

Exercise 6:

(A) hall ＿＿＿＿　sleet
(B) startling ＿＿＿＿　tar
(C) resonance ＿＿＿＿　astonishing
(D) pitch ＿＿＿＿　cart
(E) depict ＿＿＿＿　reverberation
(F) wagon ＿＿＿＿　portray

Exercise 7:

(A) net _____ tune
(B) coach _____ trainer
(C) mansion _____ balance
(D) equilibrium ____ persevere
(E) persist _____ remaining
(F) melody _____ house

Exercise 8:

(A) spontaneous ____ yarn
(B) thread _____ ledge
(C) repertoire _____ unprompted
(D) preservation ____ catalog
(E) shelf _____ conservation
(F) rhetoric _____ oratory

Exercise 9:

(A) attain _____ achieve
(B) suppose _____ bloom
(C) panel _____ back
(D) rear _____ board
(E) blossom _____ presume
(F) infect _____ contaminate

Exercise 10:

(A) release _____ cord
(B) listless _____ restrict
(C) rope _____ radical
(D) dramatic _____ languid
(E) poverty _____ lack
(F) confine _____ discharge

ANSWERS:

1	A D F B C E
2	C A B D E F
3	A F C E B D
4	B F D C A E
5	E F D A B C
6	A D B F C E
7	F B D E A C
8	B E A C D F
9	A E D C B F
10	C F D B E A

Unit 13

accelerate	endeavor	myriad	shield
adjunct	equip	neutral	simultaneous
alkali	exert	nutrition	soap
anthropology	fabric	operate	specialty
arrest	fidelity	outlying	spoon
attribute	flood	paradox	starve
ballet	fragment	peculiar	stitch
behave	gamma	personality	stroke
blow	glacial	pivot	subway
brief	hall	polished	supreme
cable	haunt	powder	symmetrical
carnivore	hollow	prestige	tavern
cellar	ideal	produce	terrace
chord	impervious	prospect	threat
coarse	infest	purification	tolerance
complement	inspire	rail	tranquil
confirm	interval	rearrange	trick
contemporary	irrigate	refer	turtle
core	kingdom	relevant	unless
crucial	ledge	repertory	variety
debris	literally	resort	vibrate
deposit	lung	rhinoceros	wander
dim	manual	rotate	whittle
distort	memorable	sanitation	yield
drift	millennium	scruple	
electron	moment	sensory	

accelerate	[æk'seləreit]
【释】	*v.* 加速；催促，促进
【例】	By centering politics on the person of the candidate, television *accelerated* the citizen's focus on character rather than issues.
【衍】	accelerated (*adj.*); acceleration (*n.*)
【近】	hasten, speed up
adjunct	['ædʒʌŋkt]
【释】	*n.* 附属物，附件
【例】	In North America, potash making quickly became an *adjunct* to the clearing of land for agriculture, for it was estimated that as much as half the cost of clearing land could be recovered by the sale of potash.
【衍】	adjunctive (*adj.*); adjunctively (*adv.*); adjunction (*n.*)
【近】	accessory, addition, attachment, appendage, affiliate, auxiliary
alkali	['ælkəlai]
【释】	*n.* ([*pl.*] alkali(e)s)碱；强碱
【例】	… an *alkali* such as soda or potash…
【衍】	alkaloid (*adj. & n.*) 含碱的；生物碱
anthropology	[ˌænθrə'pɔlədʒi]
【释】	*n.* 人类学
【例】	Most people entering historical archaeology during this period came out of university *anthropology* departments, where they had studied prehistoric cultures.
【衍】	anthropological (*adj.*); anthropologist (*n.*)
arrest	[ə'rest]
【释】	① *v.* 逮捕，拘捕
【例】	*Arrested* for breaking discriminatory laws, Dr. King went to jail dozens of times.
【近】	capture, apprehend
【释】	② *v.* 阻止，抑制
【例】	The future of our planet is dependent upon our efforts to simultaneously *arrest* the carbon dioxide buildup, protect the ozone layer, restore forests, boost energy efficiency, and further develop renewable energy sources.

Unit 13

【衍】 arrested（*adj.*）抑制的；滞留的；不良的

【近】 detain，impede，hinder

attribute ［ə'tribjuːt，'ætribjuːt］

【释】 ① *v.* 把（某事）归因于…；认为…属于

【例】 The phrase "civil disobedience" is usually *attributed* to the nineteenth-century American philosopher Henry David Thoreau.

【近】 assign，ascribe，accredit

【释】 ② *n.* 属性，特质

【例】 Both groups share two *attributes* normally associated with vertebrates.

【近】 aspect，characteristic，feature，quality，trait

ballet ［bæ'lei］

【释】 *n.* 芭蕾舞，舞剧

【例】 Before Duncan danced，*ballet* was the only type of dance performed in concert.

【衍】 balletic（*adj.*）

behave ［bi'heiv］

【释】 *v.* 行为，举止，表现

【例】 Droplets and ice crystals *behave* somewhat like dust in the air made visible in a shaft of sunlight.

【衍】 behavior（*n.*）；behavioral（*adj.*）

【近】 act，perform

blow ［bləu］

【释】 ① *v.*（blew，blown）（风）吹；（汽笛等）叫，鸣

【例】 Sea winds that *blow* inland from the west are warmed by a current of warm water that flows through the Pacific Ocean.

【衍】 blower（*n.*）

【近】 waft，gust，bluster

【释】 ② *v.*（blew，blown）（轮胎等）爆炸；【电】（灯丝等）烧断，烧坏

【例】 Paid for and maintained by "light dues" levied on ships，the original beacon was *blown* up in 1776.

【近】 explode，blast，burst

brief ［briːf］

【释】 *adj.*（时间）短暂的；（文体）简洁的；（答复等）简短的

【例】	The messages on which most of us rely are *briefer* than they once were.
【衍】	briefly (*adv.*)
【近】	concise，short，succinct

cable ['keibl]
【释】 *n.* 粗索，巨缆；电缆
【例】 Mild steel and aluminum barbed wire have two strands twisted together to form a *cable* which is stronger than single-strand wire and less affected by temperature changes.
【衍】 cablegram (*n.*) 海底电报；cable TV 有线电视
【近】 wire，rope，chain

carnivore ['kɑːnivɔː]
【释】 *n.* 食肉动物（[*opp.*] **herbivore**)
【例】 *Carnivores* greatly outnumber herbivores in the collection: for every large herbivore，there is one saber-tooth cat，a coyote，and four wolves.
【衍】 carnivorous (*adj.*)

cellar ['selə]
【释】 *n.* 地窖，地下室
【例】 Such was the dwelling on the Georgia Sea Island that sidled and leaned in Jupiter Lights with one of its roofless wings failing into the *cellar*.
【近】 basement，crypt

chord [kɔːd]
【释】 ① *n.* 腱，带
【例】 Singers practice breathing every day，as their vocal *chords* would be inadequate without controlled muscular support.
【释】 ② *n.* (琴)弦；(心)弦
【例】 Other early writers who followed Dickinson celebrated the rich and various plant and animal life of the region，striking sympathetic *chords* in the imaginations of Ralph Waldo Emerson and the English poets William Wordsworth and Samuel Taylor Coleridge.
【近】 harmony

coarse	[kɔːs]
【释】	*adj*.粗糙的([*opp*.] **fine**)；粗鲁的，粗俗的
【例】	Granite，for instance，is a *coarse*-grained igneous rock whose individual mineral crystals have formed to a size easily seen by the naked eye.
【衍】	coarsely（*adv*.）；coarsen（*v*.）（使）变粗糙
【近】	crude，vulgar
complement	['kɔmplimənt]
【释】	*v. & n.* 补足(物)；补全
【例】	By the close of the 1960's it became more common to deal gently with the existing urban fabric and to insert new buildings in such a way as to *complement* the physical and social environment.
【衍】	complementary（*adj*.）；complementation（*n*.）
【近】	supplement
confirm	[kən'fəːm]
【释】	*v*.（进一步）证实(确定)
【例】	When hypotheses are *confirmed*，they are incorporated into theories.
【衍】	confirmable（*adj*.）；confirmation（*n*.）
【近】	verify，validate
contemporary	[kən'tempərəri]
【释】	*adj. & n.* 同时代的(人)；现代的(人)
【例】	A younger *contemporary* of similar background gave the reading public an explicit feminist argument for the education of women.
【衍】	contemporarily（*adv*.）
core	[kɔː]
【释】	*n*. 果心；地核；中心
【例】	The Earth comprises three principal layers: the dense，iron-rich *core*，the mantle，made of silicate rocks that are semimolten at depth，and the thin，solid-surface crust.
【近】	center，nuclei，interior
crucial	['kruːʃəl]
【释】	*adj*.至关紧要的；决定性的

【例】 The most *crucial* factor behind this phenomenal upsurge in productivity was the widespread adoption of labor-saving machinery by northern farmers.

【衍】 crucially（*adv.*）

【近】 critical，vital，significant，essential，important

debris ['deibriː]

【释】 *n.* 碎片，破片；岩屑

【例】 Measure are already being taken to control the growth of orbital *debris*.

【近】 fragments，rubble

deposit [di'pɔzit]

【释】 ① *v.* 放置，安置；储蓄

【例】 *Deposit* the sand here.

【近】 place，drop，dump

【释】 ② *v. & n.* 淤积，沉淀；附着

【例】 The technique has uncovered new evidence from sediments that were *deposited* near the shores of the ancient oceans.

【近】 sediment，residue

dim [dim]

【释】 *adj.* 微暗的，朦胧的　*v.* （使）暗淡；（使）朦胧，（使）模糊

【例】 Place far enough away，even the blazing Sun would become a *dim* point of light；brought nearer to the Earth，a once-faint body might appear a million times as bright.

【衍】 dimly（*adv.*）

【近】 faint

distort [dis'tɔːt]

【释】 *v.* 歪扭，弄歪；曲解

【例】 These figures give a *distorted* view of the significance for the local economy.

【衍】 distorted（*adj.*）；distortion（*n.*）

【近】 deform，twist

drift [drift]

【释】 *v.* 使漂流；漂移

【例】 As they *drift* away from the polar region，icebergs sometimes move mysteriously in a direction opposite to the wind.

【衍】 adrift (*adv.*)

【近】 float, glide

electron [i'lektrɔn]

【释】 *n.* 电子

【例】 Their radio emission arises from the synchrotron process, in which *electrons* accelerated the nearly the speed of light move through magnetic fields.

【衍】 electronic (*adj.*); electronically (*adv.*)

endeavor [in'devə]

【释】 *n. & v.* 努力，尽力

【例】 This was possibly the most open scientific *endeavor* in history.

【近】 enterprise, exertion

equip [i'kwip]

【释】 *v.* 配备，装备

【例】 The cost of *equipping* and operating many thousands of conventional weather stations was prohibitively high.

【衍】 equipment (*n.*)

【近】 furnish, outfit

exert [ig'zəːt]

【释】 *v.* 用(力)，尽(努力等)；发挥(威力等)

【例】 The crossed mandibles enable the bird to *exert* a powerful biting force at the bill tips.

【衍】 exertion (*n.*) 努力，尽力

【近】 put force, endeavor

fabric ['fæbrik]

【释】 ① *n.* 结构

【例】 They were made of a top layer of woolen or glazed worsted wool *fabric*.

【近】 structure, composition, makeup

【释】 ② *n.* 编织品，织物；纤维品

【例】 Mass transportation revised the social and economic *fabric* of the American city in three fundamental ways.

【衍】 fabricate (*v.*)

【近】 textile

fidelity [fi'deləti]

【释】 *n.* 忠诚，忠实(to)；真实，确切

【例】 Determined to portray life as it was，with *fidelity* to real life and accurate representation without idealization，they studied local dialects，wrote stories which focused on life in specific regions of the country，and emphasized the "true" relationships between people.

【近】 truth，loyalty

flood [flʌd]

【释】 *n.* 洪水，水灾；大量，一大阵；滔滔不绝

【例】 A *flood* of ice would then surge into the Southern Sea.

【近】 deluge，torrent

fragment ['frægmənt]

【释】 *n.* 碎屑，碎片

【例】 With time，these patches result in layers of scales，easily seen in a *fragment* of pine bark.

【衍】 fragmental (*adj.*)

【近】 section，portion，scrap

gamma ['gæmə]

【释】 *n.* 伽马射线

【例】 The nuclear energy is released at the Sun's center as high-energy *gamma* radiation.

glacial ['gleiʃəl]

【释】 *adj.* 冰的；冰状的

【例】 Volcanic fire and *glacial* ice are natural enemies.

【衍】 glacier (*n.*)；glaciated (*adj.*)；glaciation (*n.*)

【近】 icy，chilly，cold，cool

hall [hɔːl]

【释】 *n.* 会馆，会场，会堂；展览厅

【例】 Ten years later，Ellington began giving annual concerts at Carnegie *Hall* in New York City.

haunt [hɔːnt]

【释】 *v.* 常去，常到(某地)；缠住(某人)

【例】 People in the United States in the nineteenth century were *haunted* by the prospect.

【衍】	haunted (*adj.*)
【近】	trouble，disturb，bother
hollow	['hɔləu]
【释】	*adj.* 空的，中空的；空虚的；不诚实的
【例】	All trumpets are *hollow* tubes.
【衍】	hollowly (*adv.*)；hollowware (*n.*) 锅；碟子
【近】	empty，concave，vacant，unfilled
ideal	[ai'diəl]
【释】	*n.* 理想的，典型的
【例】	The high biological productivity of the Cretaceous oceans also led to *ideal* conditions for oil accumulation.
【近】	perfect，ultimate，best
impervious	[im'pəːvjəs]
【释】	*adj.* 不可渗透的，穿不过的，透不过的
【例】	Water has trouble entering this *impervious* soil and runoff is very common during rainfalls.
【近】	impermeable，solid
infest	[in'fest]
【释】	*v.* 在…上寄生，寄生于；（指老鼠、害虫、盗贼等）大批出没
【例】	… the rat-*infested* slums where the plague flourished.
【衍】	infestation (*n.*)
inspire	[in'spaiə]
【释】	*v.* 使生灵感，使感悟，使感动
【例】	Lean but progressive，the buildings on Miami Beach *inspired* delight.
【衍】	inspiring (*adj.*)；inspiration (*n.*)
【近】	motivate，stir，arouse
interval	['intəvəl]
【释】	*n.* （时间、空间方面的）间隔
【例】	However，at *intervals* of 10 to 100 years，these glaciers move forward up to 100 times faster than usual.
【近】	period，distance
irrigate	['irigeit]
【释】	*v.* 灌溉

【例】	Therefore，if the meter indicates that a plant is warmer than the air，it may mean that it is time to *irrigate*.
【衍】	irrigation（*n.*）
【近】	water，hose
kingdom	[ˈkiŋdəm]
【释】	*n.* 王国
【例】	Members of the animal *kingdom* have developed a variety of defense mechanisms for dealing with parasites.
【近】	realm，empire，monarchy，sovereignty
ledge	[ledʒ]
【释】	① *n.* 壁架
【例】	Two *ledges* were built across from each other on the inside of the chimney.
【衍】	ledged（*adj.*）有壁架的；ledgy（*adj.*）突出物很多的
【近】	shelf
【释】	② *n.* (岩石突出的)岩架；岩礁；暗礁
【例】	On the other hand，nesting on a narrow *ledge* has its own peculiar problems，and kittiwake behavior has become adapted to overcome them.
【近】	outcrop，protuberance，protrusion
literally	[ˈlitərəli]
【释】	① *adv.* 照字义地；逐字地
【例】	The word "television"，derived from its Greek（telex distant）and Latin（visio sight）roots，can *literally* be interpreted as sight from a distance.
【衍】	literary（*adj.*）文学的；喜欢文学的；书面语的；literate（*adj.*）有学问的，有文化的；literature（*n.*）文学作品；文献
【近】	factually，accurately，exactly
【释】	② *adv.* 差不多，简直
【例】	Then for a brief time，the desert can be *literally* carpeted with color.
lung	[lʌŋ]
【释】	*n.* 肺脏，肺；(无脊椎动物的)呼吸器官；辅助呼吸的装置

Unit 13

— 281 —

【例】	The diaphragm，for example，forces the *lungs* to take in air.
【衍】	lungful（*n.*）两肺的容量

manual ['mænjuəl]

【释】 *n.* 手册；说明书；指南

【例】 Since architecture was not yet a specialized profession in the colonies，the design of buildings was left either to carpenters who undertook to interpret architectural *manuals* imported from England.

【近】 instruction booklet，handbook，guidebook

memorable ['memərəbl]

【释】 *adj.* 可记忆的，难忘的

【例】 Reliance on television means that increasingly our political world contains *memorable* pictures rather than memorable words.

【衍】 memory（*n.*）；memorial（*adj. & n.*）纪念的；纪念品；纪念碑；纪念仪式

【近】 unforgettable，impressive，remarkable

millennium [mi'leniəm]

【释】 *n.*［*pl.*］millennia 一千年（间）；千周年纪念

【例】 The very tools that the first New England furniture makers used were，after all，not much different from those used for centuries—even *millennia*.

moment ['məumənt]

【释】 *n.* 片刻，瞬息

【例】 Therefore the chorus can make a public appearance after long，leisurely preparation and add on at the last *moment* the final professional touches.

【衍】 momentary（*adj.*）瞬息间的，顷刻的

【近】 instant，second，minute

myriad ['miriəd]

【释】 *n.* 无数，极大数量 *adj.* 无数的；众多方面的

【例】 A snowfall consists of *myriads* of minute ice crystals that fall to the ground in the form of frozen precipitation.

【近】 countless，multitude，innumerable

neutral ['njuːtrəl]

【释】 ① *adj.*【化】【电】中性的；中和的；不带电的

【例】 The other tail is made of *neutral* dust particles. which get gently pushed back by the pressure of the sunlight itself.

【衍】 neutrality（*n.*）中性，中和；neutralizer（*n.*）中和器，中和剂；neutron（*n.*）中子

【近】 unbiased，impartial，disinterested

【释】 ② *adj.* 不鲜艳的，暗淡的；非彩色的(指灰、黑或白色的)

【例】 No material in modern dance was *neutral*.

【衍】 neutrally（*adv.*）；neutralism（*n.*）中立主义

nutrition [njuː'triʃən]

【释】 *n.* 营养(作用)，滋养；营养物，食物

【例】 The history of clinical *nutrition*，or the study of the relationship between health and how the body takes in and utilizes food substances，can be divided into four distinct eras.

【衍】 nutritional（*adj.*）营养的，滋养的；nutritionally（*adv.*）在营养上；nutritionist（*n.*）营养学(专)家；nutritious（*adj.*）有营养的，滋养的；nutrient（*n.*）营养品，养分，养料；undernutrition（*n.*）营养不良

【近】 nourishment

operate ['ɔpəreit]

【释】 *v.* 开动，操纵(机器等)；经营，管理；起作用，产生影响

【例】 Water and sewerage systems were usually *operated* by municipal governments，but the gas and electric networks were privately owned.

【衍】 operation（*n.*）；operating（*adj.*）；operator（*n.*）操作者；驾驶员

【近】 function，run，drive

outlying ['autlaiiŋ]

【释】 *adj.* 远离中心(主体)的，边远的

【例】 The fairs provided a means of bringing handmade goods from *outlying* places to would-be buyers in the city.

Unit 13

【衍】	outnumber（v.）数量上胜过，比…多
【近】	remote，distant，faraway

paradox ['pærədɔks]

【释】	**n. 反论，悖论；自相矛盾的话**
【例】	Certainly the greatest *paradox* was the fact that the three most pervasive friendships were the most elusive.
【衍】	paradoxical（adj.）荒谬的；悖论的
【近】	inconsistency，absurdity，irony，illogicality

peculiar [pi'kju:ljə]

【释】	***adj.* 独特的，特有的(to)；特别的，特异的，罕见的；奇怪的**
【例】	On the other hand，nesting on a narrow ledge has its own *peculiar* problems.
【衍】	peculiarity（n.）
【近】	odd，weird，unusual，strange

personality [ˌpə:sə'næləti]

【释】	**n. 个性，【心理学】性格；人格，品格；做人，为人；容貌**
【例】	A number of factors related to the voice reveal the *personality* of the speaker.
【衍】	personalize（v.）
【近】	character，trait，behavior

pivot ['pivət]

【释】	**v. 把…放在枢轴上，旋**
【例】	To be able to do this，the muscle must be attached to the bone at an angle. By pulling，the muscle can cause the bone to *pivot*.
【衍】	pivotal（adj.）中枢的，枢要的；主要的
【近】	turn，rotate，spin

polished ['pɔliʃt]

【释】	***adj.* 擦亮的，光亮的，磨光的**
【例】	Wooden planks were joined，covered with gesso to prepare the surface for painting，and then *polished* smooth with special tools.
【衍】	polisher（n.）
【近】	refined，elegant，cultured，graceful

powder ['paudə]

【释】 *n.* 粉，粉末

【例】 After further research they eventually reduced their substance to a fine，yellow *powder*.

【衍】 powdery（*adj.*）

【近】 dust，residue

prestige [pre'sti:ʒ]

【释】 *n.* 威信，威望，声望；声誉

【例】 No other colonial artisans rivaled the silversmiths' *prestige*.

【衍】 prestigious（*adj.*）

【近】 status，standing，reputation，regard

produce ['prɔdju:s，'prəu-]

【释】 *n.* 农产品

【例】 Winter *produce* will cost more for the next few weeks.

【近】 good，crop

prospect ['prɔspekt]

【释】 *n.* 眼界，风景，景色；展望

【例】 Their *prospects* for patronage in their own country were uncertain.

【衍】 prospective（*adj.*）将来的，未来的（[*opp.*] retrospective）

【近】 scene，view，vision，outlook

purification [ˌpjuərifi'keiʃən]

【释】 *n.* 清洗，洗净；净化(作用)，提纯，精制

【例】 These serve as an air *purification* scheme by allowing the compounds to move from the air to the water or soil.

【衍】 purify（*v.*）

【近】 cleansing，refining

rail [reil]

【释】 *n.* 轨道；钢轨；铁路

【例】 The city has a superb natural harbor，as well as excellent *rail* connections.

【衍】 railhead（*n.*）轨道终点；railroading（*n.*）铁路建设事业

【近】 railroad，railway

rearrange [ˌriːəˈreindʒ]

【释】 *v.* 重新整顿，重新布置，重新排列

【例】 She lights the construction，then ***rearranges*** and rephotographs it until she arrives at a final image.

【衍】 arrange（*v.*）；rearrangement（*n.*）

【近】 reorganize，reshuffle

refer [riˈfəː]

【释】 ① *v.* 涉及(to)，说到

【例】 Situation ***refers*** to the general position in relation to the surrounding region，whereas site involves physical characteristics of the specific location.

【衍】 reference（*n.*）；referee（*n. & v.*）仲裁，裁判

【释】 ② *v.* 表示，指示

【例】 The term "autonomic nervous system" ***refers*** to the parts of the central and peripheral systems that supply and regulate the activity of cardiac muscle，smooth muscle，and many glands.

【释】 ③ *v.* 参考，引证，引用；翻阅，查看(账簿等)

【例】 Slang，***refers*** to words and expressions understood by a large number of speakers but not accepted as good，formal usage by the majority.

【衍】 reference（*n.*）；referenced（*adj.*）参考的；引用的

relevant [ˈrelivənt]

【释】 *adj.* 有关的；适当的，贴切的，中肯的

【例】 The new goal was to make the university ***relevant*** to the real pursuits of the world.

【衍】 irrelevant（*adj.*）；relevantly（*adv.*）

【近】 pertinent，related

repertory [ˈrepətəri]

【释】 *n.* (尤指知识等的)贮藏，搜集；贮藏所

【例】 As the appropriate brain maturation occurs，the various emotions appear in an infant's ***repertory***.

【近】 reservoir

resort [riˈzɔːt]

【释】 ① *n.* 热闹场所，娱乐场所；胜地

【例】 Miami Beach's was the ***resort***—the tropical escape from Depression doldrums.

【释】 ② *v.* 倚靠，凭借 *n.* 手段

【例】 It is pleasant to imagine a woodworker，carefully matching lumber，joining a chest together without *resort* to nails or glue.

【衍】 resource（*n.*）资源；resourcefulness（*n.*）足智多谋

【近】 alternative，route

rhinoceros ［rai'nɔsərəs］

【释】 *n.* 犀牛

【例】 The long-haired *rhinoceros*，and other mammals have been periodically exposed in the tundra of Siberia，the hair and red flesh still frozen in cold storage.

rotate ［rəu'teit］

【释】 ① *v.* 旋转；轮转；循环；自转；使旋转(轮转)；使循环

【例】 Jupiter *rotates* very fast，once every 98 hours.

【衍】 rotation（*v.*）；rotator（*n.*）

【近】 turn，revolve，swivel

【释】 ② *v.* 轮流，交替，轮换

【例】 Committee membership *rotates* every year，so that new voices and opinions are constantly heard.

【近】 take turns，alternate，replace

sanitation ［ˌsæni'teiʃən］

【释】 *n.* 公共卫生；卫生设备；下水道设备

【例】 And in Sacramento an excavation at the site of a fashionable nineteenth-century hotel revealed that garbage had been stashed in the building's basement despite *sanitation* laws to the contrary.

【衍】 sanitary（*adj.*）卫生(上)的

【近】 hygiene，cleanliness

scruple ['skru:pl]

【释】 *n.* 顾虑；迟疑；犹豫

【例】 Sectional jealousies and constitutional *scruples* stood in the way of action by the federal government，and necessary expenditures were too great for private enterprise.

【衍】 scrupulously（*adv.*）顾虑多地，小心谨慎地，严谨地

【近】 doubt，hesitation，qualm

Unit 13

sensory ['sensəri]

【释】 *adj*. 感觉(上)的；感官的；知觉器官的

【例】 It can only evolve in species with sense organs that are well enough developed so that continuous *sensory* contact can be maintained.

【衍】 sensor（*n*.）感受器，传感器

shield [ʃi:ld]

【释】 *v*. 防护；屏蔽　*n*. 罩；屏；防御物

【例】 Locks and escutcheon plates—the latter to *shield* the wood from the metal key—would often be imported.

【衍】 shielding（*adj*.）

【近】 protect，guard，shelter

simultaneous [ˌsaiməl'teiniəs]

【释】 *adj*. 同时发生的，同时做的，同时的

【例】 These ponderous machines—sometimes pulled by as many as 40 horses—reaped the grain, threshed it, and bagged it, all in one *simultaneous* operation.

【衍】 simultaneously（*adv*.）

【近】 concurrent，synchronized，coincident

soap [səup]

【释】 *n*. 肥皂

【例】 Potash and soda are not interchangeable for all purposes, but for glass—or *soap*-making either would do.

【衍】 soapy（*adj*.）；soaping（*n*.）皂洗；soaper（*n*.）肥皂制造商

specialty ['speʃəlti]

【释】 *n*. 特制品；新产品；专门，专业

【例】 Export merchants became differentiated from their importing counterparts, and *specialty* shops began to appear in addition to general stores selling a variety of goods.

【衍】 special（*adj*.）；specially（*adv*.）；specialize（*v*.）；specialization（*n*.）；specialist（*n*.）

【近】 area of expertise

spoon [spu:n]

【释】 *n*. 匙，调羹

【例】	A hormone labeled cholecystokinin（CCK），produced by the mucosa of the upper intestine，tells you when you have had enough to eat and should promptly put down your *spoon*.
【衍】	spoonful（*n.*）一匙的量，一满匙
【近】	ladle

starve [stɑːv]

【释】	*v.* 使饿死；使饥饿
【例】	If it were not for this faculty，they would devour all the food available in a short time and would probably *starve* themselves out of existence.
【衍】	starvation（*n.*）
【近】	go hungry，be malnourished，waste away

stitch [stitʃ]

【释】	*v.* 缝，缝合；钉
【例】	Wealthy and socially prominent settlers made quilts of the English type，cut from large lengths of cloth of the same color and texture rather than *stitched* together from smaller pieces.
【衍】	stitcher（*n.*）订书机
【近】	sew，darn，suture

stroke [strəuk]

【释】	*n.* 笔画
【例】	Scratches made with a left-to-right *stroke* direction（by right-handers）are more common than scratches in the opposite direction（made by left-hander）.

subway ['sʌbwei]

【释】	*n.* 地道；地下铁道(列车)
【例】	After the stock exchange collapse of 1873，the *subway* was sealed up and forgotten.
【近】	passageway，channel

supreme [sjuː'priːm]

【释】	*adj.* 最高的，无上的，最优秀的；最重要的
【例】	Each state has its own system of courts composed of civil and criminal trial courts，sometimes intermediate courts of appeal，and a state *supreme* courts.

Unit 13

【衍】supremely（*adv.*）；supremeness（*n.*）；supremacy（*n.*）最高地位，无上权威

【近】extreme，superlative，best

symmetrical [si'metrikəl]

【释】*adj.* 对称的，匀称的，相称的，平衡的（[*opp.*] asymmetrical）

【例】The elliptical galaxies have a *symmetrical* elliptical or spheroidal shape with no obvious structure.

【衍】symmetrically（*adv.*）

【近】balanced，proportioned，regular

tavern ['tævən]

【释】*n.* 酒馆，小旅馆，客栈

【例】It was there that Crane met his wife，who at that time ran a popular *tavern* in the town.

【近】inn，pub，bar，lodge

terrace ['terəs]

【释】*n.* 台地，平台 *v.* 使成台地，筑坛建造成平顶

【例】The largest，later named Pueblo Bonito(Pretty Town) by the Spanish，rose in five *terraced* stories，contained more than 800 rooms，and could have housed a population of 1,000 or more.

【衍】terraced（*adj.*）台地的，有平台的

【近】veranda，patio，porch

threat [θret]

【释】① *n.* 凶兆，危险

【例】The ever-watchful plover can detect a possible *threat* at a considerable distance.

【近】danger，hazard，peril

【释】② *n.* 恐吓，威吓，威胁

【例】At one stroke of the pen and without even a *threat* of war，the Louisiana Purchase doubled the size of the United States，and secured the Mississippi River as a highway for Western trade.

【衍】threaten（*v.*）；threatened（*adj.*）受到威胁的，濒危的；threatener（*n.*）；threatening（*adj.*）威胁的；危险的

【近】	menace，intimidation，warning
tolerance	[ˈtɔlərəns]
【释】	***n.*** 忍受；容忍；耐性；耐受性
【例】	Other animals have a wider ***tolerance*** for changes of bodily temperature.
【衍】	tolerant（*adj.*）；tolerate（*v.*）；tolerable（*adj.*）；intolerance（*n.*）
【近】	broadmindedness，acceptance，forbearance
tranquil	[ˈtræŋkwil]
【释】	***adj.*** 平静的；安静的，镇静的；稳定的
【例】	A computer programmer from New York City moves to the ***tranquil*** Adirondack Mountains and stays in contact with her office via computer.
【衍】	tranquilly（*adv.*）；tranquility（*n.*）
【近】	calm，peaceful，quiet
trick	[trik]
【释】	① ***n.*** 奸计，诡计，骗术 ***v.*** 欺骗
【例】	Plovers also have an effective repertoire of ***tricks*** for distracting potential nest predators from their exposed and defenseless eggs or chicks.
【衍】	trickery（*n.*）；tricky（*adj.*）狡猾的，机智的；trickish（*adj.*）狡猾的
【近】	deception，hoax，swindle
【释】	② ***n.*** 戏法；快手把戏；幻术
【例】	In the speed of its execution，the righting of a tumbling cat resembles a magician's ***trick***.
【近】	knack，technique，secret
turtle	[ˈtəːtl]
【释】	***n.*** 龟，海龟
【例】	Rattles were made of gourds or of ***turtle*** shells filled with pebbles or seeds.
【衍】	turtleback（*n.*）龟甲
unless	[ʌnˈles]
【释】	***conj.*** 如果不，要是不，除非
【例】	Technique is of no use ***unless*** it is combined with musical knowledge and understanding.

Unit 13

【近】	save，except
variety	[vəˈraiəti]
【释】	*n.* 种类；项目
【例】	Composers today use a wider *variety* of sounds than ever before，including many that were once considered undesirable noises.
【近】	diversity，assortment
vibrate	[ˈvaibreit]
【释】	*v.* 摇动，振动；颤动
【例】	The ground shook and the cliffs seemed to *vibrate*.
【衍】	vibration（*n.*）；vibrant（*adj.*）
【近】	shake，tremble
wander	[ˈwɔndə]
【释】	*v.* 漫步；漫游
【例】	Small tribes such as the Shoshone and Ute *wandered* the dry and mountainous lands between the Rocky Mountains and the Pacific Ocean.
【衍】	wanderlust（*n.*）流浪癖
【近】	ramble，roam
whittle	[ˈ(h)witl]
【释】	*v.* 切；削；削减，减少
【例】	For example，in its pure form，aluminum is soft enough to *whittle*.
【近】	cut，carve
yield	[ji:ld]
【释】	*v.* 生出；产生（作物、报酬、利益等）
【例】	The cores of sediment drilled by the Glomar Challenger have also *yielded* information critical to understanding the world's past climates.
【近】	produce，bear，generate

Exercise of Unit 13

左列单词在右列中有一个同义词，请找出并在相应的位置写上正确答案。

Exercise 1:

(A) accelerate _____ cleansing
(B) adjunct _____ accessory
(C) ledge _____ shelf
(D) tranquil _____ turn
(E) rotate _____ hasten
(F) purification _____ calm

Exercise 2:

(A) behave _____ shake
(B) flood _____ diversity
(C) vibrate _____ deluge
(D) personality _____ hygiene
(E) sanitation _____ character
(F) variety _____ act

Exercise 3:

(A) irrigate _____ water
(B) deposit _____ place
(C) crucial _____ danger
(D) impervious _____ sediment
(E) deposit _____ critical
(F) threat _____ impermeable

Exercise 4:

(A) confirm _____ concise
(B) endeavor _____ ramble
(C) wander _____ verify
(D) drift _____ textile
(E) fabric _____ enterprise
(F) brief _____ float

Exercise 5:

(A) fabric _____ alternative
(B) ideal _____ structure
(C) resort _____ waft
(D) powder _____ scene
(E) blow _____ perfect
(F) prospect _____ dust

Exercise 6:

(A) hollow _____ nourishment
(B) relevant _____ motivate
(C) inspire _____ basement
(D) cellar _____ truth
(E) nutrition _____ empty
(F) fidelity _____ pertinent

Exercise 7:
(A) rail _____ period
(B) chord _____ railroad
(C) unless _____ save
(D) interval _____ harmony
(E) neutral _____ cut
(F) whittle _____ unbiased

Exercise 8:
(A) blow _____ sew
(B) core _____ center
(C) stitch _____ explode
(D) produce _____ good
(E) distort _____ balanced
(F) symmetrical ____ deform

Exercise 9:
(A) pivot _____ assign
(B) attribute _____ turn
(C) coarse _____ trouble
(D) myriad _____ crude
(E) outlying _____ remote
(F) haunt _____ countless

Exercise 10:
(A) attribute _____ aspect
(B) fragment _____ faint
(C) dim _____ take turns
(D) repertory _____ reservoir
(E) rotate _____ broadmindedn
(F) tolerance _____ section

ANSWERS:

1	F B C E A D
2	C F B E D A
3	A B F E C D
4	F C A E B D
5	C A E F B D
6	E C D F A B
7	D A C B F E
8	C B A D F E
9	B A F C E D
10	A C E D F B

Unit 14

access	endow	mystery	shift
administrate	equivalent	niche	sink
alligator	exhaustion	objective	soaring
antibiotic	facade	opinion	species
artery	figure	output	sprawl
auditory	flour	parallel	stately
barb	frame	pedagogy	stock
belief	gap	perspective	stroll
boast	gland	plague	succeed
brilliance	hallmark	poll	surge
calcium	hazard	practical	sympathy
carpenter	hominid	presumably	tax
cellular	identical	productive	terrain
choreograph	implement	prosper	thresh
coat	inflation	pursue	tomato
complex	install	rainfall	transaction
conflict	intervene	rebel	trigger
content	isolate	refine	twig
correlate	kitchen	reliable	unlikely
crude	legal	repetitive	various
decay	lithosphere	respect	vigorous
depress	lure	rhythm	wane
dime	marble	rote	wholesale
distract	mental	satellite	youngster
drip	millimeter	sculptor	
elegance	monetary	sentimental	

access	['ækses]
【释】	① *n.* 进路，入口
【例】	A sunken plaza, complete with gardens and fountains, was designed to provide *access* to these shops.
【衍】	accessible (*adj.*); inaccessible (*adj.*); accessibility (*n.*)
【近】	entry, entrance, gate, door
【释】	② *v.* 接近
【例】	Walking or leaping species *access* the outer twigs either by snapping off the whole branch.
【近】	approach, get in
administrate	[əd'ministreit]
【释】	*v.* 管理；支配
【例】	development of a welfare state *administrated* by the federal government
【衍】	administrative (*adj.*) 管理的；行政的；administration (*n.*) 行政机关；局(处、署)；[美] 政府
【近】	control, govern, manage
alligator	['æligeitə]
【释】	*n.* 短吻鳄，鳄(鱼)
【例】	Chinese *alligator* 扬子鳄
【近】	crocodile
antibiotic	[,æntibai'ɔtik]
【释】	*n.* 抗生素
【例】	Certain fungi and even some kinds of bacteria secrete substances known as *antibiotics* into their external environment.
【衍】	antibiosis (*n.*) 抗生；antibiotically (*adv.*)
artery	['ɑːtəri]
【释】	*n.* 动脉；要道；中枢
【例】	The leadership of New York City as an ocean port, along with its proximity to major *arteries* of land transportation, was a local factor that helped to make the city an irresistible magnet.
【衍】	arterial (*adj.*)
【近】	blood vessel, route, channel

auditory [ˈɔːditəri]

【释】 *adj.* 耳的，听觉的

【例】 Within the first month of their lives, babies' responses to the sound of the human voice will be different from their responses to other sorts of *auditory* stimuli.

【衍】 auditorium (*n.*) 讲堂，教室；会厅，大会堂，大礼堂

【近】 aural, acoustic

barb [bɑːb]

【释】 *n.* 倒钩，倒刺

【例】 Single-strand wire, round or oval, is made from high-tensile steel with the *barbs* crimped or welded on.

【衍】 barbed (*adj.*)

belief [biˈliːf]

【释】 *n.* 信，信任；相信(in)；信仰；信心

【例】 As with most aspects of Plains Indian culture, music was closely bound up with religious *beliefs*.

【衍】 believe (*v.*); believing (*adj.*)

【近】 faith, conviction; dogma, doctrine, tenets

boast [bəust]

【释】 *v.* 以有…而自豪，有…可以夸耀；包含；吹嘘

【例】 When the state's project has been completed, California will *boast* the most extensive water transport system in history.

【衍】 boaster (*n.*); boastful (*adj.*)

【近】 have, possess

brilliance [ˈbriljəns]

【释】 *n.* 光彩，光辉，光泽，【光】亮度

【例】 Louis Armstrong's instrumental *brilliance*, demonstrated through extended solos, was a major influence in this development.

【衍】 brilliant (*adj.*)

【近】 brightness, vividness, radiance

calcium [ˈkælsiəm]

【释】 *n.* 钙

【例】 Generally, it is the inorganic hard parts, composed mostly of *calcium* carbonate, that form the vast majority of unaltered fossils.

【衍】	calcareous (*adj.*) 含钙的，石灰质的
carpenter	[ˈkɑːpintə]
【释】	*n.* 木匠，木工(尤指粗木工)
【例】	The *carpenter's* shop probably provided the frame and perhaps supplied the panel，and yet another shop supplied the gold.
cellular	[ˈseljulə]
【释】	*adj.* 细胞的，细胞质(状)的
【例】	Active plant defense mechanisms are comparable to the immune system of vertebrate animals，although the *cellular* and molecular bases are fundamentally different.
【衍】	cell (*n.*)
choreograph	[ˈkɔriəgrɑːf]
【释】	*v.* 设计舞蹈动作
【例】	She had not only produced a technique of the dance，*choreographed* and taught it，but her disciples have gone out to fill the modern dance world.
【衍】	choreographer (*n.*) 舞蹈动作设计者；choreography (*n.*) 舞蹈艺术，舞蹈表演
【近】	compose，design
coat	[kəut]
【释】	① *v.* 包上，涂上，盖上
【例】	The steel wires used are galvanized—*coated* with zinc to make them rustproof.
【近】	cover，paint，smear
【释】	② *n.* (动物的)毛皮；(植物的)表皮；(漆等的)涂层
【例】	A bird's feathery *coat* is good insulation against the cold.
【近】	fur，wool，fleece，hair，hide，skin
complex	[ˈkɔmpleks]
【释】	*n.* 【化】络合物；复合物，综合体
【例】	But around the year 700 A. D.，the Anasazi began to build their homes above ground and join them together into rambling multistories *complexes*，which the Spanish called pueblos or villages.
conflict	[ˈkɔnflikt]
【释】	*n. & v.* 冲突，矛盾

【例】 Expressive leaders are less concerned with the overall goals of the group than with providing emotional support to group members and attempting to minimize tension and *conflict* among them.

【衍】 conflicting（*adj.*）

【近】 variance，divergence

content ［kən'tent，'kɔntent］

【释】 ① *adj.* 满足的，甘心的

【例】 Those who could afford them were quite *content* to remain in the more sumptuous，single-family homes.

【近】 satisfied，happy

【释】 ② *n.* 容量，含量

【例】 Therefore the higher the clay *content* in a sample，the more refined and durable the shapes into which it can be molded.

【释】 ③ *n.*［*pl.*］内容，内含物；（一本书的）目次，目录

【例】 In addition to revealing the primary concerns of a society，the *contents* of that society's art may also reflect the culture's social stratification.

【近】 substance

correlate ['kɔrileit]

【释】 *v. & n.* 互相关联，相互关系（with；to）

【例】 It is not enough to observe behaviors and *correlate* them with physiological events that occur at the same time.

【衍】 correlation（*n.*）

【近】 associate

crude ［kruːd］

【释】 *adj.* 天然的，未加工的

【例】 His well began to yield 20 barrels of *crude* oil a day.

【衍】 crudely（*adv.*）；crudeness（*n.*）

【近】 raw，natural，coarse

decay ［di'kei］

【释】 *v. & n.* 腐朽，腐烂；衰减，衰退

【例】 San Antonio，Texas，offers an object lesson for numerous other cities combating urban *decay*.

【近】 decompose，rot，molder

depress [di'pres]

【释】 ① v. 压下，压低(声调等)，放低([opp.] raise)

【例】 The drought *depressed* the water level in the reservoirs.

【近】 lower，press

【释】 ② v. 使沮丧；使萧条

【例】 He was *depressed* because he had not passed his examinations.

【衍】 depression (n.) 萧条，不振；沮丧，消沉

【近】 sadden，dispirit，demoralize

dime [daim]

【释】 n. (美、加)一角银币

【例】 Following the admission of Tennessee in 1796，for example，some varieties of half-*dimes*，dimes，and half-dollars were produced with sixteen stars.

distract [dis'trækt]

【释】 v. 分散(注意力等)，岔开(念头等)([opp.] attract)

【例】 Plovers also have an effective repertoire of tricks for *distracting* potential nest predators from their exposed and defenseless eggs or chicks.

【衍】 distraction (n.)

【近】 divert

drip [drip]

【释】 n. 水滴 v. 滴下

【例】 Water from the surface *drips* down through cracks.

【衍】 drippy (adj.) 滴水的；dripless (adj.) 不滴水的

【近】 trickle，leak，dribble

elegance ['eligəns]

【释】 n. 雅致，风雅，优美，高尚

【例】 The *elegance* of this first subway will probably never be surpassed.

【衍】 elegant (adj.)

【近】 grace，style，chic，sophistication

endow [in'dau]

【释】 v. 捐赠

【例】 The director refused her offer before she even had a chance to express her intention to build and *endow* a Whitney wing.

【衍】	endowment（n.）
【近】	donate，bestow
equivalent	[i'kwivələnt]
【释】	***adj. & n.*** 相当(的)，相同(的)，同等的(物)；等价的(物)
【例】	Perhaps the nearest modern ***equivalent*** in Anglo-America is the Amish.
【衍】	equivalence（n.）；equivalency（n.）
【近】	counterpart，parallel
exhaustion	[ig'zɔːstʃən]
【释】	***n.*** 疲惫，衰竭
【例】	Stuck，the unfortunate beasts would die of ***exhaustion*** and hunger or fall prey to predators that often also became stuck.
【衍】	exhaust（v.）用尽，耗尽(资源等)，使筋疲力尽
【近】	fatigue，weariness
facade	[fə'sɑːd]
【释】	***n.*** 【建】正面；外表，外观；(掩饰真相的)门面
【例】	In spite of Hunt's inviting ***facade***，the living space was awkwardly arranged.
【近】	mask，frontage
figure	['figə]
【释】	① ***n.*** 画像，塑像
【例】	With the turn-of-the-century crafts movement and the discovery of nontraditional sources of inspiration，such as wooden African ***figures*** and masks，there arose a new urge for hands-on，personal execution of art and an interaction with the medium.
【近】	statue，portrait
【释】	② ***n.*** 人物
【例】	Iry Lejeune became a pivotal ***figure*** in the revitalization of Cajun music，his untimely death in 1955 only added to his legendary stature.
【近】	personage，celebrity
flour	['flauə]
【释】	***n.*** 面粉；谷粉

【例】 In contrast，wheat and wheat *flour* composed only 6 percent of the value of American exports in that year.

frame [freim]

【释】 *n.* 机构；组织　*v.* 构造；给…装框子

【例】 Panels were fitted into slots on the basic *frames*.

【衍】 frameless（*n.*）；framework（*n.*）

【近】 structure

gap [gæp]

【释】 *n.* 裂缝；豁口，缺口

【例】 The crossbill snakes its long tongue into the *gap* and draws out the seed.

【衍】 gapped（*adj.*）

【近】 rent，gulf

gland [glænd]

【释】 *n.* 腺

【例】 The modulation of chemical signals occurs via the elaboration of the number of exocrine *glands* that produce pheromones.

【衍】 glandular（*adj.*）

hallmark ['hɔːlmɑːk]

【释】 *n.* 标志；特点

【例】 It's a technique that has become the *hallmark* of Amber Films.

【近】 characteristic，trait，brand

hazard ['hæzəd]

【释】 *n.* 碰巧；机会；偶然的事；孤注一掷，冒险

【例】 By such ingenious adaptations to specific pollinators, orchids have avoided the *hazards* of rampant cross-breeding in the wild.

【衍】 hazardous（*adj.*）

【近】 danger，risk，chance

hominid ['hɔminid]

【释】 *n.* 人科（Hominidea），原始人类

【例】 The best-known specimens were left by small *hominids* around 3.6 to 3.75 million years ago.

【衍】 hominization（*n.*）（灵长类动物等的）人化，人化过程

【近】	primitive
identical	[ai'dentikəl]
【释】	*adj*. 同一的；同样的
【例】	No two comets ever look *identical*，but they have basic features in common，one of the most obvious of which is a coma.
【衍】	identity（*n*.）一致；同一性
【近】	equal，alike，indistinguishable
implement	['implimənt]
【释】	① *n*. 工具；器具
【例】	Other Stone Age *implements* were made by or for left-handers.
【近】	tool，instrument，utensil
【释】	② *v*. 执行，履行
【例】	The plan impressed university officials，and in time many of its recommendations were *implemented*.
【衍】	implementation（*n*.）
【近】	apply，execute
inflation	[in'fleiʃən]
【释】	*n*. 膨胀；【经】通货膨胀（[*opp*.] **deflation**)
【例】	They were spurred by the *inflation* of the 1970's，which combined with California's rapid population growth，pushed housing prices，as well as rents，to record levels.
install	[in'stɔːl]
【释】	*v*. 任命，使就(职)；把…安插到(in)
【例】	Professor Sawyer was formally *installed* as President last Thursday.
【衍】	installation（*n*.）
intervene	[ˌintə'viːn]
【释】	*v*. 插进；介入
【例】	In a year，it crosses nearly ten trillion kilometers，about six million miles，of *intervening* space.
【衍】	intervention（*n*.）
isolate	['aisəleit]
【释】	*v*. 隔离，使孤立

【例】 Deep-ocean sediments are largely *isolated* from the mechanical erosion and the intense chemical and biological activity that rapidly destroy much land-based evidence of past climates.

【衍】 isolable（*adj.*）；isolation（*n.*）

【近】 insulate，detach，segregate，seperate

kitchen ['kitʃin]

【释】 *n.* 厨房

【例】 Education can take place anywhere，whether in the shower or on the job，whether in a *kitchen* or on a tractor.

legal ['li:gəl]

【释】 *adj.* 法律(上)的；法定的，合法的，正当的

【例】 The study area usually coincides with a natural physiographic region；unfortunately these seldom coincide with the *legal* jurisdiction of country and state boundaries.

【衍】 legalize（*v.*）法律认可，使合法；legality（*n.*）合法性，法律性；守法主义；legacy（*n.*）【法】(动产的)遗赠，遗产；传代物，传统，遗教

【近】 lawful，officially permitted，permissible

lithosphere ['liθəˌsfiə]

【释】 *n.* 岩石圈，陆界

【例】 Since the size of the Earth is essentially constant，new *lithosphere* can be created at the mid-ocean ridges only if an equal amount of lithospheric material is consumed elsewhere.

【衍】 lithospheric（*adj.*）；lithograph（*n.*）石(平)版画；平版印刷

lure [luə]

【释】 *v.* 引诱，诱惑 *n.* 魅力；诱惑品，诱饵

【例】 Many adults，poor and disillusioned with farm life，were *lured* to the cities by promises of steady employment，regular paychecks，and expanded social opportunities.

【近】 entice，tempt，attract

marble ['ma:bl]

【释】 *n.* 大理石 *adj.* 大理石(似)的；有大理石纹彩的

【例】 A few *marble* memorials with carved busts，urns，or other decorations were produced in England and brought to the colonies to be set in the walls of churches—as in King's Chapel in Boston.

【近】 mineral，granite

mental ['mentəl]

【释】 *adj.* 智(脑)力的；精神的，思想的；心理的([*opp.*] corporal)

【例】 Slow-wave sleep may be especially helpful in restoring muscle control，whereas REM sleep may be more important for *mental* activity.

【衍】 mentally (*adv.*)

【近】 cerebral，mind，psychological

millimeter ['milimi:tə]

【释】 *n.* 毫米(千分之一米)

【例】 In many instances the specimens are less than one-tenth of a *millimeter* in a diameter.

monetary ['mʌnitəri]

【释】 *adj.* 货币的；金钱的；金融的；财政(上)的

【例】 Today electronic *monetary* systems are gradually being introduced that will transform money into even less tangible forms，reducing it to arrays of "bits and bytes."

【衍】 monetarily (*adv.*)

【近】 financial，economic，fiscal

mystery ['mistəri]

【释】 *n.* 神秘，秘密；神秘的事物

【例】 Just how salt became so crucial to our metabolism is a *mystery*；one appealing theory traces our dependence on it to the chemistry of the late Cambrian seas.

【衍】 mysterious (*adj.*) 神秘的；暧昧的；故弄玄虚的；mysteriously (*adv.*)；mystical (*adj.*) 神秘的，秘诀的；mystify (*v.*) 使神秘化；蒙蔽，迷惑

【近】 secrecy，obscurity，inscrutability

niche [nitʃ]

【释】 ① *n.* 适当地位，活动范围

【例】 Later ancestral horse types moved from their forest *niche* out onto the grassy plains.

【衍】 niched（*adj.*）放在适当位置的

【近】 place，position，forte

【释】 ② *n.* 壁龛（搁雕像、花瓶等的墙壁凹处）

【例】 Some kivas contained *niches* for ceremonial objects，a central fire pit，and holes in the floor for communicating with the spirits of tribal ancestors.

【近】 recess，alcove，nook

objective ［əb'dʒektiv］

【释】 ① *n.* 目的，目标，任务

【例】 A draft plan has been prepared，with the *objective* of maintaining traditional economic uses but limiting new development that would damage park resources.

【近】 object，purpose，aim

【释】 ② *adj.* 客观的；真实的（［*opp.*］subjective）

【例】 Because Sioux names almost always were based on something *objective*，they could easily be rendered as pictographs.

【衍】 objectify（*v.*）；objectively（*adv.*）；objectiveness（*n.*）

【近】 unprejudiced，impartial，detached

opinion ［ə'pinjən］

【释】 *n.* 意见；看法；见解；［常 *pl.*］主张

【例】 Committee membership rotates every year，so that new voices and *opinions* are constantly heard.

【衍】 opinioned（*adj.*）有意见的；opinionated（*adj.*）固执己见的，武断的；opinionative（*adj.*）固执己见的，武断的

【近】 view，estimation，attitude

output ［'autput］

【释】 *n.* 产量；生产，出产；产品；输出量，输出

【例】 The *output* of light and heat of the sun requires that some 600 million tons of hydrogen be converted into helium in the sun every second.

【近】 production，yield

parallel ［'pærəlel］

【释】 *adj.* 平行的；并行的（to；with）；【电】并联的

【例】	Equally important is the fact that the execution of multiple-step tasks is accomplished in a series-*parallel* sequence.
【衍】	parallelism（*n*.）【数】平行，对应，类似
【近】	similar，equivalent，matching

pedagogy [ˈpedəgɒgi]

【释】	*n*. 教育学；教授法；儿童教育；教师职业
【例】	The second calls of "scientific *pedagogy*," a science of childhood based on observation.
【衍】	pedagogic（*adj*.）

perspective [pəˈspektiv]

【释】	*n*. 观点；看法
【例】	What they do is look at familiar conditions from a *perspective* that makes these conditions seem foolish，harmful，or affected.
【衍】	perspectively（*adv*.）
【近】	outlook，view

plague [pleig]

【释】	*n*. 瘟疫，传染病；灾害
【例】	They outlasted recurrent *plagues* of smallpox and malaria and a steady progression of natural accidents.
【近】	disease，infection，pestilence

poll [pəul]

【释】	*n*. 民意测验
【例】	In the United States，the best-known surveys are the Gallup *poll* and the Harris poll.
【近】	survey

practical [ˈpræktikəl]

【释】	① *adj*. 有实效的；可行的
【例】	But it may not seem such a great amount if we consider that improvements allowed steamboats to remain *practical* for most commercial transport in Canada until the mid-nineteenth century.
【衍】	practically（*adv*.）；impractical（*adj*.）
【近】	useful，functional
【释】	② *adj*. [贬]只讲实用的

【例】 In documenting geographical variation in butterfly diversity, some arbitrary, *practical* decisions are made.

presumably [pri'zjuːməbli]

【释】 *adv.* 推测起来；假定；大概，大抵，可能

【例】 Answering echoes were returned from intermediate depths, *presumably* from schools of fish, whales, or submarines.

【衍】 presumable (*adj.*)

【近】 seemingly, apparently

productive [prə'dʌktiv]

【释】 *adj.* 生产的，生产性的；有生产力的；多产的

【例】 Schools tried to educate young women so they could occupy *productive* places in the urban industrial economy.

【衍】 product (*n.*) 产品，产物；productivity (*n.*) 生产力

【近】 creative, prolific, industrious, fruitful

prosper ['prɔspə]

【释】 *v.* (使)兴隆，(使)繁荣；(使)成功

【例】 Holding a large stake in the community, they exercised power to make it *prosper*.

【衍】 prosperity (*n.*)；prosperous (*adj.*)

【近】 thrive, flourish, boom

pursue [pə'sjuː]

【释】 *v.* 追，追赶，追踪；纠缠

【例】 Toward these ends the federal government *pursued* several courses of action.

【衍】 pursuit (*n.*)

【近】 follow, chase, hunt, track

rainfall ['reinfɔːl]

【释】 *n.* 下雨，降雨量

【例】 If all of water were condensed in liquid form, it would cover the entire surface of the Earth with one inch of *rainfall*.

【近】 rain, rainwater

rebel ['rebəl]

【释】 *n.* 造反者，反叛者；起义者，反抗者

【例】 She insists she never started out to be a *rebel*.

【衍】	rebellion（*n.*）
【近】	revolutionary，dissenter
refine	[ri'fain]
【释】	① *v.* 精炼，精制；纯化，提纯
【例】	Crude oil could be *refined* into many products.
【衍】	refiner（*n.*）；refinement（*n.*）；fine（*v.*）把…提纯
【近】	purify，get rid of impurities，distill
【释】	② *v.* 使优美，使精致；琢磨（文章等），推敲
【例】	On this perfect surface，the artist would sketch a composition with chalk，and then *refine* it with inks.
【衍】	refinement（*n.*）
【近】	improve，perfect，polish
reliable	[ri'laiəbl]
【释】	*adj.* 可靠的，确实的（[*opp.*] **undependable**）
【例】	They offered the traveler *reliable* transportation in comfortable facilities—a welcome alternative to stagecoach travel.
【衍】	reliably（*adv.*）；reliance（*n.*）；reliant（*adj.*）信赖的；依靠的
【近】	dependable，trustworthy
repetitive	[ri'petitiv]
【释】	*adj.* 反复的，重复的
【例】	Art deco used plant motifs，but regularized the forms into abstracted *repetitive* patterns rather than presenting them as flowing，asymmetrical foliage.
【衍】	repetitively（*adv.*）
【近】	cyclic，recurring，cyclical
respect	[ri'spekt]
【释】	*n.* 关系；着眼点，方面；细目
【例】	The lithosphere is divided into a few dozen plates of various sizes and shapes，in general the plates are in motion with *respect* to one another.
【衍】	respective（*adj.*）各自的；respectively（*adv.*）
【近】	detail，regard，sense
rhythm	['riðəm]
【释】	*n.* 节奏；韵律

Unit 14

— 309 —

【例】 In playing hot, a musician consciously departs from strict meter to create a relaxed sense of phrasing that also emphasizes the underlying *rhythms*.

【衍】 rhythmic (*adj.*); rhythmics (*n.*) 韵律学; rhythmical (*adj.*)

【近】 beat, pace, tempo

rote [rəut]

【释】 *n.* 机械方法; 刻板办法; 死记, 死背

【例】 Drilling and learning by *rote* were replaced by the German method of lecturing, in which the professor's own research was presented in class.

satellite [ˈsætəlait]

【释】 *n.* 卫星; 人造卫星

【例】 Craters scar the surface of every planet and *satellite* in the inner solar system (Mercury, Venus, Earth, and Mars).

sculptor [ˈskʌlptə]

【释】 *n.* 雕刻(塑)家; 雕刻(塑)工人

【例】 Or the belief in the supernatural powers of a stone or tree may cause a *sculptor* to be sensitive to that material.

【衍】 sculpt (*v.*) 雕; 刻; sculpture (*n.*) 雕塑; sculptural (*adj.*)

sentimental [ˌsentiˈmentəl]

【释】 *adj.* 多愁善感的; 感伤的; 动情的

【例】 Satire tends to remind people that much of what they see, hear, and read in popular media is sanctimonious, *sentimental*, and only partially true.

【衍】 sentiment (*n.*) 情感情绪; sentimentality (*n.*) 多愁善感; sentimentalism (*n.*) 感情主义; sentimentalize (*v.*) 伤感

【近】 over-romantic, gushy, maudlin

shift [ʃift]

【释】 *v. & n.* 变迁; 变化; 变换

【例】 That yellow "hump" will *shift* as the Sun evolves, and the light of day will change accordingly.

【衍】	shifty (*adj.*); shiftable (*adj.*)
【近】	transfer，alter，change

sink ［siŋk］

【释】	① *v.* 下沉，下陷
【例】	The warmer and lighter bottom layer then tends to rise and the cooler layer tends to *sink* in a continuous cycle.
【衍】	sunken (*adj.*) 沉没的，沉下去的；sinkable (*adj.*)；sinkage (*n.*)
【近】	descend
【释】	② *v.* 衰颓，沦落，败落，堕落
【例】	How then could half of them be left to *sink* under an enormous debt，whilst others are enabled to replace all their expenditures from the hard earnings of the whole confederacy?
【近】	decline，worsen，deteriorate

soaring ［'sɔːriŋ］

【释】	*adj.* 翱翔的(鹰等)；高耸云霄的(尖塔等)
【例】	Thus，when Alexander Calder designed one of his last，mobiles—a *soaring* creation eighty feet long—his choice of aluminum over steel cut two tons from its weight.
【衍】	soar (*v.* & *n.*) 翱翔；耸立
【近】	towering，high，high-ceilinged

species ［'spiːʃiːz］

【释】	*n.* (［*sing.*］，［*pl.*］)种类；【生】(物)种
【例】	The tar pats were found to contain the remains of scores of *species* of animals from the last 30,000 years of the Ice Age.

sprawl ［sprɔːl］

【释】	*n.* 蔓延　*v.* (难看地)爬行
【例】	These excesses underscore a feature of residential expansion related to the growth of mass transportation: urban *sprawl* was essentially unplanned.
【近】	spread out，extend over，stretch

stately ［'steitli］

【释】	*adj.* 庄严的，堂皇的；宏伟的，华贵的
【例】	They are graceful，*stately*，inspiring—calm，sunlit seas.

【近】	grand，splendid，majestic
stock	[stɔk]
【释】	① *n.* 股份，股票
【例】	After the *stock* exchange collapse of 1873，the subway was sealed up and forgotten.
【衍】	stocky（*adj.*）矮胖的；结实的；stockings（*n.*）长袜
【释】	② *n.* 库存品，存货，贮存；买进的货，进货
【例】	By 1870，the resident *stock* company was at the peak of its development in the United States.
【衍】	stockpile（*v. & n.*）储备；准备急用的备用原料或物资
【近】	store，supply，hoard
stroll	[strəul]
【释】	*v.* 慢慢地走，散步，闲逛，游荡
【例】	A *strolling* gibbon reminds one of a tightrope walker.
【衍】	stroller（*n.*）散步的人；流浪者
【近】	leisurely walk，saunter，promenade
succeed	[sək'siːd]
【释】	*v.* 接连；继承；继续，接着…发生
【例】	From that time on her poetry has been read with interest by *succeeding* generations of poets and readers.
【衍】	succeeding（*adj.*）随后的；successive（*adj.*）接连的，相继的；succession（*n.*）
【近】	follow，come next，ensue
surge	[səːdʒ]
【释】	*n. & v.* 汹涌；(感情等)起伏，高涨
【例】	The interaction of improved processing and high demand led to the rapid spread of the cultivation of cotton and to a *surge* in production.
【衍】	surging（*n. & adj.*）
【近】	rush，gush，pour
sympathy	['simpəθi]
【释】	*n.* 同感，赞成；一致，协调；同情(心)，怜悯
【例】	They offer *sympathy* when someone experiences difficulties or is subjected to discipline，are quick to lighten a serious moment with humor，and try to resolve issues that threaten to divide the group.

| 【衍】 | sympathetic (*adj*.); sympathize (*v*.) |
| 【近】 | understanding, compassion, empathy |

tax [tæks]

【释】 *n.* 税，租税　*v.* 对…抽税，征税

【例】 While they levied heavy *taxes* to repay state war debts, their larger neighbors might retire debts out of land-sale proceeds.

【衍】 taxation (*n*.) 征税，抽税

【近】 duty, levy, tariff

terrain ['terein]

【释】 *n.* 地形，地势

【例】 The remainder is buried anywhere from 3 to 12 feet, depending largely upon the type of *terrain* and the properties of the soil.

【近】 topography, landscape

thresh [θreʃ]

【释】 *v. & n.* 脱粒；打谷

【例】 These ponderous machines—sometimes pulled by as many as 40 horses—reaped the grain, *threshed* it, and bagged it, all in one simultaneous operation.

【衍】 thresher (*n*.) 打谷机；threshing (*n*.) 打谷，脱粒；threshold (*n*.) 开始，开端

tomato [tə'meitəu]

【释】 *n.* 番茄，西红柿

【例】 In the past oysters were raised in much the same way as dirt farmers raised *tomatoes*—by transplanting them.

transaction [træn'zækʃən]

【释】 *n.* 交易；业务，事务

【例】 In most financial institutions today the client is serviced by any employee who happens to be free at the time, regardless of the nature of the *transaction*.

【衍】 transact (*v*.); transactor (*n*.); transactional (*adj*.)

【近】 deal, business, operation

trigger ['trigə]

【释】 *v.* 触发，激起

【例】 The factors that *trigger* migratory behavior in birds are difficult to explain.

Unit 14

【衍】	triggered（*adj.*）
【近】	activate，cause，elicit

twig ［twig］

【释】	*n.* 丫枝，细枝
【例】	The stick caterpillar is well named，because it is hardly distinguishable from a brown or green *twig*.
【衍】	twiglike（*adj.*）细枝状的；twiggy（*adj.*）多细枝的
【近】	limb，stick，branch，stem

unlikely ［ʌnˈlaikli］

【释】	*adj.*［后接不定式，可用作表语］不大可能的，不一定有把握的
【例】	It is highly *unlikely* that the artist's hand applied every stroke of the brush. More likely，numerous assistants，who had been trained to imitate the artist's style，applied the paint.
【近】	improbable，implausible

various ［ˈvɛəriəs］

【释】	*adj.* 不同的，各种各样的
【例】	Adjustments in *various* places，however，show that this standard is not immutable.
【衍】	variously（*adv.*）
【近】	diverse，numerous

vigorous ［ˈvigərəs］

【释】	*adj.* 精力旺盛的，强健的
【例】	The Anasazi Indians were an ingenious，*vigorous*，adaptable people whose highly developed society prospered despite an exceedingly inhospitable—if spectacular—environment.
【衍】	vigorously（*adv.*）；vigor（*n.*）精力，活力
【近】	energetic，vibrant，strong

wane ［wein］

【释】	*v.*（月）缺损，亏；（［*opp.*］wax）；（光、势力等）衰落，衰微；减少
【例】	Not only had household production *waned*，but technological improvements were rapidly changing the rest of domestic work.

【近】	diminish，vanish，decline，disappear
wholesale	['həulseil]
【释】	① *n.* & *adj.* & *adv.* 批发(的、地)
【例】	Warehouse clubs allow members to buy goods at *wholesale* prices.
【衍】	wholesaler（*n.*）批发商
【释】	② *adj.* 大规模的
【例】	From Boston to Los Angeles，from New York City to Chicago to Dallas，museums are either planning，building，or wrapping up *wholesale* expansion programs.
【近】	extensive，comprehensive
youngster	['jʌŋstə]
【释】	*n.* 年轻人；小孩子
【例】	A *youngster* with a learning disability can find his or her own level without being separated from the other pupils.
【近】	child，kid，teenager，adolescent

Exercise of Unit 14

左列单词在右列中有一个同义词，请找出并在相应的位置写上正确答案。

Exercise 1:

(A) access _____ entry
(B) poll _____ store
(C) monetary _____ survey
(D) belief _____ insulate
(E) isolate _____ faith
(F) stock _____ financial

Exercise 2:

(A) opinion _____ improbable
(B) hallmark _____ crocodile
(C) hazard _____ view
(D) alligator _____ danger
(E) figure _____ characteristic
(F) unlikely _____ statue

Exercise 3:

(A) crude _____ production
(B) equivalent _____ divert
(C) sink _____ cover
(D) distract _____ descend
(E) coat _____ raw
(F) output _____ counterpart

Exercise 4:

(A) presumably _____ decompose
(B) implement _____ useful
(C) refine _____ tool
(D) practical _____ seemingly
(E) decay _____ improve
(F) various _____ diverse

Exercise 5:

(A) elegance _____ grace
(B) sink _____ secrecy
(C) mystery _____ decline
(D) succeed _____ follow
(E) facade _____ outlook
(F) perspective _____ mask

Exercise 6:

(A) implement _____ apply
(B) depress _____ understanding
(C) productive _____ creative
(D) reliable _____ substance
(E) content _____ dependable
(F) sympathy _____ lower

Exercise 7:
(A) auditory _____ entice
(B) lure _____ aural
(C) figure _____ transfer
(D) objective _____ personage
(E) shift _____ unprejudiced
(F) correlate _____ associate

Exercise 8:
(A) identical _____ trickle
(B) drip _____ fatigue
(C) legal _____ purify
(D) refine _____ equal
(E) exhaustion _____ lawful
(F) parallel _____ similar

Exercise 9:
(A) prosper _____ fur
(B) content _____ deal
(C) endow _____ satisfied
(D) stately _____ donate
(E) transaction _____ thrive
(F) coat _____ grand

Exercise 10:
(A) gap _____ cerebral
(B) respect _____ structure
(C) access _____ rent
(D) mental _____ approach
(E) frame _____ sadden
(F) depress _____ detail

ANSWERS:
1 A F B E D C
2 F D A C B E
3 F D E C A B
4 E D B A C F
5 A C B D F E
6 A F C E D B
7 B A E C D F
8 B E D A C F
9 F E B C A D
10 D E A C F B

Unit 15

accident	endure	myth	shine
admire	era	nickel	skeleton
alloy	exhibit	oblige	sodium
anticipate	Fahrenheit	opportunity	specify
article	filter	outstanding	springboard
auger	flourish	paramount	stationary
bare	freight	peer	stomach
belong	garbage	pervasive	structural
bodily	glare	plain	succinct
brim	hallway	pollen	surgeon
calendar	heal	practitioner	symphony
carriage	homogeneous	pretension	team
cellulose	identify	profession	terrestrial
chorus	implicit	protagonist	thrive
cohesive	influx	puzzle	tongue
complicated	instant	rally	transcend
conform	intestine	rebuild	trillion
context	issue	reflection	twine
correspond	label	relief	unprecedented
crust	legend	replenish	varnish
deceive	litter	respond	vinegar
deprive	lust	ribbon	ward
dimension	margin	rough	widespread
distribute	mention	satire	zigzag
droplet	mimic	scurry	
elevate	monochrome	separately	

accident [ˈæksidənt]

【释】 *n.* 故障，事故，偶发事件；偶然

【例】 All these things survived in the public domain，if only by *accident*.

【衍】 accidental（*adj.*）；accidentally（*adv.*）

【近】 disaster，misfortune，mishap

admire [ədˈmaiə]

【释】 *v.* 赞美，称赞；惊异(at)

【例】 Copper was used for practical items，but it was not *admired* for its beauty.

【衍】 admirer（*n.*）赞美者；敬慕者；情人；admiring（*adj.*）赞美的；羡慕的

【近】 approve of，esteem，respect

alloy [ˈæləi]

【释】 *n.* 合金

【例】 Brass is an *alloy* of copper and zinc.

anticipate [ænˈtisipeit]

【释】 *v.* 预期，预料，预测；指望，期待

【例】 Britain *anticipated* Napoleon's imminent invasion and decided that its only hope was to take the offensive immediately.

【衍】 anticipation（*n.*）

【近】 expect，foresee，predict

article [ˈɑːtikl]

【释】 *n.* 物品；制品

【例】 Unlike the silver coins from which they were made，silver *articles* were readily identifiable.

【近】 object，item

auger [ˈɔgə]

【释】 *n.* 螺(丝)钻；钻孔器，钻孔机

【例】 The very tools that the first New England furniture makers used were，after all，not much different from those used for centuries—even millennia: basic hammers，saws，chisels，planes，*augers*，compasses，and measures.

bare [beə]

【释】 *adj.* 裸的，裸体的；仅有的；极少的

【例】 Cow's skulls and other *bare* bones found in the desert were frequent motifs in her paintings.

【衍】 barely (*adv*.)

【近】 naked, unclothed, exposed, nude

belong [bi'lɔŋ]

【释】 *v.* 属，属(某人)所有，应归入(某)部类(to; among; in; under; with)

【例】 While still growing, crops *belonged* to the men who, in contrast to most other Native American groups, planted them.

bodily ['bɔdili]

【释】 *adj.* 躯体的，身体的，肉体的

【例】 Even though cells can survive wider fluctuations, the integrated actions of *bodily* systems are impaired.

【衍】 body (*n*.)

【近】 physical, corporal

brim [brim]

【释】 *n.* (杯、碗等容器的)缘，边

【例】 The wide *brim* of the "ten-gallon hat" could be turned down to shade the eyes or drain off rainfall.

【衍】 brimful (*adj*.)

【近】 edge, top, rim, lip

calendar ['kælində]

【释】 *n.* 日历

【例】 The physical attributes of the site allow its use as a natural *calendar*/clock.

【近】 agenda, schedule

carriage ['kæridʒ]

【释】 *n.* 车; (四轮)马车

【例】 In the mid-eighteenth century, painters had been willing to assume such artisan-related tasks as varnishing, gilding teaching, keeping shops, and painting wheel *carriages*, houses, and signs.

【近】 cart, wagon, stagecoach, coach

cellulose	['seljuləus]
【释】	*n.* 细胞膜质；纤维质，纤维素
【例】	Furthermore the walls of fungal cells are not made of *cellulose*, as those of plants are, but of another complex sugarlike polymer called chitin.
【近】	fiber
chorus	['kɔːrəs]
【释】	*n.* 合唱；合唱队；合唱歌(曲)
【例】	This is why the woods in late summer often seem so quiet, when compared with the exuberant *choruses* of spring.
【近】	choir, chorale
cohesive	[kəu'hiːsiv]
【释】	*adj.* 凝聚性的；有结合力的
【例】	The *cohesive* political and social organization of the Anasazi made it almost impossible for other groups to conquer them.
【衍】	cohesion (*n.*)（各部的）结合；coherent (*adj.*) 紧密地结合着的；coherence (*n.*) 凝聚；统一
complicated	['kɔmplikeitid]
【释】	*adj.* 复杂的，错杂的
【例】	But this type of engine was expensive and *complicated*, requiring many precision-fitted moving parts.
【衍】	uncomplicated (*adj.*); complicatedly (*adv.*); complication (*n.*)
【近】	complex, intricate, involved, elaborated
conform	[kən'fɔːm]
【释】	*v.* 使一致；依照(习惯)；使遵照(to)
【例】	Nevertheless, the ability of children to *conform* to grammatical rules is only slightly more wonderful than their ability to learn words.
【衍】	conformation (*n.*); conformity (*n.*)
【近】	match
context	['kɔntekst]
【释】	*n.* (事情等的)范围，场合，处境

Unit 15

【例】 In the *context* of extreme competitiveness and dizzying social change，the household lost many of its earlier functions and the home came to serve as a haven of tranquility and order.

【近】 background，circumstance

correspond [ˌkɔri'spɔnd]

【释】 *v.* 与…一致，符合(**to**; **with**)

【例】 The variation between the hemispheres *corresponds* to which side of the body is used to perform specific activities.

【衍】 corresponding（*adj.*）；correspondingly（*adv.*）；correspondence（*n.*）

【近】 match，relate，coordinate

crust [krʌst]

【释】 *n.* 外皮，壳；地壳

【例】 The Earth comprises three principal layers: the dense, iron-rich core，the mantle，made of silicate rocks that are semimolten at depth，and the thin，solid-surface *crust*.

【衍】 crustacean（*adj. & n.*）甲壳类的(动物)

【近】 shell，skin，layer

deceive [di'siːv]

【释】 *v.* 欺，瞒

【例】 Mimicry is not an active strategy on the part of an individual plant；flowers do not deliberately trick or *deceive* animals into visiting them.

【衍】 deceptive（*adj.*）骗人的；靠不住的；deceptively（*adv.*）；deception（*n.*）

【近】 trick，misled，swindle

deprive [di'praiv]

【释】 *v.* 剥夺，使不能享受

【例】 But if the body is *deprived* of salt，the effects soon become dangerous，despite compensatory mechanisms.

【衍】 deprivation（*n.*）

【近】 divest，rob

dimension [di'menʃən]

【释】 *n.* 尺寸；【数】维(数)；［*pl.*］容积；面积；大小，规模，范围

【例】 The *dimensions* of the cosmos are so large that using familiar units of distance，such as meters or miles，chosen for their utility on Earth，would make little sense.

【衍】 dimensional（*adj.*）；dimensionally（*adv.*）在尺寸上，在幅员上

【近】 measurement

distribute ［disˈtribjuːt］

【释】 *v.* 分配，分给；分布，散布（over）

【例】 ... cities from which goods could be readily *distributed* to interior settlements.

【衍】 distribution（*n.*）

【近】 dispense

droplet ［ˈdrɒplit］

【释】 *n.* 小滴

【例】 *Droplets* and ice crystals behave somewhat like dust in the air made visible in a shaft of sunlight.

elevate ［ˈeliveit］

【释】 *v.* 举起，抬高（声音、炮口等）

【例】 A little more than half of the pipeline is *elevated* above the ground.

【衍】 elevator（*n.*）电梯，升降机；elevation（*n.*）【建】正视图

【近】 raise，promote

endure ［inˈdjuə］

【释】 *v.* 忍耐，忍受；容忍

【例】 They cannot move about or take shelter but must be equipped to *endure* whatever weather conditions are likely to occur.

【衍】 endurance（*n.*）

【近】 bear，tolerate，suffer

era ［ˈiərə］

【释】 *n.* 纪元；年代，时代

【例】 Their *era* ended with them，and their dance values nearly disappeared.

【近】 epoch，period，eon，age，time

exhibit [ig'zibit]

【释】 *v. & n.* 陈列（品），展览（品）

【例】 Three of the pictures were ***exhibited*** in the Museum of Modern Art，and in 1940 she had her first exhibition in New York.

【衍】 exhibition（*n.*）

【近】 display，demonstrate，show

Fahrenheit ['færənhait]

【释】 *n. & adj.* 华氏温度计（的）

【例】 The temperature of the Sun is over 5,000 degrees ***Fahrenheit*** at the surface.

filter ['filtə]

【释】 *n.* 滤器，滤纸 *v.* 过滤

【例】 Then she lights them and adds color from lights covered with colored ***filters***.

【近】 sieve，strainer，mesh

flourish ['flʌriʃ]

【释】 *n.* 繁荣，茂盛；兴旺

【例】 With it Neolithic peoples ***flourished***，fashioning an energetic.

【衍】 flourished（*adj.*）；flourishingly（*adv.*）

【近】 thrive，prosper，boom

freight [freit]

【释】 *n.* 货运列车（＝freight train）

【例】 Equally important to everyday life were the slow ***freight*** trains chugging through industrial zones.

【衍】 freighter（*n.*）货船

【近】 cargo，shipment

garbage ['gɑːbidʒ]

【释】 *n.* 垃圾，废物

【例】 Urban slums such as Chicago's nineteenth ward often had no sewers，***garbage*** collection，or gas or electric lines.

【近】 trash，junk，refuse，waste

glare [glɛə]

【释】 *n.* 闪耀，闪光；炫目的光，强烈的光

| 【例】 | The corona can be seen only when special instruments are used on cameras and telescopes to shut out the *glare* of the Sun's rays. |
| 【衍】 | glaring (*adj.*) |

hallway ['hɔːlwei]
【释】 *n.* 门厅，过道
【例】 There was a *hallway* with closed doors.
【近】 entry, corridor, passageway

heal [hiːl]
【释】 *v.* 医治，治愈(病伤等)，使恢复；使和解
【例】 Medical authorities and textbooks of that day counseled merely rest, cold, and opium, leaving the body to *heal* itself.
【衍】 healing (*adj.*); healer (*n.*)
【近】 cure, mend, repair

homogeneous [ˌhɔməu'dʒiːnjəs]
【释】 *adj.* 同种的，同质的，纯一的；均匀的
【例】 A folk culture is small, isolated, cohesive, conservative, nearly self-sufficient group that is *homogeneous* in custom and race.
【衍】 Homo (*n.*) 人类
【近】 uniform, standardized, identical

identify [ai'dentifai]
【释】 *v.* 辨认，识别
【例】 It reflects badly on the order of priorities in our society that schoolchildren can tell you the make of many cars on the road but cannot *identify* any but the most familiar trees and wildflowers.
【衍】 identifiable (*adj.*); identification (*n.*)
【近】 recognize

implicit [im'plisit]
【释】 *adj.* 含蓄的，不讲明的([*opp.*] explicit)
【例】 There is also an *implicit* subtext: She who follows the crowd has a weak sense of direction.
【近】 implied

influx ['inflʌks]
【释】 *n.* 流入，注入

— 325 —

【例】 Matching the *influx* of foreign immigrants into the larger cities of the United States during the late nineteenth century was a domestic migration.

【近】 arrival

instant ［'instənt］

【释】 *adj.* 立即的，直接的

【例】 Eventually she makes *instant* color prints to see what the image looks like.

【衍】 instantly（*adv.*）；instantaneous（*adj.*）；instantaneously（*adv.*）

【近】 immediate

intestine ［in'testin］

【释】 *n.*（常［*pl.*］）肠

【例】 Examples of exocrine glands are the tear glands，and the pancreas，which secretes pancreatic juice through a duct into the *intestine*.

【衍】 intestinal（*adj.*）

issue ［'isjuː］

【释】 ① *n.* 论点；争端

【例】 Biological diversity has become widely recognized as a critical conservation *issue* only in the past two decades.

【近】 subject，matter，concern

【释】 ② *v.* 颁布，发行

【例】 Most of the coins *issued* from about 1799 to the early years of the twentieth century bore thirteen stars representing the thirteen original colonies.

【近】 publish，release，announce

【释】 ③ *v.* 流出，涌出

【例】 In the modern manufacturing process，liquid glass is fed directly from a glass-melting furnace into a bushing，a receptacle pierced with hundreds of fine nozzles，from which the liquid *issues* in fine streams.

【近】 emanate，emit，well，erupt

label ［'leibl］

【释】 *n.* 贴条，标签；标记，符号　*v.* 贴标签于；把…叫做；分类，把…列为

【例】 A hormone *labeled* cholecystokinin（CCK），produced by the mucosa of the upper intestine，tells you when you have had enough to eat and should promptly put down your spoon.

【衍】 labellum（*n.*）唇瓣

【近】 tag，brand

legend ['ledʒənd]

【释】 *n.* 传说；神话

【例】 The great number of tales，*legends*，and myths about these birds indicates that people have been exceptionally interested in them for a long time.

【衍】 legendary（*adj.*）；legendarily（*adv.*）；legendry（*n.*）传说；传奇文学

【近】 fable，myth，tale

litter ['litə]

【释】 ① *n.* 枯枝层，落叶层；(兽类睡眠用的)褥草，垫圈

【例】 The leaf *litter* often promotes successful germination of acorns—and perhaps blue jays.

【释】 ② *n.* (猪等)同胎生下的小崽

【例】 An average reading of 36 degrees Fahrenheit or less produces an all-female clutch；at 93 degrees or above all the young are males；anything in between produces a mixed *litter*.

【近】 family，brood，set of offspring

【释】 ③ *v.* 乱丢东西，乱丢废物(垃圾等)

【例】 Kittiwakes defecate over the edge of the nest，which keeps it clean，but this practice，as well as their tendency to leave the nest *littered* with eggshells，makes its location very conspicuous.

【近】 scatter，spoil，drop litter

lust [lʌst]

【释】 *v.* 渴望，热烈追求 *n.* 欲望，贪欲

【例】 In the back of the race are those who wear costumes and *lust* for fun. In 1993 there was a group of men all of whom dressed up like Elvis Presley.

【近】 yearn，desire，long for

margin [ˈmɑːdʒin]

【释】 *n.* 边缘；边缘部分；范围，限界

【例】 If by "suburb" is meant an urban *margin* that grows more rapidly than its already developed interior，the process of suburbanization began during the emergence of the indus-trial.

【衍】 marginal（*adj.*）边缘的；旁注的；marginalia（*n.*）旁注；次要的东西；marginalize（*v.*）忽略，排斥，使边缘化，使处于次要地位

【近】 edge，periphery，boundary，fringe

mention [ˈmenʃən]

【释】 *v. & n.* 说到，提及；提述；提名表扬

【例】 Nesting material should be added in sufficient amounts to avoid both extreme temperature situations *mentioned* above and assure that the eggs have a soft，secure place to rest.

【衍】 mentionable（*adj.*）可以提起的，值得一提的

【近】 state，cite，declare

mimic [ˈmimik]

【释】 *n.* 仿造物　*adj.* 模仿的，模拟的，假的

【例】 Mimetic traits may include morphological structures，color patterns，behaviors or other attributes of the *mimic* that promote its resemblance to a model.

【衍】 mimicry（*n.*）模仿，模拟；仿造品；mimetic（*adj.*）模仿的，模拟的，巧于模仿的

【近】 imitate，impersonate，copy

monochrome [ˈmɔnəukrəum]

【释】 *adj.* 单色的，一色的　*n.* 单色画(照片)

【例】 Glass can be colored or colorless，*monochrome* or polychrome，transparent，translucent，or opaque.

【衍】 monochromatic（*adj.*）一色的；单色光的

【近】 toneless，colorless

myth [miθ]

【释】 *n.* 神话；神怪故事

【例】 The great number of tales，legends，and *myths* about these birds indicates that people have been exceptionally interested in them for a long time.

【衍】	mythology（n.）神话，神话集；神话学；mythological（adj.）
【近】	legend，fable，saga

nickel [ˈnikəl]

【释】 **n.** 镍

【例】 It is almost certainly made of iron，mixed with smaller amounts of other elements such as **nickel**.

【衍】 nitinol（n.）镍钛诺（镍和钛的非磁性合金）

oblige [əˈblaidʒ]

【释】 **v.** 迫使；责成

【例】 Members of Congress had hotly debated the question of a permanent home for themselves and for those departments which even the sketchiest of central governments would feel **obliged** to establish.

【衍】 obligatory（adj.）

【近】 force，obligate，compel

opportunity [ˌɔpəˈtjuːnəti]

【释】 **n.** 机会，好机会；凑巧；方便

【例】 By 1929，Whitney owned more than five hundred works by artists from the United States，and she felt the public should have an **opportunity** to see the collection.

【近】 chance，occasion，opening

outstanding [ˌautˈstændiŋ]

【释】 **adj.** 显著的；凸出的，杰出的

【例】 The quality of preservation is **outstanding**，but what is even more impressive is the number of ichthyosaur fossils containing preserved embryos.

【衍】 outstandingly（adv.）

【近】 wonderful，excellent，marvelous

paramount [ˈpærəmaunt]

【释】 **adj.** 最高的，至上的，卓越的；胜过…的（to）

【例】 Tradition is **paramount**，and change comes infrequently and slowly.

【衍】 paramountcy（n.）最高权威

【近】 supreme，chief，dominant，top

peer [piə]

【释】 **n.** 同辈，同事，伙伴；同等的人

【例】 What he dreamed of was an expanding union of self-governing commonwealths, joined as a group of *peers*.

pervasive [pəˈveisiv]

【释】 *adj.* 普遍的；深入的

【例】 But the total result is a *pervasive* pattern that continues to give New England its distinctive flavor.

【衍】 pervasion (*n.*)

【近】 invasive, all-encompassing

plain [plein]

【释】 *n.* 平地，平原，旷野

【例】 They developed permanent squints from peering into the glaring sunlight of the treeless *plains*.

【衍】 plainly (*adv.*)

pollen [ˈpɔlin]

【释】 *n.* 花粉

【例】 For example, a worker honeybee that has found a rich source of nectar and *pollen* flies rapidly home to the hive to report.

【衍】 pollination (*n.*); pollinate (*v.*) 给…授粉；pollinator (*n.*)

practitioner [prækˈtiʃənə]

【释】 *n.* 从业者(尤指医生、律师等)；老手

【例】 Furthermore, like the artisans of the Arts and Crafts Movement in England, art deep *practitioners* considered it their mission.

pretension [priˈtenʃən]

【释】 *n.* (有根据的)要求；主张

【例】 Brave new world ridicules the *pretensions* of science; a modest proposal dramatizes starvation by advocating cannibalism.

profession [prəˈfeʃən]

【释】 *n.* 职业，(特指)知识性专门职业([*opp.*] **trade, business**)

【例】 Architecture was not yet a specialized *profession* in the colonies.

【衍】 professional (*adj.*); professor (*n.*)

【近】	job，business，work，career
protagonist	[prəuˈtægənist]
【释】	*n.* (戏剧的)主角；(小说的)主人翁；领导者
【例】	Although she several times takes such potential leaders for her *protagonists*，she never shows in detail how they rise to power.
【近】	character，hero，leading role
puzzle	[ˈpʌzl]
【释】	*n.* 难题；迷惑；(字谜、书谜等的)谜
【例】	These double radio sources present astronomers with a *puzzle*.
【衍】	puzzling (*adj.*)
【近】	dilemma，mystery，enigma，riddle
rally	[ˈræli]
【释】	*v.* 召集，纠合，团结
【例】	The graduates of Harvard College simultaneously *rallied* to relieve the college's poverty and demand new enterprise.
【近】	unite，assemble，gather
rebuild	[ˌriːˈbild]
【释】	*v.* 重建，使复原，改造
【例】	Molt requires that a bird find and process enough protein to *rebuild* approximately one-third of its body weight.
【近】	reconstruct，restore，restructure
reflection	[riˈflekʃən]
【释】	*n.* 反映；倒影，(映在水等中的)影像
【例】	These are powerful images，but they are a limited *reflection* of reality.
【衍】	reflect (*v.*)；reflective (*adj.*)
【近】	mirror image，indication
relief	[riˈliːf]
【释】	*n.* 浮雕；浮雕品
【例】	Stoneware grew increasingly ornate throughout the nineteenth century，and in addition to the earlier scratched and drawn designs，three-dimensional molded *relief* decoration became popular.

Unit 15

【近】	sculpture，rilievo

replenish [ri'pleniʃ]

【释】 *v.* 装足，装满，补充(钱袋等)；加强([*opp.*] **deplete** *v.* 减少，损耗)

【例】 An equally important adaptation is the ability to *replenish* this water loss at one drink.

【衍】 replenishable (*adj.*)；replenisher (*n.*)；replenishment (*n.*)

【近】 refill，stock up，restock

respond [ri'spɔnd]

【释】 *v.* 回答；响应(**to**)；(对刺激等)感应，反应

【例】 Some city and state governments *responded* by regulating the utility companies，but a number of cities began to supply these services themselves.

【衍】 respondent (*adj.*)；response (*n.*)

【近】 act in response，reply，react

ribbon ['ribən]

【释】 *n.* 带状物

【例】 The residues from these explosions left huge black marks on the face of Jupiter，some of which have stretched out to form dark *ribbons*.

【近】 strip，tie

rough [rʌf]

【释】 ① *adj.* 粗略的，大体的，大致的([*opp.*] **exact**)

【例】 Although the birth rate continued to decline from its high level of the eighteenth and early nineteenth century，the population *roughly* doubled every generation during the rest of the nineteenth centuries.

【衍】 roughly (*adv.*)

【近】 approximate，sketchy，estimated

【释】 ② *adj.* 粗鲁的，粗暴的([*opp.*] **gentle**)

【例】 Edwin's job caused the family to move from town to town，and the girls' interest in *rough* sports and shooting rats raised eye-brows wherever they went.

【衍】 roughly (*adv.*)

【近】 violent，forceful，brutal

satire ['sætaiə]

【释】 *n.* 讽刺诗(文)；讽刺作品；讽刺

【例】 *Satire* tends to remind people that much of what they see, hear, and read in popular media is sanctimonious, sentimental, and only partially true.

【衍】 satiric (*adj.*)；satirical (*adj.*)；satirist (*n.*)

scurry ['skʌri]

【释】 *v.* 快步急跑；疾走

【例】 The effect mimics a *scurrying* mouse or vole, and the behavior rivets the attention of the type of predators that would also be interested in eggs and chicks.

【近】 rush, hurry, bustle

separately ['sepərətli]

【释】 *adv.* 分别地，个别地，分离地

【例】 The two wires that make up the line wire or cable are fed *separately* into a machine at one end.

【衍】 separate (*adj.* & *v.*)；separating (*adj.*)；separation (*n.*)

【近】 one by one, discretely, individually

shine [ʃain]

【释】 *v.* 明显流露

【例】 The more thoroughly scientists investigate the universe, the more clearly its simplicity *shines* through.

skeleton ['skelitən]

【释】 *n.* 骨骼，骸髅；骨架；(叶子的)脉络；筋

【例】 Muscle tissue covers the body in sheets and bands that lie between the skin and the *skeleton*.

【衍】 skeletonize (*v.*)

【近】 frame, carcass, framework

sodium ['səudiəm]

【释】 *n.* 钠

【例】 The rocks of the crust are composed mostly of minerals with light elements, like aluminum and *sodium*, while the mantle contains some heavier elements, like iron and magnesium.

specify ['spesifai]

【释】 *v.* 指定；具体说明，详细说明

【例】	Another method of determining soil texture involves the use of devices called sediment sieves，screens built with a *specified* mesh size.
【衍】	specific（*adj.*）；specifically（*adv.*）；specification（*n.*）；specified（*adj.*）
【近】	stipulate，indicate，denote

springboard ['sprɪŋbɔːd]

【释】	*n.* 跳板，出发点
【例】	The American civil rights movement，for example，first targeted discrimination on public transportation，then used its victories as a *springboard* to address other injustices.
【衍】	spring（*n. & v.*）跳跃；反弹；springtime（*n.*）春季，春天
【近】	launch pad，facilitator，spur

stationary ['steɪʃənəri]

【释】	*adj.* 静止的，不变的；固定的
【例】	Subsequently，manufacturers made use of new improved *stationary* steam engines to power their mills.
【衍】	stationariness（*n.*）
【近】	motionless，fixed，immobile

stomach ['stʌmək]

【释】	*n.* 胃；[口]肚子
【例】	A very dehydrated person cannot drink enough water to dehydrate at one session，because the human *stomach* is not sufficiently big.
【衍】	stomachache（*n.*）胃痛，肚子痛；stomachic（*adj.*）健胃的，助消化的；stomachy（*adj.*）易怒的；肚子大的
【近】	abdomen，belly，tummy

structural ['strʌktʃərəl]

【释】	*adj.* 构造上的，结构上的，组织上的
【例】	Accompanying that growth was a *structural* change that featured increasing economic diversification and a gradual shift in the nation's labor force from agriculture to manufacturing.
【衍】	structure（*n. & v.*）；structurally（*adv.*）

succinct [sək'siŋkt]
【释】 *adj.* 简洁的，简明的([*opp.*] lengthy)
【例】 A decision-making worksheet begins with a *succinct* statement of the problem that will also help to narrow it.
【衍】 succinctly (*adv.*)；succinctness (*n.*)
【近】 concise，brief，laconic

surgeon ['səːdʒən]
【释】 *n.* 外科医生；【军】军医；船医
【例】 Newspapers in Chicago played up the operation，and Dr. Williams became widely hailed as the first heart *surgeon* in the world.
【衍】 surgery (*n.*) 外科(学)；外科手术；外科手术(实验)室；医院；诊所
【近】 doctor，doctor of medicine，general practitioner

symphony ['simfəni]
【释】 *n.* 交响乐，交响曲
【例】 In combination with the larger and deeper-sounding members of the same family，the violins form the nucleus of the modern *symphony* orchestra.
【衍】 symphonic (*adj.*) 交响乐(式)的；谐音的；symphonious (*adj.*) 谐音的，调和的；symphonist (*n.*) 交响乐作曲家
【近】 sonata，concerto

team [tiːm]
【释】 *n.* 队，团；工作队，工作组
【例】 A hearing test that analyzes brain waves for subconscious responses to sound has recently been devised by a *team* of specialists at the University of Iowa.
【衍】 teammate (*n.*) 同队队员；teamwork (*n.*) 协同工作
【近】 lineup，group，band

terrestrial [tə'restriəl]
【释】 ① *adj.* 地球(上)的；陆地的，陆生的，陆栖的
【例】 Butterflies are perhaps the best group of insects for examining patterns of *terrestrial* biotic diversity and distribution.

【衍】 terrestrialization（*n.*）；subterranean（*adj.*）地下的，地中的

【近】 earthly

【释】 ② *adj.* 人间的，现世的

【例】 In *terrestrial* affairs we think of "big" as being complicated；a city is more intricate than a village，an ocean more complicated than a puddle.

【近】 earthly，worldly，global

thrive ［θraiv］

【释】 *v.* 兴旺，繁荣；苗壮成长，繁茂，蔓延

【例】 The polar bears of Hudson Bay are a distinct population *thriving* at the southern end of their range.

【衍】 thrived（*adj.*）；thriving（*adj.*）

【近】 flourish，prosper，boom

tongue ［tʌŋ］

【释】 *n.* 舌；舌状物

【例】 Next，the crossbill snakes its long *tongue* into the gap and draws out the seed.

【衍】 tongueless（*adj.*）无舌头的；缄默的，哑的；tongued（*adj.*）说话的

transcend ［træn'send］

【释】 *v.* 超出，超过(经验、理性、信念、理解力等)

【例】 Murray's Cleaner essays published in the 1790's *transcended* the boundaries of her world in recognizing the need for training women to earn their own living.

【衍】 transcendence（*n.*）；transcendent（*adj.*）卓越的，超群的；transcendentle（*adj.*）卓越的；玄妙的；超越的；transcendentalism（*n.*）超越论；超越哲学

【近】 go beyond，exceed，surpass，tower

trillion ［'triljən］

【释】 *n. & adj.* 万亿的，兆的；大量的

【例】 The human body，which consists of about 60 *trillion* living cells，sheds exposed skin at a rate of 50 million cells a day.

【衍】 trillionth（*n. & adj.*）万亿(百亿亿)分之一；(第)万亿(百亿亿)的

twine	[twain]
【释】	① *v.* 捻，搓；织，编
【例】	Most groups made all their basketwork by *twining*—the twisting of a flexible horizontal material, called a weft, around stiffer vertical strands of material, the warp.
【衍】	twiner (*n.*); twined (*adj.*) 成双的；搓成的
【近】	coil, twist, weave
【释】	② *n.* 两股(以上的)线；细绳；麻线(绳)
【例】	By 1880 a self-binding reaper had been perfected that not only cut the grain, but also gathered the stalks and bound them with *twine*.
【近】	string, cord, thread
unprecedented	[ʌn'presidəntid]
【释】	*adj.* 空前的；无比的
【例】	These innovations in manufacturing boosted output and living standards to an *unprecedented* extent.
【近】	unparalleled, extraordinary
varnish	['vɑːniʃ]
【释】	*n.* 清漆 *v.* 给…上清漆
【例】	In the mid-eighteenth century, painters had been willing to assume such artisan-related tasks as *varnishing*, gilding teaching, keeping shops, and painting wheel carriages, houses, and signs.
【近】	glaze, finish, polish
vinegar	['vinigə]
【释】	*n.* 醋
【例】	Quite literally, they find each others presence repulsive. A good illustration of this aversion is homemade oil-and-*vinegar* salad dressing.
【衍】	vinegarish (*adj.*)
ward	[wɔːd]
【释】	① *v.* 挡住，击退，防止(off)
【例】	When attacked by disease-causing fungi or bacteria, many kinds of plants produce chemicals that help to *ward* off the invaders.

Unit 15

【近】defense，repel

【释】② *n.* (行政)区

【例】Urban slums such as Chicago's nineteenth *ward* often had no sewers，garbage collection，or gas or electric lines；and tenements lacked both running water and central heating.

【近】district，region

【释】③ *n.* 病房，病室

【例】When resisted，as they were at Bellevue in efforts，to install trained nurses on the maternity *wards*，they went over the heads of the doctors to men of their own class of greater power and authority.

【近】sickroom

widespread ['waidspred]

【释】*adj.* 广泛的，普遍的

【例】Perhaps no single phenomenon brought more *widespread* and lasting change to the United States society than the rise of industrialization.

【衍】widespreadly（*adj.*）；widespreadness（*n.*）

【近】pervasive，prevalent

zigzag ['zigzæg]

【释】*adj.* 之字形的，锯齿形的，曲折的

【例】Resting on H-shaped steel racks called "bents"，long sections of the pipeline follow a *zigzag* course high above the frozen earth.

【近】wind，crisscross

Exercise of Unit 15

左列单词在右列中有一个同义词，请找出并在相应的位置写上正确答案。

Exercise 1:

(A) ward _____ raise
(B) distribute _____ dispense
(C) elevate _____ sickroom
(D) influx _____ unite
(E) symphony _____ arrival
(F) rally _____ sonata

Exercise 2:

(A) bare _____ choir
(B) outstanding _____ reconstruct
(C) chorus _____ wonderful
(D) freight _____ cargo
(E) rebuild _____ naked
(F) context _____ background

Exercise 3:

(A) correspond _____ coordinate
(B) thrive _____ match
(C) instant _____ bear
(D) conform _____ immediate
(E) anticipate _____ flourish
(F) endure _____ expect

Exercise 4:

(A) oblige _____ dilemma
(B) twine _____ display
(C) era _____ epoch
(D) exhibit _____ string
(E) ward _____ force
(F) puzzle _____ district

Exercise 5:

(A) heal _____ cure
(B) homogeneous _____ legend
(C) dimension _____ uniform
(D) myth _____ recognize
(E) identify _____ concise
(F) succinct _____ measurement

Exercise 6:

(A) pervasive _____ toneless
(B) litter _____ entry
(C) lust _____ invasive
(D) monochrome _____ yearn
(E) hallway _____ scatter
(F) complicated _____ complex

— 339 —

Exercise 7:

(A) relief _____ object
(B) stationary _____ motionless
(C) article _____ lineup
(D) twine _____ sculpture
(E) team _____ defense
(F) ward _____ coil

Exercise 8:

(A) rough _____ trash
(B) issue _____ state
(C) mention _____ publish
(D) mimic _____ tag
(E) garbage _____ violent
(F) label _____ imitate

Exercise 9:

(A) protagonist _____ character
(B) implicit _____ supreme
(C) scurry _____ cart
(D) specify _____ stipulate
(E) carriage _____ rush
(F) paramount _____ implied

Exercise 10:

(A) legend _____ trick
(B) ribbon _____ chance
(C) rough _____ frame
(D) deceive _____ strip
(E) skeleton _____ approximate
(F) opportunity _____ fable

ANSWERS:

1	C B A F D E
2	C E B D A F
3	A D F C B E
4	F D C B A E
5	A D B E F C
6	D E A C B F
7	C B E A F D
8	E C B F A D
9	A F E D C B
10	D F E B C A

Unit 16

acclaim	energetic	nail	shock
admission	erect	nickname	skeptical
allude	exhilarating	obscure	solder
antiquate	faint	oppose	specimen
articulate	fine	outward	sprout
authentic	fluctuate	paraphrase	statistics
barge	frequent	penalty	stony
belt	gear	petal	struggle
boil	glassy	planetary	suffer
brittle	halt	pollutant	surpass
calorie	heed	prairie	symptom
cart	honor	prevail	tear
Celsius	ideology	proficiency	terrible
chunk	imply	protection	throw
coil	ingenious	pyramid	toothed
component	instinct	ranch	transfer
confront	intimate	recall	trip
continual	jar	reform	twist
corridor	laboratory	relieve	unravel
crystal	legislation	replicate	vary
declare	livelihood	responsible	violate
derive	luxury	rid	ware
dinosaur	maritime	rounded	widow
district	merchant	satisfy	zinc
drought	mineral	seal	
elicit	monotonous	sequence	

acclaim [ə'kleim]

【释】 *n.* 喝彩，欢呼

【例】 These artists achieved widespread popular success and *acclaim*.

【衍】 acclaimed (*adj.*)

【近】 applause，compliment

admission [əd'miʃən]

【释】 ① *n.* 允许进入；许可入场（入学、入会）

【例】 Standards of *admission* were sharply advanced in 1872—1873 and 1876—1877.

【释】 ② *n.* 承认；首肯

【例】 Following the *admission* of Tennessee in 1796，for example，some varieties of half dimes，dimes，and half-dollars were produced with sixteen stars.

allude [ə'lju:d]

【释】 *v.* 暗指，暗示

【例】 Were you *alluding* to me?

【衍】 allusive (*adj.*)

antiquate ['æntikwit]

【释】 *v.* 使变旧；使过时

【例】 Television brought candidates into voters' living rooms，thereby *antiquating* some of the communication and education functions of party workers.

【衍】 antiquated (*adj.*) 陈旧的，旧式的，过时的；antiquity (*n.*) 古代；[*pl.*] 古物，古迹，古代文物

articulate [ɑ:'tikjulit]

【释】 *n.* 有节体的动物   *adj.* 有关节的；有节的；接合起来的   *v.* 用关节连接

【例】 It is this *articulating*，or moveable joint that makes the koala a good climber.

authentic [ɔ:'θentik]

【释】 *adj.* 可信的；可靠的；真的，真正的

【例】 The phrase，"the real McCoy"，has become a common term for "genuine" or "*authentic*".

【衍】 authentically (*adv.*)；authentication (*n.*) 鉴定，证明；认证

【近】 real，genuine，true，reliable

barge [bɑːdʒ]

【释】 *n.* 大平底船，驳船

【例】 Major *barge* canals generally range from 6 to 9 feet in depth.

belt [belt]

【释】 *n.* 带，皮带；线条

【例】 Viewed from outer space，auroras can be seen as dimly glowing *belts* wrapped around each of the Earth's magnetic poles.

【衍】 belted（*adj.*）

【近】 strap，girdle，buckle

boil [bɔil]

【释】 *v.* 沸腾，达到沸点，开，滚，煮滚；汽化

【例】 Comets grow tails only when they get warm enough for ice and dust to *boil* off.

【衍】 boiling（*adj. & adv.*）

【近】 simmer，bubble，heat，fume

brittle ['britl]

【释】 *adj.* 易碎的，脆的；脆弱的；易损坏的

【例】 This material was of little practical use；the fibers were *brittle*，ragged，and no longer than ten feet.

【近】 fragile，breakable，frail，weak

calorie ['kæləri]

【释】 *n.* 卡（路里）（热量单位）

【例】 The energy content of food is measured in *calories*.

cart [kɑːt]

【释】 *n.* （二轮运货）马车，大车；手推车

【例】 Flatcars carried rails to within hall a mile of the railhead；there the iron was loaded onto *carts*.

【近】 wagon，stagecoach，coach，carriage

Celsius ['selsjəs]

【释】 *adj.* 摄氏的

【例】 The temperature may fall unusually low by dawn，as low as 34 degrees *Celsius* in the camel.

【近】 centigrade

chunk [tʃʌŋk]

【释】 *n.* 大块

【例】 The world anxiously watched as, every few hours, a hurtling *chunk* of comet plunged into the atmosphere of Jupiter.

【衍】 chunky (*adj.*) 矮胖的；结实的

【近】 mass, lump

coil [kɔil]

【释】 *n.* (一)卷，(一)盘，(一)圈；【电】线圈 *v.* 卷，盘绕

【例】 A variation of barbed wire is also used for military purposes. It is formed into long *coils* or entanglements called concertina wire.

【近】 loop, spiral, twist

component [kəm'pəunənt]

【释】 *n.* 部分，成分

【例】 The use of home bases is a fundamental *component* of human social behavior; the common meal served at a common hearth is a powerful symbol, a mark of social unity.

【衍】 componential (*adj.*)

【近】 agent, constituent, ingredient, element

confront [kən'frʌnt]

【释】 *v.* (困难等)横阻在…的面前

【例】 As protector of her family's health, the pioneer woman *confronted* situations she never imagined before crossing the Mississippi.

【近】 face, meet

continual [kən'tinjuəl]

【释】 *adj.* 不断的，连续的

【例】 The school has been in *continual* use since 1883.

【衍】 continually (*adv.*); continuation (*n.*)

【近】 incessant, constant, continuous

corridor ['kɔridɔː]

【释】 *n.* 走廊；通路

【例】 Moreover, the railroad nurtured factory complexes, coat piles, warehouses, and generating stations, forming along its right-of-way what has aptly been called "the metropolitan *corridor*" of the American landscape.

【近】 passage，hallway

crystal ['kristəl]

【释】 *n. & adj.* (结)晶体(的)；水晶(制的)

【例】 A snowfall consists of myriads of minute ice *crystals* that fall to the ground in the form of frozen precipitation.

【衍】 crystalline (*n. & adj.*)（眼球）水晶体的；crystallize (*v.*)；crystallization (*n.*)

declare [di'klɛə]

【释】 *v.* 声称；宣布

【例】 Joseph Jefferson III also *declared* that he was a pioneer in the movement.

【衍】 declaration (*n.*)

【近】 announce，proclaim

derive [di'raiv]

【释】 *v.* 得到；导出(**from**)

【例】 Babies obviously *derive* pleasure from sound input.

【衍】 derivation (*n.*)；derivable (*adj.*)

【近】 stem，originate

dinosaur ['dainəsɔː]

【释】 *n.* 恐龙

【例】 The extinction of the *dinosaurs* was caused by some physical events，either climatic or cosmic.

district ['distrikt]

【释】 *n.* 区；管区；行政区

【例】 The downtown business *district* did not grow apace with the city as a whole.

【近】 region，area，quarter，ward

drought [draut]

【释】 *n.* 旱灾，干旱

【例】 But in the dry grazing lands of the West，that familiar blue joint grass was often killed by *drought*.

elicit [i'lisit]

【释】 *v.* 引出，探出(事实等)；诱出(回答等)

Unit 16

【例】 Even questions that are less structured must be carefully phrased in order to *elicit* the type of information desired.

【衍】 elicitation（*n.*）

【近】 extract，obtain，educe

energetic [ˌenə'dʒetik]

【释】 *adj.* 精力旺盛的

【例】 With it Neolithic peoples flourished，fashioning an *energetic*，creative era.

【衍】 energy（*n.*）；energetically（*adv.*）

【近】 vigorous，strong，enthusiastic，exuberant

erect [i'rekt]

【释】 *v.* 使直立，树立

【例】 Wilton also made a lead equestrian image of King George III that was *erected* in New York in 1770 and torn down by zealous patriots six years later.

【衍】 erectable（*adj.*）；erection（*n.*）

exhilarating [ig'ziləreitiŋ]

【释】 *adj.* 使人高兴的，令人兴奋的

【例】 After that *exhilarating* experience，Lucinda Childs "wasn't sure she even wanted to be an actress anymore".

【衍】 exhilaratingly（*adv.*）；exhilaration（*n.*）

【近】 exciting，elating

faint [feint]

【释】 *adj.* 稀薄的；暗淡的；模糊的

【例】 Place far enough away，even the blazing Sun would become a dim point of light；brought nearer to the Earth，a once-*faint* body might appear a million times as bright.

【衍】 faintly（*adv.*）

【近】 dim，pale，weak

fine [fain]

【释】 ① *adj.* 精制的；华美的；细致的，细微的，纤细的

【例】 Pamphlets and chapbooks did not require *fine* paper or a great deal of type to produce.

【释】 ② *n. & v.* 罚款

【例】 He was also *fined* $150 for unprofessional conduct.

fluctuate [ˈflʌktjueit]

【释】 *v.* 波动，起伏

【例】 The result, under favorable conditions, is a dynamic equilibrium in which neither fluid volume nor sodium concentration *fluctuates* too dramatically.

【衍】 fluctuation (*n.*); fluctuant (*adj.*)

【近】 changing, swing, turbulent

frequent [ˈfriːkwənt]

【释】 *adj.* 屡次的，常见的；频繁的

【例】 Maneuvering for position by various regional interests produced *frequent* changes in tariff rates throughout the nine-teenth century.

【衍】 frequently (*adv.*); frequency (*n.*)

【近】 recurrent, repeated

gear [giə]

【释】 *n.* 齿轮，(齿轮)传动装置，齿链；排挡

【例】 Gas pressures increase rapidly during a dive made with scuba *gear*.

【衍】 geared (*adj.*) 连接的；gearing (*n.*) 传动装置

【近】 cog, device

glassy [ˈglɑːsi]

【释】 *adj.* 玻璃质的，玻璃状的

【例】 Some of the glacier melted on contact, but suddenly there also appeared a huge black mass of *glassy* stone.

halt [hɔːlt]

【释】 *v.* 停止；暂停前进

【例】 Even the most efficient of operations had to be *halted* until the machines were oiled to reduce the wear and tear of friction.

【近】 stop, break, pause

heed [hiːd]

【释】 *n. & v.* 注意，留意

【例】 We must pay close *heed* to the practical needs of society.

【衍】 heedful (*adj.*); heedfully (*adv.*)

【近】 notice, regard, attention

Unit 16

honor [ˈɔnə]

【释】 *n. & v.* 尊敬，敬重

【例】 They have been *honored* with exhibitions, degrees, and medals.

【衍】 honorable (*adj.*); honorably (*adv.*)

【近】 respect, admiration, credit, reputation

ideology [ˌaidiˈɔlədʒi]

【释】 *n.* 意识形态，思想方式

【例】 Their distrust was caused, in part, by a national *ideology* that proclaimed farming the greatest occupation and rural living superior to urban living.

【近】 belief, thought, dogma

imply [imˈplai]

【释】 *v.* 暗示；包含；含有…的意思

【例】 This is not to *imply* that sunken ships are always found intact.

【衍】 implication (*n.*)

【近】 entail, involve, mean

ingenious [inˈdʒiːnjəs]

【释】 *adj.* 别出心裁的，巧妙的

【例】 The Anasazi Indians were an *ingenious*, vigorous, adaptable people whose highly developed society prospered despite an exceedingly inhospitable—if spectacular—environment.

【衍】 ingeniously (*adv.*); ingenuity (*n.*)

【近】 resourceful

instinct [ˈinstiŋkt]

【释】 *n.* 本能，才能

【例】 But like most animals without a backbone, flatworms act mostly by *instinct* and reflex.

【衍】 instinctive (*adj.*); instinctively (*adv.*)

【近】 nature, intuition

intimate [ˈintimət]

【释】 *adj.* 亲密的，亲近的，密切的

【例】 Lesser trees, however, have played an *intimate* role in the lives of people since they first appeared on Earth.

【衍】 intimately（*adv.*）；intimateness（*n.*）
【近】 close，cherished

jar ［dʒɑː］
【释】 ① *v.* 使震动，使摇动
【例】 Satire *jars* us out of complacence into a pleasantly shocked realization.
【近】 bump，hit
【释】 ② *n.* (圆柱形、大口的)罐子，坛子，瓶子
【例】 Beekeepers remove honey from the hives and pack it in bottles or *jars*.
【近】 pot，container

laboratory ［ˈlæbərətəri］
【释】 *n.* 实验室，化验室，研究室
【例】 It is in the *laboratory* that most discoveries about past cultures are actually made.
【衍】 laborer（*n.*）工人，劳工，劳动者；laborious（*adj.*）费力的，麻烦的；laboriously（*adv.*）；laborsaving（*adj.*）节省劳力的

legislation ［ˌledʒisˈleiʃən］
【释】 *n.* 立法；法规；立法机构的审议事项
【例】 The intent of this *legislation* was to provide protection to selected coastal habitats similar to that existing for land areas designated as national parks.
【衍】 legislative（*adj.*）立法的；legislator（*n.*）立法者，议员，立法委员；legislature（*n.*）立法机关，立法部，议会

livelihood ［ˈlaivlihud］
【释】 *n.* 生活，生计
【例】 Experts in specific trades had developed their own techniques and guarded their knowledge to prevent others from stealing their *livelihood*.
【衍】 lively（*adj.*）活泼的，愉快的；liveliness（*n.*）；livestock（*n.*）家畜，牲畜
【近】 living，income，source of revenue

luxury ［ˈlʌkʃəri］
【释】 *n. & adj.* 奢侈(的)；奢侈品(的)

【例】	Passenger terminals，like the *luxury* express trains that hurled people over spots，spotlight the romance of rail-roading.
【衍】	luxuriate（*v.*）生活奢华，沉迷，享受；luxurious（*adj.*）豪华的，奢侈的
【近】	lavishness，sumptuousness，extravagance

maritime ['mæritaim]

【释】	*adj.* 海的，海上的
【例】	The *maritime* life harvested by the women not only provid-ed food，but also supplied more of the raw materials for making tools than did the fish gathered by the men.
【衍】	marine（*adj.*）；mariner（*n.*）水手，船员
【近】	marine，nautical，naval，aquatic

merchant ['mə:tʃənt]

【释】	*n.* 商人　*adj.* 商人的；商业的
【例】	For as long as *merchants* have set out their wares at day break and religious services have begun on the hour，people have been in rough agreement with their neighbors as to the time of day.
【衍】	mercantile（*adj.*）贸易的，商业的；重商主义的；merchandise（*n.*）商品，货；商业；merchandize（*n.*）商品，货物
【近】	mercantile，commercial，trade

mineral ['minərəl]

【释】	*n.* 矿物；无机物
【例】	As magma rises under the mid-ocean ridge, ferromagnetic *minerals* in the magma become magnetized in the direction of the geomagnetic field.
【衍】	mineralize（*v.*）；mineralization（*n.*）

monotonous [mə'nɔtənəs]

【释】	*adj.* 单调的，无变化的
【例】	While factory work was less creative and more *monotonous*，it was also more efficient and allowed mass production of goods at less expense.
【衍】	monotonously（*adv.*）；monotony（*n.*）单调，无变化，千篇一律，无聊

【近】 dull，repetitive，tedious

nail [neil]

【释】 *n.* 钉子

【例】 While it is pleasant to imagine a woodworker，for example，carefully matching lumber，joining a chest together without resort to *nails* or glue.

【近】 pin，spike，tack，peg

nickname ['nikneim]

【释】 *n.* 诨名，绰号；略称，爱称

【例】 However，a man who had a distinguishing characteristic was forever known by an apposite *nickname*，such as Big Hand.

【近】 moniker，epithet，pet name

obscure [əb'skjuə]

【释】 *adj.* 不清楚的，含糊的　*v.* 使不明显

【例】 The origins of nest-building remain *obscure*，but current observation of nest-building activities provides evidence of their evolution.

【衍】 obscurely（*adv.*）；obscurity（*n.*）

【近】 vague，ambiguous，obfuscate

oppose [ə'pəuz]

【释】 *v.* 反对，反抗，对抗

【例】 They have no use for anyone who wishes something better for them；they *oppose* civic reform cultural and educational projects.

【衍】 opponent（*n.* & *adj.*）反对者，对手，敌手；opposing（*adj.*）反作用的，反向的；opposition（*n.*）；opposite（*adj.* & *n.*）相对的，对立的，相反的事物(人)，对立面

【近】 resist，counter，contradict

outward ['autwəd]

【释】 *adv.* 向外；在外；表面上([*opp.*] inward)

【例】 The Sun's outermost layer begins about 10，000 miles above the visible surface and goes *outward* for millions of miles.

【衍】 outwards（*adv.*）在外，向外；outwardly（*adv.*）外表上；outwardness（*n.*）客观存在，客观性

Unit 16

【近】	external，away from，towards the outside
paraphrase	['pærəfreiz]
【释】	*n. & v.* 释义；意译
【例】	When a thing has been said so well that it could not be said better，why **paraphrase** it?
【近】	rephrase，summarize，reword，translate
penalty	['penəlti]
【释】	*n.* 刑罚，惩罚，罚款，报应
【例】	Finally，those protesting must understand the **penalties** their acts entail usually jailing and be willing to accept those **penalties**.
【衍】	penal (*adj.*)
【近】	punishment
petal	['petəl]
【释】	*n.* 花瓣
【例】	Surrounding the column are three sepals and three **petals**.
planetary	['plænitəri]
【释】	*adj.* 行星的
【例】	It would suggest that comets form within the **planetary** orbits.
【衍】	planet (*n.*)；planetoid (*n.*) 小行星
pollutant	[pə'luːtənt]
【释】	*n.* 污染物(尤指放入水中和空气中的有害化学物质)
【例】	As the earth developed，the concentrations of these **pollutants** were altered by various chemical reactions.
【衍】	pollution (*n.*) 污染；pollute (*v.*)
【近】	contaminant，impurity
prairie	['preəri]
【释】	*n.* 大草原，牧场，草原地带
【例】	In their collector's enthusiasm，they even floated a **prairie** dog out of its burrow by pouring in five barrelfuls of water.
【近】	plain，grassland，pasture，ranch
prevail	[pri'veil]
【释】	*v.* 胜，压倒，占优势；普遍；传开，盛行
【例】	Most goods are handmade，and a subsistence economy **prevails**.
【衍】	prevailing (*adj.*) 普遍的，流行的

【近】	triumph
proficiency	[prə'fiʃənsi]
【释】	*n.* 精通，熟练(**in**)
【例】	Musicians have to have the muscular *proficiency* of an athlete or a ballet dancer.
【衍】	proficient (*adj.*)；proficiently (*adv.*)
【近】	skill，talent，ability，expertise
protection	[prə'tekʃən]
【释】	*n.* 保护，保卫，防御，掩护，包庇
【例】	Civilian officials often called on the army for *protection*.
【衍】	protectionist (*n.*) 保护贸易论者；protective (*adj.*)
【近】	defense，guard
pyramid	['pirəmid]
【释】	*n.* 金字塔
【例】	They sprouted from tiny seeds about the time the Egyptian *pyramids* were being built.
ranch	[ræntʃ]
【释】	*n.* 大牧场，大农场 *v.* 经营牧场
【例】	"Combines" were also coming into use on the great wheat *ranches* in California and the Pacific Northwest.
【衍】	rancher (*n.*)；ranching (*n.*)
【近】	farm，pasture，meadow
recall	[ri'kɔːl]
【释】	*v.* (使)想起；(使)回忆
【例】	Sleepers who are awakened during this rapid-eye-movement sleep will often *recall* the details of dreams they have been having.
【衍】	recaller (*n.*)；recallability (*n.*)；recallable (*adj.*)
【近】	bring to mind，remind，remember
reform	[ri'fɔːm]
【释】	① *v. & n.* 改革，改良，革新(制度、事业等)
【例】	Subsequent *reforms* have made these notions seem quite out-of-date.
【衍】	reforming (*adj.*)；reformer (*n.*)；reformism (*n.*) 改革主义
【近】	revolutionize，ameliorate，improve

Unit 16

【释】② *v.* 改过自新，矫正(品性等)

【例】Amelia's parents did not pressure her to *reform* as she grew older, even when she dabbled in the domains of science and automobile mechanics.

relieve [ri'li:v]

【释】*v.* 减轻，缓和；解除；救济

【例】The graduates of Harvard College simultaneously rallied to *relieve* the college's poverty and demand new enterprise.

【衍】relief (*n.*) 慰藉，安慰；relievable (*adj.*)；relieved (*adj.*)

【近】alleviate, ease, lessen

replicate ['replikit]

【释】*v.* 复制，反复

【例】The virus *replicates* by attaching to a cell and injecting it nucleic acid.

【衍】replication (*n.*)；replicative (*adj.*)

【近】duplicate, copy, imitate

responsible [ri'spɔnsəbl]

【释】*adj.* 有责任的，应负责任的

【例】Critics respond that this very distance may also be *responsible* for the Academy's inability to perceive accurately authentic trends in the literary world.

【衍】responsibility (*n.*) 责任；responsive (*adj.*) 回答的；反应迅速的

【近】accountable, liable, answerable

rid [rid]

【释】*v.* 使脱除，使摆脱

【例】When it is short of water, a plant cannot *rid* itself of the heat it absorbs from sunlight or the heat that may build up from its own metabolism.

【衍】riddance (*n.*)

【近】free, liberate, relieve, get rid of

rounded ['raundid]

【释】① *adj.* 圆形的；球形的

【例】Rod-shaped bacteria are usually from two to four microns long, while *rounded* ones are generally one micron in diameter.

【衍】round（*adj.* & *v.*）圆的；弄成圆的；环绕，包围；roundup（*n.*）围捕

【近】round，curved，smoothed

【释】② *adj.* 多样的；多面的

【例】*Rounded* comers made life smooth, Finals, parapets and tall signs lettered with hotel names reached for futuristic fantasies.

satisfy ['sætisfai]

【释】*v.* 使满足，使满意，符合(标准)，达到(要求)

【例】Neither the farmers of the west nor the merchants of the east were completely *satisfied* with this pattern of trade.

【衍】satisfied（*adj.*）；dissatisfied（*adj.*）不满意的；satisfactory（*adj.*）令人满足（满意）的；satisfying（*adj.*）使人满足的，令人满意的

【近】please，gratify，suit

seal [siːl]

【释】① *n.* 海豹

【例】Polar bears live on *seals*，and to hunt them the bears must have ice to where the seals are.

【衍】sealing（*n.*）猎海豹业；sealskin（*n.*）海豹皮

【释】② *v.* & *n.* 关闭；密闭，密封；隔离

【例】After the stock exchange collapse of 1873，the subway was *sealed* up and forgotten.

【衍】sealant（*n.*）密封胶；sealed（*adj.*）密封的，未知的

【近】close up，shut，stick down

sequence ['siːkwəns]

【释】*n.* 顺序

【例】More complex behavior patterns, such as crawling, standing, and walking, come much later in the developmental *sequence* than head movements do.

【衍】sequent（*adj.*）连续的，随着…而发生的；sequential（*adj.*）连续的，随着…而发生的

【近】series，order，chain

shock [ʃɔk]

【释】*v.* & *n.* (使)震惊；(使)惊骇

【例】 Satire jars us out of complacence into a pleasantly *shocked* realization that many of the values we unquestioningly accept are false.

【衍】 shocked（*adj.*）震惊的，震动的；shocking（*adj.*）让人震惊的

【近】 astonish，fright，astound

skeptical ［'skeptikəl］

【释】 *adj.* 怀疑性的，好怀疑的（［*opp.*］convinced）

【例】 Samuel Clemens，who adopted the pen name Mark Twain，became the country's most outstanding realist author，observing life around him with a humorous and *skeptical* eye.

【衍】 skepticism（*n.*）怀疑态度；怀疑论；skeptic（*n.*）怀疑者；无神论者

【近】 doubtful，incredulous，cynical

solder ［'sɔldə］

【释】 *v.* 焊；接合；锡焊；焊接；（使）结合

【例】 They were made by shaping or casting pads separately and then *soldering* them together.

【衍】 solderability（*n.*）可焊性；solderer（*n.*）焊工；soldering（*n.*）焊接

【近】 fuse，join，connect

specimen ［'spesimən］

【释】 *n.* 样本，样品；实例，例子；标本

【例】 Researchers make tools that replicate excavated *specimens* as closely as possible and then try to use them as the originals might have been used.

【近】 example，sample，case

sprout ［spraut］

【释】 *v.* 发芽，萌芽

【例】 To protect themselves from this competition，some shrubs give off a substance that kills young plants that *sprout* too close to them.

【衍】 sprouting（*n.*）发芽，萌芽

【近】 grow，germinate，bud

statistics ［stə'tistiks］

【释】 *n.* 统计学；统计法；统计数字(资料)

【例】 Descriptive *statistics* is a tool for describing or summarizing or reducing to comprehensible form the properties of an otherwise unwieldy mass of data.

【衍】 statistical (*adj.*); statistically (*adv.*)

【近】 figures, data, info

stony ['stəuni]

【释】 ***adj.*** 石的,石头的,石质的, 像石头(一样硬)的, 多石的

【例】 A *stony* meteorite has beauty of its own, but it only appears under the microscope: to the unaided eye, *stony* meteorites appear to be—indeed they are—rather homely black or gray rocks.

【衍】 stone (*n.*); stoneware (*n.*) 缸瓦器,粗陶器; stonework (*n.*) 砖石部分; 石制品; stonemason (*n.*) 石匠

【近】 rocky, pebbly, gravelly

struggle ['strʌgl]

【释】 ***v. & n.*** 挣扎; 努力, 奋斗; 同…斗争

【例】 One of the advantages of the awards is that many go to the *struggling* artists, rather than to those who are already successful.

【近】 effort, strive, work hard

suffer ['sʌfə]

【释】 ① ***v.*** 遭受, 蒙受; 经受; 忍受

【例】 But at least the child knows something of geometry and numbers, and it will always retain some memory of the early halcyon days, no matter what vicissitudes it may *suffer* later on.

【衍】 sufferable (*adj.*); sufferance (*n.*)

【近】 undergo, experience, endure

【释】 ② ***v.*** 受害, 受损失, 受苦

【例】 The cost of the First World War to the United States, exclusive of the loss of life and *suffering* involved and the subsequent payments to veterans, runs into figures almost beyond human comprehension.

【衍】 sufferer (*n.*) 受害者; suffering (*adj. & n.*) 痛苦的; 痛苦, 苦难

【近】 be ill with

surpass [sə'pɑːs]

【释】 ***v.*** 超过; 优于, 胜过

【例】	The elegance of this first subway will probably never be *surpassed*.
【衍】	surpassable（*adj.*）；surpassing（*adj.*）
【近】	exceed，go beyond，beat

symptom ['simptəm]

【释】	*n.* 症状，征候；征兆
【例】	Much of the focus of this education was on the recognition of vitamin deficiency *symptoms*.
【衍】	symptomless（*adj.*）没有征兆的
【近】	syndrome

tear

【释】	① [teə] *v.* 撕，扯；裂开，拉破 *n.* 裂缝，绽线的地方；撕裂
【例】	The mother may *tear* off the top layer of the nest，sometimes even carrying the young to the water in her mouth.
【衍】	teardown（*v.*）拆卸；tearing（*adj.*）
【近】	rip，scratch，slit
【释】	② [tiə] *n.* 泪滴
【例】	Examples of exocrine glands are the *tear* glands，and the pancreas，which secretes pancreatic juice through a duct into the intestine.
【衍】	teardrop（*n.*）泪滴，泪状物；teargas（*n.*）催泪毒气

terrible ['terəbl]

【释】	*adj.* 非常的；厉害的；极度的
【例】	As she pointed out the *terrible* deficiencies in education for women at all levels，she suggested that "if we mean to have Heroes，Statesmen and Philosophers，we should have learned women."
【衍】	terribly（*adv.*）
【近】	extreme，excessive

throw [θrəu]

【释】	① *v.* 扔，摔，投，掷
【例】	Stinging cells in the tentacles *throw* out tiny poison threads that paralyze other small sea animals.
【衍】	throwaway（*adj. & n.*）可扔掉的；广告传单
【近】	fling，toss，hurl
【释】	② *v.* 摔倒，使翻倒；（将船等）冲上（暗礁等）；（马）把…摔下来

【例】	They protected the riders' legs from injury if they fell from their horses or when they had to ride *thrown* cactus, sagebrush, or other thorny plants.
toothed	[tu:θt]
【释】	*adj.* (装)有牙齿的；锯齿状的([*opp.*] smoothed)
【例】	Direct competition may have brought about the demise of large carnivores such as the saber-*toothed* cats.
【衍】	tooth (*n.*)；toothless (*adj.*)；toothpaste (*n.*) 牙膏
【近】	jagged, notched, saw-toothed
transfer	['trænsfə:]
【释】	① *v. & n.* 转移；传递；转送
【例】	There would be a limit to the phlogiston *transfer*, since a given volume of air could absorb only so much phlogiston.
【衍】	transferable (*adj.*)；transference (*n.*)；transferred (*adj.*)
【近】	transport, convey, transmit
【释】	② *v. & n.* 交付，转让，(股票等的)过户划拨，汇划，汇兑
【例】	Electronic fund *transfer* allows money to be instantly sent and received by different banks, companies, and countries through computers and telecommunications devices.
【衍】	transferential (*adj.*) 转让的，让渡的
trip	[trip]
【释】	*n.* (短程)旅行，航行
【例】	Telecommuting—substituting the computer for the *trip* to the job—has been hailed as a solution to all kinds of problems related to office work.
【近】	journey, jaunt, tour
twist	[twist]
【释】	① *v.* 扭转；转身；扭伤
【例】	As the cat rote as the front of its body clockwise, the rear and tail *twist* counterclockwise, so that the total spin remains zero, in perfect accord with Newton's laws.
【衍】	twisting (*n.*)；twisty (*adj.*) 扭曲的，不正直的
【近】	contort, warp, distort
【释】	② *v.* 缠上，卷住，盘绕
【例】	Most groups made all their basketwork by twining—the *twisting* of a flexible horizontal material, called a weft, around stiffer vertical strands of material, the warp.

Unit 16

— 359 —

【近】 coil，weave，twine

unravel [ʌn'rævəl]

【释】 *v.* 解开，拆散，拆

【例】 In less than two centuries，by significantly reducing the variety of species on Earth，human beings have *unraveled* cons of evolution and irrevocably redirected its course.

vary ['vɛəri]

【释】 *v.* 使变化，使多样化

【例】 Other trends and inventions had also helped make it possible for Americans to *vary* their daily diets.

【衍】 variety（*n.*）；various（*adj.*）

【近】 change，alter，adapt，modify，adjust

violate ['vaiəleit]

【释】 *v.* 违犯，违反，破坏

【例】 Landscapes that were *violated* by the slowly moving glaciers would carry the scars of this advance far into the future.

【衍】 violated（*adj.*）；violation（*n.*）

【近】 breach，break，abuse

ware [wɛə]

【释】 *n.* 制品，成品，器皿，物件

【例】 Articles for nearly every household activity and ornament could be bought in Rockingham *ware*.

【衍】 warehouse（*n.*）大零售店

widow ['widəu]

【释】 *n.* 寡妇

【例】 Education could provide independence for women in need，whether they were unmarried women or *widows* or wives.

zinc [ziŋk]

【释】 *n.* 锌(Zn)

【例】 They also mixed it with *zinc* to make brass for maritime and scientific instruments.

Exercise of Unit 16

左列单词在右列中有一个同义词，请找出并在相应的位置写上正确答案。

Exercise 1:

(A) component _____ coil
(B) twist _____ agent
(C) energetic _____ stop
(D) boil _____ recurrent
(E) halt _____ simmer
(F) frequent _____ vigorous

Exercise 2:

(A) symptom _____ syndrome
(B) specimen _____ region
(C) sequence _____ transport
(D) transfer _____ passage
(E) corridor _____ example
(F) district _____ series

Exercise 3:

(A) nickname _____ moniker
(B) ranch _____ exciting
(C) brittle _____ extract
(D) belt _____ strap
(E) exhilarating _____ fragile
(F) elicit _____ farm

Exercise 4:

(A) vary _____ mass
(B) gear _____ change
(C) twist _____ cog
(D) chunk _____ contort
(E) suffer _____ rip
(F) tear _____ undergo

Exercise 5:

(A) faint _____ resist
(B) fluctuate _____ dim
(C) suffer _____ triumph
(D) oppose _____ changing
(E) maritime _____ marine
(F) prevail _____ be ill with

Exercise 6:

(A) livelihood _____ living
(B) struggle _____ exceed
(C) imply _____ wagon
(D) cart _____ journey
(E) trip _____ effort
(F) surpass _____ entai

Exercise 7:

(A) declare _____ accountable

(B) merchant _____ mercantile

(C) paraphrase _____ rephrase

(D) monotonous _____ dull

(E) responsible _____ announce

(F) prairie _____ plain

Exercise 8:

(A) pollutant _____ loop

(B) coil _____ real

(C) honor _____ resourceful

(D) ingenious _____ alleviate

(E) authentic _____ respect

(F) relieve _____ contaminant

Exercise 9:

(A) shock _____ fuse

(B) sprout _____ grow

(C) acclaim _____ applause

(D) proficiency _____ skill

(E) intimate _____ close

(F) solder _____ astonish

Exercise 10:

(A) instinct _____ vague

(B) replicate _____ pin

(C) terrible _____ nature

(D) obscure _____ duplicate

(E) nail _____ extreme

(F) Celsius _____ centigrade

ANSWERS:

1	B A E F D C
2	A F D E B C
3	A E F D C B
4	D A B C F E
5	D A F B E C
6	A F D E B C
7	E B C D A F
8	B E D F C A
9	F B C D E A
10	D E A B C F

Unit 17

accommodate	engage	naked	shore
admit	erode	nitrogen	sketch
alter	exocrine	observatory	soldier
anxiety	fair	optical	spectacle
artifact	finish	outweigh	spur
autobiography	fluid	parasite	stature
bark	friction	penchant	storage
bend	generalization	petroleum	stub
bond	glaze	plank	sufficient
broadcast	hammer	polygon	surplus
camel	height	praise	synchronous
cartoon	hook	prevent	technical
census	ignorant	profit	territory
circuit	impose	protein	thrust
coincide	ingredient	quadrilateral	topic
compose	institute	random	transformation
congestion	intoxication	recede	triumph
continuous	jaw	refreshing	typical
corrosion	lace	religion	urban
cube	leisure	representation	vast
decline	lizard	restore	violent
descend	lyric	ridge	warfare
dioxide	marrow	routine	willow
disturb	merciless	saturated	zone
dull	miniature	search	
eligible	monster	serene	

accommodate [əˈkɔmədeit]

【释】 ① v. 适应，调节

【例】 Their teeth had to *accommodate* to hard siliceous grass.

【衍】 accommodating（*adj.*）随和的，善于适应新环境的；accommodatingly（*adv.*）

【近】 get used to，adapt，adjust，acclimatize

【释】 ② v. 留宿，招待

【例】 Canals are often classified by the size of vessel they can *accommodate*.

【衍】 accommodation（*n.*）

【近】 house，contain，lodge

admit [ədˈmit]

【释】 ① v. 承认，容许

【例】 In Ontario，Canada，Queen's University was the first to *admit* women into degree programs.

【衍】 admitted（*adj.*）被承认了的；admittedly（*adv.*）明白地；admission（*n.*）允许进入；承认；首肯

【近】 give access，permit

【释】 ② v. 收容，容纳

【例】 As more states were *admitted* to the Union，however，it quickly became apparent that this scheme would not prove practical and the coins from 1798 on were issued with only thirteen stars—one for each of the original colonies.

alter [ˈɔːltə]

【释】 v. 变更；改变

【例】 Functionalism emerged as the dominant influence upon designers *altered* the First World War.

【衍】 altered（*adj.*）；unaltered（*adj.*）；alterable（*adj.*）；alterability（*n.*）

【近】 change，modify，adjust

anxiety [æŋˈzaiəti]

【释】 n. 悬念，挂念，忧虑；切望，渴望

【例】 Her *anxiety* about the world was amplifying her personal fears about her future.

【衍】 anxious（*adj.*）；anxiously（*adv.*）

【近】	concern，worry
artifact	[ˈɑːtifækt]
【释】	*n.* 人工制品；人为现象
【例】	This vertical movement of the fieldstones is not simply an *artifact* of soil erosion; it is the result of frost heaving.
【衍】	artificial（*adj.*）人工的，人造的；人为的；artificially（*adv.*）
【近】	synthetic(s)
autobiography	[ˌɔːtəubaiˈɔgrəfi]
【释】	*n.* 自传；自传文学
【例】	He wrote an *autobiography* in 1956，and also published several collections of poetry.
【衍】	autobiographic（*adj.*）；autobiographically（*adv.*）；autobiographer（*n.*）
【近】	memoir，biography
bark	[bɑːk]
【释】	*n.* 树皮
【例】	Stone，wood，tree *bark*，clay，and sand are generally available materials.
bend	[bend]
【释】	*v.* 弄弯，使弯曲
【例】	To *bend* the arm at the elbow，the muscle at the front of the upper arm has to shorten and bunch up.
【衍】	bender（*n.*）
【近】	curve，turn，crook，twist
bond	[bɔnd]
【释】	*n.* 结合(物)，结合力，黏合(剂)，联结，束缚，羁绊
【例】	That *bond* constitutes the social unit out of which all higher orders of society are constructed.
【衍】	bonder（*n.*）连接器，接合器；bonded（*adj.*）抵押的，有担保的
【近】	tie，connection，link，union
broadcast	[ˈbrɔːdkɑːst]
【释】	*adj.* 撒播的，广泛散布的；播音的，广播的
【例】	We are most familiar with *broadcast* television because it has been with us for about thirty-seven years.

Unit 17

— 365 —

【衍】 broadcasting（n.）

【近】 transmit，air，show

camel [ˈkæməl]

【释】 *n.* 骆驼

【例】 Creatures such as the *camel* and the penguin are so highly specialized that they have an extremely limited distribution.

cartoon [kɑːˈtuːn]

【释】 *n.*（报刊上的）漫画；连环画

【例】 The concept of obtaining fresh water from icebergs that are towed to populated areas and arid regions of the world was once treated as a joke more appropriate to *cartoons* than real life.

【近】 animation

census [ˈsensəs]

【释】 *n.* 人口普查

【例】 In the 1880's engineer Herman Hollerith was searching for a way to record *census* information.

【近】 poll，survey

circuit [ˈsəːkit]

【释】 ① *n.*【电】电路，线路；回路

【例】 But widespread link-ups of television systems for personal communications are economically impossible because a standard picture requires about one thousand times more information than a telephone *circuit* can carry.

【近】 route，course，path

【释】 ② *n.* 巡回，周游

【例】 By the end of the First World War the brothers had changed their names to Chico, Gummo, and Zeppo, respectively; Zeppo, who had been too young to play the *circuit*, replaced Gummo.

【近】 tour

coincide [ˌkəuinˈsaid]

【释】 *v.* 与…一致，相合，符合，相符，相巧合（with）

【例】 The study area usually *coincides* with a natural physiographic region such as the watershed of a major river or some other logical unit of land; unfortunately these seldom *coincide* with the legal jurisdiction of country and state boundaries.

【衍】 coincidence (*n.*)；coincident (*adj.*)；coincidently (*adv.*)

compose [kəm'pəuz]

【释】 ① *v.* 组成，构成(be composed of)

【例】 The best fossils are those *composed* of unaltered remains.

【衍】 composition (*n.*) 组成，组织；composite (*n.*) 合成物

【近】 comprise，consist

【释】 ② *v.* 创作(诗歌、乐曲等)

【例】 Certain films had music especially *composed* for them.

【衍】 composition (*n.*) 作品；文章；composer (*n.*) 作曲家；作者

【近】 create，compile，assemble

congestion [kən'dʒestʃən]

【释】 *n.* 拥挤；充斥；充血

【例】 The confusion and *congestion* of individual citizens looking for their letters was itself enough to discourage use of the mail.

【近】 blockage，jam，clog

continuous [kən'tinjuəs]

【释】 *adj.* 连续的，继续的

【例】 The warmer and lighter bottom layer then tends to rise and the cooler layer tends to sink in a *continuous* cycle.

【衍】 continuously (*adv.*)

【近】 incessant，constant，continual

corrosion [kə'rəuʒən]

【释】 *n.* 腐蚀，侵蚀

【例】 Copper's ability to conduct heat efficiently and to resist *corrosion* contributed to its attractiveness.

【衍】 corrode (*v.*)；corrosive (*adj.*)

【近】 decay，deterioration，decomposition

cube [kju:b]

【释】 *n.* 立方体(形)；三次幂

【例】 Streams of melting ice and snow tunnel through the glaciers the same way that water from a faucet melts it way through an ice *cube*.

【衍】 cubic (*adj.*)；cubism (*n.*)(艺术上的)立体派；cubist (*n.*) 立体派艺术家

decline ［di'klain］
【释】 **v. & n. 下降；衰老**
【例】 After the peak year of 1957，the birth rate in Canada began to *decline*.
【衍】 declination（n.）下降；偏差；declinational（adj.）偏差的
【近】 fall，drop

descend ［di'send］
【释】 **v. 下降（[opp.] ascend）；下斜；传下，遗传**
【例】 Other oceans，such as the Pacific，are shrinking as seafloor *descends* under their fringing coastlines or offshore arcs of islands.
【衍】 descent（n.）；descendant（n.）子孙，后代（[opp.] ancestor）

dioxide ［dai'ɔksaid］
【释】 **n. 二氧化物**
【例】 In photosynthesis，energy from sunlight converts carbon *dioxide* and water to sugar.

disturb ［di'stə:b］
【释】 **v. 扰乱；打扰**
【例】 The smooth surface of the lake is *disturbed* by several fallen leaves.
【衍】 disturbance（n.）
【近】 agitate，stir

dull ［dʌl］
【释】 **adj. 单调的，枯燥的，无聊的，沉闷的**
【例】 At the time when *Main Street* was published Lewis was accused of hating *dull* people.
【近】 dreary，boring，tedious，monotonous

eligible ['elidʒəbl］
【释】 **adj. 胜任的，合格的，适当的**
【例】 Members of the Academy and Institute are not *eligible* for any cash prizes.
【衍】 eligibility（n.）；ineligible（adj.）
【近】 entitled，qualified，suitable

engage ［in'geidʒ］
【释】 **v. [多用被动语态] 使从事，使忙于（in）**

【例】 In the early 1800's, over 80 percent of the United States labor force was *engaged* in agriculture.

【近】 devote, dedicate

erode [i'rəud]

【释】 *v.* 侵蚀，腐蚀

【例】 But because they are similar to Earth material and therefore *erode* easily, they are often difficult to find.

【衍】 erosion (*n.*)

【近】 corrode, decay

exocrine ['eksəkrain]

【释】 *n. & adj.* 外分泌(的)

【例】 ... *exocrine* gland

fair [fɛə]

【释】 ① *n.* 定期集市，庙会

【例】 The most eagerly anticipated social events were the rural *fairs*.

【近】 exposition, exhibition

【释】 ② *adj.* 公平的，合理的

【例】 Proponents of these reforms argued that public ownership and regulation guarantee a *fair* price.

【衍】 unfair (*adj.*)

【近】 just, reasonable

finish ['finiʃ]

【释】 *v.* 给…抛光；给…最后加工；润饰　*n.* 最后一道工序；抛光；终饰

【例】 Since surface *finishes* provided a pleasing appearance and also improved the durability in day-to-day use, the potter smoothed the exterior surface of the pot with wet hands.

【近】 varnish, glaze, polish

fluid ['fluːid]

【释】 *n.* 流体，液

【例】 In the simplest cases, convective flow begins when a *fluid* is heated from below.

【衍】 fluidal (*adj.*)

【近】 liquid, juice, solution

Unit 17

friction [ˈfrikʃən]

【释】 *n.* 摩擦，阻力

【例】 The forward movement of a small animal is seriously reduced by the air *friction* against the relatively large surface area of its body.

【衍】 frictionless（*adj.*）；frictional（*adj.*）

generalization [ˌdʒenərəlaiˈzeiʃən]

【释】 *n.* 一般化，普遍化

【例】 Scientific explanation comes in two forms *generalization* and reduction.

【衍】 generalist（*n.*）多面手；general（*adj.*）普通的

glaze [gleiz]

【释】 *v.* 镶玻璃于，装玻璃于；打光，擦亮；给…上釉

【例】 The name of the ware was probably derived from its resemblance to English brown-*glazed* earthenware made in South Yorkshire.

【衍】 glazing（*n.*）；glazed（*adj.*）

【近】 varnish，finish，polish

hammer [ˈhæmə]

【释】 *n.* 铁锤

【例】 The very tools that the first New England furniture makers used were, after all, not much different from those used for centuries—even millennia: basic *hammers*, saws, chisels, planes, augers, compasses, and measures.

height [hait]

【释】 *n.* 高，高度；身高；海拔

【例】 Desert mammals allow their temperatures to rise to what would normally be fever *height*.

【衍】 heighten（*v.*）

【近】 stature，tallness，elevation，altitude

hook [huk]

【释】 *v.* 钩住；沉迷

【例】 She *hooks* up her telephone modem connections and does office work between calls to the doctor.

【衍】 hooked（*adj.*）

【近】 clasp，clip，catch

ignorant [ˈignərənt]

【释】 *adj*. 无学识的，无知的，愚昧的

【例】 Critics *ignorant* of western conditions often attacked it as wasteful and dangerous.

【衍】 ignorance（*n*.）

【近】 unaware，uninformed

impose [imˈpəuz]

【释】 *v*. 征收(税等)；使…负担

【例】 The railroad was not the first institution to *impose* regularity on society，or to draw attention to the importance of precise timekeeping.

【近】 oblige，force，compel

ingredient [inˈgriːdiənt]

【释】 *n*. (混合物的)组成部分，成分，要素

【例】 As early marine species made their way to freshwater and eventually to dry land，sodium remained a key *ingredient* of their interior，if not their exterior，milieu.

【近】 element，component，constituent，agent

institute [ˈinstitjuːt]

【释】 *n*. 协会，学会；学院

【例】 He turned down many offers to leave Tuskegee *Institute* to become a rich scientist in private industry.

【近】 society

intoxication [inˌtɔksiˈkeiʃən]

【释】 *n*. 中毒；醉

【例】 At a depth of 5 atmospheres，nitrogen causes symptoms resembling alcohol *intoxication*，known as nitrogen narcosis.

【衍】 intoxicate（*v*.）；toxic（*adj*.）

jaw [dʒɔː]

【释】 *n*. 颌，颚

【例】 These flying reptiles had large，tooth-filled *jaws*.

【近】 chin，jawbone，jowl

lace [leis]

【释】 ① *n*. 带子，花边

【例】 Drums generally were made by soaking a strip of wood in hot water and bending it into a circle; then the drum skin was tightly strapped over the circle with rawhide *laces*.

【衍】 laced（*adj.*）有花边的，绑带子的；laceless（*adj.*）没有带子的，不镶花边的；lacelike（*adj.*）带子般的，花边状的

【近】 tie，cord，shoelace

【释】 ② *v.* 交织

【例】 New York and Philadelphia, by contrast, served a rich and fertile hinterland *laced* with navigable watercourses.

【近】 line，mix

leisure [ˈleʒə, ˈliːʒə]

【释】 *n. & adj.* 空闲(的)，闲暇(的)；悠闲(的)，安逸(的)

【例】 What we today call America folk art was, indeed, art of, by, and for ordinary, everyday "folks" who, with increasing prosperity and *leisure*, created a market for art of all kinds, and especially for portraits.

【衍】 leisureless（*adj.*）无空闲的；leisurely（*adj. & adv.*）从容不迫(的/地)，悠闲(的/地)；leisureliness（*n.*）悠然，从容

【近】 free time，relaxation

lizard [ˈlizəd]

【释】 *n.* 蜥蜴

【例】 *Lizards*, platypuses, sheep, and humans could hardly be more different in anatomy or eating habits, yet the salt content in the fluid surround their blood cells is virtually identical.

lyric [ˈlirik]

【释】 *n.* 抒情诗；抒情作品

【例】 The clear, spare, and energetic *lyrics* of H. D.'s early poems, with their classical images, later became fuller, freer, and more "open" philosophic explorations of the world.

【衍】	lyrical (*adj.*)；lyricism (*n.*) 抒情诗体，抒情语句；lyricist (*n.*) 抒情诗人
marrow	[ˈmærəu]
【释】	***n.*** 髓，骨髓；精髓
【例】	The application of this method of analysis to stone tools indicates that an important function of early stone tools was to extract highly nutritious food—meat and *marrow*—from large animal carcasses.
【近】	essence，substance
merciless	[ˈməːsilis]
【释】	***adj.*** 冷酷无情的，狠心的，残忍的
【例】	Pushing evolutionary theory to its limits，they wrote of a world in which a cruel and *merciless* environment determined human fate.
【衍】	mercy (*n.*) 仁慈，怜悯；mercilessly (*adv.*)；mercilessness (*n.*)
【近】	cruel，hardhearted，unpitying
miniature	[ˈminiətʃə]
【释】	***adj.*** 小型的，缩小的；小规模的
【例】	Their clothes and their homes act as a sort of "*miniature* climate" that can be taken with them everywhere.
【衍】	minimal (*adj.*) 最小的，最低（限度）的；minimalist (*n.*) 最简单派艺术家；minimize (*v.*) 使减到最少，按最小限度估计；minimum (*n.*) 最小，最低，最少限度，极小(值)
【近】	small，minute，diminutive
monster	[ˈmɔnstə]
【释】	***n.*** (想象中的)怪物；(尤指史前的)怪兽，巨兽
【例】	While Lewis and Clark failed to meet the mythological *monsters* reputed to dwell in the West，they did unearth the bones of a 45-foot dinosaur.
【衍】	monstrous (*adj.*) 可怕的；穷凶极恶的
【近】	fiend，ogre，mammoth
naked	[ˈneikid]
【释】	***adj.*** 裸体的；露出的

Unit 17

【例】The faintest star visible to the **naked** eye has m = 6, and is 100 times fainter than a star of m = 1.
【衍】nakedly（*adv.*）光着身子地，赤裸裸地
【近】bare，nude，exposed

nitrogen ['naitrədʒən]
【释】*n.* 氮，氮气
【例】Many of the more important air pollutants, such as sulfur oxides, carbon monoxide, and **nitrogen** oxides, are found in nature.
【衍】nitrogenous（*adj.*）

observatory [əb'zɔːvətəri]
【释】*n.* 气象台，天文台
【例】Evidence obtained from a site known as the Hole in the Rock, indicates that it might have been used as an **observatory** by a prehistoric people known as the Hohokam.
【衍】observation（*n.*）；observe（*v.*）；observer（*n.*）；observing（*adj.*）注意周到的；观察力敏锐的

optical ['ɔptikəl]
【释】*adj.* 眼的；视觉的；视力的；帮助视力的；光学(上)的
【例】The new X-ray microscopes considerably improve on the resolution provided by **optical** microscopes.
【衍】optically（*adv.*）
【近】visual，ocular

outweigh [ˌaut'wei]
【释】*v.* 比…重；比…重要；胜过，强过
【例】In potential food value, however, plankton far **outweighs** that of the land grasses.
【衍】outwork（*n.*）户外工作
【近】overshadow，prevail over，be more important than

parasite ['pærəsait]
【释】*n.* 寄生物；寄生虫；寄生菌；食客
【例】They are **parasites**, requiting human, animal, or plant cells to live.
【衍】parasitic（*adj.*）

penchant ['pentʃənt]
【释】*n.* (强烈的)倾向，嗜好，爱好(for)

【例】	But the beaver's ***penchant*** for building dams, lodges, and canals has got it into a lot of hot water lately.
【近】	fondness, desire, inclination

petroleum [pi'trəuliəm]

【释】	***n.*** 石油
【例】	First, industry requires an abundance of natural resources, especially coal, iron ore, water, ***petroleum.***
【衍】	petrol (*n.*) 汽油；petrolatum (*n.*)【化】矿脂；石油冻
【近】	fuel, oil, gasoline, petrol

plank [plæŋk]

【释】	***n.*** 板，厚板
【例】	Wooden ***planks*** were joined, covered with gesso to prepare the surface for painting.
【衍】	plankton (*n.*) 浮游生物
【近】	board, lath

polygon ['pɔligən]

【释】	***n.*** 多边形，多角形
【例】	There is another regular ***polygon*** (a ***polygon*** whose angles, and sides, are equal) that can tile the plane: the hexagon.
【衍】	polygonal (*adj.*)

praise [preiz]

【释】	***n. & v.*** 称赞；赞扬，表扬
【例】	She has also been ***praised*** for her "sense of form, which is basic and remarkable."
【近】	honor, admire, commend, extol

prevent [pri'vent]

【释】	***v.*** 阻止，阻挡；制止；妨碍(**from**)
【例】	There was no way to ***prevent*** spoilage.
【衍】	prevention (*n.*)；preventive (*adj.*)
【近】	stop, avoid, put off

profit ['prɔfit]

【释】	***n.*** [常 *pl.*] 盈余，利润，赚头（[*opp.*] **loss**）；利润率
【例】	The colonists in North America wanted the right to the ***profits*** gained from their manufacturing.
【衍】	profitability (*n.*) 收益性，利益率；profitable (*adj.*)
【近】	income, earnings, revenue, proceeds

protein ['prəutiːn]

【释】	***n.*** 朊，蛋白(质)

【例】 When the *protein* breaks down into ammo acids，the chlorophyll disintegrates.

【衍】 proteinase（*n.*）【生化】蛋白酶

quadrilateral [ˌkwɔdriˈlætərəl]

【释】 *n. & adj.* 四边形(的)

【例】 As it turns out，any triangle or *quadrilateral*，no matter how devoid of regularity，will tile the plane.

【近】 rectangle，square

random [ˈrændəm]

【释】 *adj.* 任意的，随机的

【例】 The rate at which a molecule of water passes through the cycle is not *random* but is a measure of the relative size of the various reservoirs.

【衍】 randomly（*adv.*）；randomize（*v.*）；randomness（*n.*）

【近】 casual，chance，haphazard

recede [riˈsiːd]

【释】 *v.* 后退，退却（[*opp.*] advance）

【例】 Many of these buildings were shaped in the ziggurat form，a design that *recedes* in progressively smaller stages to the summit.

【近】 retreat，withdraw，draw back

refreshing [riˈfreʃiŋ]

【释】 *adj.* 使人身心爽快的，使人精神振作的；使人耳目一新的

【例】 Satires are stimulating and *refreshing* because with commonsense briskness they brush away illusions and secondhand opinions.

【衍】 refresh（*v.*）；refreshingly（*adv.*）；refreshment（*n.*）点心；饮料；精力恢复

【近】 stimulating，invigorating

religion [riˈlidʒən]

【释】 *n.* 宗教，宗派，信仰

【例】 Secular institutions，of control such as the police and army take the place of *religion* and family in maintaining order，and a money-based economy prevails.

【衍】 religionist（*n.*）；religious（*adj.*）

【近】 religious conviction，faith，belief

representation [ˌreprizen'teiʃən]

【释】 ① *n.* 表示，表现，描画，描述

【例】 Thus a symbolic *representation* of the human world was a cross within a circle, the cross representing the intersecting lines and the circle the shape of This World.

【衍】 representational（*adj.*）

【近】 symbol, depiction, illustration, description

【释】 ② *n.* 代理，代表

【例】 Nearly every major type of plant and animal has some *representations* there.

【衍】 represent（*v.*），representative（*n.* & *v.*）代表

【释】 ③ *n.* 上演，演出；扮演

【例】 Eventually such dramatic *representations* were separated from religious activities.

restore [ri'stɔː]

【释】 *v.* 恢复原状；恢复；修复

【例】 Slow-wave sleep may be especially helpful in *restoring* muscle control, whereas REM sleep may be more important for mental activity.

【衍】 restoration（*n.*）；restorative（*adj.*）有助复原的；restorable（*adj.*）可恢复的

【近】 recover, rehabilitate

ridge [ridʒ]

【释】 *n.* 脊；脊背；山脊；分水岭

【例】 New oceanic crust is formed along one or more margins of each plate by material issuing from deeper layers of the Earth's crust, for example, by volcanic eruptions of lava at mid-ocean *ridges*.

【衍】 ridgepole（*n.*）栋梁

【近】 rim, crest, edge

routine [ruː'tiːn]

【释】 *n.* 例行公事，日常工作；常规；惯例 *adj.* 日常的，常规的

【例】 In the countryside farmers therefore relieved the burden of the daily *routine* with such double purpose relaxations as hunting, fishing, and trapping.

【衍】 routinely (*adv*.); routinize (*v*.)

【近】 schedule, regular, habitual

saturated [ˈsætʃəreitid]

【释】 *adj*. 饱和的；浸透的，湿透的

【例】 When the air had become *saturated*, no additional amounts of phlogiston could leave the combustible substance, and the burning would stop.

【衍】 saturant (*adj*.) 使饱和的；(*n*.) 饱和剂；saturate (*v*.); saturation (*n*.); saturable (*adj*.); saturator (*n*.)

【近】 soaked, drenched, inundated

search [səːtʃ]

【释】 *v. & n*. 搜索；搜寻；探求，调查；检查

【例】 Many artists late in the last century were in *search* of a means to express their individuality.

【衍】 searching (*adj. & n*.) 仔细(的)；搜索的；彻底的；searchless (*adj*.) 无法探究的；searchlight (*n*.) 探照灯

【近】 look for, hunt, investigate

serene [siˈriːn]

【释】 *adj*. 宁静的；(性情)沉静的

【例】 They especially emphasized the need for natural *serene* settings where hurried urban dwellers could periodically escape from the city.

【衍】 serenely (*adv*.); sereneness (*n*.)

【近】 tranquil, calm, peaceful

shore [ʃɔː]

【释】 *n*. 岸；海岸；滨

【例】 Women also specialized in the gathering of the abundant shellfish that lived closer to *shore*.

【衍】 shorebird (*n*.); shoreline (*n*.) 海岸线；shoreside (*adj*.) 沿岸的，岸上的；shoreward (*adj. & adv*.) 面向岸(的)，面向陆地(的)；shorefront (*n*.) 沿岸陆地

【近】 beach, coast, seashore

sketch [sketʃ]

【释】 *v*. 草拟；勾画，描画，描述 *n*. 草图，素描；概略，大意

【例】 She visits each location several times to make *sketches* and test shots.

【衍】	sketchy（*adj.*）速写的；粗略的；贫乏的，肤浅的
【近】	draft，drawing，outline

soldier [ˈsəuldʒə]

【释】	*n.* 军人；(陆军)士兵；战士
【例】	Interest and demand were especially strong among returning *soldiers*, tired of foreign wars and foreign affairs, who wanted only to get back to the comfort and security of their own culture.
【衍】	soldierly（*adj.*）像军人的；勇敢的；soldiery（*n.*）军人，军队，军事训练；soldiership（*n.*）军人身份
【近】	warrior，combatant，fighter

spectacle [ˈspektəkl]

【释】	*n.* 光景，景象；状况；奇观，壮观
【例】	Scientists who tracked Kohoutek the ten months before it passed the Earth predicted the comet would be a brilliant *spectacle*.
【衍】	speck（*n.*）斑点；spectacular（*adj.*）场面富丽的，壮观的，惊人的；spectacularly（*adv.*）；spectator（*n.*）观众
【近】	sight，scene，vision

spur [spəː]

【释】	① *n.* 踢马刺，靴刺
【例】	But every item of dress had a useful purpose，from the broadbrimmed had that kept sun and rain off his head to the *spurs* fastened to the backs of his boots.
【近】	spike，spine，barb
【释】	② *v.* 刺激；推动，鞭策，鼓舞
【例】	They were *spurred* by the inflation of the 1970's，which combined with California's rapid population growth，pushed housing prices，as well as rents，to record levels.
【近】	urge，incite，impel

stature [ˈstætʃə]

【释】	① *n.* (特指人的)身长，身材
【例】	If there had been other choreographers with Graham's gifts and her *stature*，her work might have seemed a more balanced part of the story of American dance.

【近】 physique，figure，size

【释】 ② *n.* 发展、成长的状况或高度；才干

【例】 Violin's *stature* as an orchestral instrument was raised further when in 1626 Louis XIII of France established at his court the orchestra known as Les vingt-quatre violons du Roy（The King's 24 Violins）.

【近】 importance，prominence，rank

storage ['stɔːridʒ]

【释】 *n.* 贮藏(量)，存储(量)；(仓库)保管

【例】 The electric eel is an amazing *storage* battery.

【衍】 store（*v.*）；storehouse（*n.*）；storeroom（*n.*）；storing（*n.*）

【近】 storage space，cargo space，storeroom

stub [stʌb]

【释】 *n.* 剩余部分；残留部分

【例】 He went into shock，indicating that the *stub* in the chest had penetrated to his heart.

【近】 remains，stump，remnant

sufficient [sə'fiʃənt]

【释】 *adj.* 充分的，足够的（[*opp.*] inadequate）

【例】 Nesting material should be added in *sufficient* amounts to avoid both extreme temperature situations mentioned above and assure that the eggs have a soft，secure place to rest.

【衍】 sufficiently（*adv.*）；sufficiency（*n.*）充足，满足；自满，自负

【近】 enough，adequate，plenty

surplus ['səːpləs]

【释】 *n.* & *adj.* 剩余(的)；过剩(的)

【例】 Of course，many were never occupied；there was always a huge *surplus* of subdivided，but vacant，land around Chicago and other cities.

【衍】 surplusage（*n.*）剩余；过剩；冗词；废话；枝节问题

【近】 extra，excess，leftover

synchronous ['siŋkrənəs]

【释】 *adj.* 同时的，同期的；同步的

【例】 Most systems use *synchronous* satellites that stay in one position over the Earth.

【衍】	synchronously（*adv.*）；synchronize（*v.*）；synchroniza-tion（*n.*）；synchrotron（*n.*）【原子能】同步加速器
technical	[ˈteknikəl]
【释】	*adj.* 技术(性)的；专门(技术)的
【例】	Their reports，highly *technical* and sometimes poorly written，went unread.
【衍】	technically（*adv.*）；technician（*n.*）技师；专家；tech-nique（*n.*）专门技术；(艺术上的)技巧，技能；technolo-gy（*n.*）技术，工程，工艺；technological（*adj.*）
【近】	technological，scientific，methodological
territory	[ˈteritəri]
【释】	① *n.* 领土，版图，领地
【例】	The six states holding no claim to the region doubted whether a confederacy in which *territory* was so unevenly apportioned would truly prove what it claimed to be，a union of equals.
【衍】	territorial（*adj.*）
【近】	country，land
【释】	② *n.* (野鸟的)生活范围
【例】	Muskrats build their dome-shaped houses throughout the marshes，and their *territory* is now shared by the larger nutria.
【近】	area，field
【释】	③ *n.* (科学知识、行动等的)领域，范围
【例】	Martha Graham's *territory* of innumerable dances and self-sufficient dance technique is a vast but closed *territory*，since to create an art out of one's experience alone is ultimately a self-limiting act.
【近】	subject，field
thrust	[θrʌst]
【释】	*n.* 推挤；推力，侧向压力
【例】	In a very cold winter there may actually be two *thrusts* per freeze.
【衍】	thrusting（*adj.*）自作主张的；盛气凌人的；无情的
【近】	shove，push，drive
topic	[ˈtɔpik]
【释】	*n.* 论题，题目；话题；标题，细目

Unit 17

【例】 The marketing of wheat became an increasingly favorite *topic* of conversations.

【衍】 topical（*adj.*）论题的；有关时事的

【近】 theme，subject，issue

transformation [ˌtrænsfəˈmeiʃən]

【释】 *n.* 转变，变形；（尤指昆虫的）转化、变态；改造，改革

【例】 The real *transformation* of human life occurred when huge numbers of people began to rely primarily and permanently on the grain they grew and the animals they domesticated.

【衍】 transform（*v.*）；transformative（*adj.*）

【近】 alteration，conversion，change

triumph [ˈtraiəmf]

【释】 *v. & n.* 欢庆胜利，大成功，功绩（[*opp.*] failure）

【例】 Yet they did compete，and often they *triumphed* finally despite the odds.

【衍】 triumphal（*adj.*）；triumphalism（*n.*）必胜信念；triumphant（*adj.*）

【近】 victory，achievement，success

typical [ˈtipikəl]

【释】 *adj.* 代表的，典型的

【例】 Thus，the *typical* court case begins in a trial court—a court of general jurisdiction—in the state or federal system.

【衍】 typically（*adv.*）；typify（*v.*）成为…的典型；typifier（*n.*）典型代表者；typification（*n.*）典型化

【近】 characteristic，distinctive，representative

urban [ˈəːbən]

【释】 *adj.* 城市的（[*opp.*] rural）

【例】 The principle difference between *urban* growth in Europe and in the North American colonies was the slow evolution of cities in the former and then rapid growth to the latter.

【衍】 urbanite（*n.*）城市居民；urbanize（*v.*）使城市化；rbanization（*n.*）；urbanism（*n.*）城市生活的特点；城市化

【近】 municipal，metropolitan

vast	[vɑːst]
【释】	*adj.* 广大的，辽阔的；许许多多的
【例】	As Philadelphia grew from a small town into a city in the first half of the eighteenth century, it became an increasingly important marketing center for a *vast* and growing agricultural hinterland.
【衍】	vastly (*adv.*)
【近】	immense, enormous
violent	['vaiələnt]
【释】	*adj.* (风、爆炸等)猛烈的，狂暴的
【例】	It was not a sudden and *violent* overturning of the political and social framework, such as later occurred in France and Russia, when both were already independent nations.
【衍】	violently (*adv.*)；violence (*n.*)
【近】	fierce, furious, ferocious
warfare	['wɔːfɛə]
【释】	*n.* 战争，战争状态(行为)
【例】	These tribes probably influenced by Meso-American cultures through trade and *warfare*.
【近】	conflict, rivalry, war, fight
willow	['wiləu]
【释】	*n.* 柳
【例】	The warp was always made of *willow*, and the most commonly used weft was sedge root, a woody fiber that could easily be separated into strands no thicker than a thread.
zone	[zəun]
【释】	*n.* (地)带
【例】	Solar astronomers do know that the Sun is divided into five layers or *zones*.
【衍】	zonal (*adj.*) 区域(地区)性的；zonation (*n.*) 成带(现象)
【近】	region, district, sector

Unit 17

Exercise of Unit 17

左列单词在右列中有一个同义词，请找出并在相应的位置写上正确答案。

Exercise 1:
(A) finish _____ blockage
(B) serene _____ fall
(C) quadrilateral _____ vanish
(D) violent _____ tranquil
(E) congestion _____ rectangle
(F) decline _____ fierce

Exercise 2:
(A) cartoon _____ importance
(B) restore _____ recover
(C) disturb _____ conflict
(D) stature _____ draft
(E) warfare _____ agitate
(F) sketch _____ animation

Exercise 3:
(A) thrust _____ victory
(B) triumph _____ house
(C) dull _____ decay
(D) corrosion _____ poll
(E) accommodate ___ shove
(F) census _____ dreary

Exercise 4:
(A) artifact _____ fiend
(B) stature _____ sight
(C) monster _____ physique
(D) ridge _____ synthetics
(E) spectacle _____ rim
(F) compose _____ create

Exercise 5:
(A) fair _____ stature
(B) glaze _____ pinnacle
(C) peak _____ tour
(D) height _____ varnish
(E) circuit _____ comprise
(F) compose _____ exposition

Exercise 6:
(A) surplus _____ chin
(B) ingredient _____ concern
(C) territory _____ element
(D) jaw _____ extra
(E) anxiety _____ area
(F) lace _____ line

Exercise 7:
(A) territory _____ clasp
(B) erode _____ characteristic
(C) hook _____ subject
(D) routine _____ corrode
(E) optical _____ visual
(F) typical _____ schedule

Exercise 8:
(A) miniature _____ small
(B) circuit _____ incessant
(C) continuous _____ devote
(D) random _____ casual
(E) recede _____ route
(F) engage _____ retreat

Exercise 9:
(A) shore _____ change
(B) spur _____ symbol
(C) representation __ cruel
(D) merciless _____ municipal
(E) urban _____ beach
(F) alter _____ urge

Exercise 10:
(A) fluid _____ spike
(B) marrow _____ unaware
(C) territory _____ liquid
(D) vast _____ essence
(E) ignorant _____ immense
(F) spur _____ country

ANSWERS:
1	E F A B C D
2	D B E F C A
3	B E D F A C
4	C E B A D F
5	D C E B F A
6	D E B A C F
7	C F A B E D
8	A C F D B E
9	F C D E A B
10	F E A B D C

accompany	engrave	narration	shortage
adobe	erupt	nomadic	skull
alternate	exotic	obsess	sole
ape	fairly	optimal	spectrum
artisan	fir	oven	squarely
automated	focus	parrot	status
barn	frigid	pendulum	storm
beneficial	generate	phase	studio
boom	glimpse	plantation	sugar
bronze	handcrafted	popularity	survey
camouflage	helium	preach	synonymous
carve	horizon	previous	tectonics
ceramics	ignore	profound	testify
circular	improvise	protest	thumb
collaboration	inhabit	qualify	topography
comprehensive	institution	rank	transit
Congress	intricate	receiver	trivial
continuum	jelly	refrigerate	tyrannical
cosmic	lamp	rely	urge
cue	lengthen	reproduce	vault
decompose	load	restrict	virtually
deserve	magical	rifle	warp
disaster	marvelous	row	windswept
ditch	mercury	save	
dumb	ministry	season	
eliminate	monument	seriously	

accompany [əˈkʌmpəni]
【释】 *v.* 陪伴；伴奏
【例】 *Accompanying* that growth was a gradual shift in the nation's labor force from agriculture to manufacturing and other nonagricultural pursuits.
【衍】 accompanying （*adj.*）; accompanied （*adj.*）; accompaniment （*n.*）
【近】 complement，supplement

adobe [əˈdəubi]
【释】 *n.* 砖坯
【例】 The Anasazi lived in houses constructed of *adobe* and wood.
【衍】 adobelike （*adj.*）

alternate [ɔːlˈtəːnit]
【释】 *adj.* 交替的，隔一的，间隔的
【例】 ... *alternate* between joy and grief.
【衍】 alternating（*adj.*）交互的; alternative（*adj.* & *n.*）随便一个（的），二中择一（的）；交替（的）; alternatively （*adv.*）交替地

ape [eip]
【释】 *n.* 猿
【例】 There are five kinds of *apes* in the world today.
【近】 chimp, chimpanzee, monkey, gorilla, orangutan, primate

artisan [ˈɑːtizən]
【释】 *n.* 工匠，手工业工人
【例】 Prehistoric *artisans* created each of their pieces individually, using the simplest technology.

automated [ˈɔːtəmeitid]
【释】 *adj.* 自动化的
【例】 As early as 1782, Oliver Evans had built a highly *automated*, laborsaving flour mill driven by water power.
【衍】 automate （*v.*）; automatic （*adj.*）; automation （*n.*）自动操作
【近】 automatic, robotic, programmed, mechanized

barn [bɑːn]
【释】 *n.* 仓，谷仓，库房

【例】 The dry summer air cured them，much as storing in a *barn* cured the cultivated grasses.

beneficial [ˌbeniˈfiʃəl]

【释】 *adj.* 有利的，有益的(to)([*opp.*] injurious)

【例】 They also enter into a number of mutually *beneficial* relationships with plant and other organisms.

【衍】 benefit (*n.* & *v.*)

【近】 helpful，useful，valuable，favorable

boom [buːm]

【释】 *n.* (城市等的)急速发展；(物价等的)暴涨；(人口等的)激增

【例】 Therefore，in the 1950's and 1960's，the baby *boom* hit an antiquated and inadequate school system.

【衍】 booming (*adj.*)；boomer (*n.*) 赶往新兴地区安家的人

【近】 prosper，prosperous，flourishing

bronze [brɒnz]

【释】 *n.* 青铜，古铜

【例】 They had invented *bronze*，an alloy that could be cast in molds，out of which they made tools and weapons.

【衍】 bronzed (*adj.*)

camouflage [ˈkæmuflɑːʒ]

【释】 *v.* & *n.* 伪装

【例】 If such traits help to *camouflage* a plant，for example，the plant is likely to have a survival advantage over other plants that are less well *camouflaged*.

【近】 disguise，pretend

carve [kɑːv]

【释】 *v.* 雕刻，刻

【例】 Some skilled craftspeople made intricately *carved* wooden ornamentations for furniture or architectural decorations，while others *carved* wooden shop signs and ships' figureheads.

【衍】 carver (*n.*)

【近】 cut，engrave，scratch，incise

ceramics [siˈræmiks]

【释】 *n.* 陶瓷学；陶瓷工艺，制陶术

【例】	The result was yellow ware, used largely for serviceable items; but a further development was Rockingham ware— one of the most important American *ceramics* of the nineteenth century.
【衍】	ceramist (*n.*)

circular ['səːkjulə]

【释】	*adj.* 圆的，圆(环)形的
【例】	Besides living quarters, each pueblo included one or more kivas—*circular* underground chambers faced with stone.
【衍】	circulation (*n.*) 循环；运行；circumference (*n.*) 圆周
【近】	round, spherical

collaboration [kəˌlæbəˈreiʃən]

【释】	*n.* 合作
【例】	It was to discover a fungicide without that double effect that Brown and Hazen began their long-distance *collaboration*.
【衍】	collaborate (*v.*); collaborator (*n.*); collaborative (*adj.*); collaboratively (*adv.*)
【近】	cooperation

comprehensive [ˌkɔmpriˈhensiv]

【释】	*adj.* 广泛的，全面的，完整的
【例】	Vascular plants, related to modern seed plants and ferns, left the first *comprehensive* mega fossil record.
【衍】	comprehensively (*adj.*)
【近】	complete, full

Congress ['kɔŋgres]

【释】	*n.* (美国)国会
【例】	Following the Revolution, members of *Congress* had hotly debated the question of a permanent home for themselves and for those departments.
【衍】	congressional (*adj.*); congressman (*n.*)

continuum [kənˈtinjuəm]

【释】	*n.* ([*pl.*]-ua) 【哲】连续(统一体)
【例】	The development of jazz can be seen as part of the larger *continuum* of American popular music, especially dance music.

Unit 18

— 389 —

cosmic [ˈkɔzmik]

【释】 *adj*. 宇宙的

【例】 The extinction of the dinosaurs was caused by some physical events, either climatic or *cosmic*.

【衍】 cosmically（*adv*.）; cosmos（*n*.）

【近】 space, celestial, extraterrestrial

cue [kjuː]

【释】 *n*. 暗示，指示，线索

【例】 Adults make it as easy as they can for babies to pick up a language by exaggerating such *cues*.

【近】 clue, prompt, sign, signal, indication

decompose [ˌdiːkəmˈpəuz]

【释】 *v*. (使)分解，分析；(使)腐烂；衰变

【例】 The earth's surface is basically rock, and it is this rock that gradually *decomposes* into clay.

【衍】 decomposition（*n*.）; decomposable（*adj*.）可分解的; decomposer（*n*.）分解体

【近】 decay, rot

deserve [diˈzəːv]

【释】 *v*. 应受，该得，值得

【例】 Three decades later, people still argue about who *deserves* the credit for the concept of the laser.

【衍】 deserved（*adj*.）该奖（罚）的；理所当然的; deservedly（*adv*.）; deservedness（*adj*.）

【近】 merit

disaster [diˈzɑːstə]

【释】 *n*. 天灾，灾害；不幸，事故

【例】 A second attempt ended in *disaster* in 1583, when Gilbert and his ship were lost in a storm.

【衍】 disastrous（*adj*.）; disastrously（*adv*.）

【近】 adversity, catastrophe, calamity, tragedy

ditch [ditʃ]

【释】 *n*. 水沟，渠

【例】 The Hopi and Zuni brought water from streams to their fields and garden through irrigation *ditches*.

【近】 channel, trench, drain, waterway

dumb	[dʌm]
【释】	*adj*. 哑的，不能说话的
【例】	Bees are often considered by their trainers to be very *dumb* beasts.
eliminate	[i'limineit]
【释】	*v*. 除去，消灭；逐出，淘汰；排出（from）
【例】	The research team has concentrated on *eliminating* low-frequency noise from ship engines.
【衍】	elimination（*n*.）
【近】	eradicate，abolish，remove，get rid of
engrave	[in'greiv]
【释】	*v*. 雕，刻
【例】	The experience was *engraved* into his memory.
【近】	carve，incise，scratch，etch
erupt	[i'rʌpt]
【释】	*v*. (火山等)迸发，喷出，爆发
【例】	As the air shot through the furnace，the bubbling metal would *erupt* in showers of sparks.
【衍】	eruption（*n*.）
【近】	emit，eject，spew，discharge，gush，issue，well
exotic	[ig'zɔtik]
【释】	*adj*.异国情调的；异乎寻常的；[口] 奇异的；吸引人的
【例】	It gave up lightness，it gave up a wealth of *exotic* color，it gave up a certain kind of theatrical wit and that age-old mobile exchange between a dancer and the dancer's rhythmical and musical material.
【衍】	exotica（*n*.）舶来品；珍品；奇风异俗；exotically（*adv*.）
【近】	foreign，alien
fairly	['fɛəli]
【释】	*adv*. 适当地，相当地
【例】	The proportion for the entire district could be estimated *fairly* accurately from a sample of as few as 100 children.
【近】	quite，rather，somehow

Unit 18

fir [fəː]

【释】 *n.* 冷杉木，枞木

【例】 Roof beams of pine or *fir* had to be carried from logging areas in the mountain forests many kilometers away.

focus ['fəukəs]

【释】 *n.* ([*pl.*] focuses, foci)焦点 *v.* 集中注意力于

【例】 By centering politics on the person of the candidate, television accelerated the citizen's *focus* on character rather than issues.

【近】 center, heart, hub

frigid ['fridʒid]

【释】 *adj.* 寒冷的

【例】 The *frigid* ground in the far north acts as a remarkable preservation for animal fossils.

【衍】 frigidness (*n.*)；frigidity (*n.*)

【近】 cold, frosty, chilly, freezing, icy

generate ['dʒenəreit]

【释】 *v.* 生殖，生育；产生，发生

【例】 If fully occupied, the two World Trade Center towers in New York City would *generate* 2.25 million gallons of raw sewage each year.

【衍】 generation (*n.*)；generator (*n.*) 发电机；generational (*adj.*)

【近】 make, produce, create, engender

glimpse [glimps]

【释】 *n.* 一瞥，瞥见

【例】 So many spectators flocked to the farm to catch a *glimpse* of Mrs. Stowe.

【近】 glance, peek, sight, peep

handcrafted ['hændkrɑːftid]

【释】 *adj.* 手工的，手工艺的

【例】 People who lived in the cities and were not directly involved in trade often participated in small cottage industries making *handcrafted* goods.

【衍】 handcraft (*n.* & *v.*)

【近】 handmade

helium ['hiːliəm]

【释】 *n.* 氦

【例】 The elements other than hydrogen and *helium* exist in such small quantities that it is accurate to say that the universe is somewhat more than 25 percent *helium* by weight and somewhat less than 75 percent hydrogen.

horizon [hə'raizən]

【释】 *n.* 地平(线)；眼界，视界；范围

【例】 They also shaped people's spiritual *horizons*.

【衍】 horizontal (*adj.*)

ignore [ig'nɔː]

【释】 *v.* 忽视，不理，不顾；抹煞(建议)

【例】 Hispanic arts to a great degree have been *ignored* by the speculative Anglo art market.

【近】 disregard, neglect, overlook

improvise ['imprəvaiz]

【释】 *v.* 即席创作，即席演奏

【例】 In early jazz, musicians often *improvised* melodies collectively, thus creating a kind of polyphony.

【衍】 improvised (*adj.*); improvisation (*n.*)

inhabit [in'hæbit]

【释】 *v.* 居住；栖息

【例】 The fact that half of the known species are thought to *inhabit* the world's rain forests does not seem surprising, considering the huge numbers of insects that comprise the bulk of the species.

【衍】 inhabitant (*n.*); inhabitation (*n.*)

【近】 occupy, dwell

institution [ˌinsti'tjuːʃən]

【释】 *n.* 惯例，制度，规定

【例】 The environmental problems of the chemical age stretch beyond the authority of existing political and social *institutions*.

【衍】 institutional (*adj.*) 惯例的，规定的，制度上的

intricate ['intrikit]

【释】 *adj.* 精致的；复杂的

【例】 Notwithstanding preening and constant care，the marvelously *intricate* structure of a bird's feather inevitably wears out.

【衍】 intricately（*adv.*）；intricateness（*n.*）

【近】 elaborated，complicated，complex，involved

jelly [ˈdʒeli]

【释】 *n.* （透明）冻（胶），胶状物，果冻，肉冻

【例】 Corals and *jelly* fish are coelenterates.

lamp [læmp]

【释】 *n.* 灯

【例】 Electric power was available for *lamps*，sewing machines，irons，and even vacuum cleaners.

【衍】 lamplight（*n.*）灯火，灯光

【近】 light，lantern

lengthen [ˈleŋθən]

【释】 *v.* 延长，伸长，拉长

【例】 By 1920 schooling to age fourteen or beyond was compulsory in most states，and the school year was greatly *lengthened*.

【衍】 length（*n.*）；lengthy（*adj.*）过长的，漫长的，冗长的

【近】 extend，elongate，stretch

load [ləud]

【释】 *n.* 装载；担子；负担；工作(负荷)量

【例】 The carrying capacity of the eagles，however，is only relative to their size and most birds are able to carry an extra *load* of just over twenty percent of their body weight.

【衍】 loaded（*adj.*）载重的，有负荷的；loading（*n.*）装货；loader（*n.*）装货的人；载货设备

【近】 weight，freight，consignment

magical [ˈmædʒikəl]

【释】 *adj.* 不可思议的

【例】 For both artisan and consumer，the Arts and Crafts doctrine was seen as a *magical* force against the undesirable effects of industrialization.

【衍】 magician（*n.*）魔术师，变戏法的人；magically（*adv.*）

【近】 supernatural，magic，mysterious

marvelous ['mɑːvələs]

【释】 *adj.* 奇异的，不可思议的，奇怪的

【例】 They made excellent pottery and wove *marvelous* baskets，some so fine that they could hold water.

【衍】 marvel（*n.*）奇迹；marvelously（*adv.*）；marvelousness（*n.*）

【近】 wonderful，amazing，stunning

mercury ['məːkjuri]

【释】 *n.* 汞，水银；（M-）水星

【例】 *Mercury* based streetlights，the most common type in cities in the United States，are especially disturbing to stargazers.

ministry ['ministri]

【释】 *n.* 牧师；部长的任务(职务、任期)；政府部门

【例】 As colleges ceased to cater more narrowly to candidates for the religious *ministry* and came to be seen as a logical continuation of secondary school，younger students began to predominate.

【衍】 minister（*n.*）牧师；部长；阁员，大臣

【近】 office，bureau，department

monument ['mɔnjumənt]

【释】 *n.* 纪念碑，纪念物，不朽的功业(著作)等

【例】 In Memphis，sculptor Richard Hunt has created a *monument* to Martin Luther King，Jr.，who was slain there.

【衍】 monumental（*adj.*）；monumentalize（*v.*）立碑纪念，树碑立传

【近】 memorial，tombstone

narration [nə'reiʃən]

【释】 *n.* 叙述；故事

【例】 Her unique art of storytelling employs iconographic elements to create a concentrated *narration*.

【衍】 narrative（*adj.*）；narrator（*n.*）

【近】 recitation，telling，recounting

nomadic [nəu'mædik]

【释】 *adj.* 游牧的；流浪的

【例】 The shared needs and pressures that encourage extended family ties are less prominent in settled than in *nomadic* societies.

Unit 18

【衍】	nomad（*n.*）；nomadically（*adv.*）；nomadism（*n.*）
【近】	itinerant，traveling

obsess ［əb'ses］

【释】	*v.* 缠住，迷住；使着迷；使烦扰
【例】	The self-educated son of a Delaware farmer，Evans early became *obsessed* by the possibilities of mechanized production and steam power.
【衍】	obsession（*n.*）摆脱不了的迷念
【近】	preoccupy，consume，grip

optimal ［'ɔptiməl］

【释】	*adj.* 最适宜的；最理想的；最好的（［*opp.*］pessimal）
【例】	But far from being random，molt is controlled by strong evolutionary forces that have established an *optimal* time and duration.
【衍】	optimization（*n.*）最佳化，最优化；optimum（*adj.*）最适宜的
【近】	best，most favorable，most advantageous

oven ［'ʌvən］

【释】	*n.* 灶，炉；炭窑；干燥炉；烘箱
【例】	Sometimes the door of the *oven* faced the room，but most ovens were built with the opening facing into the fireplace.
【衍】	ovenproof（*adj.*）耐热的
【近】	stove，stove-top，range

parrot ［'pærət］

【释】	*n.* 鹦鹉；学舌者
【例】	When *parrots* incubate their eggs in the wild，the temperature and humidity of the nest are controlled naturally.
【近】	mimic，imitator

pendulum ［'pendjuləm］

【释】	*n.* （钟等的）摆；动摇的人（物）；犹豫不决的人
【例】	They move by brachiation，by swinging like *pendulums* from branch to branch.

phase ［feiz］

【释】	*n.* 形势，局面，状态；阶段

【例】	In other words, unlike comparison between temperate and tropical areas, these patterns are still in the documentation *phase*.
【衍】	phased (*adj.*)
【近】	stage, chapter, point, part
plantation	[plæn'teiʃən]
【释】	*n.* 农场，种植园
【例】	In fact, one of the strongest factors in the selection of *plantation* land was the desire to have it front on a water highwave.
【衍】	planter
【近】	farm
popularity	[ˌpɔpju'lærəti]
【释】	*n.* 名气，名望；通俗性；大众性；流行；普及
【例】	The key to its *popularity* is its incredible versatility.
【衍】	popularize (*v.*); popular (*adj.*)
【近】	fame, status, reputation
preach	[priːtʃ]
【释】	*v.* 讲道，布道；宣扬，鼓吹
【例】	During her New York days, Mabel Dodge had *preached* the gospel of Gertrude Stein and spread the fame of her new style.
【衍】	preacher (*n.*)
【近】	speak, talk, urge, advocate
previous	['priːviəs]
【释】	*adj.* 先，前；以前的
【例】	Those birds that did not feed well on the *previous* day appear to follow those that did.
【衍】	previously (*adv.*)
【近】	earlier, prior, before
profound	[prə'faund]
【释】	*adj.* 深远的，意味深长的
【例】	The transition to settled life also had a *profound* impact on the family.
【衍】	profoundly (*adv.*)
【近】	deep, thoughtful, reflective, insightful

Unit 18

protest [prə'test]

【释】 *n.* 声明，断言，抗议

【例】 Examples range from the incidents leading up to the Revolution through the many social *protests* of the 1960's.

【衍】 protestant（*n.*）新教；新教徒

【近】 complain，objection，dissent

qualify ['kwɔlifai]

【释】 *v.* 使具有资格；准予；使适宜

【例】 A five-pointed star，for example，does not *qualify* as a convex polygon.

【衍】 qualified（*adj.*）；qualification（*n.*）

rank [ræŋk]

【释】 ① *v.* 把…分类，分等级

【例】 As early as 120 B.C.，astronomers *ranked* the stars according to six categories of luminosity.

【近】 categorize，grade，position

【释】 ② *v.* 并列；位于

【例】 From the earliest colonial times throughout the nineteenth century，disease *ranked* as the foremost problem in defense.

【近】 be placed

【释】 ③ *n.* 等级，地位

【例】 He must be treated as a hostage of high *rank*，not as a common prisoner.

【近】 status，class

receiver [ri'siːvə]

【释】 *n.* 接收器；接受者

【例】 It contains a wireless transmitter that works up to the length of a football field from the flying-saucer shaped *receiver*.

【衍】 receive（*v.*）

【近】 recipient

refrigerate [ri'fridʒəreit]

【释】 *v.* 冷藏，冷冻

【例】 After the Civil War（1861—1865），as ice was used to *refrigerate* freight cars，it also came into household use.

【衍】 refrigeration（n.）；refrigerator（n.）冰箱
【近】 store at a low temperature，chill

rely ［ri'lai］

【释】 v. 倚赖，依靠；信任，信赖
【例】 Not long after the last Ice Age，around 7,000 B. C.，some hunters and gatherers began to *rely* chiefly on agriculture for their sustenance.
【衍】 relier（n.）

reproduce ［ˌriːprə'djuːs］

【释】 ① v. 生殖，繁殖
【例】 An individual worker bee cannot *reproduce* itself.
【衍】 reproduction（n.）；reproductive（adj.）；reproducible（adj.）
【近】 produce，breed，rear
【释】 ② v. 再演；再版；转载；翻印
【例】 She was also the most successful within her lifetime and her work was *reproduced* on greeting cards and calendars and in prints.
【衍】 reproduction（n.）；reproductive（adj.）；reproducible（adj.）
【释】 ③ v. 复制；再生产；再现
【例】 Every detail of these is accurately *reproduced* in color and structure.
【衍】 reproduction（n.）；reproductive（adj.）；reproducible（adj.）
【近】 replicate，duplicate，make a replica

restrict ［ri'strikt］

【释】 v. 限制，限定
【例】 The study of fossil footprints is not *restricted* to examples from such remote periods.
【衍】 restricted（adj.）；restriction（n.）；restrictionism（n.）限制主义；restrictive（adj.）
【近】 limit，confine，put a ceiling on

rifle ［'raifl］

【释】 n. 步枪；来福枪

Unit 18

【例】 Edwin gave the girls footballs and *rifles*, while Amy shocked the community by dressing them in gym suits instead of skirts.

【衍】 rifleman（*n.*）步枪射手

row [rau]

【释】 ① *n.* （一）排，（一）行；一排（座位）

【例】 When you ask them to work out a sum they take a piece of paper, cover it with *rows* of A's, B's, and X's and Y's, scatter a mess of flyspecks over them, and give you an answer that's all wrong.

【近】 line, string, rank

【释】 ② *n.* （两旁或一旁有房屋的）路

【例】 That lot was a rectangular area 25 feet wide by 100 feet deep—a shape perfectly suited for a *row* house.

save [seiv]

【释】 *prep.* 除…以外，除了

【例】 She had no formal education in mathematics *save* a single course required for graduation from high school in 1939.

【近】 but, except, apart from

season ['siːzən]

【释】 *v.* 风干；晒干（木材）；晾干

【例】 Ensure that new wood has been *seasoned*.

【近】 weather

seriously ['siəriəsli]

【释】 *adv.* 严肃地；认真地；严重地

【例】 Without regular supplies of some hormones our capacity to behave would be *seriously* impaired: without others we would soon die.

【衍】 serious（*adj.*）; seriousness（*n.*）

【近】 gravely, badly, sincerely

shortage ['ʃɔːtidʒ]

【释】 *n.* 不足，缺少；不足额；缺点，缺陷

【例】 In 1943 the federal government imposed rent controls to help solve the problem of housing *shortages* during wartime.

【衍】 short （ *adj.* ）； shortly （ *adv.* ）； shortness （ *n.* ）； shorten （ *v.* ）； shortcut（ *n.* ）近路，捷径

【近】 lack，scarcity，deficiency

skull ［skʌl］

【释】 *n.* 颅骨，头骨，脑壳，头盖骨

【例】 Scientists think that physical differences between the right and left sides of the interior of the *skull* indicate subtle physical differences between the two sides of the brain.

【衍】 skulled （ *adj.* ）有脑壳的

【近】 head，cranium

sole ［səul］

【释】 ① *adj.* 单独的，单一的，唯一的

【例】 Pheromones are the predominant medium of communication among insects（but rarely the *sole* method）.

【衍】 solely （ *adv.* ）；soleness （ *n.* ）；solemn （ *adj.* ）严肃的，庄严的

【近】 single，singular，solitary

【释】 ② *n.* 鞋底；脚底，袜底

【例】 Tens of thousands of rural women fabricated the "uppers" of shoes，which were bound to the *soles* by wage-earning-journeymen shoemakers in dozens of Massachusetts towns.

spectrum ［'spektrəm］

【释】 *n.* 光谱；波谱；范围，幅度

【例】 Whether a particular color is obtained by adding colored lights together or by subtracting some light from the total *spectrum* , the result looks the same to the eye.

【衍】 spectral （ *adj.* ）光谱的

【近】 range，scale，continuum

squarely ［'skwɛəli］

【释】 *adv.* 规规矩矩地；公正地；断然地（ *opp.* ］ indirectly）

【例】 From the influence of the father came modern inferential statistics，which is based *squarely* on theories of probability.

【衍】 square （ *adj. & n.* ）

【近】 exactly，directly，straight

status	['stætəs]
【释】	**n. 情形，状况，状态；地位；资格**
【例】	By the outbreak of tile Revolution against British rule in 1776，the *status* of the artist had already undergone change.
【近】	rank，position，standing
storm	[stɔːm]
【释】	**n. 风暴，风潮，骚动，动乱**
【例】	The homing pigeon is very intelligent and will persevere to the point of stubbornness；some have been known to fly a hundred miles off course to avoid a *storm*.
【衍】	stormy（*adj.*）
【近】	tempest，hurricane，explosion
studio	['stjuːdiəu]
【释】	**n. 工作室**
【例】	She aided artists in numerous other ways—sending them abroad to study，paying their hospital bills and *studio* rents，and most important，purchasing their works.
sugar	['ʃugə]
【释】	**n. 糖；【化】糖（即碳水化合物）**
【例】	In photosynthesis，energy from sunlight converts carbon dioxide and water to *sugar*.
【衍】	sugarcane（*n.*）甘蔗；sugarlike（*adj.*）似糖的
【近】	sweetie，honey
survey	[sə'vei]
【释】	**v. & n. 检查，调查；测量（土地），勘查；俯视；概论**
【例】	A *survey* is a study，generally in the form of an interview or a questionnaire，that provides information concerning how people think and act.
【衍】	surveying（*n.*）；surveyor（*n.*）
【近】	review，investigation，study
synonymous	[si'nɔniməs]
【释】	**adj. 同义词性质的；同义的（[*opp.*] antonym）**
【例】	Martha Graham and the school she has founded are virtually *synonymous* with the modern dance.
【衍】	synonymously（*adv.*）

【近】 identical，the same

tectonics [tek'tɔniks]

【释】 *n.* 筑造学，构造学

【例】 With a understanding of plate *tectonics*，geologists have put together a new history for the Earth's surface.

【衍】 tectonic（*adj.*）构造的；建筑的

testify ['testifai]

【释】 *v.* 证明；证实

【例】 Their products，primarily silver plates and bowls，reflected their exalted status and *testified* to their customers' prominence.

【衍】 testification（*n.*）；testifier（*n.*）

【近】 give evidence，confirm，bear witness

thumb [θʌm]

【释】 *n.* 拇指

【例】 On each front foot the two innermost digits can be opposed to the others like two *thumbs*，as can the innermost digits on each rear foot.

【衍】 thumbnail（*n.*）拇指甲；thumbprint（*n.*）拇指印纹；个性特征；thumbtack（*n.*）图钉

topography [tə'pɔgrəfi]

【释】 *n.* 地形，地势；地形(测量)学

【例】 He and his brothers believed that parks should be adapted to the local *topography*，utilize the area's trees and shrubs，and be available to the entire community.

【衍】 topographical（*adj.*）；topographically（*adv.*）

【近】 geography，scenery，landscape

transit ['trænsit]

【释】 *n.* 运输；通路；转变，变迁

【例】 The downtown business district did not grow apace with the city as a whole，and the rapid *transit* system designed to link the center with outlying areas withered away from disuse.

【衍】 transition（*n.*）转变，演变，变迁；transitional（*adj.*）；transitive（*adj.*）传递的；及物的；过渡的

【近】 transportation，transfer，shipment

Unit 18

trivial	['triviəl]
【释】	*adj.* 琐细的，轻微的；平常的，平凡的（[*opp.*] **crucial**）
【例】	It is far less complicated than the Earth, one of its most *trivial* members.
【衍】	trivially（*adv.*）；trivialism（*n.*）；triviality（*n.*）；trivialness（*n.*）
【近】	insignificant, unimportant, trifling

tyrannical	[ti'rænikəl]
【释】	*adj.* 残暴的
【例】	She urged her husband, the second President of the United States, to "remember the ladies" in the new code of laws, and to give married women protection from *tyrannical* husbands.
【衍】	tyrannic（*adj.*）；tyranny（*n.*）暴政，残暴；tyrannize（*v.*）施行暴政，压制
【近】	oppressive, dictatorial, cruel

urge	[ə:dʒ]
【释】	① *v.* 极力主张；强烈要求
【例】	Dr. King *urged* Blacks to use nonviolent sit-ins, marches, demonstrations, and freedom rides in their efforts to gain full freedom and equality.
【近】	exhort, ask
【释】	② *n.* 刺激；冲动；迫切要求
【例】	In time the increasing complexity of Neolithic societies led to the development of writing, prompted by the need to keep records and later by the *urge* to chronicle experiences, learning, and beliefs.
【近】	desire, longing, craving, yearning

vault	[vɔ:lt]
【释】	*n.* 拱顶，穹窿
【例】	Previously the poor quality of the iron had restricted its use in architecture to items such as chains and tie bars for supporting arches, *vaults*, and walls.
【近】	arc, arch, arcade, curve

virtually	['və:tjuəli]
【释】	*adv.* 实际上，实质上，事实上

【例】	Young ravens, for example, first attempt to build with sticks of quite unsuitable size, while a jackdaw's first nest includes *virtually* any movable object.
【衍】	virtual (*adj.*)
【近】	actually, practically, in effect

warp	[wɔːp]
【释】	*v. & n.* (使)卷曲，翘曲，弯曲
【例】	It should have prevented rain water *warping* the door trim.
【衍】	warpage (*n.*)
【近】	distort, deform, bend, twist

windswept	['windswept]
【释】	*adj.* 暴露在风中的
【例】	The steel pipe crosses *windswept* plains and endless miles of delicate tundra that tops the frozen ground.
【近】	bare, exposed

Exercise of Unit 18

左列单词在右列中有一个同义词，请找出并在相应的位置写上正确答案。

Exercise 1:

(A) circular _____ identical
(B) collaboration ____ cooperation
(C) season _____ round
(D) reproduce _____ stage
(E) synonymous _____ weather
(F) phase _____ produce

Exercise 2:

(A) testify _____ head
(B) skull _____ clue
(C) disaster _____ give evidence
(D) popularity _____ complete
(E) comprehensive___ fame
(F) cue _____ adversity

Exercise 3:

(A) decompose _____ sweetie
(B) engrave _____ rank
(C) sugar _____ carve
(D) ditch _____ eradicate
(E) eliminate _____ channel
(F) status _____ decay

Exercise 4:

(A) optimal _____ emit
(B) parrot _____ replicate
(C) erupt _____ mimic
(D) intricate _____ elaborated
(E) load _____ best
(F) reproduce _____ weight

Exercise 5:

(A) camouflage _____ exactly
(B) handcrafted ____ foreign
(C) profound _____ deep
(D) exotic _____ exhort
(E) urge _____ disguise
(F) squarely _____ handmade

Exercise 6:

(A) save _____ status
(B) shortage _____ limit
(C) magical _____ lack
(D) marvelous _____ supernatural
(E) rank _____ wonderful
(F) restrict _____ but

Exercise 7:

(A) warp _____ extend
(B) plantation _____ farm
(C) storm _____ actually
(D) carve _____ tempest
(E) lengthen _____ cut
(F) virtually _____ distort

Exercise 8:

(A) narration _____ complain
(B) fairly _____ disregard
(C) protest _____ quite
(D) obsess _____ make
(E) generate _____ recitation
(F) ignore _____ preoccupy

Exercise 9:

(A) trivial _____ chimp
(B) frigid _____ light
(C) deserve _____ insignificant
(D) receiver _____ cold
(E) ape _____ merit
(F) lamp _____ recipient

Exercise 10:

(A) sole _____ single
(B) glimpse _____ arc
(C) focus _____ prosper
(D) vault _____ space
(E) boom _____ glance
(F) cosmic _____ center

ANSWERS:

1	E B A F C D
2	B F A E D C
3	C F B E D A
4	C F B D A E
5	F D C E A B
6	E F B C D A
7	E B F C D A
8	C F B E A D
9	E F A B C D
10	A D E F B C

Unit 19

accomplish	enhance	narrow	shovel
adolescent	escape	nonetheless	skyrocket
altitude	expertise	obstacle	solidify
apprentice	faith	oral	speculation
ascend	fist	overall	squash
autonomy	fog	partially	steady
barrel	frontier	penetrate	stout
besiege	generous	phenomenon	stylized
boost	global	plasma	suit
bubble	handedness	populous	survival
camp	hemisphere	precarious	synthesis
cast	hormone	prey	tedious
ceremony	illuminate	progress	textile
circumstance	impulse	prototype	thunder
collective	inherent	quantity	tornado
compress	instruct	rare	translation
conjunction	intriguing	recent	trolley
contribute	jewel	refurbish	ultimate
costume	landmark	remainder	usher
culminate	lens	reptile	vegetation
decorate	locality	resume	virtue
designate	magma	rift	warrant
discard	mason	rub	wipe
dive	mere	scar	
dwarf	mint	seasonal	
elliptic(al)	mood	session	

accomplish [əˈkɔmpliʃ]
【释】 *v.* 成就，完成；贯彻(计划等)；达到(目的)；实行
【例】 Equally important is the fact that the execution of multiple-step tasks is *accomplished* in a series-parallel sequence.
【衍】 accomplished (*adj.*)；accomplishment (*n.*)
【近】 achieve，brought about，carry out，realize

adolescent [ˌædəuˈlesənt]
【释】 *adj.* 青年期的，青春期的   *n.* 少年
【例】 Those especially vulnerable to calcium deficiency are women: *adolescent* girls and middle-aged women.
【衍】 adolescence (*n.*) 青年期，青春期，青春
【近】 juvenile，pubertal

altitude [ˈæltitjuːd]
【释】 *n.* 高，高度；海拔(高度)
【例】 Synchronous satellites are launched to an *altitude* of 22,300 miles.
【近】 height，elevation

apprentice [əˈprentis]
【释】 *n.* 学徒
【例】 In 1905 he was sent to Paris as an *apprentice* to an art dealer.
【近】 trainee，learner，tyro，novice

ascend [əˈsend]
【释】 *v.* 上升；登高
【例】 To avoid this event, a diver must *ascend* slowly...
【衍】 ascent (*n.*)
【近】 mount，scale

autonomy [ɔːˈtɔnəmi]
【释】 *n.* 自治；自治权
【例】 Graham had achieved her *autonomy* by 1931.
【衍】 autonomic (*adj.*)
【近】 independence，sovereignty

barrel [ˈbærəl]
【释】 *n.* 桶，装满的桶，桶装
【例】 The ashes were placed in a *barrel* with holes in the bottom.

Unit 19

【近】	tub，container，drum，cask

besiege [bi'siːdʒ]

【释】 *v.* 围，包围，围困，围攻

【例】 Almost daily the public is *besieged* by claims for "no-aging" diets, new vitamins, and other wonder foods.

【衍】 besieger（*n.*）

【近】 surround，siege，encircle，blockade

boost [buːst]

【释】 *v.* 推，升，提；支援；增加；提高；促进

【例】 Post chapels provided a setting for religious services and *boosted* morale.

【衍】 booster（*n.*）

【近】 increase，improve，enhance，advance

bubble ['bʌbl]

【释】 *n.* 泡，水泡；气泡；泡沫

【例】 By careful kneading, the potter removed the air *bubbles* and made the clay as plastic as possible.

camp [kæmp]

【释】 *n.* 野营；露营地

【例】 Another realist, Bret Harte, achieved fame with stories that portrayed local life in the California mining *camps*.

【近】 site，encampment，campground

cast [kɑːst]

【释】 ① *v.* 浇铸，铸造

【例】 They had invented bronze, an alloy that could be *cast* in molds, out of which they made tools and weapons.

【衍】 typecast（*v.*）铸字，浇字

【释】 ② *v.* 丢弃，抛弃；脱掉(衣服)；(蛇)脱(皮)；(鸟)换(毛)；(鹿)换(角)；(树)落(叶)；(马)脱落(铁掌)

【例】 It also *casts* off attached structures such as tentacles.

【近】 shed

ceremony ['seriməni]

【释】 *n.* 典礼，仪式

【例】 In public *ceremonies* singing was combined with dancing and with music from a variety of instruments.

【衍】 ceremonial（*adj.* & *n.*）

【近】	rite，ritual，ceremonial
circumstance	[ˈsəːkəmstəns]
【释】	*n.* (常 [*pl.*]) (周围的)情况，情形，环境
【例】	A number of *circumstances* contributed to the meteoric rise of Los Angeles.
【近】	condition，situation
collective	[kəˈlektiv]
【释】	*adj.* 集合的；共同的
【例】	All such work was done by *collective* enterprise in the workshops.
【衍】	collectively (*adv.*)；collectivism (*n.*)；collectivistic (*adj.*)
【近】	cooperative，united
compress	[kəmˈpres]
【释】	*v.* 压缩，浓缩
【例】	Snow accumulating yearly in Rainier's summit craters is compacted and *compressed* into a dense form of ice called firm.
【衍】	compression (*n.*)
【近】	compact，condense
conjunction	[kənˈdʒʌŋkʃən]
【释】	*n.* 结合，连接
【例】	Pullman, Illinois, and Gary, Indiana, were likewise one-industry towns created in *conjunction* with the much broader economy of nearby Chicago.
contribute	[kənˈtribjuːt]
【释】	*v.* 出力，做出贡献
【例】	The economic depression in the late-nineteenth-century United States *contributed* significantly to a growing movement in literature toward realism and naturalism.
【衍】	contribution (*n.*)；contributive (*adj.*)
costume	[ˈkɔstjuːm]
【释】	*n.* 服装
【例】	Her second contribution lies in dance *costume*.
【近】	garb，attire，clothes
culminate	[ˈkʌlmineit]
【释】	*v.* 达到极点，达最高潮；告终(**in**)

Unit 19

【例】	They had an argument, which *culminated* in Tom getting drunk.
【衍】	culmination (*n.*); culminant (*adj.*)
【近】	finish, close, conclude

decorate ['dekəreit]

【释】	*v.* 修饰,装饰,布置
【例】	Glass can be *decorated* in multiple ways and its optical properties are exceptional.
【衍】	decorative (*adj.*); decoratively (*adv.*); decoration (*n.*)
【近】	adorn, ornament, embellish

designate ['dezigneit]

【释】	*v.* 指出,指明
【例】	Two and a half decades later, only fifteen sanctuaries had been *designated*, with half of these established after 1978.
【衍】	designated (*adj.*) 指定的,派定的; designative (*adj.*); designation (*n.*)
【近】	assign, delegate

discard [dis'kɑːd]

【释】	*v.* 放弃,抛弃
【例】	Squirrels pry off the caps of acorns, bite through the shells to get at the nutritious inner kernels, and then *discard* them half-eaten.
【衍】	discarded (*adj.*)
【近】	abandon, cast off, forsake

dive [daiv]

【释】	*v.* 潜水;【泳】跳水;俯冲
【例】	The eagle *dived* down on the rabbit.
【衍】	diver (*n.*) 潜水员

dwarf [dwɔːf]

【释】	*n.* 矮小的(动)植物 *v.* 使矮小,使相形见绌
【例】	Cotton became the main American export, *dwarfing* all others.
【衍】	dwarfish (*adj.*) 比较矮小的

elliptic(al) [i'liptik(əl)]

【释】	*adj.* 椭圆(形)的
【例】	There are three main types of galaxy: spiral, *elliptical*, and irregular.

【衍】	ellipse (*n.*); elliptically (*adv.*)
【近】	oval
enhance	[in'hɑːns]
【释】	*v.* 提高；增强
【例】	These strange adaptations to life represent just a few of the sophisticated means by which plants *enhance* their chances of survival.
【衍】	enhancement (*n.*)
【近】	improve, boost, increase
escape	[is'keip]
【释】	*v.* 逃走，逃脱，逃逸；避免
【例】	Therefore, organisms must be buried rapidly to *escape* destruction by the elements and to be protected against agents of weathering and erosion.
【近】	flee, run off
expertise	[ˌekspə'tiːz]
【释】	*n.* 专门技能，专门知识
【例】	This specialization allows Congress to compete with the executive branch in assembling information and applying *expertise* to given problems.
【近】	skill, proficiency
faith	[feiθ]
【释】	*n.* 信仰，信心
【例】	This awareness of education's value, rooted in the Enlightenment *faith* in human potentiality, had feminist implications before there was a feminist ideology.
【衍】	faithful (*adj.*)
【近】	belief, conviction, loyalty
fist	[fist]
【释】	*n.* 拳头
【例】	An iron *fist* policy or approach is one which deals with people and situations in a very strict and cruel way.
fog	[fɔg]
【释】	*n.* 雾
【例】	Many conditions such as flying at night and landing in dense *fog* require a pilot to use radar.

Unit 19

【衍】	foggy (*adj.*)
【近】	mist，smog，haze，vapor

frontier [ˈfrʌntjə]

【释】	*n.* 边疆；边界，边缘
【例】	The ocean bottom is a vast *frontier* and even today it is largely unexplored and uncharted.
【近】	border，boundary，edge

generous [ˈdʒenərəs]

【释】	*adj.* 宽大的，慷慨的，大方的，丰盛的，丰富的
【例】	In their *generous* conceptions, play harmlessly and experimentally permits us to put our creative forces into action.
【衍】	generosity (*n.*)；generously (*adv.*)
【近】	kind，giving，liberal，bighearted

global [ˈgləubəl]

【释】	*adj.* 球面的，球状的；全球的，世界的
【例】	On a *global* basis, nature's output of these compounds dwarfs that resulting from human activities.
【衍】	globe (*n.*)；globalism (*n.*)；globalist (*n.*)；globalization (*n.*)
【近】	worldwide，international，universal

handedness [ˈhændidnis]

【释】	*n.* 惯用左手(右手)
【例】	Anthropologists have pieced together the little they know about the history of left-*handedness* and right-*handedness* from indirect evidence.
【衍】	handed (*adj.*) 惯用…手的
【近】	hander

hemisphere [ˈhemisfiə]

【释】	*n.* 半球
【例】	The variation between the *hemispheres* corresponds to which side of the body is used to perform specific activities.

hormone [ˈhɔːməun]

【释】	*n.* 荷尔蒙，激素，内分泌
【例】	Without regular supplies of some *hormones* our capacity to behave would be seriously impaired.

【衍】	hormonal (*adj.*)
illuminate	[i'lju:mineit]
【释】	*v.* 照亮，照明
【例】	The light that highlights the figures of the sailors also *illuminates* the scales of the fish in the bottom of the boat.
【衍】	illumination (*n.*)
【近】	light
impulse	['impʌls]
【释】	*n.* 冲动；冲量
【例】	This was not something the Presidents themselves would try to resolve the disputes, but rather try to give a new *impulse* to them in terms of trying to resolve them.
【衍】	impulsive (*adj.*)
inherent	[in'hiərənt]
【释】	*adj.* 内在的，固有的，生来的
【例】	Why do homing pigeons fly home? They are not unique in this *inherent* skill; it is found in most migratory birds, in bees, ants, toads, and even turtles.
【衍】	inherently (*adv.*); inherence (*n.*)
【近】	intrinsic, innate, inbuilt, natural, inborn
instruct	[in'strʌkt]
【释】	*v.* 教，指示
【例】	All but one member of each group had been *instructed* to agree upon a wrong answer for a majority of the trials.
【衍】	instructive (*adj.*); instructor (*n.*); instruction (*n.*)
【近】	teach, introduce
intriguing	[in'tri:giŋ]
【释】	*adj.* 引起兴趣的；有魅力的
【例】	To lure their pollinators from afar, orchids use appropriately *intriguing* shapes, colors, and scents.
【衍】	intrigue (*n. & v.*) 阴谋，密谋；使发生兴趣；使着迷
【近】	absorbing, fascinating
jewel	['dʒu:əl]
【释】	*n.* 宝石，宝玉，宝石饰物
【例】	They were carved from precious *jewels* instead of ice.

Unit 19

【衍】	jeweler（*n.*）宝石商，宝石匠；jewelry（*n.*）珠宝，珠宝类
landmark	[ˈlændmɑːk]
【释】	*n.* 路标，地界标，里程碑；划时代的事
【例】	Perhaps most telling is the preservation of the huge Ghirardelli sign as an important *landmark*；it is such improbable，irrational，and cherished idiosyncrasies which give cities identity and character.
【近】	signpost，pointer，milestone
lens	[lenz]
【释】	*n.* （[*pl.*] lenses）透镜；一组透镜
【例】	Once the new *lens* became available，it suddenly became possible to see a rather interesting effect by combining two *lenses*.
【衍】	lensed（*adj.*）有透镜的；lensing（*n.*）透镜化
locality	[ləuˈkæləti]
【释】	*n.* 地点，位置，场所；方向；地区；（植物的）产地；环境
【例】	In addition，depending on the *locality*，other resources may be accessible：shells，horns，gold，copper，and silver.
【衍】	local（*n.* & *adj.*）；locale（*n.*）现场，地点，场所；localize（*v.*）局限；集中；localization（*n.*）；locate（*v.*）确定…的位置；location（*n.*）
【近】	area，district，region
magma	[ˈmægmə]
【释】	*n.* （矿物、有机物等的）稀糊状混合物；岩浆；稠液
【例】	As *magma* rises under the mid-ocean ridge，ferromagnetic minerals in the *magma* become magnetized in the direction of the geomagnetic field.
【近】	lava
mason	[ˈmeisən]
【释】	*n.* 石匠；（中世纪的）石匠协会会员
【例】	Where stone was the local building material，a *mason* was sure to appear on the list of people who paid taxes.
【衍】	masonry（*n.*）石工技术；石工行业；石造建筑
mere	[miə]
【释】	*adj.* 仅仅的，只不过的；全然的；纯粹的

【例】 Archaeological data are historical documents in their own right, not *mere* illustrations to written texts.

【衍】 merely (*adv.*)

【近】 simple, sheer, plain

mint [mint]

【释】 *v.* 铸造(货币) *n.* 造币厂

【例】 With the issue of the Lincoln penny, Congress and the federal *mint* realized that great men like Lincoln and Washington would not be treated as deities but as paragons of freedom and liberty.

【衍】 minter (*n.*) 造币厂工人，造币者

【近】 cast, imprint, issue

mood [mu:d]

【释】 *n.* (一时的)心情，情绪

【例】 Tiny amounts of some hormones can modify our *moods* and our actions, our inclination to eat or drink, our aggressiveness or submissiveness, and our reproductive and parental behavior.

【衍】 moody (*adj.*) 喜怒无常的；郁郁不乐的

【近】 frame of mind, temper, feel

narrow ['nærəu]

【释】 ① *adj.* 狭窄的，狭隘的 *v.* 弄窄，收缩([*opp.*] wide)

【例】 The trumpet family is much more than a group of related instruments that can stir one with their sound, or *narrow* tubes of metal capable of producing a variety of musical sounds.

【衍】 narrowly (*adv.*); narrowness (*n.*); narrowing (*n.*) 缩小，窄化

【近】 thin, fine, slim

【释】 ② *adj.* 有限的，受限制的 *v.* 限制，缩小([*opp.*] broaden)

【例】 A decision-making worksheet begins with a succinct statement of the problem that will also help to *narrow* it.

【衍】 narrowly (*adv.*); narrowness (*n.*); narrowing (*n.*) 缩小，窄化

【近】 restrict, limit, confine

Unit 19

nonetheless [ˌnʌnðəˈles]

【释】 *adv. & conj.* 仍然(还)，不过；(尽管如此)还是

【例】 Researchers were delighted *nonetheless* with the new information they were able to glean from their investigation of the comet.

【近】 nevertheless，however，even so

obstacle [ˈɔbstəkl]

【释】 *n.* 障碍(物)；妨害，阻碍，干扰

【例】 Serious accidents and consequent loss of life can be prevented if the engineer is forewarned of a washed-out bridge or of some *obstacle* in the path of the train.

【衍】 obstruct (*v.*) 妨碍；阻挠；(给…)设置障碍

【近】 obstruction，impediment，barrier

oral [ˈɔːrəl]

【释】 *adj.* 口头的；口的；口腔发声的

【例】 To be considered genuine traditional folk songs，they must have *oral* transmission, continuity, variation, and selection.

【衍】 orally (*adv.*) 口头上

【近】 spoken，verbal，by word of mouth

overall [ˈəuvərɔːl]

【释】 ① *adj. & adv.* 全部的(地)，所有的(地)，总的(地)

【例】 Expressive leaders are less concerned with the *overall* goals of the group than with providing emotional support to group members and attempting to minimize tension and conflict among them.

【近】 generally，total，global

【释】 ② *n.* (套头)工作服；罩衫，(妇女、小儿等的)罩衣

【例】 Cowhands sometimes wore leather trousers，called chaps，over regular *overalls*.

partially [ˈpɑːʃəli]

【释】 *adv.* 部分地

【例】 Satire tends to remind people that much of what they read in popular media is sanctimonious, sentimental，and only *partially* true.

【衍】 partial (*adj.*)

【近】 partly，incompletely

penetrate ['penitreit]
【释】 *v.* 进入，渗入，穿透
【例】 Each year, the observatory's telescopes find it more difficult to *penetrate* the artificial lights.
【衍】 penetrating (*adj.*); penetration (*n.*)
【近】 enter, go through, go in

phenomenon [fi'nɔminən]
【释】 *n.* 现象；事件
【例】 The most interesting architectural *phenomenon* of the 1970's was the enthusiasm for refurbishing older buildings.
【近】 fact, event, happening, incident

plasma ['plæzmə]
【释】 *n.* 血浆；淋巴液；等离子(体)；等离子区
【例】 Outside the magnetosphere, blasting toward the Earth is the solar wind, a swiftly moving *plasma* of ionized gases.

populous ['pɔpjuləs]
【释】 *adj.* 人口稠密的，人口多的；挤满的
【例】 This was a wealthy and *populous* region and the center of a strong craft tradition.
【衍】 population (*n.*); populate (*v.*)
【近】 crowded, packed

precarious [pri'kɛəriəs]
【释】 *adj.* 不确定的，靠不住的；危险的
【例】 Hunting is at best a *precarious* way of procuring food.
【衍】 precariously (*adv.*)
【近】 shaky, unstable, insecure, unsafe

prey [prei]
【释】 *n.* 被捕食的动物，牺牲者，牺牲品
【例】 Bloodhounds are biologically adapted to trailing their *prey*.
【衍】 preyer (*n.*) 猛兽，猛禽
【近】 victim

progress ['prəugres]
【释】 *n.* 前进，进行；发育，进化
【例】 She was frequently dismayed by what economic *progress* was doing to her region.

【衍】	progressive（adj.）；progressively（adv.）日益增多地
【近】	development，growth，improvement，evolution

prototype [ˈprəutəutaip]

【释】 *n.* 原型；典型；样板；模范，标准

【例】 Engineers have produced ***prototype*** engines that are driven by the force of nitinol springing from one shape to another.

【近】 example，sample，model

quantity [ˈkwɔntəti]

【释】 *n.* 量；分量，数量；额；值，参量

【例】 There were also a number of poor-quality figurines and painted pots produced in ***quantity*** by easy，inexpensive means.

【近】 amount，measure，size，capacity

rare [rɛə]

【释】 ① *adj.* 稀少的；（空气等）稀薄的；（群岛、星等）稀疏的

【例】 Home base behavior does not occur among nonhuman primates and is ***rare*** among mammals.

【衍】 rarely（adv.）；rarefied（adj.）纯净的，稀薄的

【近】 uncommon，infrequent，unusual

【释】 ② *adj.* 稀有的，珍奇的；极好的，珍贵的

【例】 A sunken ship，therefore，can be a ***rare*** window through which a moment in time is glimpsed.

【衍】 rarely（adv.）；rarer（adj.）更稀罕的，更珍贵的；rarest（adj.）

【近】 scarce，sparse，scant

recent [ˈriːsənt]

【释】 *adj.* 近来的，近代的

【例】 In one ***recent*** year，the addition of 17 million square feet of skyscraper office space in New York City raised the peak daily demand for electricity by 120,000 kilowatts.

【衍】 recently（adv.）；recentness（n.）

【近】 current，modern，latest

refurbish [riˈfəːbiʃ]

【释】 *v.* 再刷新；整修；翻新

【例】 The most interesting architectural phenomenon of the 1970's was the enthusiasm for *refurbishing* older buildings.

【衍】 refurbishment (*n.*)

【近】 renew, renovate

remainder [ri'meində]

【释】 *n.* 剩余物，残余　*adj.* 剩余的

【例】 They saved the best to the harvest for seeds or for trade, with the *remainder* eaten right away or stored for later use in underground reserves.

【衍】 remain (*v.*)

【近】 remnants, residue, leftovers

reptile ['reptail]

【释】 *n.* 爬行动物

【例】 Over the years, thousands of specimens of marine *reptiles*, fish and invertebrates have been recovered from these rocks.

【衍】 reptilian (*adj.*)

resume [ri'zju:m]

【释】 *v.* 重新开始(已停的事)，继续(中断的谈话等)

【例】 The group wintered near the Mandan villages in the center of what is now North Dakota, and *resumed* their journey in the spring of 1805.

【近】 recommence, restart, take up again

rift [rift]

【释】 *n.* 断裂

【例】 If at such a spreading contact the two plates support continents, a *rift* is formed that will gradually widen and become flooded by the sea.

【近】 crack, fissure, split

rub [rʌb]

【释】 *v.* 摩擦；使相擦

【例】 It was then *rubbed* with a round stone or similar object to give it a shiny, hard surface.

【衍】 rubber (*n.*) 橡皮，橡胶

【近】 massage, chafe, polish

scar [skɑː]

【释】 *v.* 使留伤痕，使留痕迹　　*n.* 伤痕；疤；痕迹

【例】 Craters *scar* the surface of every planet and satellite in the inner solar system（Mercury, Venus, Earth, and Mars）.

【近】 blemish，disfigurement，wound

seasonal [ˈsiːzənəl]

【释】 *adj.* 季节（性）的；周期性的（[*opp.*] irregular）

【例】 In the beginning, human beings viewed the natural forces of the world, even the *seasonal* changes, as unpredictable.

【衍】 season（*n.*）；seasonally（*adv.*）

【近】 cyclic，recurrent，regular

session [ˈseʃən]

【释】 *n.* 一次，一段时间；会议；会议的一次（一届）

【例】 A very dehydrated person, cannot drink enough water to dehydrate at one *session*, because the human stomach is not sufficiently big.

【衍】 sessional（*adj.*）开会的，开庭的

【近】 meeting，sitting，conference

shovel [ˈʃʌvəl]

【释】 *n.* 铲，铁锨　　*v.* 拿铲子铲

【例】 The Mesabi deposits were so near the surface that they could be mined with steam *shovels*.

【衍】 shoveler（*n.*）用铲子铲的人；shovelful（*n.*）满铲，一铲之量

【近】 spade，scoop，spoon

skyrocket [skaiˈrɔkit]

【释】 *v.* （使）直线上升；（物价）猛涨

【例】 Production *skyrocketed* from seventy-seven thousand tons in 1870 to over eleven million tons in 1900.

solidify [səˈlidifai]

【释】 *v.* 使凝固，固化；使结晶（[*opp.*] dissolve）

【例】 Any rock that has cooled and *solidified* from a molten state is an igneous rock.

【衍】 solid（*adj.*）；solidarity（*n.*）团结一致，共同责任，休戚相关

【近】 harden，coagulate，congeal

speculation [ˌspekjuˈleiʃən]

【释】① *n.* 沉思，思索；设想，推测

【例】This *speculation* is based on the fact that, even today, the blood serums of radically divergent species are remarkably similar.

【衍】speculate (*v.*); speculative (*adj.*); speculator (*n.*)

【近】conjecture, assumption, thought

【释】② *n.* 投机，投机事业

【例】Indian crafts, viewed as valuable art objects in themselves purchased with an eye for *speculation*.

【衍】speculate (*v.*); speculative (*adj.*); speculator (*n.*)

squash [skwɔʃ]

【释】*n.* 南瓜，西葫芦

【例】The women planted another staple, *squash*, about the first of June, and harvested it near the time of the green corn harvest.

steady [ˈstedi]

【释】*adj.* 稳固的，稳定的，不变的

【例】By far, the most appealing publishing investments were to be found in small books that had proven to be *steady* sellers, providing a reasonably reliable source of income for the publisher.

【衍】steadily (*adv.*); steadfastly (*adv.*) 坚持不变地

【近】stable, constant, balanced

stout [staut]

【释】*adj.* 结实的；坚强的；坚牢的([*opp.*] flimsy)

【例】The bills of different crossbill species and subspecies vary ... some are *stout* and deep, others more slender and shallow.

【衍】stoutly (*adv.*); stoutness (*n.*); stouten (*v.*) 坚定；stouthearted (*adj.*) 刚毅的，勇敢的

【近】sturdy, strong, tough

stylized [ˈstailaizd]

【释】*adj.* 程式化的，按固定格式的

【例】In her versions the figures became more *stylized* and the landscapes less naturalistic.

【衍】stylize (*v.*); stylization (*n.*)

suit [sjuːt]

【释】 ① *v.* 适合；相配

【例】 That lot was a rectangular area 25 feet wide by 100 feet deep—a shape perfectly *suited* for a row house.

【衍】 suited（*adj.*）；suitability（*n.*）；suitable（*adj.*）；suitably（*adv.*）

【近】 go well with，match，be appropriate

【释】 ② *n.* 申诉，起诉，诉讼；控告；讼案

【例】 Most cases go no further than the trial court，for example，the personal injury *suit* results in a judgment by a trial court.

survival [sə'vaivəl]

【释】 *n.* 生存；幸存；幸存者；成活（植株）

【例】 They continue to look for better ways to increase egg production and to improve chick *survival* rates.

【衍】 survive（*v.*）；survivable（*adj.*）可存活的；不易破坏的；survivability（*n.*）

【近】 continued existence，endurance

synthesis ['sinθisis]

【释】 *n.* 综合；合成

【例】 Site planning is the process in which the assessment of the site and the requirements of the program for the use of the site are brought together in creative *synthesis*.

【衍】 synthesize（*v.*）；synthesizer（*n.*）合成者，合成物；synthetic（*adj.*）合成的，人造的

【近】 manufacture，combination，mixture

tedious ['tiːdiəs]

【释】 *adj.* 单调沉闷的，令人生厌的，冗长乏味的

【例】 Play is release from the *tedious* battles against scarcity and decline which are the incessant，and inevitable，tragedies of life.

【衍】 tedium（*n.*）

【近】 boring，dull，monotonous

textile ['tekstail]

【释】 *n.* 纺织品；纺织原料 *adj.* 纺织（品）的

【例】 Denied Southern cotton，*textile* mills turned to wool for blankets and uniforms.

【近】	fabric，yard goods，cloth
thunder	[ˈθʌndə]
【释】	***n.*** 雷，雷声
【例】	Environmental sounds，such as ***thunder***，and electronically generated hisses and blips can be recorded，manipulated，and then incorporated into a musical composition.
【衍】	thunderous（*adj.*）雷鸣似的，轰隆响的；thunder-storm（*n.*）雷雨
tornado	[tɔːˈneidəu]
【释】	***n.*** 大旋风，龙卷风
【例】	Many of the most damaging and life-threatening types of weather—torrential rains，severe thunderstorms，and ***tornadoes***—begin quickly，strike suddenly，and dissipate rapidly.
【衍】	tornadic（*adj.*）
【近】	cyclone，hurricane，whirlwind
translation	[trænsˈleiʃən]
【释】	***n.*** 翻译；译文
【例】	Because the Akkadians thought of Sumerian as a classical language，they taught it to educated persons and they inscribed vocabulary，***translation*** exercised，and other study aids on tablets.
【衍】	translate（*v.*）；translated（*adj.*）
【近】	paraphrase，version，rendition
trolley	[ˈtrɔli]
【释】	***n.*** 手推车；(有轨)电车
【例】	By opening vast areas of unoccupied land for residential expansion，electric ***trolleys*** pulled settled regions outward four times more distant from city center than they were in the premodern era.
【衍】	trolleybus（*n.*）无轨电车
ultimate	[ˈʌltimit]
【释】	***adj. & n.*** 最终(的)，根本(的)
【例】	This is true even if the protester's ***ultimate*** goal is to alter radically the legal system.
【衍】	ultimately（*adv.*）

Unit 19

【近】	final，eventual
usher	[ˈʌʃə]
【释】	*v.* 引导，展示(in)
【例】	The quarter century immediately before 1900 was the period of invention which helped to *usher* in the machine age.
【近】	begin，initiate
vegetation	[ˌvedʒiˈteiʃən]
【释】	*n.* (集合名词)植物，植被
【例】	Solitary roosters shelter in dense *vegetation* or enter a cavity.
【衍】	vegetative (*adj.*) 植物的；蔬菜的
【近】	shrubbery
virtue	[ˈvəːtjuː]
【释】	① *n.* 价值；长处，优点
【例】	In the United States as well as in Great Britain，reformers extolled the *virtues* of handcrafted objects.
【近】	advantage，benefit
【释】	② *n.* 效能，效力，功效
【例】	Yet historically this widespread faith in the economic *virtues* of science is a relatively recent phenomenon.
【近】	effect
warrant	[ˈwɔrənt]
【释】	① *v.* 证明…具有充分根据
【例】	Matters of the global environment now *warrant* the kind of high-level attention that the global economy receives.
【近】	guarantee，assure
【释】	② *n.* 正常理由；根据
【例】	There is some *warrant* for holding back on full-scale aid.
【近】	reason，foundation
wipe	[waip]
【释】	*v.* 擦去，消除(away；off；up)
【例】	Entire crops can be *wiped* out by fugal attacks both before and after harvesting.
【近】	smear，erase

Exercise of Unit 19

左列单词在右列中有一个同义词，请找出并在相应的位置写上正确答案。

Exercise 1：

(A) ceremony _____ simple
(B) altitude _____ guarantee
(C) warrant _____ height
(D) mere _____ improve
(E) enhance _____ rite
(F) virtue _____ effect

Exercise 2：

(A) obstacle _____ crowded
(B) handedness _____ cooperative
(C) cast _____ hander
(D) besiege _____ obstruction
(E) collective _____ surround
(F) populous _____ shed

Exercise 3：

(A) compress _____ harden
(B) frontier _____ assign
(C) solidify _____ nevertheless
(D) designate _____ compact
(E) remainder _____ remnants
(F) nonetheless _____ border

Exercise 4：

(A) virtue _____ shaky
(B) precarious _____ abandon
(C) landmark _____ signpost
(D) expertise _____ skill
(E) textile _____ fabric
(F) discard _____ advantage

Exercise 5：

(A) translation _____ sturdy
(B) speculation _____ begin
(C) autonomy _____ paraphrase
(D) stout _____ independence
(E) usher _____ meeting
(F) session _____ conjecture

Exercise 6：

(A) instruct _____ lava
(B) barrel _____ mount
(C) overall _____ teach
(D) prototype _____ example
(E) magma _____ tub
(F) ascend _____ generally

— 427 —

Exercise 7:

(A) scar _____ blemish
(B) locality _____ recommence
(C) narrow _____ victim
(D) mint _____ area
(E) resume _____ thin
(F) prey _____ cast

Exercise 8:

(A) inherent _____ amount
(B) quantity _____ massage
(C) rub _____ intrinsic
(D) tedious _____ scarce
(E) circumstance ____ boring
(F) rare _____ condition

Exercise 9:

(A) vegetation _____ restrict
(B) shovel _____ spade
(C) camp _____ stable
(D) fog _____ mist
(E) steady _____ shrubbery
(F) narrow _____ site

Exercise 10:

(A) global _____ renew
(B) refurbish _____ flee
(C) apprentice _____ trainee
(D) escape _____ crack
(E) rift _____ worldwide
(F) seasonal _____ cyclic

ANSWERS:

1	D C B E A F
2	F E B A D C
3	C D F A E B
4	B F C D E A
5	D E A C F B
6	E F A D B C
7	A E F B C D
8	B C A F D E
9	F B E D A C
10	B D C E A F

Unit 20

accord	enormous	nationwide	shower
adorn	essence	nonsense	slave
aluminum	explicit	obvious	solitary
approach	falcon	orbit	sphere
asphalt	flake	overcome	squat
avant-garde	foliage	participate	steal
barren	frost	penicillin	stove
bias	genetic	philosopher	subdivide
border	glowing	plaster	sulfur
buckle	handful	pore	suspect
campaign	hence	precede	systematic
caste	horsepower	pride	teens
challenge	illusion	prolific	texture
cite	inability	province	thwart
collide	inherit	quarry	totality
comprise	instrument	rat	translucent
connoisseur	intrinsic	receptacle	troop
controversy	join	refuse	ultraviolet
cotton	larva	remark	utensil
cure	levy	republic	velocity
dedicate	locomotion	retail	virus
desirable	magnesium	rigid	wary
discern	massive	rule	wispy
divergent	Mesozoic	scarce	
dwell	minuscule	secondary	
eloquent	moral	setting	

accord [ə'kɔːd]

【释】 v. 一致，与…符合（with）

【例】 His actions *accord* with his words.

【衍】 accordingly（*adv*.）

adorn [ə'dɔːn]

【释】 v. 装饰，修饰；佩戴

【例】 Some pots were *adorned* with incised or stamped decorations.

【衍】 adornment（*n*.）；unadorned（*adj*.）

【近】 decorate，embellish，ornament

aluminum [ə'ljuːminəm]

【释】 n. 铝

【例】 Modern barbed wire is made from mild steel, high-tensile steel, or *aluminum*.

approach [ə'prəutʃ]

【释】 ① v. 向…接近

【例】 They do not run from their nests when *approached*, and if they should come near to the chiff edge, they instinctively turn back.

【衍】 approachable（*adj*.）；approachablity（*n*.）

【近】 advance，loom

【释】 ② n. 方法，手段

【例】 Nonetheless, while Edison's *approach* to invention was often cut-and-try, it was highly systematic.

【近】 method，tactic

asphalt ['æsfælt]

【释】 n. 沥青，柏油

【例】 Unwary animals would become tapped on these thin sheets of liquid *asphalt*, which are extremely sticky in warm weather.

【近】 tarmac，pitch，tar

avant-garde [ˌævɔŋ'gɑːd]

【释】 n. & adj. 先锋（的），先驱（的）

【例】 Gertrude shared, moreover, the point of view of these *avant-garde* artists.

【近】 ultramodern，advanced，futuristic

— 430 —

barren ['bærən]

【释】 *n. & adj.* (土地)荒芜(的)([*opp.*] fertile)

【例】 Americans had trampled underfoot in their haste to cross the "Great American Desert" to reach lands that sometimes proved *barren*.

【近】 arid, unproductive, infertile, sterile

bias ['baiəs]

【释】 *n.* 成见，先入之见，偏执，偏见([*opp.*] impartiality)

【例】 Humans have a *bias* toward land that sometimes gets in the way of truly examining global issues.

【衍】 biased (*adj.*)

【近】 prejudice, partiality, unfairness

border ['bɔːdə]

【释】 *n.* 边缘，边沿，框；边界，国界，国境

【例】 In 1850, for example, the *borders* of Boston lay scarcely two miles from the old business district.

【衍】 borderer (*n.*) 边境居民

【近】 edge, boundary, margin, rim

buckle ['bʌkl]

【释】 *n.* 扣子，带扣；(衣、鞋等的)扣形装饰品

【例】 He was rodeo rider hankering to show off a fancy belt *buckle* won in an arena.

【衍】 buckled (*adj.*)

campaign [kæm'pein]

【释】 *n.* 战役；竞选运动

【例】 As anyone who watches the news during presidential *campaigns* knows, these polls have become an important part of political life in the United States.

【近】 fight, battle, operation

caste [kɑːst]

【释】 *n.* (昆虫的)职别(如工蜂等)；等级(制度)

【例】 Moreover, ants specializing in particular labor categories typically constitute a *caste* specialized by age or body form or both.

【近】 class, social group

challenge ['tʃælindʒ]

【释】 *n.* 挑战

Unit 20

【例】 Life's transition from the sea to the land was perhaps as much of an evolutionary *challenge* as was the genesis life.

【例】 challenging（*adj.*）；unchallenged（*adj.*）；challenger（*n.*）

cite ［sait］

【释】 *v.* 引用，举(例)，列举

【例】 As to ràtes，some *cite* an index plus a 0.625 percent margin rounded to the highest quarter.

【近】 quote，mention

collide ［kə'laid］

【释】 *v.* (车等)碰撞(with)；(意志等)冲突，抵触(with)

【例】 This is because they *collide* with the water molecules and are pushed this way and that.

【衍】 collision（*n.*）

【近】 crash

comprise ［kəm'praiz］

【释】 *v.* 包含，包括；由…组成(合成)

【例】 The Earth *comprises* three principal layers：the dense, iron-rich core，the mantle made of silicate rocks that are semimolten at depth，and the thin，solid-surface crust.

【近】 include，consist，compose

connoisseur ［ˌkɔnə'səː］

【释】 *n.* 艺术(品)的鉴定家，行家，内行，权威(in; of)

【例】 *Connoisseurs* of dance，gathered at the Forty-eighth Street Theater in New York，witnessed Martha Graham's first foray into this new realm of dance.

【衍】 connoisseurship（*n.*）

【近】 expert，veteran

controversy ［'kɔntrəvəːsi］

【释】 *n.* 争论，辩论

【例】 Political *controversy* about the public-land policy of the United States began with the American Revolution.

【衍】 controversial（*adj.*）

【近】 argument，debate

cotton ［'kɔtən］

【释】 *n.* 棉，棉花；棉线

【例】 River boats carried to New Orleans the corn and other crops of northwestern farmers, the *cotton* and tobacco of southwestern planters.

cure [kjuə]

【释】 ① *n.* 治愈，痊愈；疗法

【例】 Hazen and Brown's work was stimulated by the wartime need to find a *cure* for the fungus infections that afflicted many military personnel.

【近】 treatment，therapy

【释】 ② *v.* (鱼等用腌、熏、晒、烤等的)加工保藏(法)

【例】 People who lived in the cities and were not directly involved in trade often participated in small cottage industries making handcrafted goods. Others *cured* meats，ran bakeries，or otherwise produced needed goods and commodities.

dedicate ['dedikeit]

【释】 *v.* 献给，奉献；(把精力、时间等)专门用于某事(to)

【例】 Modern dance *dedicated* itself to deep significance.

【衍】 dedicative (*adj.*)；dedication (*n.*)；dedicator (*n.*) 献身者

【近】 contribute，devote，donate

desirable [di'zaiərəbl]

【释】 *adj.* 理想的，希望到手的；称心的，令人满意的

【例】 If for no other reason，the prize will continue to be *desirable* for the financial rewards that accompany it.

【衍】 undesirable (*adj.*)；desirably (*adv.*)；desirableness (*n.*)

【近】 enviable，wanted

discern [di'sə:n]

【释】 *v.* 辨别，分清；看出，认出

【例】 The available weather data are generally not detailed enough to allow computers to *discern* the subtle atmospheric changes that precede these storms.

【衍】 discernible (*adj.*) 可识别的；discerning (*adj.*) 眼光敏锐的

【近】 distinguish，detect，recognize

divergent [dai'və:dʒənt]

【释】 *adj.* 叉开的；分歧的；背道而驰的

【例】 These were two widely *divergent* influences on the early development of statistical methods.

【衍】 divergence（*n.*）分歧，分岔，分出（[*opp.*] convergence 集中，收敛）

【近】 different，deviating，opposing

dwell [dwel]

【释】 *v.* [书] 住，居住

【例】 Ocean-*dwelling* organisms are lust as sensitive to climatic changes—in this case temperature and salinity—as land animals.

【衍】 dweller（*n.*）居住者，居民

【近】 reside，inhabit

eloquent ['eləkwənt]

【释】 *adj.* 雄辩的，善辩的，有口才的，有说服力的

【例】 Reverend Williams，an *eloquent* speaker，played an important role in the community since so many people's lives centered around the church.

【衍】 eloquently（*adv.*）；eloquence（*n.*）

【近】 expressive，persuasive

enormous [i'nɔ:məs]

【释】 *adj.* 巨大的，庞大的

【例】 They range in size from microscopic structures to dinosaur skeletons and complete bodies of *enormous* animals.

【衍】 enormously（*adv.*）；enormity（*n.*）

【近】 vast，massive，giant，gigantic，mammoth

essence ['esəns]

【释】 *n.* 本质（[*opp.*] phenomenon）；精髓

【例】 The *essence* of the machine age was the harnessing of steam energy to complicated devices with many moving parts.

【衍】 inessence（*adv.*）；essential（*adj.*）；essentially（*adv.*）

【近】 quintessence，core

explicit [ik'splisit]

【释】 *adj.* 明白的，明确的（[*opp.*] implicit）；直爽的，不隐讳的

【例】 A younger contemporary of similar background gave the reading public an *explicit* feminist argument for the education of women.

【衍】 explicitly (*adv.*); explicitness (*n.*)

【近】 clear, plain

falcon ['fɔːlkən]

【释】 *n.* 隼，(猎鹰的)母鹰

【例】 If it is your lucky day, you might even see the white-tailed eagle, eagle owl, peregrine *falcon*, or golden eagle.

【衍】 falconer (*n.*) 养猎鹰的人；鹰猎者；falconet (*n.*) 小鹰

【近】 eagle, condor, kestrel

flake [fleik]

【释】 *n.* 薄片

【例】 A fresh snowfall is a fluffy mass of loosely packed snow *flakes*.

foliage ['fəuliidʒ]

【释】 *n.* [集合名词] (树的)叶子

【例】 Many butterflies can suddenly disappear from view by folding their wings and sitting quietly among the *foliage* that they resemble.

【近】 leaf

frost [frɔst]

【释】 *n.* 霜；霜柱；结霜；冰冻

【例】 In theory, the upward movement of fieldstones should result in pure soil, all the stones above the *frost* line having been pushed to the surface and carried away.

genetic [dʒi'netik]

【释】 *adj.* 遗传(学)上的；发生的，发展的；创始的

【例】 Their *genetic* makeup constrains them to be insects and to share similar characteristics with 750,000 species of insects.

【衍】 genetical (*adj.*)

【近】 inherent, inherited, heritable

glowing ['gləuiŋ]

【释】 *v.* 灼热；发白热光；燃烧；放光，发热

【例】 Viewed from outer space, auroras can be seen as dimly *glowing* belts wrapped around each of the Earth's magnetic poles.

Unit 20

— 435 —

| 【衍】 | glowing（*adj.*） |
| 【近】 | burn，blaze，flame，shine |

handful ['hændfʊl]

| 【释】 | *n.* 少数，少量，一小撮 |
| 【例】 | Of the tens of thousands of ships on the ocean bottom，only a *handful*，less than 1 percent，contain negotiable treasure，such as gold and jewels. |

hence [hens]

【释】	*adv.* 从此，因此，所以，本来
【例】	Usually the creatures are cucumber-shaped— *hence* their name.
【近】	therefore，thus，so

horsepower ['hɔːsˌpauə]

| 【释】 | *n.* 马力 |
| 【例】 | The high-pressure engine was far lighter in proportion to *horsepower*. |

illusion [i'luːʒən]

【释】	*n.* 幻想；错觉
【例】	Many workers are seduced by rosy *illusions* of life as a telecommuter.
【衍】	illusive（*adj.*）
【近】	delusion，fantacy

inability [ˌinə'biləti]

【释】	*n.* 无能，无力
【例】	This may well be true，but critics respond that this very distance may also be responsible for the Academy's *inability* to perceive accurately authentic trends in the literary world.
【近】	incapacity

inherit [in'herit]

【释】	*v.* 继承；遗传而得
【例】	Preceding generations have always been concerned about the future，but we are the first to be faced with decisions that will determine whether the Earth our children will *inherit* will be habitable.
【衍】	inherited（*adj.*）；inheritance（*n.*）

instrument ['instrumənt]
【释】 *n.* 手段；工具；仪表，仪器；乐器
【例】 Of all modern *instruments*, the violin is apparently one of the simplest.
【衍】 instrumental (*adj.*); instrumentalist (*n.*)
【近】 tool, device, utensil, apparatus, implement, appliance

intrinsic [in'trinsik]
【释】 *adj.* 内部的，体内的([*opp.*] **extrinsic**)
【例】 Once the chlorophyll breaks down, however, the *intrinsic* yellow or brown color of the remaining leaf tissue appears.
【衍】 intrinsically (*adv.*)
【近】 inherent, built-in

join [dʒɔin]
【释】 *v.* 接合，连接，使结合
【例】 Wooden planks were *joined* and then polished smooth with special tools.
【衍】 joining (*n.*); joint (*n.*); joiner (*n.*) 工匠
【近】 link, connect, bond, adhere

larva ['lɑːvə]
【释】 *n.* 幼虫；幼体
【例】 They do not need to carry each task to completion from start to finish—for example, to check the *larva* first, then collect the food, then feed the larva.
【衍】 larval (*adj.*); larvicide (*n.*) 杀幼虫剂
【近】 young insect, caterpillar, worm

levy ['levi]
【释】 *v.* 征收；索取；征集，征用
【例】 While they *levied* heavy taxes to repay state war debts, their larger neighbors might retire debts out of land-sale proceeds.
【衍】 leviable (*adj.*) 可征收的(税等)，得课税的(货物等)；levier (*n.*) 强征人(尤指征税人)
【近】 tax, charge, impose

locomotion [,ləukə'məuʃən]
【释】 *n.* 运动，移动，位移；运动力，移动力，运转力

【例】 A great deal can be learned from the actual traces of ancient human *locomotion*：the footprints of early hominids.

【衍】 locomote（*v.*）；locomotive（*n. & adj.*）火车头（的）；机车（的）；运动（的）

magnesium ［mæg'niːzjəm］

【释】 *n.* 镁

【例】 The rocks of the crust are composed mostly of minerals with light elements，like aluminum and sodium，while the mantle contains some heavier elements，like iron and *magnesium*.

massive ['mæsiv]

【释】 *adj.* 大规模的；大量的；大的，重的；大块的

【例】 The United States economy underwent a *massive* transition and the nature of work was permanently altered.

【衍】 mass（*n. & v.*）

【近】 enormous，immense，huge

Mesozoic ［ˌmesəu'zəuik］

【释】 *n. & adj.* 中生代（的），中生代岩石（的）

【例】 All birds living today，from the great condors of the Andes to the tiniest wrens，trace their origin back to the *Mesozoic* dinosaurs.

【衍】 proterozoic（*n. & adj.*）元古代（的），元古界（的）

minuscule ['minəskjuːl]

【释】 *adj.* 极小的，微小的，细微的

【例】 In the twentieth century，electron microscopes have provided direct views of viruses and *minuscule* surface structures.

【近】 minute，microscopic，miniature

moral ['mɔrəl]

【释】 *adj. & n.* 道德（上的）（［*opp.*］immoral）；精神（上的）（［*opp.*］physical，practical）

【例】 Most lived on farms and in small towns and believed cities to be centers of corruption，crime，poverty，and *moral* degradation.

【衍】 morally（*adv.*）；moralize（*v.*）说教，讲道；morale（*n.*）士气，民心

【近】 ethical，decent，honorable

nationwide [ˈneiʃənwaid]

【释】 *adj.* 全国性的　*adv.* 全国性地([*opp.*] **local**)

【例】 May buildings in this style were erected *nationwide* through government programs during the Depression.

【衍】 nation（*n.*）; national（*adj.*）; nationally（*adv.*）; nationalism（*n.*）; nationalistic（*adj.*）; native（*adj.*）

【近】 countrywide, universally, national

nonsense [ˈnɔnsəns]

【释】 *n.* 无意义的话，荒谬(荒唐)的话，胡说；废话

【例】 The brothers' contrapuntal verbal styles relied for humor on puns, aphorisms, malapropism, wisecracks gags, insults, and sheer *nonsense*.

【衍】 nonsensical（*adj.*）没有意义(条理)的; nonsensically（*adv.*）

【近】 baloney, twaddle, drivel, gibberish

obvious [ˈɔbviəs]

【释】 *adj.* 明显的，明白的；显而易见的

【例】 The most *obvious* results of the process are growth rings, which are visible on the cross section of a trunk, a root, or a branch.

【衍】 obviously（*adv.*）; obviousness（*n.*）

【近】 clear, palpable, noticeable, apparent

orbit [ˈɔːbit]

【释】 ① *n.* 轨道　*v.* 沿轨道运行

【例】 A series of *orbiting* satellites and a group of sending and receiving stations located around the Earth form a communications satellite system.

【衍】 orbiter（*n.*）(绕)轨道飞行器; orbital（*adj.*）轨道的

【近】 course, path, track

【释】 ② *n.* 势力范围；(人生的)旅程；生活过程

【例】 Thousands of villages were included in its *orbit*.

【近】 range, scope, compass

overcome [ˌəuvəˈkʌm]

【释】 *v.* 打败，战胜，征服；克服(困难)

【例】 On the other hand, nesting on a narrow ledge has its own peculiar problems, and kittiwake behavior has become adapted to *overcome* them.

【近】 conquer, defeat, beat

Unit 20

— 439 —

participate [pɑː'tisipeit]
【释】 *v.* 参与，参加，有关系；分担；共享
【例】 The entire village *participated* in the occasion.
【衍】 participation（*n.*）；participator（*n.*）
【近】 join，take part，contribute，share

penicillin [ˌpeni'silin]
【释】 *n.* 青霉素，盘尼西林
【例】 In addition，fungi are the source of many of the most potent antibiotics used in clinical medicine，including *penicillin*.

philosopher [fi'lɔsəfə]
【释】 *n.* 哲学家；思想家；学者
【例】 Some *philosophers* have claimed that our playfulness is the most noble part of our basic nature.
【衍】 philosophy（*n.*）哲学；philosophic（*adj.*）

plaster ['plɑːstə]
【释】 *n.* 灰泥，石膏
【例】 Walls were made of *plaster* or wood，sometimes elaborately paneled.

pore [pɔː]
【释】 *n.* 毛孔；气孔，细孔
【例】 As new snow falls and buries the older snow，usually a year or more old，which has little *pore* space.
【近】 stoma，hole

precede [pri'siːd]
【释】 *v.* 领先于，居先于，在…之先
【例】 The idea of sea-floor spreading actually *preceded* the theory of plate tectonics.
【衍】 preceding（*adj.*）
【近】 head，lead，herald

pride [praid]
【释】 *n.* 自大，骄傲，傲慢，自豪；得意
【例】 Rather it has remained as an object of cultural *pride* and identity and not simply the product of the tastes and demands of the art market.
【衍】 prideful（*adj.*）
【近】 satisfaction，pleasure，delight

prolific [prə'lifik]

【释】 *adj*. 有生产力的；多产…的(of)

【例】 The beds of former lakes are also *prolific* sources of fossils.

【衍】 prolifically（*adv*.）；prolificacy（*n*.）

【近】 productive，abundant，plentiful

province ['prɔvins]

【释】 *n*. 省，州；[*pl*.] 地区，地方

【例】 British Columbia is the third largest Canadian *province*, both in area and population.

【衍】 provincialism（*n*.）地方风尚

【近】 region，area，state，country

quarry ['kwɔri]

【释】 *n*. 采石场，石坑，石矿

【例】 That is because of the unusual preservation in a limestone *quarry* in southern Germany of Archaeopteryx.

【衍】 quarrying（*n*.）

【近】 pit，mine，excavation

rat [ræt]

【释】 *n*. 鼠(比 mouse 要大)

【例】 These large water *rats* eat vegetation，and they make themselves unpopular by feeding in rice and sugarcane fields.

receptacle [ri'septəkl]

【释】 *n*. 容器，贮藏所

【例】 The broken valleys of the Great Basin provided ready *receptacles* for this moisture.

【近】 container，vessel

refuse [ri'fjuːz，'refjuːz]

【释】 ① *v*. 拒绝，推辞([*opp*.] accept)

【例】 Many subjects *refused* to change，and continued to hold to their independent appraisals.

【衍】 refusal（*n*.）

【近】 reject，rebuff，turn down

【释】 ② *n*. 废料，糟粕，渣滓，垃圾，废物

【例】 The researchers applied ground limestone，put a thin layer of topsoil on it，and sowed the plant seeds on the *refuse*, consisting of waste coal，rock，clay，and mining debris.

【近】 waste，garbage

remark ［riˈmɑːk］

【释】 *v.* 评论，谈论，议论

【例】 Critics and historians have *remarked* more than once that taletelling is a regional trail of the South.

【衍】 remarkable（*adj.*）显著的，非凡的；remarkably（*adv.*）

【近】 comment，statement，mention

republic ［riˈpʌblik］

【释】 *n.* 共和国；共和政体（［*opp.*］ **monarchy**）

【例】 Thomas Jefferson had presented precisely this idea，and it had been basic in his own thinking about the future of the *Republic* throughout the struggle for independence.

【衍】 republican（*adj.* & *n.*）；republicanism（*n.*）；republicanize（*v.*）

【近】 democracy，state，nation

retail ［ˈriːteil］

【释】 *adj.* & *n.* & *v.* 零售(的)（［*opp.*］ **wholesale**）

【例】 In the nineteenth century，state regulation through licensing fell especially on peddlers innkeepers，and *retail* merchants of various kinds.

【衍】 retailer（*n.*）

【近】 sell，trade，vend

rigid ［ˈridʒid］

【释】 *adj.* 刚硬的，坚定的；严格的；僵化的

【例】 The most striking single fact about chimpanzees is the flexibility of other social life，the lack of any *rigid* form of organization.

【衍】 rigidly（*adv.*）；rigidify（*v.*）；rigidity（*n.*）

【近】 inflexible，stiff，strict

rule ［ruːl］

【释】 ① *n.* 规则，定律；常例，惯例

【例】 Since most stations in the Northeast were built on rocky eminences，enormous towers were not the *rule*.

【衍】 ruleless（*adj.*）无规则的

【近】 regulation，statute，law

【释】 ② *n. & v.* 统治，支配

【例】 In the middle class especially，men participated in the productive economy while women *ruled* the home and served as the custodians of civility culture.

【衍】 ruler（*n.*）；rulership（*n.*）；ruling（*adj.*）

【近】 govern，reign，administrate

scarce ［skɛəs］

【释】 *adj.* 缺乏的，不足的；稀有的，罕见的

【例】 Labor-saving machinery naturally appeared first where labor was *scarce*.

【衍】 scarcity（*n.*）

【近】 inadequate，scant，insufficient

secondary ［ˈsekəndəri］

【释】 ① *adj.* 第二(位)的；第二次的；中级的

【例】 As colleges came to be seen as a logical continuation of *secondary* school，younger students began to predominate.

【衍】 second（*adj. & n.*）；secondhand（*adj. & adv.*）间接的(地)；二手的(地)

【释】 ② *adj.* 副(的)；从属的；次要的

【例】 It was made like a small，*secondary* fireplace with a flue leading into the main chimney to draw out smoke.

【近】 minor，inferior，derivative

setting ［ˈsetiŋ］

【释】 ① *n.* 安装；装配；装置；安放

【例】 There is no ambiguity if we can see the *setting* of a switch.

【衍】 set（*v.*）

【释】 ② *n.* 背景；(花园的)布置；环境

【例】 They especially emphasized the need for natural serene *settings* where hurried urban dwellers could periodically escape from the city.

【近】 surroundings，location，site

shower ［ˈʃauə］

【释】 *n.* 阵雨；(风雪等的)一阵；淋浴

【例】 As the air shot through the furnace，the bubbling metal would erupt in *showers* of sparks.

Unit 20

【衍】 showery（*adj.*）阵雨般的；多阵雨的

slave ［sleiv］

【释】 *n.* 奴隶；苦工

【例】 The Stowes' original intent in buying a home，which is at Mandarin on the Saint Johns River，was to create a model for the employment of former *slaves*.

【衍】 slavery（*n.*）奴隶身份；slavish（*adj.*）奴性的；无独创性的

solitary ［'sɔlitəri］

【释】 *adj.* 独个儿的，孤独的；独居的（［*opp.*］**social**）

【例】 Richly organized colonies of the kind made possible by eusociality enjoy several key advantages over *solitary* individuals.

【衍】 solitude（*n.*）；solo（*n.*）独奏（曲）；soloist（*n.*）独奏者，独唱者

【近】 private，lone，friendless

sphere ［sfiə］

【释】 *n.* 球；球体，圆体，球面，球形；天体；星，行星

【例】 The continents and the seabed are formed by the crust—a thin *sphere* of relatively light，solid rock.

【衍】 spherical（*adj.*）；spheroidal（*adj.*）扁球体的，类球体的

【近】 globe，orb，ball

squat ［skwɔt］

【释】 *v.* 蹲；坐 *n.* 蹲伏的位置（姿势） *adj.* 蹲着的

【例】 Men gossiped and exchanged rumors while whittling bits of wood or while *squatting* in the shade to get acquainted with strangers.

【衍】 squatter（*n.*）擅自占地者；在公地上定居者

【近】 sit on your heels，crouch，hunker down

steal ［stiːl］

【释】 *n.* 便宜货

【例】 At only ＄1,350，this champagne is a *steal*.

【近】 bargin，cheapie

stove ［stəuv］

【释】 *n.* 火炉，电炉，加热器

【例】	Heat was provided by wood or coal *stoves*.
【衍】	stovepipe（*n.*）火炉烟囱管
【近】	heater，wood stove，oil-burning stove

subdivide [ˈsʌbdivaid]

【释】	*v.* 再分；细分
【例】	The stony meteorites can also be *subdivided* into two categories by using nothing more complicated than a magnifying glass.
【衍】	subdivision（*n.*）；subdivisional（*adj.*）；subdividable（*adj.*）可再分的

sulfur [ˈsʌlfə]

【释】	*n.* 硫(磺)
【例】	They are composed of iron and nickel along with *sulfur*，carbon，and traces of other elements.
【衍】	sulfuric（*adj.*）；sulfurous（*adj.*）；sulfury（*adj.*）；sulfurize（*v.*）

suspect [səsˈpekt]

【释】	*v.* 怀疑，觉得可疑，猜疑 *adj.* 可疑的
【例】	Scientists *suspect* that the changing length of the day is factor that triggers migratory behavior.
【衍】	suspicion（*n.*）
【近】	suppose，think，imagine

systematic [ˌsisti'mætik]

【释】	*adj.* 有系统的，成体系的
【例】	Population growth in turn created an even greater reliance on settled farming，as only *systematic* agriculture could sustain the increased numbers of people.
【衍】	systematically（*adv.*）；systematize（*v.*）使体系化
【近】	methodical，organized，regular

teens [tiːnz]

【释】	*n.* 十多岁(13～19岁)
【例】	During her *teens* she contributed more than seventy-five poems to a Chicago newspaper.
【衍】	teenager（*n.*）十几岁的青少年
【近】	adolescence，youth，young adulthood

texture [ˈtekstʃə]

【释】	*n.* (织物的)组织，结构，质地

Unit 20

— 445 —

【例】	Igneous rocks with this coarse-grained *texture* that formed at depth are called plutonic.
【衍】	textural（*adj.*）

thwart [θwɔːt]

【释】	*v.* 反对；阻挠；挫败(对方意图等)
【例】	However there is a flaw in the argument that the evolution of wheeled animals was *thwarted* by the insoluble joint problem.
【衍】	thwarter（*n.*）横越者；thwartwise（*adj. & adv.*）横着的(地)
【近】	frustrate, spoil, prevent

totality [təu'tæləti]

【释】	*n.* 完全，完备；全体，总数
【例】	Even when an audience thinks it discerns traces of influence from other dance styles, the *totality* of Graham's theatrical idiom makes the reference seem a mirage.
【衍】	total（*adj. & v.*）合计，总的；totally（*adv.*）
【近】	entirety, whole, total

translucent [trænz'luːsənt]

【释】	*adj.* 半透明的
【例】	It can be colored or colorless, monochrome or poly-chrome, transparent, *translucent*, or opaque.
【衍】	translucently（*adv.*）; translucence（*n.*）; translucency（*n.*）
【近】	semi-transparent, see-through, lucid

troop [truːp]

【释】	*n.* 大群；群集 *v.* 成群结队地走
【例】	In 1781 twelve families *trooped* north from Mexico to California.
【衍】	troopship（*n.*）军队运输船
【近】	crowd, throng, flock

ultraviolet [ˌʌltrə'vaiəlit]

【释】	*adj. & n.* 紫外线(的)
【例】	An alternative would be sodium lights, which emit no *ultraviolet* waves and free the *ultraviolet* band that is

essential to spectral astronomy.

utensil	[juːˈtensəl]
【释】	***n.*** 器具，用具；家庭厨房用具
【例】	Each product had its own peculiar characteristics that demanded a particular way of cutting or drying the meat，and each task required its own cutting blades and other ***utensils***.
【近】	tool，apparatus，instrument，implement，appliance
velocity	[viˈlɔsəti]
【释】	***n.*** 速度，速率
【例】	The flow of traffic (number of cars per hour) can be obtained by multiplying the car density (number of cars per kilometer) by the average ***velocity*** (kilometers per hour).
【近】	speed，rate
virus	[ˈvaiərəs]
【释】	***n.*** 病毒
【例】	In the twentieth century，electron microscopes have provided direct views of ***viruses*** and minuscule surface structures.
【近】	germ
wary	[ˈwɛəri]
【释】	***adj.*** 小心的，留神的；谨慎的
【例】	National parties in the United States have generally been weak in structure and ***wary*** of ideology.
【衍】	warily (*adv.*); unwary (*n.*)
【近】	cautious，chary
wispy	[ˈwispi]
【释】	***adj.*** 细微的
【例】	The corona's rays flash out in a brilliant fan that has ***wispy*** spikelike rays near the Sun's north and south poles.
【近】	frail，delicate

Unit 20

Exercise of Unit 20

左列单词在右列中有一个同义词，请找出并在相应的位置写上正确答案。

Exercise 1:
(A) minuscule _____	class
(B) caste _____	minute
(C) secondary _____	baloney
(D) nonsense _____	expressive
(E) remark _____	minor
(F) eloquent _____	comment

Exercise 2:
(A) suspect _____	region
(B) province _____	suppose
(C) orbit _____	tool
(D) thwart _____	frustrate
(E) instrument _____	course
(F) connoisseur _____	expert

Exercise 3:
(A) controversy _____	treatment
(B) cite _____	waste
(C) inability _____	stoma
(D) cure _____	argument
(E) pore _____	quote
(F) refuse _____	incapacity

Exercise 4:
(A) nationwide _____	reside
(B) troop _____	globe
(C) sphere _____	arid
(D) barren _____	countrywide
(E) participate _____	crowd
(F) dwell _____	join

Exercise 5:
(A) rigid _____	inflexible
(B) solitary _____	private
(C) moral _____	distinguish
(D) discern _____	ethical
(E) totality _____	entirety
(F) dedicate _____	contribute

Exercise 6:
(A) quarry _____	conquer
(B) intrinsic _____	pit
(C) divergent _____	inherent
(D) overcome _____	different
(E) bias _____	prejudice
(F) approach _____	method

Exercise 7:
(A) explicit _____ clear
(B) essence _____ fight
(C) larva _____ quintessence
(D) campaign _____ edge
(E) border _____ young insect
(F) retail _____ sell

Exercise 8:
(A) falcon _____ reject
(B) refuse _____ include
(C) comprise _____ decorate
(D) adorn _____ eagle
(E) prolific _____ productive
(F) massive _____ enormous

Exercise 9:
(A) obvious _____ inherent
(B) receptacle _____ container
(C) glowing _____ burn
(D) genetic _____ therefore
(E) approach _____ clear
(F) hence _____ advance

Exercise 10:
(A) virus _____ inadequate
(B) desirable _____ enviable
(C) wary _____ govern
(D) rule _____ cautious
(E) scarce _____ germ
(F) illusion _____ delusion

ANSWERS:
1   B A D F C E
2   B A E D C F
3   D F E A B C
4   F C D A B E
5   A B D C E F
6   D A B C E F
7   A D B E C F
8   B C D A E F
9   D B C F A E
10 E B D C A F

Unit 21

account for	enroll	navigate	shrimp
advent	estimate	normal	slice
amateur	explode	occasion	solution
appropriate	fame	orchestra	spider
aspiring	flame	overlap	squeak
avenue	folk	particle	steam
barrier	frustrate	peninsula	straight
bind	genius	photograph	subjugation
botanical	glue	plastic	sum
bugle	handle	porpoise	suspend
campus	herald	precious	tactics
casual	hostile	primal	telegraph
chamber	illustrate	prominent	theater
civic	inanimate	provision	ticket
colony	inhibit	quarter	touch
conceal	insulate	ratify	transmission
conquer	intruder	reception	tropic
convection	jolt	regard	unaided
counterpart	lash	remind	utilitarian
curious	liberty	reputation	vent
defeat	lodge	retain	vision
destructive	magnetic	ring	wax
discharge	masterpiece	rumor	wit
diverse	metabolism	scatter	
dye	minutely	secret	
elusive	morphology	severe	

account for [əˈkaunt fɔː]

【释】 *v.* 证明，说明

【例】 Variations of clay composition and the temperatures at which they are fired *account for* the differences in texture and appearance between a china teacup and an earthenware flowerpot.

【近】 explain，explicate，demonstrate

advent [ˈædvənt]

【释】 *n.* (季节、事件等的)到来，出现

【例】 With the *advent* of high-resolution radio interferometers during the late 1970's，part of the answer became clear.

【近】 arrival，initiation

amateur [ˈæmətə]

【释】 *n.* 业余者，爱好者

【例】 These writers，like most of their male counterparts，were *amateur* historians.

【衍】 amateurish (*adj.*) 不熟练的；amateurism (*n.*) 业余活动；业余性质

【近】 layperson

appropriate [əˈprəupriət]

【释】 ① *adj.* 适当的，合适的

【例】 Most speakers of English will，during *appropriate* situations，select and use all three types of expressions.

【衍】 inappropriate (*adj.*)；appropriately (*adv.*)

【近】 apt，apposite，proper，suitable

【释】 ② *v.* 挪用，盗用

【例】 … *appropriate* public funds for one's own private use.

aspiring [əˈspaiəriŋ]

【释】 *adj.* 有大志的，抱负不凡的；热望的

【例】 He was once an *aspiring* writer.

【衍】 aspire (*v.*) 热望，渴望；有志于，立志要；aspiration (*n.*) 愿望，抱负；aspirant (*n. & adj.*) 有志愿(的)，抱负不凡(的)，努力向上(的)

【近】 ambitious

avenue [ˈævinjuː]

【释】 *n.* (南北向)街道(东西向称 street)

【例】	The little art gallery run by Alfred Stieglitz at 291 Fifth *Avenue*, New York, was never merely a business operation.
【近】	street, road, boulevard

barrier ['bæriə]

【释】 *n.* 栅栏，障碍；壁垒

【例】 More specifically, they learned a good deal about river drainages and mountain *barriers*.

【近】 fence, wall, blockade, obstacle

bind [baind]

【释】 *v.* 捆，扎，绑；束

【例】 A molecular biologist would "explain" these events in terms of forces that *bind* various molecules together and cause various parts of these molecules to be attracted to one another.

【衍】 binder (*n.*) 装订工；包扎者；bindery (*n.*) 装订所，装订厂

【近】 attach, connect, combine, tie

botanical [bə'tænikəl]

【释】 *adj.* 植物(学)的

【例】 Yet everyone comes unconsciously on an amazing amount of *botanical* knowledge.

【衍】 botany (*n.*) 植物学；botanist (*n.*) 植物学家

bugle ['bju:gl]

【释】 *n.* 军号，喇叭；(狩猎时用的)号，角，笛

【例】 There are cornets *bugles*, flugelhorns, and a number of others that are all similar to the trumpet in the way they are made and played.

【衍】 bugler (*n.*) 喇叭手

【近】 trumpet

campus ['kæmpəs]

【释】 *n.* 校园

【例】 According to one report, squirrels destroyed tens of thousands of fallen acorns from an oak stand on the University of Indiana *campus*.

casual ['kæʒjuəl]

【释】 *adj.* 随便的，非正式的

【例】	Naturalists and *casual* observers alike have been struck by the special relationship between squirrels and acorns（the seeds of oak trees）.
【衍】	casually（*adv.*）
【近】	informal

chamber ['tʃeimbə]

【释】	*n.* 穴；腔；室；箱
【例】	Besides living quarters，each pueblo included one or more kivas—circular underground *chambers* faced with stone.
【近】	cavity, cave, crater

civic ['sivik]

【释】	*adj.* 城市的；市民的
【例】	They have no use for anyone who wishes something better for them；they oppose *civic* reform cultural and educational projects.
【近】	municipal, public, civil

colony ['kɔləni]

【释】	① *n.* 殖民地
【例】	Another was Australia，which became a penal *colony* now that America was no longer available for prisoners and debtors.
【衍】	colonial（*adj.*）；colonist（*n.*）；colonize（*v.*）；colonization（*n.*）
【释】	② *n.* 【动】（鸟、蚁、蜜蜂等的）集团，群
【例】	Eventually there may be several hundred，or even a thousand，bees in the *colony*.

conceal [kən'si:l]

【释】	*v.* 隐藏，隐蔽
【例】	By 1800 a complete internal iron skeleton for buildings had been developed in industrial architecture replacing traditional timber beams，but it generally remained *concealed*.
【近】	hide, cover

conquer ['kɔŋkə]

【释】	*v.* 征服；攻克
【例】	The cohesive political and social organization of the Anasazi made it almost impossible for other groups to *conquer* them.

Unit 21

| | 【近】 | beat, defeat, surmount |

convection ['kən'vekʃən]

【释】 *n.* 对流，上升气流

【例】 Usually, these swarms take off from the ground against the wind, but, once airborne, they turn and fly with it, warm *convection* currents help to lift them, often to great heights.

【衍】 convective (*adj.*)

counterpart ['kauntəpɑːt]

【释】 *n.* 相对物，对应物

【例】 These writers, like most of their male *counterparts*, were amateur historians.

【近】 equivalent

curious ['kjuəriəs]

【释】 *adj.* 稀奇的，古怪的；好奇的

【例】 There is a *curious* thing about her writings in this period.

【衍】 curiously (*adv.*); curiosity (*n.*) 古玩；好奇心

defeat [di'fiːt]

【释】 ① *v.* 打败(敌人)；使受挫折

【例】 His initial expedition was *defeated* by the Spanish.

【近】 beat, crush, rout

【释】 ② *n.* 战败，失败；挫折

【例】 It represented trouble and *defeat*.

【近】 loss, setback

destructive [di'strʌktiv]

【释】 *adj.* 破坏性的；有害的

【例】 The *destructive* power of fungi is impressive.

【衍】 destruct (*v. & n.*) 破坏；自毁；destruction (*n.*) 破坏；灭亡

【近】 devastating, detrimental, negative

discharge [dis'tʃɑːdʒ]

【释】 *v.* 放出(水等)；释放；【电】放(电)

【例】 If too much volcanic heat is *discharged*, the crater's ice pack will melt away entirely and the caves will vanish along with the snows of yesteryear.

【衍】 charge (*v.*) 充(电)；使饱和；使充满

【近】 release

diverse [dai'vəːs]

【释】 *adj*. 不同的；形形色色的，多种多样的

【例】 A few species even include all three of these *diverse* forms of life.

【衍】 diversity（*n*.）；diversify（*v*.）；diversification（*n*.）

【近】 varied, various, assorted, miscellaneous

dye [dai]

【释】 *n*. 染料，染液　*v*. 染，染上，把…染色

【例】 In the subtractive process, colors are produced when *dye* absorbs some wavelengths and so passes on only part of the spectrum.

【近】 tint, pigment

elusive [i'ljuːsiv]

【释】 *adj*. 无从捉摸的，难懂的；容易忘记的

【例】 Social scientist were also using new terms to describe the *elusive*, vaguely defined areas reaching out from what used to be simple "towns" and "cities".

【衍】 elusively（*adv*.）；elusiveness（*n*.）；elusion（*n*.）逃避，回避

【近】 subtle, intangible, vague, obscure

enroll ['inrəul]

【释】 *v*. 把…记入名簿

【例】 Many of those who now *enrolled* were experiencing transition not only from a small town or rural area to an urban environment, but also from adolescence to young adulthood.

【衍】 enrollment（*n*.）

【近】 register, sign up

estimate ['estimeit]

【释】 *v*. 估计，估算

【例】 It is *estimated* that red fire ants employ at least twelve different chemical signals.

【衍】 estimation（*n*.）

【近】 guesstimate, approximate

explode [ik'spləud]

【释】 *v*. 使爆炸

【例】 Each fall，billions of green leaves *explode* into a mosaic of reds，yellows and browns.

【衍】 explosion（*n.*）；explosive（*adj.*）；explosively（*adv.*）

【近】 detonate，blast，blow

fame ［feim］

【释】 *n.* 名声，声望

【例】 Ellington soon received international *fame* for his talent as a band leader，composer，and arranger.

【衍】 famous（*adj.*）

【近】 celebrity，eminence，prominence

flame ［fleim］

【释】 *n.* 火焰；光辉，光芒　*v.* 燃烧

【例】 Jupiter might have attained internal temperatures as high as the ignition point for nuclear reactions，and it would have *flamed* as a star in its own fight.

【近】 fire，blaze

folk ［fəuk］

【释】 *adj.* 民间的　*n.* (folks)人们

【例】 What we today call America *folk* art was，indeed，art of，by，and for ordinary，everyday "*folks*" who，with increasing prosperity and leisure，created a market for art of all kinds，and especially for portraits.

frustrate ［frʌ'streit］

【释】 *v.* 挫败(敌人)；破坏(计划等)，阻挠

【例】 Institutions that are too brittle can *frustrate* policy-making，especially in periods of rapid social or political change.

【衍】 frustrated（*adj.*）；frustration（*n.*）；frustratingly（*adv.*）

【近】 prevent，hinder，obstruct

genius ［'dʒiːnjəs］

【释】 *n.* 天才，天资，天赋，天分

【例】 In later years trail，error，and *genius* founded the techniques and the principles of the movement.

【近】 intellect，brilliance，intelligence

glue ［gluː］

【释】 *n.* 胶，胶水，各种胶粘物

【例】	Some nails—forged by hand—were used but no screws or *glue*.
【衍】	gluey (*adj.*)
【近】	paste，stick，fasten，attach
handle	['hændl]
【释】	*v.* 处理；讨论(问题)
【例】	When a food object or nest intruder is too large for one individual to *handle*，nestmates can be quickly assembled by alarm or recruitment signals.
【近】	control，deal with
herald	['herəld]
【释】	*v.* 预示，预报
【例】	Their works have been *heralded* as one of the basic symbols of Canadian culture.
hostile	['hɔstəl]
【释】	*adj.* 敌人的，敌方的，怀有敌意的，敌对的
【例】	The deep-ocean bottom is a *hostile* environment to humans.
【衍】	hostility (*n.*)
【近】	unfriendly，antagonistic，intimidating
illustrate	['iləstreit]
【释】	*v.* (用例子、图解等)说明；举例证明
【例】	Of their major discovery，Brown said lightly that it simply *illustrated* "how unpredictable consequences can come from rather modest beginnings."
【衍】	illustration (*n.*)；illustrator (*n.*)
【近】	exemplify，demonstrate
inanimate	[in'ænimət]
【释】	*adj.* 无生气的，没精打采的
【例】	Too often，the interest of children in the natural world is diverted by the example of their elders into a concentration on the *inanimate* objects that money will buy.
【近】	dull，lethargic，monotonous
inhibit	[in'hibit]
【释】	*v.* 抑制，阻止
【例】	If the physical barriers of the plant are breached，then preformed chemicals may *inhibit* or kill the intruder.

Unit 21

morphology [mɔːˈfɔlədʒi]

【释】 *n.* 形态学；组织；形态

【例】 Still other evidence comes from cranial *morphology*: physical differences between the right and left sides of the interior of the skull indicate subtle physical differences between the two sides of the brain.

【衍】 morphological（*adj.*）形态学（上）的；morphologist（*n.*）形态学家

navigate [ˈnævigeit]

【释】 *v.* 航行；驾驶(船舶、飞机等)；导航

【例】 Many conditions such as flying at night and landing in dense fog require a pilot to use radar，which is an alternative way of *navigating*.

【衍】 navigation（*n.*）；navigational（*adj.*）；navigable（*adj.*）可航行的；navy（*n.*）海军

【近】 steer，find the way，pilot

normal [ˈnɔːməl]

【释】 *adj.* 正常的，平常的，普通的；正规的，标准的，额定的

【例】 Desert mammals also depart from the *normal* mammalian practice of maintaining a constant body temperature.

【衍】 norm（*n.*）规范，标准，定额；normally（*adv.*）正常情况下，通常

【近】 usual，standard，ordinary

occasion [əuˈkeiʒən]

【释】 ① *n.*（庆祝等的特殊）场合；（重大）时节，时刻

【例】 A Sioux baby was named soon after birth—usually by a medicine man or a paternal relative—and the entire village participated in the *occasion*.

【近】 time，instance，event

【释】 ② *n.* 机会；（适当的）时机

【例】 On the rare *occasion* when a fine piece of sculpture was desired，Americans turned to foreign sculptors.

【衍】 occasional（*adj.*）临时的，偶尔的；特殊场合的；occasionally（*adv.*）

【近】	chance, possibility, opportunity
orchestra	[ˈɔːkistrə]
【释】	*n.* 管弦乐；管弦乐队
【例】	Its importance as an instrument in its own right dates from the early 1600's, when it first became standard in Italian opera *orchestras*.
【衍】	orchestral (*adj.*); orchestrally (*adv.*)
【近】	pop group, ensemble, rock band
overlap	[ˈəuvəˈlæp]
【释】	*v. & n.* 重复；部分一致；重叠；复合
【例】	The two court systems are to some extent *overlapping*, in that certain kinds of disputes (such as a clam that a state law is in violation of the Constitution) may be initiated in either system.
【近】	partly cover, have common characteristics, coincide
particle	[ˈpɑːtikl]
【释】	*n.* 颗粒，微粒
【例】	The mineral particles found in soil range in size from microscopic clay *particles* to large boulders.
【近】	granule, pellet, particulate
peninsula	[piˈninsjulə]
【释】	*n.* 半岛
【例】	One of the world's largest *peninsulas*, it is partly share with Canada on the east.
【衍】	peninsular (*adj.*)
photograph	[ˈfəutəɡrɑːf]
【释】	*v.* 为…照相，为…摄影
【例】	She also *photographs* away from her studio at various architectural sites.
【衍】	photography (*n.*); photographic (*adj.*); photographer (*n.*)
【近】	shoot, take pictures of
plastic	[ˈplæstik]
【释】	*n.* 塑料；塑料制品
【例】	The first synthetic *plastic* was a thermosetting resin called ebonite, patented in 1843.

Unit 21

【例】	Nevertheless, many local residents want to *retain* the existing character of the area.
【衍】	retainer (*n.*); retentive (*adj.*)
【近】	preserve, maintain, save
ring	[riŋ]
【释】	① *n.* 环，环形物
【例】	Objects in the universe show a variety of shapes: round planets (some with *rings*), tailed comets, wispy cosmic gas and dust clouds, and so on.
【衍】	ringed (*adj.*)
【近】	circle, loop, hoop
【释】	② *v.* 围住，包围
【例】	*Ringing* the plaza were circular, ceremonial rooms, called kivas.
【衍】	ringed (*adj.*)
【近】	encircle, surround, enclose
rumor	['ru:mə]
【释】	*n. & v.* 谣言，传闻，流言；[常用被动语态]谣传
【例】	Men gossiped and exchanged *rumors* while whittling bits of wood or while squatting in the shade to get acquainted with strangers.
【衍】	rumormonger (*n.*) 造谣者
【近】	chitchat, gossip, anecdote
scatter	['skætə]
【释】	*v. & n.* 散布；散播
【例】	When you ask them to work out a sum they take a piece of paper, cover it with rows of A's, B's, and X's and Y's, *scatter* a mess of flyspecks over them, and give you an answer that's all wrong.
【衍】	scatteration (*n.*); scattered (*adj.*); scattering (*adj. & n.*)
【近】	disperse, distribute, spread out
secret	['si:krit]
【释】	*n. & adj.* 秘密(的)；机密(的)；秘诀(的)
【例】	However, glassmakers guarded their *secrets* so carefully that no one wrote about glass fiber production until the early seventeenth century.

【衍】	secretary（*n.*）秘书，书记，干事
【近】	confidential，undisclosed，clandestine
severe	［si'viə］
【释】	*adj.* 严重的，严峻的；剧烈的
【例】	Skyscrapers put a *severe* strain on a city's sanitation facilities.
【衍】	severely（*adv.*）；severity（*n.*）
【近】	harsh，rigorous，terrible
shrimp	［ʃrimp］
【释】	*n.* 小虾；河虾
【例】	A pound of these crustaceans contains about 460 calories—about the same as *shrimp* or lobster，to which they are related.
【衍】	shrimplike（*adj.*）
slice	［slais］
【释】	*v.* 把…切成薄片　*n.* 薄片，一片；一部分
【例】	After they picked it，they *sliced* it，dried it，and strung the slices before they stored them.
【衍】	sliceable（*adj.*）；slicer（*n.*）切片机
【近】	piece，segment，divide
solution	［sə'luːʃən］
【释】	① *n.* 解决，解释，解法
【例】	These possible *solutions* are called hypotheses.
【衍】	soluble（*adj.*）能解释的；能解决的
【近】	answer，explanation，way out
【释】	② *n.* 溶解；溶液，溶体，溶剂
【例】	Often a wet clay *solution*，known as a slip，was applied to the smooth surface.
【衍】	soluble（*adj.*）可溶的，易溶解的；solute（*n.*）溶质，溶解物
【近】	mixture，emulsion，liquid
spider	［'spaidə］
【释】	*n.* 蜘蛛
【例】	His fibers were short and fragile，but he predicted that spun glass fibers as thin as *spider* silk would be flexible and could be woven into fabric.

Unit 21

【近】	the stage
ticket	['tikit]
【释】	*n.* 票，入场券，车票
【例】	Now a stage full of happy and earnest oratorio singers must represent considerable potential *ticket* sales，and if this is true，it does not make much difference what work the singers select to perform.
【近】	voucher，permit，receipt
touch	[tʌtʃ]
【释】	① *v.* 触，碰，摸
【例】	In ancient times wealth was measured and exchanged tangibly，in things that could be *touched* food，tools，and precious metals and stones.
【衍】	touchable（*adj.*）
【近】	handle，contact，feel
【释】	② *v.* 使开始，激起，触发
【例】	Twain drew on his own experiences and used dialect and common speech instead of literary language，*touching* off a major change in American prose style.
【衍】	touchy（*adj.*）易怒的，暴躁的
【近】	stir
【释】	③ *n.* 修饰，添画，润色
【例】	Therefore the chorus can make a public appearance after long，leisurely preparation and add on at the last moment the final professional *touches*.
transmission	[trænz'miʃən]
【释】	*n.* 传递；传达；传送；发射；播送；通话；传输
【例】	The field of television can be divided into two categories determined by its means of *transmission*.
【衍】	transmissive（*adj.*）；transmit（*v.*）；transmitter（*n.*）
【近】	broadcast，diffusion，spread
tropic	['trɔpik]
【释】	*n.* 热带(地区)
【例】	The additional sea ice floating toward the *tropics* would increase.
【衍】	tropical（*adj.*）；tropic（*adj.*）

unaided	[ˌʌnˈeidid]
【释】	*adj.* 未受(无人)帮助的
【例】	To answer these questions, one needs to see more detail than is visible to the *unaided* human eye (肉眼).
【近】	independent
utilitarian	[ˌjuːtiliˈtɛəriən]
【释】	*adj.* 功利的；实用主义的
【例】	Beneath this glamorous but *utilitarian* garb, the cowhand was dressed like any other labor.
【衍】	utilitarianism (*n.*)
【近】	practical, functional
vent	[vent]
【释】	*n.* 裂口；通风孔
【例】	For the same reason, tornado cellars must have an air *vent*.
【近】	outlet, aperture
vision	[ˈviʒən]
【释】	① *n.* 视力，视觉
【例】	The midbrain handles *vision*, the hindbrain balance.
【释】	② *n.* [不用冠词] 先见，洞察
【例】	Edward Bellamy's utopian novel, *Looking Backward*, sold over a million copies in 1888, giving rise to the growth of organizations dedicated to the realization of Bellamy's *vision* of the future.
【衍】	visional (*adj.*) 幻想的
【近】	foresight, imagination, prediction
wax	[wæks]
【释】	*n.* (蜂)蜡；蜡状物
【例】	They are made from a variety of materials, such as *wax* and glass, so skillfully that they can scarcely be distinguished from natural flowers.
【衍】	waxy (*adj.*)
wit	[wit]
【释】	*n.* 智慧；理智；机智的人
【例】	She was direct, impulsive, original, and the droll *wit* who said unconventional things which others thought but dared not speak, and said them incomparably well.
【近】	intelligence

Unit 21

附录 1

朗文定义词汇表

* This list was extracted from Longman Dictionary (1998).

Word Class Labels

[A = Adjective]   [Av = Adverb]   [C = Conjunction]
[D = Determiner]   [P = Preposition]   [Pd = Predeterminer]
[Pn = Pronoun]   [N = Noun]   [V = Verb]

Defining Vocabulary

a	active [A]	advertisement	airport
ability	activity	advice	alcohol
about	actor	advise	alike
above [AvP]	actress	affair	alive
abroad	actual	afford	all [AvDPdPn]
absence	add	afraid	allow
absent [A]	addition	after [AvCP]	almost
accept	address	afternoon	alone
acceptable	adjective	afterwards	along
accident	admiration	againagainst	aloud
accordance	admire	age [N]	alphabet
according	admit	ago	already
according to	admittance	agree	also
account	adult	agreement	although
ache	advance [NV]	ahead	altogether [Av]
acid	advantage	aim	always
across	adventure [N]	air [N]	among
act	adverb	aircraft	amount [N]
action [N]	advertise	airforce	amuse

amusement	around	bag [N]	bell
amusing [A]	arrange	bake	belong
an	arrangement	balance	below [AvP]
ancient [A]	arrival	ball [N]	belt [N]
and	arrive	banana	bend
anger [N]	art	band [N]	beneath
angle [N]	article	bank [N]	berry
angry	artificial	bar [NV]	beside
animal	as	bare [A]	besides
ankle	ash	barrel	best [AAvN]
annoy	ashamed	base [NV]	better [AAv]
annoyance	aside [Av]	basket	between
another	ask	bath [N]	beyond [AvP]
answer	asleep	bathe [V]	bicycle [N]
ant	association	battle [N]	big [A]
anxiety	at	be	bill [N]
anxious	atom	beak	bind [V]
any	attack	beam [N]	bird
anyhow	attempt	bean	birth
anyone	attend	bear	birthday
anything	attendance	beard [N]	bit
anywhere	attention	beat [NV]	bite
apart	attract	beautiful	bitter [A]
apparatus	attractive	beauty	black [AN]
appear	aunt	because	blade
appearance	autumn	become	blame
apple	average [AN]	bed [N]	bleed
appoint	avoid	bee	bless
approval	awake [A]	beer	blind
approve	away [Av]	before	block
arch [N]	awkward	beg	blood [N]
area	baby	begin	blow
argue	back [AAvN]	beginning	blue
argument	background	behave	board [N]
arm	backward [Av]	behavior	boat [N]
armor [N]	backwards [Av]	behind [AvP]	body
arms	bacteria	belief	boil [V]
army	bad [A]	believe	bomb

diamond	drawer	elect [V]	everyone
dictionary	dream	election	everything
die [V]	dress [NV]	electric	everywhere
difference	drink	electricity	evil
different	drive [V]	elephant	exact [A]
difficult	drop	else	examination
difficulty	drown	employ [V]	examine
dig [V]	drug [N]	employer	example
dinner	drum [N]	employment	excellent
dip [V]	drunk	empty [AV]	except [CP]
direct	dry	enclose	exchange
direction	duck [N]	enclosure	excite
dirt	dull [A]	encourage	excited
dirty [A]	during	encouragement	exciting
disappoint	dust [N]	end	excuse
discourage	duty	enemy	exercise
discouragement	each	engine	exist
discover	eager	engineer [N]	existence
discovery	ear	English	expect
dish [N]	early	enjoy	expensive
dismiss	earn	enjoyment	experience
distance [N]	earth [N]	enough	explain
distant	east	enter	explanation
ditch [N]	eastern	entertain	explode
divide [V]	easy	entertainment	explosion
division	eat	entrance [N]	explosive
do [V]	edge [N]	envelope	express [V]
doctor [N]	educate	equal [ANV]	expression
dog [N]	education	equality	extreme
dollar	effect [N]	escape	eye
door	effective	especially	eyelid
doorway	effort	establish	face
dot [N]	egg [N]	establishment	fact
double [AAvPdV]	eight	even [AAv]	factory
doubt	eighth	evening	fail [V]
down [AAvP]	either	event	failure
drag [V]	elastic	ever	faint [AV]
draw [V]	elbow [N]	every	fair [A]

fairy	fifth	football	fulfill full [A]
faith	fight	footpath	fun
faithful [A]	figure [N]	footstep	funeral
fall	fill [V]	for [P]	funny
false [A]	film	forbid	fur [N]
fame	find [V]	force	furnish
familiar [A]	fine [A]	forehead	furniture
family	finger [N]	foreign	further [AAv]
famous	finish	foreigner	future
fancy [A]	fire	forest	gain [V]
far	fireplace	forget	game [N]
farm	firm [AN]	forgive	garage [N]
farmer	first [AvD]	fork [N]	garden
farmyard	fish	form	garment
fashion [N]	fisherman	formal	gas [N]
fashionable	fit [AV]	former	gasoline [petrol]
fast [AAv]	five	formerly	gate [N]
fasten	fix [V]	fort	gather [V]
fat	flag [N]	fortunate	general
fate	flame	fortune	generous
father [N]	flash [NV]	forward [Av]	gentle
fault	flat	forwards [Av]	gentleman
favor [N]	flesh	four	get
favorable	flight	fourth	gift
favorite [A]	float [V]	fox [N]	girl
fear	flood	frame [N]	give [V]
feather [N]	floor [N]	free	glad
feed [V]	flour	freedom	glass [AN]
feel [V]	flow	freeze [V]	glory [N]
feeling	flower [N]	frequent [A]	glue
feelings	fly [NV]	fresh	go [V]
fellow [N]	fold	friend	goat
female	follow	friendly	god
fence [N]	fond	frighten	God
fever	food	frightening	gold
few	fool [N]	from	golden
field [N]	foolish	front [AN]	good
fierce	foot [N]	fruit [N]	good-bye

machinery	melt	moon [N]	need
mad	member	moral [A]	needle [N]
magazine	memory	morals	neighbor
magic	mend [V]	more	neighborhood
magician	mention [V]	morning	neither
mail	merry	most	nerve [N]
main [A]	message	mother [N]	nervous
make [V]	messenger	motor [AN]	nest [N]
male	metal [N]	mountain	net [N]
man [N]	meter	mouse	network [N]
manage	method	mouth [N]	never
manager	metric	move [V]	new
manner	microscope	much	news
many	middle [AN]	mud	newspaper
map [N]	might [V]	multiply	next [AAv]
march	mile	murder	nice
mark	military [A]	muscle [N]	night
market [N]	milk	music	nine
marriage	million	musician	ninth
marry	millionth	must [V]	no [AvD]
mass [N]	mind	my	no one
master [N]	mine [NPn]	myself	noble [A]
mat	mineral	mysterious	nobleman
match	minister [N]	mystery	noise [N]
material	minute [N]	nail	none [Pn]
matter	mirror [N]	name	nonsense
may [V]	miss [V]	narrow [A]	nor
me	mist [N]	nasty	north
meal	mistake	nation	northern
mean [V]	mix [V]	national [A]	nose [N]
meaning [N]	mixture	nature	not
means	model [N]	naval	nothing
measure	modern [A]	navy	notice
meat	moment	near [AAvP]	noun
medical [A]	money	nearly	now
medicine	monkey [N]	neat	nowhere
meet [V]	month	necessary	number [N]
meeting	monthly [AAv]	neck	nurse

nut	or	park	photography
nylon	orange	parliament	phrase [N]
o'clock	order	part	physical
obedience	ordinary	participle	piano [N]
obedient	organ	particular [A]	pick [V]
obey	organization	partner [N]	picture [N]
object [N]	origin	party [N]	piece [N]
obtain	other	pass [V]	pig [N]
occasion [N]	otherwise	passage	pile
ocean	ought	passenger	pilot
odd	our	past	pin
of	ours	pastry	pink [AN]
off [AvP]	ourselves	path	pipe [N]
offend	out [AAv]	patience	pity
offense	outdoor	patient [A]	place
offensive [A]	outdoors	pattern [N]	plain [AN]
offer	outer	pause	plan
office	outside	pay	plane [N]
officer	over [AvP]	payment	plant
official	owe	peace	plastic
often	owing to	peaceful	plate [N]
oil	own [DPnV]	pen [N]	play
old	oxygen	pence	pleasant
old-fashioned	pack [V]	pencil [N]	please
on [AvP]	packet	people [N]	pleased
once [Av]	page [N]	pepper [N]	pleasure [N]
one	pain [N]	per	plenty [Pn]
oneself	painful	perfect [A]	plural
onion	paint	perform	pocket [N]
only	painting	perhaps	poem
open [AV]	pair [N]	period [N]	poet
operate	palace	permission	poetry
operation	pale [A]	permit [V]	point
opinion	pan [N]	person	pointed
opponent	paper [N]	personal	poison
oppose	parallel [AN]	persuade	poisonous
opposite	parcel [N]	pet [N]	pole [N]
opposition	parent [N]	photograph	police [N]

size [N]	song	stand [V]	struggle
skill	soon	standard	student
skillful	sore [A]	star [N]	study
skin [N]	sorrow [N]	start	stupid
skirt [N]	sorry	state	style [N]
sky [N]	sort [N]	station [N]	subject [N]
slave [N]	soul	stay	substance
sleep	sound [NV]	steady [A]	subtract
slide [V]	soup	steal [V]	succeed
slight [A]	sour [A]	steam [N]	success
slip [V]	south	steel [N]	successful
slippery	southern	steep [A]	such
slope	space [N]	stem [N]	suck [V]
slow	spacecraft	step	sudden
small	spade	stick	suffer
smell	speak	sticky	sugar [N]
smile	spear [N]	stiff [A]	suggest
smoke	special [A]	still [AAv]	suit
smooth [A]	specialist	sting	suitable
snake [N]	speech	stitch	sum [N]
snow	speed [N]	stomach [N]	summer [N]
so	spell [V]	stone [N]	sun [N]
soap [N]	spend	stop	supper
social [A]	spin [V]	store	supply [NV]
society	spirit [N]	storm [N]	support
sock [N]	spite [N]	story	suppose
soft	splendid	straight [AAv]	sure [A]
soil [N]	split [V]	strange	surface [N]
soldier [N]	spoil [V]	stranger	surprise
solemn	spoon [N]	stream [N]	surround [V]
solid	sport [N]	street	swallow [V]
some [DPn]	spot [N]	strength	swear
somehow	spread [V]	stretch	sweep [V]
someone	spring	strike [V]	sweet
something	square [AN]	string [N]	swell [V]
sometimes	stage [N]	stroke [N]	swim
somewhere	stair	strong	swing
son	stamp	structure [N]	sword

sympathetic	them	timetable [N]	trick [NV]
sympathy	themselves	tin	trip [N]
system	then [Av]	tire [tyre] [N]	tropical
table [N]	there	tire [V]	trouble
tail [N]	therefore	title [N]	trousers
take [V]	these	to	true [A]
talk	they	tobacco	trunk
tall	thick [A]	today	trust
taste	thief	toe [N]	truth
tax	thin [A]	together	try [V]
taxi [N]	thing	tomorrow	tube
tea	think [V]	tongue	tune [N]
teach	third	tonight	turn
team [N]	thirst [N]	too	twice
tear [V]	thirsty	tool [N]	twist
tear [N]	this [DPn]	tooth	type [N]
telephone	thorough	top [AN]	typical
television	those	total [AN]	ugly
tell	though	touch	uncle
temper [N]	thought	tour	under [P]
temperature	thousand	tourist	understand
temple	thousandth	towards	undo
tend	thread [N]	tower [N]	uniform [N]
tendency	threat	town	union
tender [A]	threaten	toy [N]	unit
tennis	three	track	unite
tense [N]	throat	trade [N]	universal
tent	through [AvP]	traffic [N]	universe
terrible	throw	train	university
terror	thumb [N]	translate	until
test	thunder	transparent	up [AAvP]
than	thus	trap	upper [A]
thank	ticket [N]	travel	upright [AAv]
that [CDPn]	tidy [AV]	treat [V]	upset [V]
the	tie	treatment	upside down
theater	tiger	tree	upstairs [AAv]
their	tight [A]	tremble [V]	urge
theirs	time [N]	tribe	urgent

date	n. 海枣
deal	n. (松等的)木板；木材，木料 adj. 松木的
dear	adj. 昂贵的，高价的
default	n. & v. 不履行；违约；拖欠
dock	n. 草本植物 vt. 剥夺，扣去…的应得工资
down	n. [美国] 沙丘；(蒲公英等的)冠毛；鸭绒，绒毛；(鸟的)绒羽；柔毛；汗毛，软毛，毳毛
draw	vt. 提取(钱款)；使打成平局
drill	vt. (用钢钻)钻(孔)；在…上(用钢钻)钻孔
drive	n. 冲力，动力；干劲；努力；魄力；精力
eat	vt. 蛀；腐蚀；消磨
exploit	n. 功绩，功劳，勋绩
exponent	n. 典型，样品
factor	n. 因子，因数；倍；乘数；商
fair	n. [英国] 定期集市，庙会；商品展览会，展销会，商品交易会
fashion	vt. 形成，铸成，造，作(into/to)
felt	n. 毛毡；毛布；毡制品；油毛毡
figure	n. 1. (著名)人物；2. 雕像；画像
fine	adj. 细小的
functional	adj. 从使用的观点设计[构成]的
game	n. [集合词] 猎物，野味；(鹑等的)群；野外游戏 [游猎、鹰狩等]
give	n. 弹性
hide	n. 兽皮
hit	vt. 偶然碰见，遭遇
hold	n. (货船)船舱
humor	n. (眼球的)玻璃状液体；(旧时生理学所说动物的)体液；(植物的)汁液
import	n. 意义，含义
inviting	adj. 引人注目的，吸引人的
involved	adj. 复杂的，难缠的
issue	n. & v. 流出，(血、水等的)涌出；【法律】子孙，子女
jar	vt. 1. 给人烦躁[痛苦]的感觉，刺激(on)；2. (发出刺耳声地)撞击(on/upon/against)；3. 震动，震荡(不和谐地)反响，回荡；4. (意见、行动等)不一致，冲突，激烈争吵(with)
late	adj. 已去世的，已故的

lay	*adj.* 1. 一般信徒的，俗人的，凡俗的（*opp.* clerical）；2. 无经验的，外行(人)的（*opp.* professional）
lead	*n.* 铅
leave	*n.* 1. 许可，同意；2. 告假，休假；假期
letter	*n.* 出租人；letters 证书，许可证
lot	*n.* 土地
make	*n.* 构造
measure	*n.* 准绳；韵律 a measure of＝is determined by …的体现：The rate at which a molecule of water passes through the cycle is not random but is a measure of the relative size of the various reservoirs. [9810-p01-L8]
meet	*n.* 比赛
minute	*adj.* 微小的，细小的
novel	*adj.* 新的，新颖的；新奇的，珍奇的，异常的
observe	*vi.* 陈述意见，评述，简评(on；upon)：strange to observe 讲起来虽奇怪。I have very little to observe on what has been said. 关于刚才所听到的我没什么话好讲。 *vt.* 保持；遵守：observe silence 保持沉默；observe a rule 遵守规则
organ	*n.* 【音】(教堂用的)管风琴(＝〔美国〕pipe organ)；(足踏)风琴；手摇风琴；口琴；机构；机关；机关报〔杂志〕；喉舌；报刊
outstanding	*adj.* 未付的，未清的；未解决的；未完成的
partial	*adj.* 【植物；植物学】后生的，再生的
period	*n.* 【音】乐段
pile	*n.* 1. 高大建筑；2. 痔疮；3. 软毛，绒毛，毛茸；(布、绒的)软面
pitch	*n.* 沥青；含有沥青的物质；松脂，树脂
pocket	*v.* & *n.* 【赛跑】自前后妨碍(跑的人)，四面挤轧
pool	*n.* 【医学】淤血
pound	*n.* 兽栏 *v.* (连续)猛击；乱敲；砰砰砰地乱弹(钢琴等)，乱奏(曲子)
preserve	*n.* 1. 禁猎区；2. 蜜饯
produce	*n.* 物产；产品，农产品；制品，作品
project	*v.* 使突出，使凸出；伸出：The upper storey projects over the street. 二楼伸出街上。
promise	*n.* (前途有)希望；(有)指望
pronounced	*adj.* 决然的，断然的，强硬的；明白的，显著的

附录2

provided	*conj.* 倘若…，只要，在…条件下
quality	*adj.* 1. 优质的，高级的；2. 上流社会的
quarters	*n.* 寓所，住处；【军事】营房，驻地，营盘，宿舍；岗位
rate	*v.* 1. 被估价；被评价：The ship rates as a ship of the line. 这条船列入战舰级。2. 申斥，斥责，骂
rear	*v.* 饲养（家畜等）；抚养，教养（孩子）；栽培（作物）
relief	*n.* 【雕刻】凸起；浮起，浮雕，浮雕品；【绘画】人物凸现，轮廓鲜明
rent	*v.* （rend 的过去分词）撕碎　*n.* 【地质学；地理学】断口；（意见等的）分裂，分歧；（关系等的）破裂
retire	*vi.* 就寝，去睡觉
run	*n.* 丝袜上的洞
save	*prep.* 除了
say	*n.* 发言权
scale	*n.* 阶梯，梯子；天平；鳞；锅垢，锈　*v.* 用梯子爬上；爬越，攀登；剥鳞/垢、锈
school	*n.* （鱼、鲸等水族动物的）群；队：a school of dolphins 一群海豚
score	*n.* 【音】总谱，乐谱；（电影歌舞等的）配乐
scores	*n.* 许多：scores of fossil remains
screen	*n.* 筛子
season	*vt.* 1. 使熟练；使（习）惯；2. 风干；晒干（木材）；晾干，对…进行干燥处理；使陈化；3. 使适应（气候等）；4. 给…加味［调味］；5. 给…增加趣味；6. 缓和，调和
secretary	*n.* 1. （上部附有书橱的）写字台；2. 书写体大写铅字
secure	*vt.* 搞到，把…拿到手；得到，获得
serve	*vi.* 【网球】开球；发球
shower	*n.* ［美］（为新娘等举行的）送礼会；（婚前、产后的）聚会
shrink	*n.* 精神病医师
smooth	*v.* 排除，解决（困难等）；调解
sole	*n.* 脚底，鞋底
sound	*vi.* 1. 测水深；探测（上层空气）；2. 试探（别人的意见）；调查（可能性）；3. （鱼或鲸鱼）突然潜入海底
sow	*n.* 大母猪
spell	*vt.* 1. 招致，带来；2. 轮班，换班；替班　*n.* 1. 符咒，咒语；2. 吸引力，诱惑力，魔力，魅力
spoke	*n.* （车轮的）辐条
spot	*vt.* 认出，发现，定位

spring	*n*. 弹簧；泉水　　*v*. 扭伤(腿)
staff	*n*.【音】五线谱
stand	*v*. 忍受　*n*. 床头柜
standard	*n*. 直立支柱；灯台；烛台，电杆，垂直的水管(电管)
start	*v*. (船材、钉等)松动，翘曲，歪，脱落
stem	*v*. 起源于，起因于，（由…）发生，来自（from out of）：Correct decisions stem from correct judgments. 正确的决心来自于正确的判断。
still	*n*. 蒸馏锅　*v*. 蒸馏
strain	*n*. 血统，家世；族，种；【生物学】品系，系；菌株；品种
stroke	*n*. 笔画
temper	*n*. (黏土的)黏度；(灰泥的)稠度
tender	*v*. 正式提出：tender one's resignation 提出辞呈
till	*n*.【地质学；地理学】冰碛土(物)　*v*. 耕种，翻耕，耕作
touch	*v*. 修饰，润色
trick	*n*. 窍门，绝技
utter	*adj*. 完全的，十足的
vessel	*n*. 船，舰；飞船
wage	*v*. 实行，进行，发动(战争等)(on against)
way	*adv*. [美口] … 得多，远为。与 above、ahead、behind、below、down、off、out、over、up 等副词、介词连用，以加强语气。way back 老早以前；way down upon the river Thames 在老远老远的泰晤士河边；way up 还在上面；好得多；way out of balance 逆差很大很大
weather	【地质学；地理学】[常用被动语态] 使风化
well	*n*. 井　*vt*. 涌出，喷出(up/out/forth)
wholesale	*adj*. 大规模的
wind	*n*. 肠气，屁　*v*. 1.(winded/winded)嗅出，察觉，嗅到猎物的气味；2.(winded/wound)吹(角笛、喇叭等)：wind a call 吹哨子(召唤)；3.(wound/wound)卷绕，缠绕；上发条

— 491 —

附录 2

TOEFL 考试
常见词组及搭配

a cluster of
（花）一团
a great deal
很多的
a minimum of
最低限度的
a number of
许多的
ability to do
有能力去做某事
according to
根据
account for
说明
act on
1. 遵行，奉行，按照…行动；2. 作用于，对…起作用［反应］，影响到
as far as is known
在已知的范围内
ask for
要（某物）
at least
至少
at one time
同时

bare of
无…的
be able to
能（做…）
be adapted to
适应（环境）
be appreciated for
因…而被赏识
be associated with
与…有关，由…联想到…，把…同…联系起来
be based on
以…作为…的根据
be capable of doing
能做…的
be composed of
由…组成
be concerned with
1. 对…关心的；2. 与…有关的
be considered to be
把（某人、某事）看作…，认为（某人、某事）如何
be credited with sth.
某事应归（功于某人）

be dedicated to
（把精力、时间等）专门用于某事（to）
be dependent on/upon
依靠，取决于
be derived from
由…而来［生出］
be destined to
被指派到…
be divided into
被分（割）为
be equal to
1. 等于（The supply is equal to the demand. 供求相等。Twice two is equal to four. 两个二等于四）；2. 赶得上，敌得过；3. 胜任，能干（He is equal to anything. 他事事能干）；4. 忍耐得住（be equal to any trial 经得起任何磨炼）
be familiar with
通晓、精通某事
be famous for
因…而著名

— 492 —

be filled with
被…而填满

be force to do
被迫去做…；不得不…

be found in
在…中存在；在…中
被找到

be inclined to
易于…，有…的倾向

be involved in
陷入…；涉及到…

be known as
通称，叫做…

be known for
因…而著名

be made from
由…制成

be made of
…制的，用…制成的

be noted for
因…而知名

be obtained from
从…得到

be originated from
在…开始，发生

be related to
与…相关

be resistant to
抗…的；防…的

be rich in
富于…的

be similar to
与…类似

be subjected to
易遭…的，动不动就…
的，易患…的

be suited for
适合…的

be supposed to
料想，应该…

be typical of
代表；象征

be valuable for
因…而有价值

be viewed as
被视为…

be woven from
由…构成

belong to
应归入…类

benefit from
因…而受益

break away from
1. 逃走，脱逃，脱身；
2.（柄等）脱离，离开；
3. 背弃，叛离；4. 戒
除（积习），摆脱（陈规
等）；5.（赛马时）抢先
起步

bring about
1. 造成…；带来…，
引起…；2.（使船）回
转，掉头

by means of
用…，以…，依靠…

carry on
1. 继续；经营，处理；
开展；2. 不得体［狂
乱，幼稚］地行动

close on/upon
同意，与…一致

come of
来源于…

come from
得自…

comment on
对…注释，评论，提意见

concentrate on
把…集中在…

consist of
由…组成

consist with
与…一致

consist in
存在于…

contrary to
跟…相反［相违背］

contribute to
捐助，帮助，贡献，出
力；给…投稿

convert ... into
把…转化、转变为…

date back to
回溯至…，（年代）远在…

deal with
办理，处理；对待；
与…交涉，与…交往；
与…交易

depend on
取决于，因…而定

devote to
把…专用于

differ from
1. 和…不同，和…不
一致；2. 和…意见不同

do no harm to
对…无害

due to
起因于…，由于…

feed on
靠吃…生存；用…喂养
（鸟兽等）

focus attention on
专心于…；热衷于…

give off
放出…，发散(水蒸气等)

give up doing
放弃做某事

give way to
让步于…

grant sb. sth.
答应某人某事；授予某人某物

in addition to
除…外

in comparison with
和…比起来

in connection with
与…有关系

in danger of
有…危险

in honor of
向…表示敬意，为祝贺…，为纪念…

in nature
1. 现在存在；事实上；2. [疑问词、否定语的加重语气] 究竟，什么地方也(What in nature do you mean? 你究竟是什么意思呢?)

in/with relation to
关于…，就…而论

in response to
应…而，答…而

in spite of
不管，不顾

in that
因为…

in the future
将来，今后

interfere with
与…(利害、要求等)抵触，冲突

lead to
导致；引起

meet one's goal
达到目的

native of
土著，生在…的人

on account of
因为…，因…

play a key role
在…中起重要作用

protect ... against/from
保护…免遭…(危险)

range from ... to ...
分布，蔓延，散布

refer to
使…参看；使…注意(事实等)

regardless of
不管，不顾

rely on
依靠…，信任…

rest on
根据，以…为基础

result in
结果为…

result from
由…而造成

serve as
可作…用；作为

set about
开始；下手；着手

settle down

1. 平静下来；恢复镇静；2. 沉淀；沉；3. 定居；成家；移居；4. 定下心来；定心去做

spread out
张开，伸

strive to
力求，努力

substitute for
以…代替，用…代替

take place
发生

tend to
1. 注意，照看；2. 趋向(于)…，倾向(于)…

to a great extent
很大程度上

transform into
转变为…

use up
用完，用光

usher in
宣告…的到来

逆向分类词汇表

宇宙 universe；cosmos
宇宙的 universal（*adj.*）；cosmic（*adj.*）
宇宙尘 cosmic dust
宇宙万物 cosmic inventory

天体 celestial body
天体力学 celestial mechanics；
　　mechanical astronomy
天体演化 cosmogony

星系 galaxy
河外星系 extragalactic system
总星系 metagalaxy
银河系 Galactic System；Milky Way
太阳系 solar system

星际空间 interstellar space
星团 star cluster；stellar cluster；
　　star dust
星云 nebula
星辰 stars
小星 starlet
恒星（fixed）star
彗星 comet
流星 meteor；shooting［falling］star
行星 planet

小行星 minor planet；asteroid；planetoid
卫星 satellite
星尘 dust
类星体 quasar；quasi-stellar object
　　（QSO）
发光的 luminous

金星 Venus
木星 Jupiter
水星 Mercury
火星 Mars
土星 Saturn
地球 Earth
天王星 Uranus
海王星 Neptune
冥王星 Pluto

太阳 sun
太阳光谱 solar spectrum
太阳光线 sunray
太阳黑点（子）spot；sun spot；macula
太阳粒子 solar particle
日食 solar eclipse
日冕（solar）corona

太阳中心说 heliocentricism

地球中心说 geocentricism

月亮 moon
满月 full moon
新月 crescent
月亮由亏转盈 wax (*v.*)
月亮由盈转亏 wane (*v.*)
环形山 crater
月的，月球上的 lunar
月食 lunar eclipse

公转 revolve (*v.*)；revolution (*n.*)
自转 rotate (*v.*)；rotation (*n.*)
轨道 orbit (*n.*)；orbital (*adj.*)

黑洞 black hole
真空 vacuum

红外线 infrared ray
辐射 radiation
发射 emit (*v.*)；emission (*n.*)

地壳 crust
地幔 mantle
地核 core；earth's core
半球 semisphere；hemisphere
北半球 the Northern Hemisphere

地球基本磁场 fundamental magnetic
  field of the earth
地球自转 earth rotation
地球公转 revolution of the earth
地球引力 gravity；gravitational
  attraction
地震 earthquake；seism (*n.*)；
  seismic (*adj.*)

地震波 seismic wave

南极 the Antarctic Pole
北极 the Arctic Pole
赤道 the equator
热带地区 tropics (*n.*)；tropical (*adj.*)
温带 temperate zone
寒带 frigid zone；cold zone
经度 longitude
经线 ［地］meridian (line)；［纺织］
  warp
纬度 latitude
纬线 ［地］parallel；［纺织］weft
地平线 horizon

亚洲 Asia
美洲 America
非洲 Africa
欧洲 Europe
澳洲 Australia
大洋洲 Oceania

大西洋 the Atlantic (Ocean)
北冰洋 the Arctic Ocean
太平洋 the Pacific (Ocean)
地中海 the Mediterranean (Sea)
海的 marine (*adj.*)；maritime (*adj.*)；
  oceanic (*adj.*)
边缘 fringe；margin；periphery；verge
海峡 straits；channel
海湾 gulf；bay

岛 island；isle
小岛 islet
半岛 peninsula
浮岛 floating island

群岛 archipelago
火山岛 volcanic island
珊瑚岛 coral island

板块 plate
板块边缘 plate margin
板块学说 plate tectonics
板块假说 plate hypothesis
板块碰撞 plate collision
板块运动 plate motion; plate movement
板块漂移 plate drift
大陆 continent (*n.*); continental (*adj.*)
断裂 rift; rent

地形 topography; landform; relief;
  relief feature; surface feature; terrain
高地 highland; upland; elevation; plateau
平原 plain; flatlands
低地 low; lowland
盆地 basin; saucer; bowl
地上的，陆地的 terrestrial
天上的，天体的 celestial
地下的 underground; subterranean

洞穴 cave; cavity; chamber; crater
大山洞 cavern
山脉 mountain range; mountain chain
山脊 ridge
山谷，峡谷 valley; mountain valley; dale;
  ravine; gorge; glen; gap; canyon
山崖 cliff
峭壁 barranca; precipice; steep
悬崖 bluff; escarpment; scarp
峡谷 canyon, gorge
河流 river; stream
溪 brook; streamlet; rivulet

石头 stone
卵石，砾石 pebble; rubble;
  debris; boulder
石灰石 limestone
页岩 shale
陨石 meteorite
花岗岩 granite
大理石 marble
矿石 mineral
翡翠 jadeite
绿宝石 emerald
红宝石 ruby
珍珠 pearl
宝石 gem; jewel
纹理 grain
纹理细腻的 fine-grained
纹理粗糙的 coarse-grained
有线纹的 line-grained

火山 volcano
活火山 active volcano
死火山 extinct volcano
休眠火山 dormant volcano

火山口 crater; volcanic vent;
  summit crater
火山锥 cone
火山坑 fire pit
火山腔体 chamber
火山带 volcanic belt
火山爆发 volcanic eruption
火山沉积 volcanic deposit
火山尘 volcanic dust
火山熔岩 lava; slag
熔岩湖 lava lake
熔岩瀑布 lava cascade

附录4

熔岩丘 lava dome
岩浆 magma

冰山 iceberg
冰河 glacier
冰河时代 glacial epoch
冰河学 glaciology
冰河作用 glaciation
汹涌，高涨 surge（*v.*）

化学 chemistry
成分 composition；constituent；agent
物质 substance；material
元素 element
元素周期表 periodic table［system］
  of elements
化合物 compound

金属 metal
有色金属 nonferrous metal

铂 platinum（俗称"白金"）
银 silver
铜 copper
铝 aluminium
锡 tin
铅 lead
锌 zinc
镍 nickel
镁 magnesium
钾 potassium
钠 sodium
钙 calcium
汞 mercury

氢 hydrogen

氧 oxygen
氮 nitrogen
氦 helium
氨 ammonia
碳 carbon
硅 silicon
硫 sulfur
碘 iodine

分子 molecule
原子 atom
原子核 nucleus
质子 proton
中子 neutron
电子 electron
离子 ion
粒子 particle

水蒸汽 water vapor
溶液 solution
溶解 dissolve（*v.*）；resolve（*v.*）
溶质 solute；solvent
可溶的 soluble（*adj.*）；不可溶的
  insoluble（*adj.*）
溶剂 dissolvent；solvent；resolvent
沉淀 subside（*v.*）；deposit（*v.*）；
  precipitate（*v.*）
沉淀物 subsidence（*n.*）；deposition
  （*n.*）；sediment（*n.*）；sedimen-
  tation（*n.*）；precipitate（*n.*）
凝结 coagulate（*v. & adj.*）
浓缩 condense（*v.*）；condensation（*n.*）
饱和 saturation（*n.*）；saturated（*adj.*）
晶体 crystal
结晶 crystallize（*v.*）
结晶作用 crystallization

挥发 volatilize（*v.*）；volatile（*adj.*）
蒸发 evaporate（*v.*）；evaporation（*n.*）
电解 electrolyze
电解槽 electrolytic bath

分解 decompose
腐烂 decompose；rot；decay

物理 physics
物理变化 physical change
力学 mechanics
光学 optics
电学 electricity
电 electricity
静电 static electricity
摩擦 rub（*v.*）；chafe（*v.*）
电流 electric current
直流电 direct current（dc）
交流电 alternating current（AC）
直流电变压器 direct-current
　　transformer
电路 circuit（CKT）；electric circuit
电荷 electric charge；charge
电压 electric tension；electric voltage
伏特 voltage
导电体 conductor
绝缘体 insulator
半导体 semiconductor
电池 battery
真空管 vacuum tube；valve
晶体管 transistor；crystal valve

凸透镜 convex lens
凹透镜 concave lens
显微镜 microscope
望远镜 telescope

放大镜 magnifier
光学纤维 optical fiber
光谱 spectrum
紫外线 ultraviolet rays
红外线 infra-red rays
X 光线 Roentgen rays＝X rays
透明的 transparent
半透明的 translucent
不透明的 opaque

微波 microwave
波峰 wave crest；peak；ridge
波谷 trough of wave；trough；valley
波长 wavelength
频率 frequency；rate
媒质 medium；media
震动 vibrate（*v.*）；vibration（*n.*）
回声 echo
速度 speed
速率 velocity
加速度 accelerated velocity
重力 gravity
引力 gravitation；attraction
运动 motion
移动 locomotion
惯性 inertia
动量 momentum
动力(学)的，运动的 kinetic（*adj.*）
运动摩擦 kinetic friction
冲量 impulse
势能 potential energy
阻力 resistance；drag；drag force
空气阻力 air resistance；air friction
摩擦(力) friction

歌剧 opera

附录 4

歌剧剧本 libretto
乐队 orchestra；band
乐队指挥 conductor；bandmaster
合唱；合唱队 chorus
民歌 folk song
流行歌曲 pop song；popular song
管弦乐 string orchestra
交响乐，交响曲 symphony
爵士乐 jazz
声学 acoustics
耳的，听觉的 acoustic（*adj.*）；aural
　（*adj.*）；auditory（*adj.*）
乐谱 score
五线谱 staff
乐章 movement
音符 note
曲调 tune；melody（*n.*）；melodic（*adj.*）
音高 pitch
节奏 rhythm
节拍 meter；beat
乐器 musical instrument
和音，琴弦 chord
拨弦乐器 plucked instrument
打击乐器 percussion instrument
弦乐器 stringed instrument
喇叭，号 bugle；trumpet；horn
大提琴 cello
小提琴 violin

同感 sympathy
反感 antipathy
通感 empathy

森林 forest
木材 timber；lumber
风干；晒干（木材） season（*v.*）

树冠 canopy
树枝 branch
大树枝 limb
小树枝 twig
树干 trunk
树皮 bark
树叶 leaf；foliage
灌木 bush；shrub；arbuscle
乔木 arbor
柳树 willow
松树 pine
杉 fir
雪松 cedar

植被 vegetation
苔藓 moss；lichen
蕨类植物 fern

花 flower
果树的花 blossom
草本植物的花 bloom
花瓣 petal
花叶 floral leaf
花蜜 nectar
花粉 pollen
授粉 pollinate（*v.*）；pollination（*n.*）
授粉者 pollinator
芬芳 fragrant；aroma；perfume
气味 scent；odor
臭味 stink；stench
茎 stem；stalk
根茎 rhizome
块茎 tuber
球茎 corm
受精 fertilize（*v.*）
杂交 crossbreeding

细胞 cell

细胞壁 cell wall
细胞核 nucleus；cell nucleus
细胞质 cytoplasm
纤维素 cellulose
叶绿素 chlorophyll
光合作用 photosynthesis

农业 agriculture
农产品 produce (*n.*)
主要产物(或商品)staple
谷仓 barn
梯田 terrace
灌溉 irrigate (*v.*)；irrigation
耕，犁 plough (*v. & n.*)；plow
　(*v. & n.*)
铲 shovel (*v.*)
镐 pick (*v.*)；pickaxe (*n.*)
镰刀 sickle
碾子 roller
磨 mill (*n. & v.*)；grind (*v.*)
耕种，养植 cultivate (*v.*)；till (*v.*)
收割 reap；harvest；gather in
收割机 harvester；harvesting imple-
　ments；reaper；reaping machine
拖拉机 tractor
打谷，脱粒 thresh (*v.*)；thresher (*n.*)
除草 weeding；extirpate weed；weed
　out（weeds）
杂草 weeds；rank grass；hogweed
渠 ditch；canal；channel
排水渠 drainage ditch
肥料 fertilizer；manure
农作物，庄稼 crop
谷 grain；cereal
小米，粟 millet
小麦 wheat

大麦 barley
稻子 rice；paddy
豆；蚕豆 bean
大豆 soybean
豌豆 pea
玉米 corn
棉花 cotton
蔬菜 vegetables
害虫 pest；injurious/destructive insect
杀虫剂 insecticide；pesticide；
　insectifuge
土地 land；soil
田地 farmland；field
麦田 wheatland；wheat field
犁沟 furrow
田埂 ridge
耕地 arable land
肥沃 fertile (*adj.*)
贫瘠 barren；infertile (*adj.*)；
　impoverished；sterile
干旱 drought；arid；dry
干旱地区 arid area

牧场 grazing land；pasture；meadow；
　ranch
种植园 plantation
果园 orchard
草地 grassland；meadow；lea
奶牛场 dairy
家禽饲养场 hennery
畜牧业 animal [livestock] husbandry
游牧的 nomadic (*adj.*)
苗圃 nursery
干草，(喂牲畜的)饲草 hay；forage；
　silage；fodder
兽群 herd

家畜 livestock
牛 cattle
公牛 ox；bull
母牛 cow
奶牛 dairy cattle
小牛 calf
水牛 water buffalo
牛棚 cowshed
马 horse
母马 mare
小马 pony
种马 stallion；stu
马厩，马棚 stable
马具 harness
踢马刺 spur
羊 sheep
公羊 ram
绵羊 sheep
母羊 ewe
山羊 goat
小羊 lamb
羊栏 sheepcote
猪 hog；pig；swine
母猪 sow
公猪 boar
小猪 piglet
野猪 wild boar
猪圈 pigsty
(猪等)同胎生下的小崽 litter
狗 dog
猎狗 hunting dog；hound
小狗 puppy
狗窝 kennel
繁殖，饲养 breed（v.）；rear（v.）
家禽 fowl；domestic bird；domestic
  fowl

鸡 chicken
雏鸡 chick；chicken
公鸡 cock；rooster
母鸡 hen
养鸡场 chicken farm
鸡舍 roost
鸭 duck
公鸭 drake
家[野]鸭 domestic [wild] duck
母鸭 duck
小鸭 duckling
鹅 goose
一群鹅 a drove [flock] of geese
孵卵，孵化 hatch（v. & n.）；
  incubate（v.）；incubation（n.）；
  hover（v.）

蛋 egg
蛋黄 yolk
蛋青，蛋白 albumen
蛋壳 eggshell

哺乳动物 mammal
脊椎动物 vertebrate
无脊椎动物 invertebrate
甲壳类的(动物)crustacean
节肢动物 arthropod
节体动物 articulate
啮齿动物 rodent
爬行动物 reptile
食腐动物 scavenger
反刍动物 ruminant
腔肠动物 coelenterate
灵长目动物 primate
软体动物 mollusk
水生动植物 aquatic

两栖动物[植物] amphibian
食草动物 herbivore
食肉动物；食虫植物 carnivore

纲 class
目 order
亚目 suborder
科 family
属 genus
种 species

昆虫，虫 insect；worm
卵 ovum；egg
幼虫 larva；caterpillar
茧 cocoon
颚，下巴 jaw
上[下]颚 upper [lower] jaw
蜕变 transform
害虫 destructive insect；pest
益虫 useful insect
触须 vibrissa；smeller；tentacle
蛾 moth
蚂蚁 ant
白蚁 termite
蜜蜂 bee
蜂 wasp
蜂群 swarms
毛虫 caterpillar
蝗虫 grasshopper；locust
蜘蛛 spider；arachnid
蜘蛛网 cobweb；web；spider web
群居 social (*adj.*)
独居 solitary (*adj.*)

鱼 fish
鱼类触须 barbell

鱼卵 spawn
一群鱼 a school of fish
鲨鱼 shark
鲸鱼 whale
章鱼 octopus
海参 sea cucumber
海星 starfish
海豚 dolphin

鸟 bird
鹪鹩(小型鸟的典型)wren
秃鹫(大型鸟的典型)condor
猛禽 birds of prey
鹰 eagle；falcon；hawk；kestrel；
condor
鸵鸟 ostrich
鹦鹉 parrot
鸽子 pigeon；dove
鸟嘴 bill(水禽等细长而扁平的)；猛
禽的钩状嘴通常叫 beak
迁徙 migrate
换毛 molt
栖息 perch
巢 nest
栖息处 roost；habitat
(鸟)用嘴理(毛)preen (*v.*)
蔽身之处 shelter (*n. & v.*)

兽 beast；animal
猛兽 beast of prey
怀孕 be [become] pregnant；
conceive (*adj.*)
食肉动物，捕食其他动物的动物
predator
被捕食的动物 prey
猿 ape；orangutan；primate

猩猩 chimp；chimpanzee；gorilla

狒狒 baboon

猴 monkey

类人猿 anthropoid

交配 mating；copulation

冬眠 hibernation

胎 foetus；embryo

胎儿，幼儿 infant

恐龙 dinosaur

鱼龙 ichthyosaur

翼龙 pterosaur

始祖鸟 archaeopteryx

化石 fossil

考古学 archaeology

人类学 anthropology

人种学 ethnology

原始人类 hominid；primitive

微生物 microbe

细菌 bacterium（n. 复数：bacteria）

病菌，病原体 pathogen

真菌 fungus（pl. fungi）

酵母(菌) yeast

霉菌 mould(＝mold)；mildew

蘑菇 mushroom

酶 enzyme

分泌 secrete；ooze

寄生(虫) parasite（n. & v.）；
parasitic（adj.）

共生 symbiosis（n.）；symbiotic（adj.）

免疫 immune（adj.）；immunity（n.）

过敏的 hypersensitive（adj.）

蛋白质 protein

有机物 organism

骨 bone

骨骼 skeleton

头骨 skull（n.）；cranium（n.）；
cranial（adj.）

肋骨 rib

脊柱 spinal column；spine；backbone

脊髓 spinal cord

骨髓 marrow

神经 nerve

脑神经 cranial nerve

神经中枢 nerve center；nerve center

末梢神经 nerve ending

肺 lung

呼吸器官 respiratory organ

肾 kidney

肝 liver

胃 stomach

肠 intestine

消化系统 digestive system

内分泌系统 endocrine system

胰腺 pancreas

腺 gland（n.）；glandular（adj.）

排泄系统 excretory system

心脏 heart；cardiac（n. & adj.）

静脉 vein

动脉 artery（n.）；arterial（adj.）

血管 blood vessel

毛细血管 capillary（n. & adj.）

血浆 blood plasma

红细胞 red blood cell

白细胞 leucocyte

血小板 blood platelet

凝结 coagulum

(使)充血 congest（v.）；congestion（n.）

血液循环 blood circulation

组织 tissue
器官 organ
肌肉 muscle
腹腔 abdominal cavity
腹 abdomen
胸 chest
胸腔 thorax
唾液 saliva
汗 sweat
尿 urine
排泄 excrete (*v.*); excretion (*n.*)
排泄物 excrement
呕吐 vomit (*v. & n.*)
屁 fart (*v. & n.*)

免疫系统 immune system
免疫性 immunity

脂肪 fat
脂类 lipid
蛋白质 protein
维生素 vitamin
营养 nutrition (*n.*); nutritional (*adj.*)
营养不良 undernutrition
热量 amount of heat
卡(路里)［热量单位］calorie
热度计 calorimeter
温度计 thermometer
摄氏温度 centigrade
摄氏的 Celsius (*adj.*)
华氏温度计 Fahrenheit (*n. & adj.*)

微风 breeze; gust
台风，飓风 typhoon; hurricane
旋风，龙卷风 whirlwind; tornado; cyclone
暴风 squall; storm

对流，上升气流 convection

细雨，毛毛雨 drow; drizzle
滴，流 trickle (*v.*); drip (*v.*); dribble (*v.*)
倾注 pour
阵雨 shower
倾盆大雨 downpour
暴风雨 tempest
雨滴 droplet; dew
霜 frost
雾 fog(mist)

雹，冰雹 hail
雪花 snowflake
晶体 crystal

潮湿的 damp; moist; humid
干燥的 dry; arid
温暖的 warm; cozy
寒冷的 cold; frigid; chill; chilly; icy
多雨的 rainy
多风的 windy
多云的 cloudy

大楼 mansion
公寓 apartment
庄园 manor
教学大楼 hall
建筑群 complex
摩天大厦 skyscraper
大教堂 cathedral
小教堂 chapel
草坪 lawn; sward
人造喷泉 fountain
入口 doorway; entrance; entry

附录 4

走廊 corridor；hallway；passage；
　　passageway；vestibule
大厅 hall；lobby；foyer；antechamber
横梁 span
拱顶 arch；arc；vault
天井，院子 patio
露台，阳台 balcony
地窖 crypt；pit；basement
厨房 kitchen
窗帘 curtain
壁架 ledge
小屋，帐篷 lodge

数学 mathematics
代数 algebra
线性代数 linear algebra
几何 geometry
积分 integral
微积分 calculus
统计 statistics
概率 probability
概率论 probability theory
函数 function

角 angle
内角 interior angle
外角 exterior angle
锐角 acute angle
钝角 obtuse angle
三角形 triangle
不等边三角形 scalene triangle
等边三角形 equilateral triangle
等腰三角形 isosceles triangle
直角三角形 right-angled triangle；
　　right triangle
矩形，长方形 rectangle（n.）；
　　rectangular（adj.）

对称的 symmetry（n.）；symmetrical
　　（adj.）
左右对称 bilateral symmetry

四边形 quadrilateral；tetragonum；
　　quadrangle
正方形 square
平行四边形 parallelogram；平行线
　　parallel
五边形 pentagon
五角星 five-pointed star
梯形 trapezoid

四面体 tetrahedron
六面体 hexahedron
立方体 cube；hexahedron
多面体 polyhedral；polyhedron；
　　polytope
柱状体 column
锥体 pyramis；pyramid；cone；taper

球体 sphere；orb；spheroid；spherite；
　　spheroidal
圆 round；circular；spherical
半圆 semicircle
椭圆 ellipse；ellipsoid
直径 diameter；diam
半径 radius；semidiameter
周长 circumference；perimeter
面积 area
体积 volume
曲线 curve
线性 linear
螺旋 spiral；helix；screw

交通 transportation

马车 cart；carriage；wagon；coach；stagecoach

火车 train

货运列车 freight

(火车等发动机等短而钝的)嗤嘎声 chug

站台 station；platform

交通工具 vehicle

(有轨)电车 trolley

通勤 commute（*v. & n.*）

港口 port；harbor

运河 canal

船只 boat；ship；vessel；craft；barge；canoe

船桨 paddle

小桨 scull

灯塔 beacon

公路 highway

收税高速公路 turnpike

枢纽 pivot（*adj. & n.*）；hub

腹地，内地 hinterland（复数：穷乡僻壤）

驿站 stage；post

边界贸易站 fort

市场 market house；marketplace

博览会 fair；exhibition；exposition

日用品 commodity

商品 merchandise；product

货物 goods

船货 cargo

易货交易 barter

小贩 peddler；vendor

零售 retail

零售商 retailer；retail trader；dealer

批发 wholesale

批发商 wholesaler；merchant

进口 import

出口 export

关税 tariff

征收(税金、罚款) levy

联合抵制(货物等) boycott

(商业)风险投资 venture

企业家 entrepreneur

企业 enterprise

产业 industry

城市的 urban（*adj.*）

乡下的 rural（*adj.*）

首都 metropolis；capital

首都的 metropolitan（*adj.*）

城市 city

(由中心大城市及卫星城镇构成的)集合城市 conurbation

市的，都市的；市营的 municipal（*adj.*）

自治市，自治区；市政府 municipality

城市居民 urbanite

城市的；市民的；公民的 civic

一块地 lot

平民 civilian

居民 resident；inhabitant；citizen；dweller

下水道；排水设备，排水系统 drainage；sewerage

公共卫生 sanitation

公共设施 public utilities

住处 department；quarter；tenement

留宿 accommodate（*v.*）

房客 tenant

房东 landlord

租约 lease
房租 rent
地区，区域 district；ward；area；
　　region

手工艺 handicraft
手工艺工人 craftsman；artisan
手工艺品 articles of handicraft art；
　　handicrafts
学徒 apprentice；trainee
制造 fashion；create；produce
炉 stove；furnace；oven
窑 kiln
锻造 forge；smithing；hammering；
　　blacksmithing
铁匠 blacksmith
银匠 silversmith
铜匠 coppersmith
小贩 peddler；vendor
木匠 carpenter

碟子，盘子 dishes
碗 bowls
(烧水用的)水壶 kettle
盆 basin；tub；pot
桶 barrel；bucket；pail
小桶 keg
便桶 commode
痰盂 cuspidors
罐 jar；jug；pot；tank；tin
容器 vessel

凿子 chisel
钻子 drill；auger
钳子 pincers；pliers；tongs
刨子 plane (*n.*)

刨 plane (*v.*)；shave (*v.*)
钉子 nail；tack
拔出钉子 draw [pull] out a nail
把钉子敲进去 drive [hammer；knock]
　　in a nail
粘 glue (*v.*)；stick (*v.*)；paste (*v.*)
凸 bulge (*n.*)
凸出 project (*v.*)；protrude (*v.*)
凹 concave (*adj. & n.*)；dented (*adj.*)
雄榫，榫舌 tongue；tenon

纺(拧纱；捻线)spin (*v.*)；reel (*v.*)
织 knit (*v.*)；weave (*v.*)
纺织品 textile
织物 woof；fabric；texture；drap
拼制物 mosaic
亚麻羊毛交织物 linsey-woolsey
羊毛 wool
亚麻 flax
粗布 coarse cloth；homespun cloth
织布机 loom
皮革，革制品 leather

绳 rope
钢丝绳 steel cable
麻绳 hemp rope
细绳 string
细线；棉纱；纤维 thread；fila-
　　ment；yarn；strand
纤维 fiber
(制陶)转盘；纺车 wheel
卷轴；(线、铁丝、胶片、纸、铅管
　　等的)一卷 reel；coil
蚕丝；丝；绸，绢，缎 silk
织物上纵向的纱或线 weft
织物上横向的纱或线 warp

陶器 pottery；earthenware；ware
制陶术 ceramics
陶工 potter
壶，瓶，罐 pot
黏土 clay
粗陶(器)，瓷器 stoneware
土器，陶器 earthenware
红土陶 redware
釉料，上光料 glaze（n. & v.）
抛光 finish（v. & n.）
揉，捏 knead（v.）
模子 mold
质地 texture
炉 stove；furnace；oven
窑 kiln
泥釉 slip
色素 pigment
清漆 varnish

雕塑(术) sculpture
雕刻家 sculptor
浮雕 relief
雕刻，刻 carve；engrave
(图案的)基本花纹 motif
图案 design（n.）
画像；雕像 icon
画师，画匠 limner
鉴定家，行家 connoisseur
赞助人 patron
支援，保护；赞助 patronage
文艺复兴 renaissance
评论家；鉴定家 critic

激进主义 radicalism
保守主义 conservatism
怀疑论者 doubter

不可知论者 agnostic
不信宗教的人；异教徒 infidel
异教徒，邪教徒 pagan
怀疑基督教/真理的人；怀疑宗教教
　　条者，无神论者 skeptic
愤世嫉俗者，犬儒主义者 Cynic
愤世嫉俗的 cynical（adj.）

无政府主义 anarchism
君主制 monarchy
宪法 constitution
立法 legislation
民主党 the Democrats
共和党 the Republicans
国会 congress
联邦政府 federal government
美国独立战争 American Revolution；
　　Independent War
美国内战 the Civil War
美国大萧条时期 the Great Depression
移民 immigrant
移居者 migrant
侨民 emigrant
殖民者 colonist
大多数 majority
少数派 minority

祖先 ancestors；forefathers；progenitor；
　　forbears
后代 descendant；successor；offspring；
　　progeny；inheritor；heir
子女 offspring；issue
血统 lineage；ancestry；root
传统 tradition；heritage；custom

进化 evolve（v.）；evolution（n.）
适应 adapt（v.）；adaptation（n.）

附录4

生存 survive（*v.*）；survival（*n.*）
适者生存 survival of the fittest
濒临灭绝的动物 endangered animals
灭绝 extinction（*n.*）；extinct（*adj.*）

生态系统 ecosystem
小生境 niche
植物群 flora
动物群 fauna
生物多样性 biological diversity

食物链 food chain
保护；保护森林[河道] conservation
禁猎（区）preserve

温室效应 greenhouse effect
臭氧层 ozone layer
紫外辐射 ultraviolet radiation
污染 pollute（*v.*）；pollution（*n.*）；
　　contaminate（*v.*）；contamination（*n.*）
污染物 pollutant
有毒的 poisonous（*adj.*）；noxious
　　（*adj.*）；toxic（*adj.*）
废物 rubbish；waste
废料的处理 the disposal of waste
　　material
噪音 noise
噪音污染 sound pollution
分贝 decibel

TOEFL 考试
常见前缀后缀

anti-	1. 反，排：antialien 排外的 antimilitarism 反军国主义 2. 伪，假：antipope 僭称的教皇 3. 对：antitype 原型 antithesis 对立面 4. 非：antigrammatical 不合语法的 5. 抗，阻，防：antitoxin 抗毒素 antiaircraft 防空的 6. 逆，正反对：anticyclone 反气旋 antipole 相反的极
auto-	1. 自，自己，自身：autobiography 自传 2. 自动：autoalarm 自动警报 3. 汽车：autocade 汽车队伍.
bi-	二，两，双，复：bilateral 有两面的，双边的 bicentennial 二百年，二百周年纪念 biannual 一年二次的
circum-	周，围，环：circumaviation 环绕(地球)飞行 circumpolar 极圈的
contra-	反，逆，抗：contradiction 矛盾，抵触，相反 contraoctave 中央 C 以下第二与第三 C 之间的八度
dec-	表示"十"：decagon 十边形 decameter 十米
extra-	一般加在形容词之前表示"外"，"额外"，"格外"，"临时"，"超出"：extra-fine 超级的，极好的 extraordinary 非凡的，卓绝的
hemi-	表示"半"：hemianopsia 偏盲 hemicycle 半圆形
hexa-	表示"六"[在元音前用 hex-]：hexad 成六的一组 hexagon 六角形
inter-	表示"在…中"，"在…间，""在…内"，"相互"：interact 相互作用 intercity 城市间的 interstellar 星际的

macro-	大，巨，宏，长，粗（*opp*. micro-）macroengineering 宏观工程(学)
micro-:	1. 小，微（*opp*. macro-）：microcosm 微观世界　2. 扩大：microphone 麦克风，话筒　3. 微（＝100万分之一）：microampere 微安(培) microfarad 微法(拉) micromicrofarad 微微法(拉) micromho 微姆(欧) microvolt 微伏(特)
neo-	表示"新"，"近代(的)"；"复活"：neoimpressionism 新印象主义
paleo-	表示"古，旧，原始"：paleoanthropology 古人类学
post-	表示"后，次"：postaxial 轴后的　postwar 战后的
pre-	表示"前，先，预先"：prehistory 史前史　prepay 预付 preschool 幼儿园，保育园
pseudo-	表示"伪，拟，假，赝"：pseudoarchaic 拟古的　pseudoclassical 伪古典的　pseudomartyr 假烈士　pseudoplastic 代塑料，假塑性体
retro-	表示"向后，倒退，追溯"：retrogress 退步　retrorocket 制动[减速]火箭系统
semi-	一半；（一段时期中）出现两次的：semicolony 半殖民地 semimonthly 半月刊
super-	特别；极，过度；超；总：superconductor 超导体
-cide	杀…者，杀[灭]…药：suicide 自杀　insecticide 杀虫剂
-en	加在形容词或名词后面构成动词，表示"弄"，"变"，"使"，"使有"，"变得"，"变得有"：moisten 弄湿　strengthen 加强 deepen 加深　lengthen 加长
-grained	有纹理的：line-grained 有条纹的　coarse-grained 颗粒状的
-ics	表示"…学"，"…术"：mathematics 数学　physics 物理学

-ish	1. "…一样的"：childish 幼稚的　monkish 僧侣的　2. "…似的"，"…气的"，"患…的"：fiendish 恶魔似的　foolish 愚蠢的　feverish 发烧的
-ism	"主义"，"学说"，"信仰"，"制度"：marxism 马克思主义　atomism 原子论
-let	表示 "小"：ringlet 小环　streamlet 小溪
-like	表示 "…一样"，"像…"：lilylike 像百合的　womanlike 女子气的，女人腔的
-nomy	表示 "法"，"学"：economy 经济学　astronomy 天文学
-odd	表示 "多出几个的"：twentyodd 二十几个
-logy	表示 "…学"，"…论"：philology 语文学
-sphere	表示 "…球"，"…圈"：hydrosphere 水界，水圈

附录 5